THE

IMPERIAL

INTELLECT

A STUDY OF NEWMAN'S EDUCATIONAL IDEAL

The
Imperial
Intellect

A STUDY OF NEWMAN'S EDUCATIONAL IDEAL

By A. DWIGHT CULLER

New Haven and London: Yale University Press

Originally published on the foundation
established in memory of
Philip Hamilton McMillan of the class of 1894,
Yale College.

To H.S.C.

Table of Contents

Preface

WHAT can a book on Newman do that has not been done before? To answer this question one need only go to Birmingham, to the Oratory which Newman built in 1852, and ask to be shown his room and the dark little Archivum off the corridor beside it. In the former there are cupboards, ranged almost from floor to ceiling, which contain journals, notebooks, manuscripts of published and unpublished works, proof sheets and memoranda, trinkets and account books—a veritable treasure of thousands upon thousands of pages. And in the Archivum next door there are the letters, how many one would hesitate to say, but in the loose-leaf binders and boxes in which they are stored they comprise over four hundred volumes. There is only one scholar who has ever come even close to mastering this material, and that is Newman himself. From the age of about twenty on he lived two lives, one producing these papers and another studying the papers which he had thus produced. Almost annually he would have a session "going through his papers," and this meant arranging them, copying out extracts, drawing up digests and summaries, annotating them and then annotating the annotations, tying them up in packets, writing on the packets "Nothing worth saving," and then putting them back into the cupboards to be saved. He did this because, as he said, his biographers needed "elbow-room," but the actual effect upon most of his biographers is to give them not elbowroom but agoraphobia. Viewing the prospect before them, they turn and run for the shelter of the published works, for the wilderness of the papers is too vast to contemplate. Anne Mozley, of course, had no such problem. What she published in the *Letters and Correspondence* was the selection that Newman gave her, and I at least can never read her work without feeling that this is Newman himself going through his papers posthumously. Wilfred Ward is the first independent explorer, but even there, although he struggled manfully and achieved much, the paths which he did not take are quite as numerous as those that he did. In our own time the greatest of all Newman scholars was the late Henry Tristram, whose recent death is a most tragic loss to the world of Catholic letters. But although Father Tristram knew the papers intimately and wrote the most delightful and authoritative books about them, in his modesty he simply put these books away in his own cupboard and so continued the process which Newman himself began. And as for the other New-manists, there is at least a tendency among them, although with striking exceptions, to use again and again the same threadbare anecdotes from Mozley and Ward and not to strike out into the new material of the papers.

Without pretending to be braver than anyone else, I can at least say that I have handled every manuscript at the Oratory (for this much was made necessary by the project of filming them for the Yale University Library), and I have tried to make my study dependent as much as possible on manuscript materials. Thus, even where the story that it tells is already familiar in its main outlines to Newman scholars, the details of that story, and the quotations by which it is illustrated, will often be fresh. It should of course be clear that I am not writing a general biography of Newman. The story that I tell is simply that of Newman's education, of his work as an educator of others, and of his educational thinking as expressed in the *Idea of a University*. But it also happens that one effect of this restriction is to reveal aspects of Newman's life which the general biographies have missed. For these works, following the line laid down in the *Apologia*, have concentrated upon the development of Newman's religious opinions, narrowing his life to the compass of the Tractarian movement and measuring his opinions by their approximation to Rome. What they forget is that all this while Newman was living in a university and was professionally engaged in the work of education. "Now from first to last," he wrote in 1863, "education, in this large sense of the word, has been my line," and by following out this line one discovers an interaction between Newman's educational and his religious interests which provides the central pattern of his entire life. That pattern is not the steady, in-eluctable march toward Rome, but an oscillation between an intellectual liberalism and a religious submissiveness which revealed itself most dramatically in the five crushing illnesses of Newman's adolescence and early manhood. From most biographies one would hardly know that these illnesses had occurred. Even where they are mentioned they are not related to each other nor is their significance emphasized. And yet, in my opinion, these illnesses provide an essential key to the under-standing of Newman's intellectual and religious development.

Much of the research for this book was done during two years' leave of absence from Yale University, and I wish to express my thanks to the Department of English for granting these leaves and to the University for the award of a Yale research instructorship. During the second year I enjoyed a Fulbright grant to England, and I wish to express my appreciation for this grant, and for the various courtesies which attended it, to the United States Educational Commission. To the University of Birmingham, with which I was affiliated in my year abroad, I owe many friendly attentions, but my greatest and most personal debt is to the Fathers of the Oratory in Edgbaston. To the Rev. Philip Lynch, Superior, I am inclined to say, as Newman did in the dedication of the *Idea of a University*, "Hospes eram, et collegistis me," and of Father Henry Tristram I simply can say nothing that would be at all adequate. He took me by the hand and led me through the papers of which he had the charge, and it was always an embarrassment to me to know that he could, any day, have sat down and written, almost out of his head, the book which I was laboring to construct. Indeed, he had all but done so many years before, and one day he showed me, and allowed me to read, an incompleted manuscript of his own, begun on somewhat the same plan as I had adopted for myself. To this and to his other published and unpublished works I owe many references which in my notes give an erroneous idea of my own learning.

For access to materials and for many other courtesies I am indebted to the Provost and Fellows of Oriel College and especially to the College Librarian; to the President of Trinity College; to the Curator of the Diocesan Archives, Drumcondra; to the Director of the National Library of Ireland; to the Librarian and staff of the Yale University Library; and to the anonymous donor whose generosity made possible the filming of the Newman papers.

For reading my manuscript in whole or in part and making many helpful suggestions I am indebted to Dean William C. DeVane and to Professors Davis P. Harding, Frederick W. Hilles, Maynard Mack, Louis L. Martz, Frederick A. Pottle, Gordon N. Ray, and Martin J. Svaglic.

To the editor of the *Journal of General Education* I owe the permission to use again (in Chapter 11) parts of my article, "Newman on the Uses of Knowledge."

Finally, as Browning said, "one word more," which is that this entire book really belongs to my wife, who shed both sweetness and light upon the problem of composing it. So much I wish to express by the dedication, but I ought also to particularize that she typed almost the entire first draft of the manuscript, verified the greater part of the references to published works, and helped extensively with the proofs and the index.

North Haven, Conn.
February, 1955

A Note on the References

In the Bibliographical Appendix, Part 1, the reader will find an explanation of the symbols used in referring to manuscript sources. In passages quoted from these sources my text follows the manuscript faithfully, even to preserving the ubiquitous little dash which in Newman's hand may replace almost any mark of punctuation. The only exception to this practice is that I have silently corrected a few obvious errors and have expanded a few shortened forms such as *&*, *wʰ*, *Govᵗ*, and *Univ.*

Unless otherwise noted, the fourth edition of the *Idea of a University* (1875) is the one referred to throughout.

Oxford

CHAPTER 1

Undergraduate
at Trinity

Trinity? a most gentlemanlike college.
—Dr. Nicholas

IT was said in those days that the approach to Oxford by
the Henley road was the most beautiful in the world. Soon after passing
Littlemore you came in sight of, and did not lose again, the sweet city
with its dreaming spires, driven along a road now crowded and obscured
with dwellings, open then to the cornfields on the right, to uninclosed
meadows on the left, with an unbroken view of the long line of towers,
rising out of foliage less high and veiling than after sixty more years of
growth to-day. At once, without suburban interval, you entered the finest
quarter of the town, rolling under Magdalen Tower, and past the Magdalen elms, then in full unmutilated luxuriance, till the exquisite curves
of the High Street opened on you, as you drew up at The Angel, or
passed on to the Mitre and the Star." [1]

Doubtless this was the road that Newman traveled as he went up to
Oxford with his father on December 14, 1816. He had hoped to enter
at Exeter, to which he had been directed by a friend of the family, but
there was no vacancy and so he went across the street to Trinity and
was matriculated by its president, Dr. Thomas Lee. In those days there
was no entrance examination, although it was not unusual to ask the
candidate to construe a little Latin and in other ways to show that he
had the normal equipment of the sixth-form boy. This is just about what
Newman had, being perhaps a little weaker than some in classics ("There
are several," he wrote, "who know much more than I do in Latin and
Greek—and I do not like that" [2]) and a little stronger than some in
mathematics. In age he was just short of sixteen, and this was two years
younger than most, for "no boy," his master declared, "had run through
the school, from the bottom to the top, as rapidly as John Newman." [3]

The master was the Rev. George Nicholas, head of Great Ealing
School near London, which Newman had attended from the age of seven
till nearly sixteen. It was a proprietary school of between two and three

hundred boys, was conducted on the Eton lines, and at that date "had a great name," for it was noticed that the boys "got on." [4] Two of them, for example, became lord chancellors, and among the other pupils in its best days were the sculptor Westmacott, Marryat, T. H. Huxley, W. S. Gilbert, and George Adams, son of the American minister to Great Britain. The teaching staff, apart from the headmaster, consisted of six Latin, six English, and two French masters, with eight instructors of dancing, drawing, music, fencing, and drilling.

A picture of the boy who entered this school in May, 1808 may be gained from a series of children's tales written by his sister Harriett many years later. They were called *Family Adventures*, and being designed to show that the things which happen to ordinary people do constitute real stories such as might go into a book, they are drawn faithfully from events in the Newman household. The children of the household are represented under their middle names, and Henry, the eldest, is described as "a very philosophical young gentleman, always full of thought, and never at a loss for an answer." He is sharp with company when he finds it a great bore, and no one, as his father put it, would ever call him "a pretty dear" as they do his little brother. Nevertheless, to his own family he is "observant and considerate," and his mother gives him a very real compliment by saying on the occasion of some thoughtful act, "You always understand about everything." [5]

What Newman learned in the "little school" to which he went for the first year at Ealing we do not know, but his progress through the higher forms is meticulously recorded in a notebook of the period.[6] On May 11, 1810 he began Latin prosody and got into Ovid a fortnight later. On November 16 he began Virgil and started doing Latin verses the next February and themes in March. Among his subjects were "Napoleon to his sister from St. Helena," the Battle of Waterloo, the Popish Plot, and the address of an injured horse to its master, "done without any assistance whether from book or master or English." Somewhat later he went on in his reading to Juvenal and Persius in the Delphin edition,[7] to Horace, and in 1816 to Cicero's *Cato major* and *Laelius*.[8]

Meanwhile, along with Latin came Greek, which Newman began on May 25, 1810. His first reader was *Aesop's Fables*, which he exchanged for Homer in the spring of 1812 and for Herodotus the following May. Also in 1812 he began studying a Greek life of Christ compiled from the Four Gospels by the Hebrew professor at Oxford, Dr. Joseph White. This was the Dr. White who wrote his lectures first and then had the style put on afterward, thus providing Newman with an illustration in his lecture on "Literature" of what literature can never be.[9] French he was studying by 1814 and perhaps earlier, and music by 1811, when he began the practice of the violin, which delighted him almost throughout his life. In mathematics he got through five books of Euclid and also a work by Charles Hutton called *The Compendious Measurer*, which treated, so said the title page, of decimal and duodecimal arithmetic, practical geometry, and mensuration.

Much more exciting than these formal exercises, however, were the three "Grand Nights" which the school was given every year, alternately in June and September, with a Latin play on each of the three nights, and on the morning of the third "speeches." The boys were trained for the speeches by two rhetorical readers, William Enfield's *Exercises in Elocution* and John Walker's *Academic Speaker*, and prize books were given to those who did well. The books which Newman selected (for they were allowed to choose their own) were Lamb's *Tales from Shakespear*, Vivant Denon's *Travels in Upper and Lower Egypt* (which turned out to be too expensive, though eventually he was given an English abridgment in 16mo), Milton's poems, and Cowper's Homer.[10] The first two of these books still survive, but they are less interesting than the copy of Terence which was used by Newman in doing the Latin plays, and which, with its notes on how to read the various lines and its indication of a "Salmon colour silk coat" for one of the actors, looks more like a prompter's book than a school lesson. Newman himself played the roles of Hegio in *Phormio*, Pythias in *Eunuchus*, Syrus in *Adelphi*, and Davus in *Andria*,[11] and the fact that fifty years later he revived the custom of the Latin play in his own Oratory School at Birmingham shows how valuable he had found the experience to be.

Indeed, his predilections were strongly literary and dramatic. Inside the classroom he wrote the usual themes on "Pride," "Roman History," "The consequences of the fall of Carthage [to] Rome," "Learning," and "Prodigality," [12] but outside he wrote an even greater quantity of poems, satires, burlesque operas, romantic dramas, and vast cabalistic periodicals such as the *Spy* and *Anti-Spy*, the *Portfolio* and *Beholder*, which combined the style of Addison with the materials of Mrs. Radcliffe. His reading seems to have united these same strains, for on the one hand we find the usual eighteenth-century poets and essayists and on the other the romances of Mrs. Radcliffe and Miss Porter, and especially of the beloved author of *Waverley*, whose works he read in bed in the early summer mornings when they first came out.[13]

So far, then, there was little to distinguish Newman from any superior schoolboy with literary inclinations, but in the autumn of 1816 he experienced the religious conversion which he ever after regarded as the most momentous event of his entire life. Its precise nature is difficult to establish, but it seems to have been the first in a series of acute psychological crises which extended from the onset of adolescence until the beginning of middle age and which, though varying in intensity and circumstance, always followed the same general pattern. In every case there was a period of expanding intellectual powers and self-confidence which was then checked by some sharp affliction, either an external calamity or simply a breakdown from overwork, and finally the interpretation of this as God's chastisement for intellectual pride. At the time of the first crisis, for example, which occurred toward the end of Newman's school career when he was feeling a natural pride in his medals and other accomplishments, he seems to have fallen into the habit, not uncommon among adolescents, of toying with the arguments for infidelity. "When I was fourteen," he confessed in the *Apologia*, "I read Paine's Tracts against the Old Testament, and found pleasure in thinking of the objections which were contained in them. Also, I read some of Hume's *Essays*; and perhaps that on *Miracles*. So at least I gave my Father to understand; but perhaps it was a brag. Also, I recollect copying out some French verses, perhaps Voltaire's, against the immortality of the soul, and saying to myself something like 'How dreadful, but how plausible.' " [14] At the same time he used to think that he should like to be virtuous but not religious. "There was something in the latter idea I did not like," and he also professed not to know what it meant to "love God." [15]

Then, on March 8, 1816, his father's bank closed, and the family was thrown into a panic.[16] The girls were sent away to relatives, and Newman, as the eldest son, was summoned home to have the whole situation explained to him. He bore it well, but to one of his sensitivity it was a humiliating experience. The beloved cottage at Norwood where the children spent their summer vacations had to be sold, the London house was stripped of its grandeur, and in the autumn the family moved to Alton, in Hampshire, where the father was to begin life over as the manager of a brewery. Newman was spared the disorder of these moves by being kept on at school through the summer vacation, but while he was there he fell seriously ill. "Another thought has come on me," he wrote many years later in his private journal, "that I have had three great illnesses in my life, and how have they turned out! The first keen, terrible one, when I was a boy of 15, and it made me a Christian - with experiences before and after, awful, and known only to God." [17]

The human means of his conversion was one of the masters at Ealing, the Rev. Walter Mayers, a devout evangelical.[18] In the absence of the other boys Newman was thrown much into his company, and they took walks together, talked about religious problems, and read together in books of the school of Calvin. Then, at the end of the summer, the conversion followed, and it was so definite an experience that Newman could date its first and last days as August 1 and December 21, 1816.[19] He nowhere tells us exactly what it was like, except to say that it lacked the violence and did not follow the pattern of the usual evangelical conversion as described in books. Nevertheless it left him almost a different person from what he had been before. Writing in 1885, he said, "Of course I cannot myself be the judge of myself; but, speaking with this reserve, I should say that it is difficult to realise or imagine the identity of the boy before and after August 1816. . . . I can look back at the end of seventy years as if on another person." [20]

It was one week before the last day of his conversion that Newman went up to Oxford to matriculate, but it was not until the following June that he was actually called into residence. The intervening months he used largely for study, and although he says he was "not allowed or able to read much" [21] because of trouble with his eyes, he apparently averaged about five hours daily. He would begin in the mornings with perhaps a hundred verses of Sophocles, then do a page of Greek exercises and half a dozen Latin sentences, leave that for two chapters of Cicero's De officiis, then four propositions of Euclid, and finally either some English verse translation or simply an ode of Horace. In this way, between the middle of March and the first of June he read five plays of Sophocles, some of them twice over; Cicero's De officiis, De amicitia, and De senectute; four satires of Juvenal, about twenty selections from Horace, and fourteen chapters from the Gospel of St. Matthew in Greek. In addition, he did the first book of Euclid, various Greek and Latin exercises, a theme on the subject "non nobis solum," and some translations of Ovid and Horace into English verse. All this was cut short, however, when he was suddenly summoned up to Oxford on June 8 to take possession of a room which had unexpectedly fallen vacant.

He arrived just as everybody else was leaving and so spent the first three weeks feeling very solitary and very conspicuous. He had to dine alone in hall with half a dozen servants standing behind his back watching, and as he wandered about the streets and quadrangles he fancied he was being "silently stared at" and laughed at because of his dress.[22] Indeed, his feelings about Oxford were strangely ambivalent. When he first told Dr. Nicholas the name of his new college, which he did rather timidly because he had never heard of it before, he received the "reassuring" reply, "Trinity? a most gentlemanlike college—I am much pleased to hear it." [23] But it was not altogether reassuring to a young evangelical to learn that his college was "gentlemanlike." Gentlemen did things that evangelicals did not, and Mr. Mayers had warned him that he would need all his staunchness of spirit if Oxford were not to be for him an occasion of sin. In later years he recollected "with what awe and transport he had first come to the University, as to some sacred shrine," [24] but within a single week an episode had occurred by which the shrine was desecrated and his transport turned to disgust. "Hollis," he wrote to his father, ". . . asked me to take a glass of wine with two or three others of the College, and they drank and drank and drank all the time I was there. . . . They sat down with the avowed determination of each making himself drunk. I really think, if any one should ask me what qualifications were necessary for Trinity College, I should say there was only one,—Drink, drink, drink." [25]

"My dear Friend," wrote Mr. Mayers in reply to a similar communication, "I did not expect you would be so soon called upon to reduce to practice the good resolutions you had formed. Your letter convinces me that I have not overstated the dangers of a residence at the seat of learning, and convey[s] a hope that you will be on the alert against your numerous enemies. . . . For you to mix at a venture with such a society I conceive very dangerous. . . . You will find the ridicule of the world among the strongest weapon[s] Satan can employ and one very frequently assumed by the Logicians of O[xford], but on such occasions we must appeal to higher authority and I am sure you never will be of that school the favorite tenet of which is that 'Ridicule is the test of truth.'" He recommended to Newman that he inform his tutor that "you by no means intend to associate with any who may be dissipated" and request him "to introduce you to a select few." [26]

Fortunately Newman was busy with other problems at the moment. As yet he had not received any instruction, and indeed it was not intended that he should. He had been summoned up to Oxford merely to take advantage of a delightful fiction whereby three weeks of residence counted as a full term toward the degree. Nevertheless he did not like to go home without learning what books he should read in the Long Vacation, and therefore, when he discovered that he could not leave in any case without the permission of the president, he determined to take that opportunity to inquire.[27] The first day he waited an hour and a half and finally discovered it was a mistake—the President was not in.[28] The second day he was received but was gently informed that all such matters were left in the hands of the tutors. This was fine, for the problem was now narrowed to finding a tutor. At last, on a Sunday evening in the Park, he saw one in top boots on horseback, obviously leaving for the country. It seemed like a last chance, so he dashed into the street and accosted him abruptly. The reply, we are told, was kindly and referred him to a colleague still in residence, who ultimately did give to the unfortunate youth the information he required.

We can guess what the information was from the record of Newman's studies during the summer months.²⁹ He read the first book of the *Aeneid*, part of it twice, the *Germania* of Tacitus, the first seven chapters of Genesis in the Septuagint, and the little *Rudiments of Logic* extracted from Aldrich; but his main effort was spent on Herodotus (Book I), the seven plays of Sophocles, Euclid (Books I–III), mathematics, and Latin composition. With the aim of perfecting himself in the latter he rendered many sentences out of Valpy's *Elegantiae latinae* and committed to memory many of its precepts. He translated a *Spectator* paper into Latin and turned some Cicero into English and then, after an interval, back into a Latin version which he compared with the original. For two full weeks, we are told, he wrote Latin verses daily.

By mid-October he was back in Oxford and for the first time saw his college in full residence. The sight must have been frightening and a little repellent. Sixty lively youths, all of them older than Newman and none of them sharing in the deeply moving experience of the year before—how could they know what was passing in his mind, and how could he care for the pursuits which occupied them? Twice more during the autumn term he was subjected to the acutely agonizing experience of a wine party (it was a common trick to make freshmen drunk), and although his diary records one evening spent among those who "de artibus, scientiis loqui non recusant" ³⁰—who do not refuse to speak of their studies—it is clear that he regarded the youths about him as strangely alien from his own concerns. In all the letters he has left from these years, and they are numerous and full, there is not one which mentions any boyish prank or escapade, any sport or game or comradely excursion, any new-found friend or widening circle of companions. He was not aloof from his fellow collegians nor was he disliked by them, but it would be quite wrong to describe his years at Trinity as spent in the midst of sixty tumultuous undergraduates. They were spent with one undergraduate, his friend John W. Bowden, and for the rest with his teachers, his books, and his private devotions.

The officers of the college at this time consisted of a president, Dr. Thomas Lee; a dean, the Rev. W. Morgan Kinsey; and two tutors, John Wilson and the Rev. Thomas Short. Mr. Short, who was Newman's tutor, had just returned from a second mastership at Rugby to replace Mr. Ingram, and the significance of this change was put succinctly by the first undergraduate Newman met. "Mr. Ingram," said the youth, "was very much liked; he was very good natured. . . . Mr. Short on the

contrary is not liked; he is strict; all wish Mr. Ingram were Tutor still." [31]
All, that is, but John Newman, who wrote home that he "rejoiced" at
the change. Actually, Mr. Short was not excessively strict and in time
he came to be liked too, but his advent does symbolize the transformation which Trinity was just then undergoing. From a "most gentlemanlike" college it was becoming, not indeed the rival of Oriel and Balliol,
but at least a place perfectly alive to the spirit of reform which was then
rising in the university. A quarter of a century before, Oxford had been
notorious for the easy indolence of its ways. It was a world (so Gibbon
tells us) in which the greater part of the professors had given up even
the pretense of lecturing, in which examinations were simply a tedious
interlude between the port which preceded and the congratulatory
dinner which followed them, and in which the Latin disputations,
handed down from generation to generation, were heard only by the
four walls of a dusty room. Then, in the year 1800, the New Examination Statute was passed, and although this measure did nothing to improve the actual teaching of the place, it did establish a final public
examination which was both honest and exacting, and it provided the
possibility of Honors in the two Schools of Literae Humaniores and
Mathematics and Physics. In other words, it gave an incentive to both
teacher and taught, and although at first there was some falling off of
candidates, gradually, as the effect of the reform spread out over the
Oxford community, touching one reluctant college after another, a
spirit of emulation developed among the better undergraduates, and in
several colleges the tutors were there to guide it.

Short was such a tutor in Trinity. No scholar himself, he was yet a
patient and exacting master, "*the* famous tutor of his day," [32] according
to his biographer. Ten years later he was to lose the headmastership of
Rugby to Arnold by only one vote, but at this date he was concerned
with his own college and in particular was attempting to raise its standards by throwing open its scholarships to all comers. Trinity "wishes to
rise in the University," wrote Newman in November, 1817, "and is
rising fast. . . . In discipline it has become the strictest of Colleges.
There are lamentations in every corner of the increasing rigour; it is
laughable, but it is delightful, to hear the groans of the oppressed." [33]

Like every boy who has been considered "sharp" at school, Newman
was eager that his tutor should not be too long in discovering that this
was the case, and the story of his first full term at Oxford is the story of
his gradual "approximation," as he called it, to Mr. Short. On October
22: "Mr. Short has not spoken to me, though Lectures have begun. I of
course do not attend." [34] On the 28th: "Mr. Short has not examined
me, but he has appointed me some lectures. I have one in Tacitus, every

morning but Thursday; one in Cicero on Wednesday, Mathematics three times a week. This is little enough, but of course they begin with little to see what I can do." [35] Indeed, in mathematics Newman was "rather astonished" to hear his class begin with "*the Ass's bridge*, a proposition quite at the beginning of Euclid, nor was my amazement in the least degree abated, when my turn came, to hear my Tutor say with a *condescending* air, 'I believe, Sir, you never saw Euclid before?' - I answered I had - 'How far?' - I had been over five books (then he looked surprised) but I added I could not say I knew them *perfect* by any means. I am sure by his manner he then took it into his head that I was not well-grounded; for he proceeded to ask me what a point was, and what a line, and what a plane angle." [36] As a result of this quizzing Newman was put into the higher division, which was already in the fourth book, and there he had the satisfaction of seeing his tutor descend through the degrees of donnishness from a stiff "sir" to a cordial admission, when Newman had demonstrated a tough one from the fifth book, that he had done it "very correctly" indeed.[37] A few days later Short lent him a book on mathematics, and the next morning invited him to breakfast. The book was Edmund Scarburgh's *The English Euclide* (1705), from which Newman made four pages of extracts [38] and learned all there was to know "about Multiple superparticular, submultiple superparticular, subsuperpartient of the less inequality, sesquialteral, sesquintal, supertriquartal and subsuperbitertial." [39] He wrote out a dissertation on the fifth book and found himself dreaming of "four magnitudes, being proportionals." Indeed, the pace was rather fast, and soon all the other pupils except one discovered that they liked logic better than Euclid, and Newman was left alone with the one undergraduate whom he had learned to know the previous term, his friend John W. Bowden. Bowden was "pretty assiduous," but "I disdain to say he goes too fast," [40] and so they fagged together through Books IV–VI and XI–XII and were into algebra by December 6.[41]

In classics the story was about the same. Early in November he had a declamation to do, and not realizing that it was a mere form, actually wrote one out, indeed taking a great deal of pains with it. It was not until he read it aloud in hall that he discovered his mistake, and yet, he thought, "I have not laid out my time for nothing, for it must improve my writing Latin." [42] But virtue in this instance did not have to be its own reward, for the Dean, who looked over all the declamations, stopped Newman as he was going to lecture and told him that his did him much credit.[43] The two lectures Newman found "childishly easy," [44] the entire reading being the first book of the *De officiis* and Tacitus' *Germania* and *Agricola*, none of which was entirely new to him. Short promised books for the next term that would give him more trouble, but meanwhile the mischief was done, for when he came to select a Greek author to take up for Collections (the college terminal examination), instead of choosing Herodotus, which would have advanced him somewhat, he chose a book which he had already read, Xenophon's *Anabasis*, because he judged from the standard of the lectures that it was not customary to take up anything higher. Nevertheless, even here he made "something like a dash" and was a little anxious lest he should not fulfill his engagement. "Every one must take some Greek, Latin, Mathematics, and Divinity," he explained to his mother. "I have taken the whole of Xenophon's Anabasis . . . (*one* book would have done and I have chosen all *seven*) two tracts of Tacitus, the 5th B[ook] of Euclid (the hardest book of Euclid - tell Harriett and Jemima it is the *ratio of ratios* Book) and the Gospels of Luke and John. This is rather fagging for a month or six weeks." [45] Nevertheless he carried it off on December 13, and the next day went home for a vacation in which he read four books of Herodotus and did some algebra and trigonometry.[46]

During the next term the "approximation" of Newman with his tutors became complete. In mid-February, when he notified them of the subjects he proposed to take up for Collections—five books of Herodotus, Virgil's *Aeneid*, mechanics, and the Pentateuch, together with Joshua, Judges, and Ruth—they shook his hand warmly, and Wilson was inspired to promise him a copy of Port's *Lexicon ionicum*.[47] Actually, when the time came on March 14, Newman increased his mathematics by the addition of plane trigonometry,[48] but his main effort during the term was spent on the two classical authors, together with Terence, in whom he had a lecture. He acquitted himself so well that when his father came up at the end of term Mr. Short grasped him by the hand and said, "Oh, Mr. Newman! what have you given us in your son!" or words to that effect.[49]

It was perhaps this remark which suggested to Mr. Newman that his son should stand for a scholarship, but John himself was rather doubtful. During the Easter Term he would have Euclid, Herodotus, Terence, Virgil, and conic sections; [50] he would have to pass his Responsions in May; and thus, "if I tried for a scholarship, I should have my Collections, responsions, and examination for scholarship, which I think I should [not] be able to manage." [51] Mr. Short, however, wishing that the newly opened scholarships should go to worthy candidates—and the more glory to Trinity if they were in-college men—was very urgent that Newman should stand, and on April 29 he agreed to do so.[52] How his heart beat within him at the thought that he might attain this honor! Did he desire it too much? There was certainly some spiritual pride, for he was haunted by the fear of a *turpis repulsa*,[53] and also some intellectual pride, for he was sanguine beyond all reason. Therefore he prayed for help and confided his prayer to his private diary.

> O God of heaven and earth, Thou hast been pleased of Thine infinite goodness to impart Thy Holy Spirit to me and to enlighten my soul with the knowledge of the truth. Therefore, O Lord, for our Blessed Saviour's sake, hearken to the supplication which I make before Thee. Let me not rely too much on getting this scholarship - Let me not be led away from Thee by the hopes of it. So let me order my spirit, that, if I get it not, I may not be disappointed but may praise and bless Thy name, as knowing better than myself what is good for me. O Lord God of hosts, grant it not to me, if it is likely to be a snare to me, to turn me away from Thee.[54]

It seemed best not to tell his parents that he was standing until after the event was known, though in his suppressed excitement he dropped hints which they must have been very dull not to interpret correctly. "Next Monday," he wrote, "is an important day. It is our Gaudy, as well as election for Fellows and Scholars. We are all anxious to see who is to assume the dimidated sleeve and the £60 a year. I will tell you something now concerning the scholarship. The candidates are eleven in number - five in-college men, and six out-college. . . . They were examined yesterday and the greater part of today, and I understand they will be kept two more days at it. I hope, but scarcely hope, (mysterious words!) to send you a letter full of news soon." [55] The examination ranged over a wide field—Latin verse, Latin theme, English theme, Latin translation, Euripides (a choral passage), Plato, Xenophon, Lucretius, and Livy, the translation being done orally and at sight,[56] and there was mathematics as well. Coxe of Worcester was very near to winning, but Newman's superiority in mathematics is said to have turned the scale in his favor.[57] Most people, including his friend Bowden, had not credited him with much of a chance, "but I, when I heard the voice of the Dean summoning me before the Electors, seemed to myself to feel no surprise. I am told I turned pale." [58] With what may seem like undue haste he ran out at once to buy his scholar's gown, but in his notebook he declared that it was not his work but God's—"est Deo gratia." [59] "I prayed, and He was pleased to hear my petition, and yesterday, out of his infinite loving kindness He gave me the scholarship." [60]

After the excitement of this contest Responsions must have seemed very tame indeed, for it required of the candidate only one Greek and one Latin author, portions of either Euclid or Aldrich, and translation from English into Latin. Newman had chosen the last five books of

Herodotus and the odes and epodes of Horace for his authors, and in Euclid he was required to "shew how a circle may be inscribed in a rhombus." [61] This he showed on May 30, and with that his Latin diary ceases to record any studies until December of the next year.

Newman liked at this time to compare the undergraduate residence of three years to "a picture of a whole life, of youth, of manhood, and of old age," [62] and certainly his own career falls into three distinct periods, the first extending to his winning the scholarship in May, 1818; the second to April, 1819, when he began studying in earnest for the Final Examination; and the third to December, 1820, when he took his degree. The simile only fails in that with Newman the solemnity of old age came first, and his wild oats were sown in the middle period. From June, 1818 to April, 1819 he confesses to having been "idle," [63] but by this he signified merely that he was very busy about things which did not directly relate to his college studies. Actually, the only time that he was off these studies completely was in the Long Vacation of 1818, when he was taken up with Gibbon and Locke to the exclusion of everything else. Once he returned to Oxford he exchanged the historian and philosopher of his own land for those of Patavium and Stagira in quite a dutiful way. In Michaelmas and Hilary terms he apparently had lectures in Thucydides, Livy, Aristotle's *Rhetoric* (the last two with Kinsey, the dean), and algebra,[64] and continued with the study of Old Testament history. In December he wrote out an analysis of the eight books of Thucydides, whether for his own use or because it was required for Collections is not certain. He began it in "that pseudo-Gibbonian style, in which it amused me at this time to compose," [65] but the style proved tedious to maintain and so after a few pages he lapsed into giving the substance without the flourish. Livy he analyzed more barely—at least all that survives is an eight-page summary of Books XXVI–XXX of the second decade, and then a summary of the summary to bring out the principal events more clearly.[66] There is also an elaborate analysis of the *Rhetoric* which was made in 1819, whether at the beginning of the year or when he returned to that work in December is uncertain.[67] For algebra something more special was required. Everyone who contemplated Honors in the Schools was almost obliged at this time to supplement the regular collegial instruction with that of a private tutor, and as early as February, 1818 Newman had made inquiries on the subject.[68] At that time he thought the price very high and so did nothing about it, but in November he and his friend Bowden engaged themselves to J. A. Ogle,[69] who had taken a First in mathematics five years before and later was to become Aldrichian and Clinical Professor of Medicine. They spent two hours a day with him from November until February, when he became a regular college tutor in the place of Wilson and so could give them only one hour, which it appears they were very glad to have.[70] In view of these studies it could hardly be said that Newman was a wastrel during these two terms, but he did go about things in a more cavalier spirit. "I write standing in great haste," he said to his mother, "to say, that, in the midst of three books of Thucydides, five of Livy, one of Aristotle [Rhetoric], fourteen Prophets, and the last half of Algebra, (for such are my Collections) I am going to Concerts!" [71]

Newman never ceased to love concerts, but he did cease to admire the spirit which prompted this remark. One can imagine him reading this letter over in later years and commenting in the margin, as he loved to do, that its tone betrayed the author to be emphatically "young," and to be in that mood of heady intoxication with his own powers where the garb of the mere student seemed drab and he was pleased to exchange it for the brighter colors of the dilettante and the man of the world. And it is true that just about this time Newman began to see himself in this pleasing character. "What? Can any one fag, fag and be an author?" [72] he exclaimed, for he was writing verses on "The Coliseum" in competition for the Newdigate prize (which he did not get), and he and Bowden had just published the second canto of their poem, *St. Bartholomew's Eve.* The poem, moreover, was merely introductory to a larger project, nothing less than a periodical entitled *The Undergraduate*, which Newman and Bowden conducted through six numbers in February and March, 1819,[73] and which is very interesting as revealing their attitude toward themselves and their university at this time. The first number is a Johnsonian essay on the difficulties of commencing such a periodical when one must please all the various classes of undergraduates. There is the reading man and then, of the nonreading men, there are those who openly attack study, those who would study if their health permitted, those who simply "do not see the *good* of it," [74] those who procrastinate, and those who with imposing words conceal their total neglect of study. The *Undergraduate* would address all of them and yet none of them—rather, says the editor, it would address the literary person. The editor, indeed, fancies that he himself is such a person, for in the second number he displays his progress through the university, first in the character of a Rustic, then of a Dandy, and now of an Author. It is in that character, in the third number, that he takes Ariosto's hippogriff on a flight to the moon, where all things lost on earth are stored, and finds in various small packages "the wit of a Don," "the lenity of an Examining Master," and two commodities which he is assured would be highly valued at Oxford if they were made known, namely "the practical utility of Aristotle" and "the sense and advantage of Logic." [75] This paper is nearly contemporaneous with J. S. Boone's *The Oxford Spy*, a rather witty undergraduate poem in five dialogues which spied out the very abuses enumerated by the *Undergraduate*—the pedantic concern with detail, the exclusive devotion to ancient authors, and especially the emphasis on Aristotle and logic. Newman has noted that this poem illustrates "the vague dissatisfaction of the young 50 years ago with the Oxford curriculum of studies," [76] but it was apparently a dissatisfaction which he shared, for the whole significance of the *Undergraduate* is the feeling to which it testifies that so much of the process of education, if it is to be real education, must lie outside of the academic routine. This feeling becomes especially clear in a paper which Newman wrote for the *Undergraduate* but never published. It proposes a debating society (the present Union was not founded till 1830) which should meet fortnightly in the music room to debate questions covering "the whole range of history, poetry and the fine arts, indeed nothing should be excluded but the politics of the last fifty [on second thought he substituted "100"] years." Each college should send three members (but six from Christ Church and one from each hall), and "it would be a school for the future senator or lawyer, it would enlarge and refine the mind, it would be a most agreeable relaxation after the toils of the day." [77]

Such grandiose ideas were furthered by an incident which occurred just at this time and which, though trivial in itself, remained vivid in Newman's memory for many years. "I was a youth of eighteen," he wrote, "and was leaving my University for the Long Vacation, when I found myself in company in a public conveyance with a middle-aged person, whose face was strange to me. However, it was the great academical luminary of the day, whom afterwards I knew very well. Luckily for me, I did not suspect it; and luckily too, it was a fancy of his, as his friends knew, to make himself on easy terms especially with stage-coach companions. So, what with my flippancy and his condescension, I managed to hear many things which were novel to me at the time." [78] One point that his companion was strong upon was "the material pomp and circumstance which should environ a great seat of learning," and especially that Oxford ought to stand in a domain of its own surrounded by an ample range of wood and meadow not less than four miles in extent. What other "novel" things Newman heard we are not told, nor are we told whether his companion was Edward Copleston, the provost, or Richard Whately, the Fellow and Tutor of Oriel, but certainly it was one of the two.

Newman's longing for a broader educational experience was also fostered by his friendship with the dean of his college, the Rev. W. Morgan Kinsey. Kinsey belonged to that new race of tutors which Reginald Heber discovered on revisiting Oxford in 1818. "The old boys never stirred from home," he wrote; "these pass their whole vacations on the continent, are geologists, system-mongers, and I know not what." [79] Kinsey was no system monger, but he was a more liberal and easy personality than Mr. Short. He ranged about more in his lectures and inspired affection where the other inspired merely respect.[80] He treated Newman "with the familiar kindness of an elder brother," [81] and in the summer term of 1819 took him to Professor Buckland's lectures in geology, that "new and interesting science" [82] which was just then delighting the younger dons. Buckland was a fine lecturer, clear and eloquent, overflowing with witty illustrations and wont to enforce his points by dashing down among his auditors, like Samson, wielding the jaw of a cave bear or the thighbone of a hyena.[83] Newman found this "entertaining" but feared he did not fully understand the lectures "from not knowing the principles of the science," [84] as, indeed, neither did Buckland. Buckland's geology was wholly in the service of natural theology, but despite its perfectly innocent character it was just a little ominous that Newman should be attending such lectures at all. Was it not possible that the breadth of his intellectual interests would once again lead him into a kind of worldliness? Indeed, so it seemed to be doing, for in the Long Vacation of 1819 he reread Gibbon and found that he liked him even better than he had before. The elegance of his style seemed to palliate the fact that he was not "a better man," and if this were true, was it not silently implied that one who had modeled his own style upon that elegance might also model himself upon the character of the man? Not that Newman could ever become a nineteenth-century Gibbon, but he did become half conscious of "some mental and moral change" within himself. He found he was beginning to hope "great things" for himself and to have "dreams of a secular ambition." [85] For some years his father had been intending him for the bar, and now, in November, 1819, this intention was put in motion by having his name entered at Lincoln's Inn.[86] Clearly, the "school for the future senator or lawyer" was to be a school for himself, and he records that he was so calculating as to attend Dr. Nares's lectures on modern history merely because he heard that the names were reported to the minister in London.

How is one to interpret this period of Newman's studies? To many it will seem a perfectly natural unfolding of normal, healthy desires, and so it seemed to Newman at the time. But by the autumn of 1820, when the press of work for the Final Examination was upon him, the conviction grew in his own mind that he had been "idle." It was forced upon him how much there was to know in the central core of his classical and mathematical books without scampering about the periphery of new sciences and modern authors. Thus these scamperings became "idleness," and the spirit which had prompted them became intellectual pride. The pride, he saw, had resulted from gaining the scholarship, and his prayer to be saved from sin had apparently not been answered. He turned again to the private journal in which this prayer was copied, and as he read it over he trembled at the recollection. "Could I thus so earnestly pray that obtaining the object of my prayers might be no snare to me, and could I faint after a time, and, on gaining the scholarship, grow cold and remiss and ungrateful? Could I be so lowly and resigned beforehand, so thankful on succeeding, and yet in a few short weeks become so vain, so puffed up, so quarrelsome, so very wicked?" [87]

Obviously, what seemed like wickedness to Newman would make very tolerable behavior for most pople, but the important question is not what Newman was, but what, by his own standards, he seemed to himself to be. And there is no question that by the autumn of 1820 he came to believe that his scholarship had led him into sin. "No one can imagine," he wrote to Mr. Mayers in October, "the sins into which I fell after I got the Scholarship"; [88] and to his sister he declared, "I am very vain, and the least success is apt to alter me, - witness my getting the Trinity scholarship." [89]

Long before Newman came to perceive his sin, however, he had more or less freed himself from it by the renewed diligence which he showed in the spring of 1819. From that time until his examination in November, 1820 his life was "almost one continued *mass* of reading." [90] He had decided to attempt Honors in both classics and mathematics, and the books which he intended to offer were the following: in Greek, Aeschylus, Sophocles, Thucydides, Herodotus, Xenophon's *Hellenica*, Books I and II, Polybius, Book I, Aristotle's *Ethics*, *Rhetoric*, and *Poetics*; in Latin, Virgil, Horace, and two decades of Livy; in mathematics, Euclid, Bridge's *Algebra* and *Trigonometry*, Newton's *Principia* (three sections), Robertson's *Conic Sections*, Vince's *Fluxions*, *Hydrostatics*, and *Astronomy*, Wood's *Mechanics* and *Optics*.[91] This list was neither more nor less than was usual, but it was enough to keep him busy. In the Long Vacation of 1819 he took home a "horrid" number of books [92] and, despite his Gibbon, read for nine hours a day, chiefly, it would seem, in the Greek historians. From August 9 to September 9 he did for Herodotus what he had already done for Thucydides—filled a large copybook with an analysis of the history, and on the blank facing pages copied out the relevant notes from the editions of Larcher and Major Rennell.[93] By October, when he joined Bowden at Oxford, the pace was increased to eleven or twelve hours daily, and they determined to sweep "on, on, like the Destroyer" in Southey's poem until they arrived at "the ocean of great-goes." [94] The course took them through Aeschylus and Sophocles and Aristotle's *Rhetoric*, which last Newman offered for Collections in December,[95] and by Christmas vacation he was alone again in London, doing algebra, conic sections, and mechanics.[96]

Life was not yet a continual grind. In February he joined a music club at St. John's which gave weekly private concerts, he himself playing the first violin in quartets by Haydn and Mozart.[97] He read *Ivanhoe* on its first appearance, and though forced to observe that it had no plot in the true Aristotelian sense, declared that the second volume was "unequalled in all the requisites of fine writing. I never read any thing that surpassed it. . . . O what a poet! . . . Author of Waverley, thou art a second Shakespeare." [98] With the value of modern literature brought thus sharply before him, he and eleven of his fellow undergraduates established, on February 29, the Trinity College Book Society, whereby books which were proposed by the various members were purchased, passed around to be read, and then bought at half price by the proposer or anyone else who cared to bid higher.[99] We may imagine that it was through this society that Newman became acquainted with Crabbe's *Tales of the Hall*, a work of which he was "excessively fond" and in which he never ceased to delight throughout his entire life.[100] Nevertheless, the time for even such modest diversions was coming to an end. As the Long Vacation drew near he announced that he would be home for intervals of only three weeks during the summer, and that for the rest, "the Green Gate and venerable roof of Trinity College will, I hope, keep me in an uninterrupted, calm, delightful course of study." [101]

In the event, the three weeks turned to four,[102] but except for that time and for Sundays, on which he never worked, every day of the last twenty-four weeks before the examination was a day of intensive study. He rose at half past four, read four hours before breakfast, hardly allowed himself time for his meals, and before retiring had put in an average of twelve hours of study.[103] Generally it was exactly that, but at least it was that average: if one day he worked only nine hours, the next day it was fifteen, and so on. As usual, he and Bowden studied together, and the method they adopted was to keep several things going at once, for the sake of variety, and to go back over them again and again so that they really stuck, rather than to do them once and for all, though ever so thoroughly, and then dismiss them. They would begin the morning with one proposition of conic sections and one of mechanics and then go on to the principal book they were working up at the time. If Livy, they would do some thirty chapters; if a play, some five to six hundred verses, and then go back and review the work which they had done a week or two weeks before. At no time was their reading merely passive. They accompanied it with all kinds of written and oral exercises designed to fix the material in their minds, to set it in new and meaningful relationships, and to give a genuine, working mastery over it. They filled copybook after copybook with their mathematical problems, made chronologies and abstracts of their histories, quizzed each other on Aristotle's *Ethics* in the manner of a *viva voce*, and analyzed various plays of Aeschylus in the light of the principles laid down by Aristotle. In this manner they had completed by the end of October all of mechanics, conic sections, Newton, Xenophon, Polybius, and Livy, had read the plays of Aeschylus and Sophocles from two to four times each, with further attention to the choruses, had done the *Poetics* twice with Twining's notes, and in a most careful manner had gone three times through the *Ethics*.[104] The *Ethics* at this period was the great "stock-in-trade" [105] of the examiners, and since Newman apparently felt that his major historians were well in hand and his mathematics might wait for a final review, he thought himself justified in spending part of six full weeks on this major work. Indeed, toward the end of his review he devoted several days to writing out practice answers to questions on the *Ethics* which had been given in the Schools in previous years. This, then, was his course of study, and it was, as he insisted, "real reading," "*bona fide* reading," [106] in which his attention was alive throughout.

At the beginning of the summer Newman felt quite confident of success, and although he had little flurries of fear as time went on, he still considered that he had advanced much more quickly than he expected, and by the end of September he was so easy in his mind as to hope that he would have little or nothing to do the week before his examination.[107] But the solitariness of Oxford, so conducive to study, was also conducive to searching the heart, and as the crisis approached Newman began to see that its real significance was spiritual rather than intellectual. The event, properly considered, was not in his hands but in the hands of God, and since God would use it for his servant's good, though 'not necessarily for his success, it was not only a duty but a privilege to take no thought for the morrow.[108] Labor he must to provide the means of success, but he must not allow his heart to be set too avidly upon it. "It is my daily, and (I hope) heartfelt prayer," he wrote to his brother, "that I may not get any honours here, if they are to be the least cause of sin to me." [109] But, as always, the situation was made more painful by the fact that there were others besides himself who would be disappointed if he failed. For seven years now Trinity had not secured a single First. Christ Church, during the same period, had secured forty-two, Oriel fifteen, Balliol and Brasenose each eleven, but

Trinity, despite the late spirit of reading, had not achieved a single success, and there was a feeling that it never would. "Unless success . . . attends on Trinity this examination," Newman was told, "we have determined it is useless to read." [110]

Under this pressure and that of his own eager hopes, Newman continued to pray, "Let me get no honours here, if they are to be the slightest cause of sin to my soul." Yet with all the earnestness he assumed, he felt how little his heart went with his words. His very prayer, it seemed, was an instrument of hypocrisy. "I am buoyed up by the secret idea, that by thus leaving the event in the hands of God, when I pray, He may be induced, as a reward for so proper a spirit, to grant me my desire. Thus," he confessed, with echoes of a famous scene in *Hamlet*, "my prayer is a mockery." [111] This fear was perhaps an overrefinement, but it did not exaggerate the perils of an intellectual triumph. Surely the scholarship had taught him that much. His mind reverted to the prayer he had offered at that period, and suddenly his whole conduct of the past two years was set, not in the satisfying glow of his earlier triumph, but in the harsh light of his approaching ordeal. Thus seen, all the enlarging of his hopes, the dreams of authorship and of prominence at the bar, the excursions into novel sciences and modern authors, seemed to be merely the shallow egotism of one who had made a religion out of his own mind. "What a lesson for me!" he exclaimed. "Now, before my examination, I feel, by the grace of God, warm, resigned and teachable; I pray Him not to let me succeed, if success would cause me to commit the least sin . . . and yet, yet, if I *am* successful, what may happen! may I not fall as before? is it not likely? what a heart is mine! So trifling a good fortune, and it must stop my prayers, lull my watchfulness, blind me, lead me back to wallow in the mire! What *would* happen, were I to get this greater success? my mouth is stopped. . . . How probable, then, since I have prayed the Lord that I may *not* succeed if sin must follow, how probable I shall fail!" [112]

As Newman pursued this thought during the coming weeks, his dilemma seemed increasingly clear. He was striving toward an intellectual triumph which, if he achieved it, would most likely carry him into spiritual sin. It had happened so once—how could he desire it should happen so again? "The recollection of my ingratitude," he wrote Mr. Mayers, "this it is that hangs heavy on my heart, and unnerves my arm in the day of battle." [113] What is more, with the loss of his religious integrity he found that his intellectual integrity had suffered too. His thoughts became scattered and disorganized, and even the reading of the past few months was jumbled together "so very irregularly and out of place that my mind is a labyrinth more than anything else." [114] On

October 16 he turned from classics to mathematics and was so dismayed at all that remained to do that he became panicky, declaring that he would have to throw his classics overboard to bring his mathematics into port; and even then he thought it "highly probable" that he would fail.[115] In this distress Mr. Wilson kindly came to the rescue, gave him some two to five hours daily of his time, and persuaded him to jettison only Aristotle's *Rhetoric*, though to do even so much meant abandoning all hopes of a First in classics. With this help Newman steadied a bit and by mid-November declared that he was "quite the reverse of nervous." True, he had "moments of terror" but otherwise was in good spirits, and, judging calmly, thought he would get a First in mathematics and a Second in classics.[116]

He was doomed to be disappointed. On November 25, a day sooner than he expected, he was suddenly called into the Schools and found himself so nervous that he could not answer half a dozen questions. The examiners gave him every consideration, but nothing would do. Whenever he approached the room a great depression came over him. He was nervous in the extreme, a thing he declared he had never before experienced and did not expect. His memory was gone; his mind was altogether confused; and he dragged on a sickly examination from Saturday to Friday, when he was finally obliged to retire from the contest.[117]

"It is all over," he wrote his father, "and I have *not* succeeded. The pain it gives me to be obliged to inform you and my Mother of it I *cannot* express. What I feel on my own account is indeed nothing at all, compared with the idea that I have disappointed you; and most willingly would I consent to a hundred times the sadness that now overshadows me if so doing would save my Mother and you from feeling vexation. . . . I have done everything I could to obtain my object, I have spared no labour and my reputation in my College is as solid as before, if not so splendid. If a man falls in battle after a display of bravery he is honoured as a hero; ought not the same glory to attend him who falls on the field of literature?" [118]

From this dramatic epistle Newman's parents quite naturally concluded that he had been "plucked"; [119] but the fact was that his degree was safe, although he had gained no Honors in mathematics and in classics was a Second "under the line," that is, the lowest possible class. Nevertheless, to have the thing over was an inexpressible relief. Before, "there was a darkness and dread - I saw the cataract, to which I was hurrying without the possibility of a rescue. It was as if a surgical operation was day after day being carried on upon me, and tearing away something precious," [120] but now there was only a wonderful calmness and peace of mind. It was perhaps a trifle boyish of him to declare that he was less disappointed at his failure than he would have been at having torn his hat or got his coat wetted by the rain, but when a friend said, "Well, Newman, I would rather have your philosophy than the high honours to which you were aspiring," [121] he must have felt that this was really true, though perhaps it was a pity one could not have both.

Newman never admitted, of course, that his failure in the Schools was any measure of his real intellectual capacity. But if not, how did it happen that he failed? Was it, as Geoffrey Faber has suggested in his brilliant character study of the Oxford movement, that there was a sense in which Newman wanted to fail, that his loss of memory, his nervousness, his confusion were simply an escape mechanism whereby he avoided a competition in which he knew that he could not succeed? [122] It may well be, for certainly by failing in this spectacular way Newman did keep his reputation intact, which he could not have done if he had gone into the examination with all his faculties about him and performed in a merely mediocre or undistinguished way. And yet the question arises, why did Newman need an escape mechanism? He was paralyzed by guilt, no doubt, but if he had been really prepared for the examination there would have been nothing to feel guilty about. It was not guilt that made him fail but the apprehension of failure that made him feel guilty, and if this be so, then there must have been some other cause, of an intellectual character, which had brought him to the point of a breakdown and made an escape seem necessary. In later years Newman was inclined to see this cause as a failure of system, a failure to give his studies form, whether that of genuine education or the special form required by the Oxford examination.

For the two were not the same. Improved only a decade before, the examination was already being widely criticized for giving the palm, so people said, to facility of response rather than depth of understanding or elegance of taste. Being largely viva voce, it was almost limited to the routine problems of sight translation, ready construing, and quick answers to factual questions; what is more, since it was open to the public these questions had to be answered in an atmosphere which was strained and hectic, almost that of a gladiatorial contest. Obviously there was a special technique about preparing for such an examination, and in Newman's day this technique was a kind of guild secret possessed by some colleges and not by others. Their men got the Firsts, and then, on becoming tutors and examiners, passed the tradition on to their pupils, thus continuing the process by which they themselves had been produced. Oriel, Balliol, and Christ Church were within this charmed circle but Trinity was not, and in after years Newman was aghast at what little guidance he had received in his preparation. The way to study for such an examination, according to a Christ Church tutor, was to spend two and a half years reading the classics in lecture in the ordinary way, and then, during the last year, to read them over again in exactly the same way. The aspirant "cannot be much encouraged to analyze what he has read, or to compare it with the opinions of those who have written on the same subjects: because so much time is necessary for things absolutely required, that he dares not diverge from the beaten track." [123] This, however, is exactly what Newman did. He wrote out lengthy analyses of Herodotus [124] and Thucydides, spent hours copying out the notes of Larcher and Major Rennell, and wrote Aristotelian critiques of the plays of Aeschylus. All this may have been good discipline, but it was of no service in the Schools, and no one informed him that such would be the case. "I have not been advised," he wrote shortly before his examination, "or have been advised wrongly, what books to read. I have fagged at books which will be of no service to me, and this to such an extent that I think six months of very hard reading have been thrown away." [125] This was also his mature opinion. Over thirty years later, in a letter written for the *Catholic University Gazette* but withheld from publication, he explicitly laid his failure to the "little or no guidance" which he had received throughout his entire course of studies.[126]

And yet he had been equally unable to guide himself. Being very young, "he had not that experience for shaping for himself his course of reading, or that maturity of mind for digesting it, which a longer time would have given him." [127] But not having this, he really had nothing at all.

> When I look back upon those anxious, toilsome years and their event [he wrote in 1854], I seem to myself to see a type of Protestantism;—zeal, earnestness, resolution, without a guidance; effort without a result. It was a pattern instance of private judgment and its characteristics. I think of the words you have lately quoted, and apply them to myself, though it was only an Undergraduate life I lost, which is retrievable,—"Heu, vitam perdidi, operosè nihil agendo!"
>
> You will say that what I lost was, not mental advancement, but academical honors; I think I lost both.[128]

CHAPTER 2

Fellow of Oriel

Behold you now a Fellow of Oriel. . . .
—F. R. Thresher to Newman, 1822

IN 1821 Newman wrote an "Essay on the Study of Modern History" which he submitted for the English essay prize. It failed to win, and on looking it over in later years he thought that he understood why. "This Essay," he wrote, "gives evidence I had not yet attended to *composition* - i.e. taking an *idea* and developing it. I believe the same fault is to be found in my Essay on ancient Slavery. Perhaps I did not begin to attempt this difficult accomplishment (which even now, November 1851, is what tries and distresses me in writing) till I had been writing Sermons for some time." [1]

That the problem of composition, that is, of ordering his materials in accordance with a central idea, was really a major one for Newman appears from the account he has given, in the *Catholic University Gazette*,[2] of his lifelong quest for a Latin style. From earliest years, he says, one of the wishes nearest to his heart had been to write Latin well, but although he had some idea of the style of English authors, he never could understand what was meant by good Latin style—he did not have the *idea* of it. When the books told him, "This is neat Ciceronian language" or "This is pure and elegant Latinity," he agreed perforce but without understanding why. Then, in October, 1817, just before going up to Oxford for his first full term, he fell upon an article in the *Quarterly Review*[3] which noticed a Latin history of the Rebellion of 1745 and which, though he did not know it at the time, was the work of Edward Copleston, the provost of Oriel. The criticisms in this article seemed so trenchant and judicious that he copied them out and nearly got them by heart. "Indeed for a long time, wandering as I was without a guide, wishing to write Latin and having no one to inform [me] how to set about it, those criticisms were my only comfort, the only remarks which seemed vigorous and certain, and on which I felt I could lean." [4] The difficulty was that they were purely verbal, and hence they "did but lead me deeper into the mistake to which I had already been introduced,—

that Latinity consisted in using good phrases." [5] He made lists of these phrases and tried to introduce them into his own compositions, and whenever he fell in with new authors, such as Tacitus or Erasmus, he skimmed the cream of their vocabulary and added it to his own. Once again, however, "the labour . . . of years came to nothing." "When I was twenty I knew no more of Latin composition than I had known at fifteen," and the reason was that "I was aiming to be an architect by learning to make bricks." [6]

Indeed, even after Newman's examination was over and he was free for that silent, inward communion which was always his deepest need, he seems to have done nothing to make this communion possible. Instead he threw himself into a variety of projects which had no relation to each other and no very prominent relation to himself. At one moment he would conduct experiments in chemistry and congratulate his sister for "her skill in steaming away the superfluous water of the nitro-sulphate of copper." [7] A little later he would transform himself into Signor Giovanni Enrico Neandrini, the famous composer, and write a piece of music which he triumphantly described as "light and airy," until, on hearing it played, he discovered to his chagrin that it was really "very heavy." [8] Or perhaps he would decide to be a linguist, mastering the Persian, Arabic, Italian, German, and Anglo-Saxon tongues, whether simultaneously or not is uncertain.[9] In any case these studies were not to interfere with the "various excursions" which he planned to the British Museum "for the sake of the minerals." He had already ridden over to Abingdon with Kinsey to view the mineralogical collection of "a gentleman of the name of Bowles," [10] and he was also attending Buckland's lectures on the subject. These latter, which cost him two guineas, he found "very simple and intelligible even to children," and he took down the substance of them in notes.[11] Buckland's geology lectures, however, which cost only one guinea, he did not take down, largely because of the very desultory way in which the information was imparted. "For, to tell the truth," he wrote to his mother, "the science is so in its infancy, that no regular system is formed. Hence the lectures are rather an enumeration of facts from which probabilites are *deduced*, than a consistent and harmonious theory of certainties *illustrated* by occasional examples." [12]

The state of geology was the state of Newman's studies, and one may wonder if this was to be another period, like the "idle" one after gaining the scholarship, for which Newman would later be repentant? Superficially it would appear so, but actually, amid the minerals and the music, the nitrosulphate and the Arabic, there was a deep and continuing concern with religion. "Easter and Act Term [1821]," wrote Newman in his private journal, "I devoted nearly entirely to religion,—for about six weeks, and July in the vacation, I was employed on that collection of texts, which I have not yet finished." [13] The collection still survives, consisting of six copybooks filled with passages of scripture arranged under such topics as "The unconverted man," "The law," "The unswerving justice of God," and "The scheme of salvation." [14] These matters, then, were Newman's real preoccupation during these months. If he studied mathematics, he also wrote an essay on how the mysteries of mathematics prepare the mind for receiving the mysteries of religion.[15] If, in the daytime, he attended lectures on geology, at night he dreamed that a spirit came to him and "discoursed about the other world. . . . Among other things it said that it was absolutely impossible for the reason of man to understand the mystery of the Holy Trinity . . . but that everything in another world was so very, very plain that there was not the slightest difficulty about it." [16] In September he quarreled with his father about the propriety of writing a letter on Sunday, and the following January he wrote a dialogue about a young man who tried to pay a bill on Sunday and was refused—and he added an appendix of supporting "Passages from the writings of the Church of England divines." [17] In other words, his surface concerns were not his real ones. Where previously he had dabbled in these things in a spirit of intoxication and following a triumph, now he dabbled in them idly, in a spirit of absence of mind, as something to be doing while he recovered from defeat. Disparate as these occupations were, he was not dissipating himself with them. Rather he was gathering himself together, nourishing his forces from within, finding in his collection of texts that "consistent and harmonious theory" which he could not find in Buckland. To Buckland he listened with one ear, but to the visiting spirit, who told him how the mysteries of religion would be made "very, very plain," he listened with his whole heart. Here was a luminous kind of order which he could realize, and it in turn would give order to all the world. Knowing this, he could afford to bide his time, and therefore as he waited he silently applied to himself the line from Gray's "Bard,"

And hushed in grim repose expects his
evening prey.[18]

But what should this prey be? That was the question. Climbing one autumn evening to the top of Trinity Chapel tower, he meditated upon this theme, and while the friend who had mounted with him made observations on the stars, he, "earthly-minded youth [looked] down into the deep gas-lit, dark-shadowed quadrangles, and [wondered] if he should ever be Fellow of this or that college, which he singled out from the mass of academical buildings." [19] If his gaze carried so far as Oriel, it was indeed prophetic, for only a few weeks later, on Novmber 15, 1821, a cousin of Kinsey's happened to mention in his presence the Oriel Fellowship examination,[20] and it flashed through his mind that this, perhaps, was the "prey" for which he had been waiting.

An Oriel Fellowship at this period was "the great object of the ambition of half the Bachelors of Oxford." [21] To Mark Pattison it was held up as "the ideal prize to which I was to aspire," [22] and a clerical friend of the Newman family declared that although it was "great in point of emolument, in point of character it was immortality." The lustrous names of Copleston, Whately, and Hawkins, of Keble, Pusey, and R. H. Froude, of the two Arnolds and the poet Clough all belong to the Oriel of these years, for in the early nineteenth century talent flowed Orielwards, said the college historian, as if by a natural law. That law was simply the manner in which elections to Fellowships were made, for in Oriel they were conducted more purely on a basis of merit than was the case anywhere else in the university. In other colleges most of the Fellowships were confined by the terms of their foundation to persons who were already members of the college or to candidates from a particular locality, but Oriel had never had any of the first sort and only a few of the second. Moreover, ever since the end of the eighteenth century there had been a distinct tendency to relax even the few restrictions that did exist, and the result of this tendency was that by 1822 Oriel had almost a free choice among the best minds of the university.[23]

The striking thing, however, was the use which the college made of this freedom. Where the elections elsewhere went largely by interest or congeniality and were openly canvassed for like any sinecure or political office, the Oriel elections went strictly by examination and that an examination of a very peculiar kind. "The questions," wrote Dean Church, "were very general, not involving directly much knowledge, but trying how a man could treat ordinary questions which interest cultivated men. It was altogether a trial, not of how much men knew, but of *how* they knew, and what they could do." [24] "Their style of philosophical question and essay," says Mark Pattison, "was a peculiar one. . . . Instead of the eclectic, incoherent ten questions, ranging over the surface of philosophy, and papers by which knowledge rather than original power is tested, their paper had a uniform colour, as if the work of a single examiner. It proposed the simple but everlasting problems of morals and logic in such a way that a candidate, who had thought more than he had read, was inevitably impelled to pour out his very self upon it." [25]

It would not be surprising if the results of such an examination were very different from those of the Schools, and in point of fact it was almost the intention of the college that they should be. "Every election to a fellowship," wrote Copleston, "which tends to discourage the narrow and almost technical *routine* of public examinations, I consider as an important triumph." [26] The trouble was that too many such "triumphs" might give rise to a cry of favoritism, and this had actually happened in the election of 1821. In that year the winners were both second-class men, and among the rejected was a first-class man, D. K. Sandford of Christ Church, a son of the Bishop of Edinburgh and subsequently professor of Greek at Glasgow. The conflict was rendered dramatic by the fact that Sandford won the English essay prize at the same time that one of the successful competitors, C. J. Plumer, won the Latin essay prize. Thus, when they appeared together at the ensuing commencement to recite their essays, it seemed a kind of appeal to a larger audience, and the more popular English essay carried away some sympathy. But the affair did not end there. The July number of the *Edinburgh Review* contained an article in which Sandford, under the cover of anonymity and in the course of reviewing a volume of lectures on the ancient Greeks, issued a vindictive attack on the integrity of the Oriel electors. The attack provoked a reply and a counterreply,[27] and although Sandford later made a sincere and candid apology, the effect of his action at the time might well have been to make the electors somewhat cautious in their choice. To elect another Second would be to defy their critics and invite a renewal of the attack, but to choose one who was "under the line"—this was something which the electors themselves had never seen fit to do in the entire history of the college.[28]

Newman realized that this was so. "Who indeed will not rightly wonder," he wrote, "at the audacity of him, who, being an Under-the-line himself, presumes to contend with some of the first men in the University, for a seat by the side of names like Keble and Hawkins?" [29] Some of his friends thought the attempt unwise, for if he failed, as he was sure to do, would not this second rebuff have the effect of confirming the first and set a definite stamp upon his name? To such counsels Newman replied that he had no thought of succeeding—he merely wished to gain experience which would help him on a later attempt, either at Oriel or some place else—but the truth is that he had a strange anticipation of success almost from the beginning. This troubled him, as indicating a resurgence of worldly passions which he had thought were stilled. "After my failure last November," he wrote in his diary, "I thought that they never would be unruly again, for I felt so resigned through God's grace that it seemed as if the honours of the world had no longer any charm in themselves to tempt me with. Alas! no sooner is any mention made of my standing for a fellowship, than every mound and barrier seems swept away, and the tides of passion spread and over-flow and deluge me in every direction, and without Thy help, O Lord, what will be the end of this?" [30] A short time later, on December 15, he told Mr. Kinsey of his intention to stand, and was shown an essay by the successful candidate of the year just passing. As he read it he thought to himself, "I could do as well, or better," and the thought "threw me into such a fever, I do not know when I shall recover it. If the distant and improbable shadow of success affects me so, what would the reality!" [31]

Reflections like these continued through the winter until they culminated in a letter of March 6, 1822. Newman was replying to his mother's birthday congratulations, and after some solemn thoughts on his coming of age, he added, "Not that I am sorry so great a part of life is gone—would that all were over!—but I seem now more left to myself, and when I reflect upon my own weakness I have cause to shudder." [32] Quite naturally, his mother remonstrated at the tone of his letter and urged him to take more air and exercise, to allow himself a proper quantity of wine, and not to be overanxious about anything. Indeed, she seemed so genuinely concerned about the state of his health and spirits that Newman asked Mr. Kinsey and his brother Frank to write her something reassuring. He himself appealed to "facts." "To take last week,—I dined out once, and was three times out in the evening; to two music parties and one dance. I have walked out an hour and a half every day (except two or at most three rainy days) for the last month. I bathe most regularly. I do not read an average of 4 to 5 hours a day" [33]—in short, the sentiments which he expressed did not arise out of nervousness or ill health, and neither did they make him morose. "Take me when I am most foolish at home . . . ," he said; "stop me short and ask me then what I think of myself. . . . I should seriously return the same answer, that 'I shuddered at myself.' " [34] A few days later he explained that this did not mean that he undervalued himself "*relatively* to others." [35] What it did mean, presumably, was that he felt his utter nothingness before God, and that the religious ideal of self-abnegation was now being intensified, as it had been twice before, by being forced into conflict with the ideal of self-development demanded by the coming examination.

Nevertheless, on this occasion the conflict was less acute than it had been before. The cruder forms of intellectual pride, if indeed they had ever existed, were chastened now, and success in this examination was not so closely associated with a worldly way of life as it had been in the others. Indeed, during the previous year Newman had been under pressure to decide what he was going to do with himself, and in January,

1822, he definitely rejected the bar and decided upon the church. It is possible that this decision may even have been forwarded by his hopes for a fellowship, for fellows normally proceeded to orders, and the fact that he intended to do so would not be held against him in the decision. He even thought it politic to circulate the news of his intention as quietly as he could,[36] and although it is unlikely that this maneuver had any effect upon the judges, it certainly did have an effect upon the judged, for it placed the Oriel Fellowship in just that different light from the Trinity Scholarship and the lost Honors of the Schools as enabled Newman to proceed toward it with some degree of equanimity.

The examination was to be held in Easter week, and as the time approached, Newman became more and more sanguine. On February 5 he called upon the Provost to gain his leave to stand,[37] and on March 7 he made a similar call on the Dean. From both interviews he emerged strangely elated. "I do not know how it happens," he wrote, "but I certainly feel very confident with respect to Oriel, and seem to myself to have a great chance of success. God keep me from setting my heart upon it, and feeling any disappointment, if I fail. . . ." [38] On March 18 he wrote the customary Latin letter to the Provost setting forth his reasons for wishing to be a fellow, and in his diary he noted that his feelings were quite the reverse of what they had been before the Schools. Then, "every day made my hopes fainter," but now "they seem to swell and ripen, as the time approaches." [39]

The basis of these hopes was partly a kind of intuition that his time had come but more especially a feeling that this examination was the kind in which he could do well. He had ascertained that Latin composition was "the principal thing," [40] although a metaphysical turn was a great advantage and general mathematics was also required. It was, he said, the sort of examination for which one could not prepare, and yet no one would have a chance who had not been preparing for it most of his life. It was an examination which tested what you were rather than what you knew. It demanded no specific information but merely a general ability to think, and Newman considered that if his education had done anything for him at all, it must have done something like this. "I lay great stress," he noted in his diary, "on the attention I have given to mathematics . . . on account of the general strength it imparts to the mind . . . ," [41] and when forced by his parents' letters to speak of his chances relative to others, he declared that "few have attained the facility of comprehension which I have arrived at from the regularity and constancy of my reading, and the laborious and nerve-bracing and fancy-repressing study of Mathematics, which has been my principal subject." [42]

Such preparations as could be made, however, he gladly set about making. He took up logic, which he had never attended to very seriously, and wrote out some "Casual Observations on the *Modes &c. of Syllogisms*." [43] To acquire a "metaphysical turn" he attended a course of lectures in natural philosophy given by Rigaud, Savilian Professor of Geometry, and he also reviewed his mathematics. But of what avail was all this when "the principal thing" was Latin composition, and he, by his own admission, knew no more of the subject now than he had at the age of fifteen? At that time he had been led by Copleston's article into the mistaken idea that Latinity consisted "in using good phrases," but now, by a lucky chance, he was destined to be set right by the same authority who had led him astray. Early in 1822 he fell in with a volume of Latin lectures, or *Praelectiones*, which Copleston had delivered as professor of poetry from 1802 to 1812. The Latin of these lectures Newman was later to characterize as "very good, but Coplestonian, not Ciceronian," [44] and yet what he meant by this was simply that they were display lectures and as such required "a style less simple, less natural and fresh, than Cicero's, more studied, more ambitious, more sparkling; heaping together in a page the flowers which Cicero scatters over a treatise." [45] On that very account, however, they were more fitted for teaching the inquiring student what Latin was, and Newman used them accordingly. "No man in Oxford," said Tom Mozley, "ever so studied and admired Coplestone's famous Praelections as Newman did," [46] and what he learned from them was to begin with the whole and proceed from that to the part. He learned, in other words, that Latin has a peculiar genius or structure and that once a feeling for this structure is developed, individual words and phrases, which before had remained stubbornly English, would fall naturally into place and become Latin. Not that they would do so by any magical process or that the "idea of Latinity" could be mystically attained, far from it. The method was the same arduous one which he had used before, going through the writings of Cicero and carefully entering into blank books every peculiarity of every individual sentence—the force of particular words, their combination into phrases, the breaking up of a sentence into clauses, and the evasion of its categorical form—but as he now saw it, these peculiarities were not themselves the hallmark of good Latin, but were simply the materials from which the principles of good Latin could be induced. [47] Two years later Newman actually did draw out these principles in a paper called "Hints on Latin Composition," [48] but at the moment what he needed was practice in applying them. To give himself an object he decided to write for the Latin essay prize, the subject for that year being "An, re vera, praevaluerit apud eruditiores antiquorum polytheismus."

His notes show that he did extensive preparatory reading,[49] but what he learned about the subject of polytheism among the ancients was less important than what he learned about Latin, for it was in the course of doing this essay that he grasped, with the aid of the *Praelectiones*, the "*idea* of Latin composition"; [50] and although the idea came too late to save the essay, his progress thereafter was extremely rapid.

During the following weeks he did other practice themes, timing himself as he did them, and by March 18 his hopes were extremely high. They were too high to last. Five days later, with the examination only a fortnight off, his nerves gave way completely and he found that all his hard-earned Latin had left him. "See," he exclaimed, "God can take away the fruit of my labour at a stroke." [51] But it was not so. By the 29th he had recovered enough to do a practice theme on a subject which must have been suggested by his state of mind, "Splendida peccata," [52] but he felt "very little sanguine" and thought he most certainly should fail. "And therefore," he added, "[I] have cause to look forward for some great trials this next year; for how am I to live?" [53]

At length the day came—Saturday, April 6. There were eleven candidates competing for two vacancies, and Newman's record was the least distinguished of all. The examination was held in Oriel Hall beginning each morning at ten and continuing without break until dusk made it too dark to write, for candles were not allowed. Lunch, consisting of sandwiches, fruit, cake, jellies, and wine, was brought in at one, and there was a blazing fire.[54] The examination was to last for five days, with written papers on Saturday, Monday, and Tuesday, and viva voce on Tuesday through Thursday. The decision was made Thursday night and the result announced Friday morning, which was the day of the college Gaudy.

Newman's examination paper still exists,[55] and thus we can follow his course with great detail. On the first day the task was to translate into Latin a portion of *Spectator* No. 291,[56] which is one of the critiques of *Paradise Lost*, and to write an English essay on the subject of a motto from Cicero. Afterward Newman fancied that the Latin translation was one of the two things he had done best,[57] but at the time he had no inkling of his success. He was only "stiff, oh how stiff" [58] from sitting nearly nine hours on hard benches, and the next day he crawled about in misery, rehearsing in his mind all the careless blunders he had made and squirming at the thought of what the Fellows must think. Indeed, by nighttime he had made himself quite ill. He felt a heat in his back, almost as if there were an eruption *on* his spine, and he decided he would have to go to the doctor in the morning. Morning came, however, and with it some refreshment, and so he went back into the examination.

THE IMPERIAL INTELLECT

The problem on that day was a Latin essay on the subject, "Exiguum est ad legem esse bonum," and twelve mathematical and philosophical questions. As Newman was the only mathematician in the group he should have had an advantage here, but by midday he was again so ill that he was obliged to walk up and down the hall, and thus at the end of nine hours, what with "despair, headache, and dimness of the twilight," he had answered only five questions [59] and had to send in his essay uncorrected. By Tuesday morning he was "very, very nervous, and I prayed earnestly for strength, and God gave it me most wonderfully." [60] Thus he was enabled to answer nine out of the ten logical questions, there being only a single paper that day, and in the afternoon he went up to the tower to take his turn at the viva voce. He was placed at a table amid the assembled Fellows with a number of Greek and Latin texts before him, and was told to translate either at sight or after a brief interval from the various authors. During that day and the two following he was put upon nine books—Euripides (iambics), Aeschines, Euripides (chorus), Thucydides, Aristotle (*De caelo*), Juvenal, Cicero (*De oratore*), Lucretius, and Pliny.[61] Only two of the passages had he seen before.

Meanwhile, the Provost and several of the Fellows had been so impressed by Newman's first paper that on Tuesday afternoon they sent three of their number over to Trinity to make discreet inquiries about his character and antecedents. When they left, Kinsey clapped his hands in ecstasy and Short was so excited that nothing would do but he must send for Newman at once. He found him, as is well known, so despondent that he had about decided to retire from the contest, but Short made him sit down to an early dinner of lamb cutlets and fried parsley, and though of course he could not tell what he knew, still, by his encouraging words, as also by the lamb cutlets and parsley, he instilled into Newman such confidence that on Wednesday morning he construed some part of his passages "with very great readiness and even accuracy." [62] Alas! the confidence did not continue, and on the final day he had to seek comfort from the motto high up in the window of Oriel Hall, *Pie repone te*. "Thank God," he wrote in his journal, "I am now going to bed, and have been very calm the whole evening. How can I sufficiently praise Him! Before I look at this book again, it will be decided. God grant grace!" And the next day, "Friday, April 12. I have this morning been elected Fellow of Oriel. Thank God, thank God." [63]

Newman was ever conscious of anniversaries, but there was no anniversary, not his birthday nor even that of his conversion, which he kept more faithfully than that of his election to Oriel. Year after year, in letter after letter, he remarks quietly and yet movingly upon it. At the

[32]

age of sixty-two, when he was looking back over a life which had been rich in inward happiness but empty of public recognition, he could think of only two joyful events which had happened to him in his entire life, his winning the scholarship at Trinity and his election as Fellow of Oriel.[64] It was not exactly a turning point in his life; it was rather, in a worldly sense, its beginning. It brought him out onto the platform of life, gave him a position from which he could speak, and made possible the great and unparalleled influence which he later enjoyed over the young men of his day.

Why was it, one may ask, that Newman did so brilliantly at Oriel when he had done so poorly in the Schools? Partly, of course, because of the difference between the two examinations. When Copleston declared, in the letter already quoted, that every election which discouraged the narrow and technical routine of the Schools was an important triumph, he went on to observe that "Newman himself was an example. He was not even a good classical scholar, yet in mind and powers of composition, and in taste and knowledge, he was decidedly superior to some competitors who were a class above him in the schools." [65] But the answer is also to be found in the very different spirit in which Newman approached the Oriel examination. When he went into the Schools he was tortured by the thought of his vanity—"this it is that . . . unnerves my arm in the day of battle"—but when he stood for Oriel, although again there were flutterings of worldly passion, he was not conscious of any unusual sin and he even hoped that this second event might undo what the first had done. By God's grace it might furnish the prey which had escaped him then, and with this feeling he went into the examination with his wits about him. His mother, failing to detect the confidence and even eagerness which lay beneath his self-depreciatory letters, had scolded him sharply. "I see one great fault in your character," she wrote, "which alarms me, as I observe it grows upon you seriously; and as all virtues may degenerate into vices, it is everyone's duty to have a strict guard over themselves to avoid extremes. Your fault is a want of self-confidence and a dissatisfaction with yourself." [66]

It is a curious coincidence that only a few weeks after receiving this letter Newman went into the Oriel examination and found himself obliged to write an essay on this very subject! The point of departure was Cicero's statement that "the saying 'Know thyself' should be used not only to chasten arrogance but also to make us conscious of our good qualities," [67] and Newman's development of this theme is simply an analysis of his own difficulties during the previous two years. The very imagery he uses is that of his letters home. He had announced his failure in the Schools by exclaiming, "If a man falls in battle after a display of bravery he is honoured as a hero; ought not the same glory to attend him who falls on the field of literature?" and now he declares, "If a man refuse to fight from an ignorance of his own strength and a dread of being worsted, he is called coward and despised accordingly; but he who from a like ignorance of his mental powers and the fear of defeat shrinks from any literary challenge . . . is called bashful, modest, diffident." [68] Diffidence, he says, arises from "an excessive fear of shame; - a shuddering at repulse, defeat, or even criticism," and is no more a virtue than is its opposite, arrogance. The true mean (and here he is echoing both Aristotle [69] and his own mother) is that "selfconfidence which lies between the extremes of self conceit and diffidence," and he proceeds to explain how this quality is compatible with humility. "The arrogant man thinks himself positively excellent; the person, who forms a proper estimate of his own powers, is aware his excellence . . . is relative only: - and reflecting on the superiority he may possess over his own race, he is led to figure to himself beings of such comprehensive powers, that the difference which exists in mental ability or cultivation between himself and his fellow creatures dwindles into nothing. . . . he humbles himself before the mysteries of the book of nature, and with still deeper abasement before those of a still holier nature; from him we may expect at once caution and enterprise, being alike removed from the self-sufficiency of the arrogant and the despair of the diffident." [70]

There is no doubt that Newman intended this as an account of the position he had now reached. On the one hand he "shuddered at himself," but on the other he did not disvalue himself "relatively to others." In the latter respect he differed from the youth who had been taken ill in the Schools, but in the former he also differed from the youth who had been made giddy by winning a scholarship. No longer shuddering at the thought of a repulse, he was yet conscious that before God his powers were nothing. For this reason he found comfort in the motto, *Pie repone te*, which he might have translated, "Rest in the Lord." From high up in the window of Oriel Hall this message came flooding down upon him in words which were never thereafter lost to his consciousness. *Pie repone te*. In 1836, in the midst of the Hampden controversy, when he was filled with alarm about the state of the church, he wrote to Pusey, "Keep quiet in *mind* as well as body. . . . Pie repone te. I recollect when I was in at the examination for fellowship at Oriel and very much harassed and almost sinking, I happened to look up at the window and saw that motto on the painted glass. The words have been a kind of proverb to me ever since. Really we have nothing to fear - and after all it will be a great thing if 'in that Day' our own 'life be given us as a prey.' " [71] Here was the true view. So far was our "evening prey" from being anything we had a right to expect, that we should be blessed indeed if "in that Day" we were given our own life as a prey. In this view lay quietness of mind, and also that humility which was not diffidence, and that oneness with God which was a precondition of being at one with ourselves.

So it was, then, that Newman became a Fellow of Oriel. On the Friday morning when his election was announced he had to proceed "to the very tower, which had been the scene of torture, to receive the congratulations of the assembled Fellows. I could bear the presence of Copleston," he said, "and many other of the lights of Oriel; but when Keble advanced to take my hand, I quite shrank and could have nearly sunk into the floor, ashamed at so great an honour." [72] He was installed (literally) in the chapel at one o'clock, and though he did not take rooms in college until four years later, he began to dine there at once. "Indeed I am absolutely a Member of the Common Room - am called by them 'Newman,' and am abashed to find I must soon learn in turn to call them 'Keble,' 'Hawkins,' 'Tyler.' " [73]

Had Newman continued the list, it would have included Edward Copleston, the provost; Richard Whately, William James, Henry Jenkyns, Joseph Dornford, Samuel Rickards, and R. W. Jelf. Moreover, lingering in the background, their presence still felt though they themselves had lately resigned, were John Davison, Thomas Arnold, and R. D. Hampden, and to these should be added the name of one soon to join the college as an honorary member, Joseph Blanco White. This company was not all of a piece, but there was a group within it, including Copleston, Davison, Hawkins, Whately, Arnold, and Hampden, whose thought had a tone of its own and who were recognized by the *Edinburgh Review* as forming "the School of Speculative Philosophy in England." [74] More familiarly they were known as "the Noetics," and it was they who gave to the Oriel common room its traditional and distinctive character.

What was this character? One element in it was a deep seriousness of purpose, what the age called a "high tone." Newman wrote to his brother the day after his election that the Fellows were "kind, liberal, candid, moderate, learned, and pious men," [75] and this eulogium, comprehensive as it is, is no more than the facts can bear. The famous Oriel teapot, which replaced the pottle of wine that was usual in most college common rooms, was a symbol of the correctness of their lives.[76] They were evolving a new conception of the life of a don, namely that it involved something more than port mingled with an idle and elegant scholarship, that there was hard work to be done, and that those in a university had a special call to do it.[77] Therefore in their writings they ranged broadly over political, economic, and educational affairs, and even in their own persons they tended to pass beyond the college into the more active positions of the church and the world.

The center of their interest, however, was always theological, and here they were of no definite school, either High or Low, but were characterized by the "spirit of moderation and comprehension" [78] with which they treated all theological questions. They could hardly be called latitudinarian, which in that day was nothing so definite as a party, but they were the progenitors of the liberal theologians of a later time. "A school arose," wrote William Palmer of Worcester College, "whose conceit led them to imagine that their wisdom was sufficient to correct and amend the whole world. . . . With boundless freedom [they] began to investigate all institutions, to search into the basis .of religious doctrines, and to put forth each his wild theory or irreverential remark. All was pretended to be for the benefit of free discussion, which was substituted for the claims of truth. This school came from Oriel College." [79]

The real interest of the Noetics, as Palmer suggests, is less in their theological conclusions than in their method of arriving at them, for they were agreed in regarding dialectic as the only valid approach to truth. In the common room they all "practised. . . the Socratic method of improving thought by constant cross-questioning," and this to such a degree that G. A. Denison said they were afraid of one another.[80] Indeed, estimates of the habit varied. What Pattison described as "a wholesome intellectual ferment," Mozley characterized as "a morbid intellectual restlessness," [81] but intellectual they certainly were and always on the move. The trouble was they moved from premise to conclusion rather than from book to book—they reasoned more than they read—and thus their weakness as critics was that they were very restricted in their information, especially of history and continental thought. Pattison says they were the product of the French Revolution, and in a mild and English sense this was perfectly true, but they had not read the writings of Rousseau and Voltaire and they knew nothing of Kant. British philosophy they did know, especially Locke, Hume, Paley, and Adam Smith, but the thinker to whom they were most deeply indebted was Aristotle. In his *Organon* they found an instrument, and in his popular treatises a mode of applying it to human problems, which precisely suited their needs. They employed him, therefore, not as an authority but rather as a precedent for dispensing with authorities and relying simply on their own powers. "They called everything in question," said Pattison; "they appealed to first principles, and disallowed authority as a judge in intellectual matters." [82]

Such a spirit is immensely attractive to youth, and Newman soon felt that in these men he had discovered a living embodiment of his intellectual ideal. On February 2, 1823, he delivered a Latin oration before them, the customary exercise of the probationary Fellow, in which he gave vent to his enthusiasm for his new college. The oration is less interesting for itself, however, than for the note which he wrote across the top of it in 1874: "I read this now for the first time this 51 years," he says, "with sad tenderness, as if I loved and pitied the poor boy, so ignorant of the future, who then wrote and delivered it before the Provost and Fellows, now almost all dead, but to whom I then looked up with great reverence and loving pride." [83] The reverence and pride which he felt were for all the Fellows, but most of all for Copleston, Whately, and Hawkins.

Edward Copleston was a famous name in Oxford. He had a robust independence of mind which made him, in the cautious words of a contemporary, "a great man (academically speaking)." [84] Tom Mozley, who entered Oriel the same year that Newman became a Fellow, found Copleston "the most substantial and majestic and, if I may say so, richly-coloured character within my knowledge of Oxford." [85] To others he was the very essence of Oxford, "the representative man of University culture," [86] and it was said that to praise Oxford and dispraise Copleston was "like admiring Scotland, yet decrying Scott; or . . . like loving a species from aversion to its special characteristic." [87]

It is right to identify Copleston so closely with Oxford, for the various stages of his career were all associated with events momentous to the university. His election as Fellow of Oriel in 1795 was that which set the college upon its path of choosing strictly for merit and so led to its greatness in future years. Moreover, to be in Oriel at that time was to be in the center of the movement for university reform, for the provost of Oriel was John Eveleigh, the chief author of the New Examination Statute of 1800, and through him Copleston too was brought into the work of reform and became one of the first examiners under the new system. Then, in 1808–09, when Oxford was attacked by the *Edinburgh Review*, it was he who went forth, in Newman's words, "single-handed, with easy gallantry, to encounter and overthrow the charge of three giants of the North combined against him." [88] He became professor of poetry at the age of twenty-six and provost of Oriel at thirty-eight, and the years of his headship (1814–28) are considered by the college historian to be the golden years of the society. He brought together a distinguished company of fellows, built up an effective tutorial system, and generally raised the college to its most flourishing state.

He was himself a great teacher, and in his college lectures, which were so famous that Whately said he would "limp upstairs on one leg" [89] to attend them, he developed the peculiar type of instruction which characterized all the best Oxford colleges in the early part of the century. His method was a rigorous kind of catechism or dialectic which he applied with such force that although the undergraduates had only one lecture a day, we are told that the preparation of this one, to the degree of accuracy which he required, taxed the industry of even the most attentive. *Multum, non multa* was his motto, and as this is but a short way of expressing the Oxford ideal, so we may say that Copleston was the first to formulate this ideal distinctly and fully for the Noetic school. "The more I think on it," he wrote to a friend, "the more am I convinced that, to *exercise* the mind of the student is the business of education, rather than to pour in knowledge." [90]

Newman's relations with Copleston were never easy, for the two men were very different in temperament and in the early years Newman was terribly shy. Indeed, all the fellows were somewhat troubled by this raw, admiring youth who sank through the floor at their approach and who, despite their efforts, could not be persuaded to talk. They began to fear that they had made a mistake, and at last some of them had the brilliant idea of turning him over to Whately. Whately could find out what was in him if anyone could, and sure enough, in a few months' time the report came back that they need not worry, whatever they had drawn it was certainly not a dud. [91]

"The first time I saw Whately," said Hawkins, "he wore a pea-green coat, white waistcoat, stone-coloured shorts, flesh-coloured silk stockings. His hair was powdered." [92] Styles changed soon after this, and presumably Newman never saw him in anything so bright. Nevertheless he was a memorable figure in any dress. He used to scandalize the Provost by throwing stones at birds, and amazed Blanco White by playing at ducks and drakes with the latter's pupil "and beating him hollow." [93] To some he was known for his dog Sailor, whom he had taught to climb trees in Christ Church meadow and drop from their overhanging branches into the Cherwell; to Mrs. Baden-Powell it was for the day he plunged and shifted upon her spider-legged chair until it crumpled under him and was tossed upon a sofa without any interruption of the talk. [94] Shyness with such a man would suffer the same fate as the chair, and so Newman quickly found himself at home with this fascinating companion who drew him out and cultivated him in the summer of 1822. "He used to take me out walking and riding," wrote Newman, "and used to talk; and thus he was the first person who opened my mind, that is, who gave it ideas and principles to cogitate upon." [95]

To Whately, who was "a Noetic of the Noetics," this was the true task of education. In teaching his children he forbade them to memorize anything they had not really understood, for "to teach thus mechanically," he used to say, "in the hope that the children would afterwards find out the meaning of what they had learned, was to make them 'swallow their food first, and chew it afterwards.' " [96] So too with his students. "Shall I form your mind," he asked his pupil Hinds, "or cram you for a First?" But the idea of Whately "cramming" is too incongruous even to imagine. He used to lecture lying on a sofa, with his leg dangling over the back or one end,[97] and this dissociation from his books, which rested on a window seat at the far side of the room, was the state most congenial to his mind. He and Thomas Brown, according to J. S. Mill, were the two modern philosophers whose reading was scantiest in proportion to their intellectual abilities,[98] and Whately justified this imperfect knowledge by distinguishing between two kinds of "smattering," the superficial knowledge of a subject which is given by a little random information, and the elementary knowledge which is given by a grasp of its principles. "My own learning," he admitted, "is of a very singular kind, being more purely elementary than anyone's I know. I am acquainted with the elements of most things, and that more accurately than many who are much versed in them, but I know nothing thoroughly, except such studies as are intrinsically of an elmentary character, viz. grammar, logic, metaphysics, ethics, rhetoric." [99] His favorite authors, as ministering to these studies, were Aristotle, Thucydides, Bacon, Bishop Butler, Warburton, and Adam Smith, but above all Aristotle. The introduction of the *Ethics* and *Rhetoric* into the Schools was perhaps the work of Dr. Sheppard, who was examiner in 1809, but it was Whately who made them for many years the leading class-books of his university. For the deep Aristotelian character of Oxford minds, in both his own generation and the generation thereafter, no one was so responsible as Whately.[100]

In 1822, as a result of his marriage the year before, Whately relinquished his Fellowship and was passing the summer in lodgings in Oxford, previous to entering upon a rectorship in Suffolk. It was in these months, from early June until his departure on August 6, that he "opened Newman's mind and gave it ideas and principles to cogitate upon." He did this by the characteristic method of getting Newman to help him with an article on logic which he had engaged to write for the *Encyclopaedia Metropolitana*, and since logic is the distinctive mark of the Noetic mind and plays so large a part in the formation of Newman's intellectual ideal, this episode will be recounted in some detail.

In the first quarter of the century the study of logic was in a very low state at Oxford. The reformers of 1800 had given it a prominent place in the system of examinations, making it essential to the degree and allowing it to replace Euclid, if the candidate so wished, in the preliminary examination of Responsions. But they had done nothing to make it worthy of this place. The text commonly used was the little *Rudiments* of Aldrich, and the manner of teaching was perfunctory. The mysterious terms of "barbara" and "bokardo," "subaltern" and "subcontradictory" were simply laid before the student to understand if he could or to learn by rote if he could not, and the result was that the subject was utterly despised. The undergraduate poem, the *Oxford Spy* (1818), is chiefly a protest against it, and Whately himself was forced to admit "that a very small proportion even of distinguished students ever become proficients in Logic; and that by far the greater part pass through the University without knowing any thing at all of the subject." [101]

Only at Oriel were things somewhat different. When Copleston had become tutor and found himself obliged to lecture on logic, he had set about reading books and working up a syllabus [102] which later formed the basis of Whately's lectures and eventually of the book which he was just bringing into shape in 1822. In the dedication of this work Whately acknowledged (with too much generosity, according to Newman) that the book was not more than half his own; but whether his or his master's it quickly put the subject on a more respectable basis and remained the standard text for nearly twenty years, until it was superseded by the *Logic* of Mill.

Aldrich, Whately, and Mill—these names designate the three phases of logical instruction in Oxford in the early nineteenth century. Each was perfectly characteristic of its own time, but the reign of Whately, which was the shortest of the three, was definitely transitional. In substance he added little or nothing to Aldrich, but in spirit he prepared the way for Mill. He brought logic out of Latin and into English, out of the disputation into the daily converse of men, out of the memory and into the understanding—but it remained the same logic as before. He could not invent a new instrument or even greatly improve upon the old, but he understood what the old was for and he conveyed this understanding to others. How he did it may be seen by a single glance at his work. Where Aldrich began with terms and proceeded through propositions to syllogisms, Whately, though preserving this synthetical treatment in the body of his work, began with a general view of the drift and purpose of logic and then descended through its various elements, analyzing each in the light of that purpose. The syllogism was not a special form of reasoning but was the form to which all correct reasoning could ultimately be reduced. It was not opposed to induction or common sense but was involved in them. True, there were things it could not do. It could not discover absolutely new truths, but it could elicit from materials already present in our minds truths which were previously unknown to us and in that sense were new. In short, it was simply the science which analyzed the mental process involved in all correct reasoning and the art which guided us in keeping that process correct. And since reasoning, the drawing of premises from conclusions, was what all men, whatever their profession, were continually engaged in, since it was, indeed, "the most appropriate intellectual occupation of MAN, *as man*," [103] logic certainly deserved a place among the studies of a liberal education.

For Newman this view cast a new light on a subject which he had hitherto despised and neglected. Five years before, in the Long Vacation after his first term at Oxford, he had read through the little *Artis logicae rudimenta*, a copy of which he had also purchased; but in the following year he chose Euclid for Responsions and apparently did not take up the subject again until he began preparing for the Schools. At that time he reviewed it briefly, and on November 6, 1821 he purchased another copy of the *Rudimenta* with extensive notes and illustrations in English. This he used in preparing to meet the logicians of Oriel, and in February or March, 1822 he even wrote out some "Casual Observations on the *Modes &c. of Syllogisms*" for his own guidance. Nevertheless, when he was turned over to Whately in the spring of that year, the subject was still "quite a novelty" [104] to him, and as this was a condition which Whately could not tolerate, he soon lent to Newman the manuscript of two of his papers, one a discussion "Of Fallacies" and the other a series of five dialogues "On Reasoning" and "The Province of Reason." Newman took copies of both these, transcribing the latter himself on June 12 and asking his brother Frank to transcribe the other, probably between June 19 and 28 when they were together at home.[105] On July 1 he was back at Oxford and noted in his private journal, "Whately has proposed to me to undertake part of an article on Logic in the *Encyclopaedia Metropolitana*." [106]

It was Whately's peculiarity, Newman explains, to write his books by the medium of other men's brains, a process which "did not detract at all from the originality of what he wrote." [107] He would seize upon some young disciple, expound his ideas to him, make him expound them back again, and sometimes even have him write them down in a sketch, which would then be used in the preparation of the final work. It was in this way that his treatise on logic was composed, and Newman's part was to cast the five Analytical Dialogues "into the shape of a synthetical treatise," [108] and also to write a short history of logic for the introduction. Both of these tasks he accomplished in the month of July.[109]

It was partly from Newman's "synthetical treatise" that Whately rewrote the final draft of his article, which was published in the *Encyclopaedia Metropolitana*, then being issued in parts. Four years later he revised it slightly, adding some notes and a long appendix on ambiguous terms, and issued it as a separate volume under the title *The Elements of Logic*. In this form it contained the generous dedication to Copleston and a preface with the following notice: "I have also to acknowledge assistance from several friends who have at various times suggested remarks and alterations. But I cannot avoid particularizing the Rev. J. Newman, Fellow of Oriel College, who actually composed a considerable portion of the work as it now stands, from manuscripts not designed for publication, and who is the original author of several pages." [110] To this notice Newman replied on November 14, 1826:

> My dear Principal,
>
> I have just received through Hinds your kind and valuable present, for which accept my best thanks. . . . I cannot tell you the surprise I felt on seeing you had thought it worth while to mention my name, as having contributed to the arrangement of its materials. Whatever I then wrote was written, I am conscious, almost as an Undergraduate exercise, and consequently of little value, except as regards my own improvement in doing it. Yet, while on this ground I take the liberty of questioning the necessity of your mentioning my name, I cannot regret that in the composition of your work you have introduced it in some sort of connexion with your own. There are few things which I wish more sincerely than to be known as a friend of yours; and, though I may be standing on the verge of propriety in the earnestness with which I am expressing myself, yet you must let me give way to feelings, which never want much excitement to draw them out, and now will not be restrained.
>
> Much as I owe to Oriel, in the way of mental improvement, to none, as I think, do I owe so much as to you. I know who it was that first gave me heart to look about me after my election, and taught me to think correctly, and (strange office for an instructor) to rely upon myself.[111]

Whether Whately really failed to catch Newman's drift through the tortuous phrases of his letter or whether he deliberately chose to misunderstand is not known, but on November 20 he replied as follows:

"You certainly are right in your complaint that I have not done justice to your labours. I ought to have mentioned that what you wrote was several years ago, when you were just a graduate, and done as an exercise for your own improvement; so that it is not to be taken as a fair sample of your powers, since you can write much better now. This shall be added in a future edition. It is true I let it stand as you wrote it, because I could not make it any better; but it does not follow that you could not." [112] On this strange reply Newman comments, "This was unfair. I wrote in great surprise that he should have thought my part in the Logic *worth* his noticing, in the Preface, and thanking him *most cordially* for it. I think that I desired nothing better than that my name should be associated with his." [113]

Throughout 1823 Newman continued his study of logic. He filled copybooks with "Casual observations on Fallacies," "Miscellaneous questions on the three parts of Logic," and remarks "On Hypothetical Syllogisms," [114] all arising out of his work with Whately and showing a tendency, perhaps, to probe beyond it. But as time went on, both Whately and the science he represented became less congenial to Newman's mood, and by 1834, when Whately asked him to help in preparing a new edition of *"our* Logic," Newman wrote that the press of engagements would not allow it.[115] Perhaps he had already come to the conclusion which Tom Mozley heard him express "that Whately's Logic was a most interesting book, but that there was one thing not to be found in it, and that was logic." [116]

When Newman wrote to Whately, in the letter quoted above, "Much as I owe to Oriel, in the way of mental improvement, to none, as I think, do I owe so much as to you," the rough draft of the letter shows that the sentence originally concluded, ". . . to none, as I think, do I owe so much as to yourself (and Hawkins)." [117] The period of Whately's greatest influence on Newman was 1822 and 1825–28; that of Edward Hawkins was in between these two dates, and especially 1824–25. In June of 1824 Newman had become curate of St. Clement's Church in Oxford and so was bound by his parochial duties to residence throughout the year. At the same time Hawkins was vicar of St. Mary's, and therefore the two men were thrown much into each other's company, especially during the Long Vacation when they had the hall and common room almost to themselves. "They dined and read the papers," wrote Newman, speaking of himself in the third person; "they took their evening walk, and then their tea, in company; and, while Mr. Newman was full of the difficulties of a young curate, he found in Mr. Hawkins a kind and able adviser." There was a difference of twelve years between them, but in mind Hawkins was older than his years and Newman younger, so that "the intercourse between them was virtually that of tutor and pupil." [118]

The pupil found his tutor to be "clear-headed and independent in his opinions, candid in argument, tolerant of the views of others, honest as a religious inquirer, though not without something of self-confidence in his enunciations." [119] His principal trait, all testimony agrees, was an extreme conscientiousness, not only in matters of duty but also in matters of fact; and therefore to many people who really loved him he gave an impression of sharpness, dryness, and even pedantry which their love had some difficulty in overcoming. Golightly, searching for an epithet which would least express his character, hit upon "gushing." "Yes," he said. "*That* is precisely what the dear man *never* was." [120] But the fact that he was never gushing sometimes gave him an appearance of being harsh. Early one morning during his provostship an undergraduate fell to his death in the Oriel quadrangle, and while others rushed out half dressed to see what had happened, it was an hour later before Hawkins appeared, and then, according to an onlooker, "*his bands were tied perfectly square.*" [121] The end of the story, which is usually omitted, is that long after the others had forgotten the incident, the Provost was still seeing the young man's pale, shattered features in his dreams. He was not unfeeling, then, but merely precise. "*Exactness,*" said the Bishop of Rochester, "was a passion with him. He would have set a King right, if his Majesty had slipped in a date." [122]

Under the tuition of such a person Newman profited immensely. Hawkins read his sermons and the essays he was writing for university prizes and checked him severely for their looseness. Of his first sermon, for example, which divided the Christian world into two classes, the one all darkness, the other all light, Hawkins pointed out that such a division was unreal; and this advice had its consequence not only in Newman's theology but in his habit of mind as well. Hawkins "was the first," said Newman, "who taught me to weigh my words, and to be cautious in my statements. He led me to that mode of limiting and clearing my sense in discussion and in controversy, and of distinguishing between cognate ideas, and of obviating mistakes by anticipation, which to my surprise has been since considered . . . to savour of the polemics of Rome." [123]

The combination of Hawkins' precision with Whately's originality was a gift much to be desired, but Newman's debt to Oriel did not end with what any one Fellow, or any two taken together, could do for him. It extended to the intellectual life of the college as a whole. In the conversation of the common room, with its wide-ranging dialectic, was to be found what no individual could provide, namely a comprehensiveness or catholicity of mind for which Newman had felt the need ever since he was an undergraduate. His proposal for a debating society which would treat "the whole range of history, poetry, and the fine arts" was partly an expression of this need, and although the youth of his day were not ready for his proposal, here, in the Oriel common room, was the debating society of the oldsters, and Newman was perfectly entranced at what he saw. How good the debates were we have no way of knowing. G. A. Denison found them "dull," and it was whispered by others that Whately and Davison crammed for postprandial talk.[124] But despite the pretentious and even ridiculous character which this famous room may have had, the talk was certainly substantial and informing and probably was sometimes brilliant. To a man like Whately the common room was "not a mere place of resort for relaxation and recreation, but a school for sharpening his argumentative powers," [125] and he declares that he owed more to it than to his college lectures. So too did Newman, for it was in the Oriel common room, with its daily collision of mind with mind, that he found embodied the very idea of a university. Later, of course, he was to have his doubts. If it was a university in essence, it was not so in integrity. It had the strength of the intellect but also the weakness of the intellect insufficiently guided by religion. But within these limits it remains true that Newman's idea of a university was first formed on the model of the Oriel common room.

CHAPTER 3

Tutor of Oriel

As we all have the good of the college at heart,
The men are divided and each has a part;
The lecture we give to the general stock,
But each has besides a particular flock;
And them we are gratis to superintend,
And act as a sort of tutorial friend.
　　—"Letter from a Tutor [of Oriel] at Oxford,
　　　to his Friend in the Country," from
　　　The Undergraduate (1819)

ALTHOUGH no one ever stops learning, we all recognize in the learning process a point where it ceases to be something we do for ourselves and becomes something we do for a purpose beyond ourselves. What we write is no longer written as an exercise but for the use of others, and the subjects we get up are those made necessary by the work which we have in hand. Our mind is no longer an instrument being fashioned but an instrument at work, and it is well, in the case of so delicate an instrument, if there can be some period when the further improvement of the mind and the beginning of its work go on concurrently. With Newman this period was found in the years 1822 to 1826. His election to Oriel in the earlier year marked the end of his formal education, and his becoming tutor of Oriel in 1826 was the real beginning of his work. In between these dates his studies were transitional in character. On the one hand, he wrote several times for the chancellor's essay prize,[1] always unsuccessfully, and these were exercises, done for the sake of education; but he also wrote for the *Encyclopaedia Metropolitana* and for various reviews, and these were works done, the product of education. In 1826 he fulfilled a long-cherished ambition by starting the study of Hebrew, and before he gave it up at the end of the next summer he had worked through Genesis and Exodus and mastered a part of Lee's *Hebrew Grammar*.[2] He was going about it, however, in a way which Whately would have called "superficial" rather than "elementary," that is, he was trying to get a working knowledge of the language itself rather than using the language (as he had his Latin and Greek)

as a means of improving his own mind. So also with German. He had
begun German as early as 1822, borrowing a set of books from his friend
Bowden for the purpose, but although he fretted over the thing for a
dozen years and urged upon himself the practical ends of knowing German divinity and being able to read the "useful books . . . in my line," [3]
in the end he gave it up because, as Bowden put it, it was only an "*indirect* labour for the Church," [4] and indirect labors were a luxury he could
no longer afford. Indeed, the melancholy fact was being forced upon him
that, for better or for worse, his own education was over and he must
now devote himself to the education of others.

He began, as did every university man in those days, by taking private
pupils, and because of his low degree he at first experienced some difficulty in securing them. In June, 1821, Mr. Short got him one man from
Trinity to begin after the Long Vacation, but he found no others until
the next January.[5] Then three came at once, two from Ogle and Kinsey
for termtime and a third for the Long Vacation at Oxford, the last paying fifty guineas for instruction and thirty-five for board.[6] The money was
badly needed, but Newman had to admit that it was hardly worth it, for
his classics were still weak and the lad was just mischievous enough to
enjoy exposing him when he could. He left at last, however, and Newman jumped about for very joy. "Liber sum," he wrote to his sister, "and
I have been humming, whistling, and laughing out loud to myself all
day." [7] Gradually, however, by dint of going for weeks on end with only
four hours of sleep a night,[8] he got his classics in shape, and now that he
was a Fellow of Oriel new pupils came in abundance. By February he
had four, one being "very docile and very *nice*," [9] and three more offered themselves within the next three months. Altogether he seems
to have had over a dozen private pupils before he became tutor of Oriel
in 1826,[10] and of course he had many more afterward. They provided
good experience and a fair income, but the work was obviously of a
temporary nature, and in May, 1823, when Copleston offered him the
chance of a private tutorship in Lord Lansdowne's family, he refused
without much pondering.[11]

The shift from private to public tutor came two years later, when
Whately was appointed principal of Alban Hall. On the day of his
induction, March 25, 1825, he offered Newman the vice-principalship,
which the latter accepted the following morning.[12] "It is a post of considerable authority and responsibility," he wrote to his mother. "I am
Dean, Tutor, Bursar and all - in his [Whately's] absence indeed, Principal." [13]

Whately was absent for the first two weeks of the new term, and thus
Newman had all the opening duties on himself. Indeed, throughout the

year he seems to have been almost entirely responsible for the instruction, the discipline, and even the practical arrangements of the Hall. He did most of the lectures himself, set the weekly compositions, and looked over the finished essays. He dined three times a week with the men and read prayers in hall on Sunday. He admonished the wayward, he discharged the butler, and he kept the accounts.[14]

As there were only a dozen undergraduates in residence, these duties would not have been exacting had it not been for the special character of Alban Hall. All the halls were in a low state at this period, but St. Alban's in particular had degenerated into a kind of Botany Bay of the university. Youths who could not secure admission to a college or were unable to persevere in the one to which they had been admitted drifted into the shallows of Alban Hall, and there, in a time when many were idle, they became known as the most idle of the university. It was even said that some had been allowed to try for their degree as often as a dozen times.[15] In any case, they formed a small but affable society whose ways, at least in their own eyes, had the sanction of a long-standing tradition, and one may well imagine that to place Newman in charge of them was like entrusting the Roaring Boys of London to the tender mercies of Savonarola. He was, as he said later, "a new broom," and when he resigned at the end of the year he noted in his diary, "I trust I have done good at Alban Hall. I have had a divinity lecture three times a week." And then, as a solitary instance of the opposition he had met, "I am very good friends with the men. They saw, I think, they had not hurt me [last Michaelmas Term]; on my part I think myself much more culpable than I did." [16] How had they tried to hurt him? And what had he done that he considered culpable? We do not have the precise answer, but as this fracas was simply the prelude to a much greater one at Oriel the following year, and as that was occasioned by the peculiar conception which Newman had of the office of tutor, the general nature of both affairs will probably be illumined by noting the unusual spirit in which he had entered upon his new duties.

It will be remembered that in January, 1822 Newman had rejected the law in favor of the church, and it does not appear that he ever wavered in this decision. He was aware, however, that the church may be served in various ways, and during the next four years he was deliberately considering which of these ways he ought to choose. Should he be a college tutor or a parish priest or a missionary to the heathen? These were the three ways which seemed open to him, and they were contrasted in his mind not merely in the degree of heroism which they involved but also in the scope they offered to intellectual aspirations. In the first these aspirations would be fulfilled, in the second they would have some scope but hardly a wide one, and in the last they would be completely renounced. Nevertheless, it was to this last course that Newman was attracted, and by the very renunciation which it involved. He was deeply affected by the life of Henry Martyn, the missionary, which he was just then reading,[17] for Martyn had had a brilliant undergraduate career at Cambridge, becoming Senior Wrangler and First Smith's Prizeman in mathematics, and then, under the influence of the Rev. Charles Simeon, had turned to God and gone out as a chaplain with the East India Company to Dinapore. He had translated the New Testament into Hindustani and Persian and after a few years of heroic service had died of the plague in a strange land, a very symbol of great intellectual abilities devoted to the service of God. It was Newman's strong desire in the years 1823 and 1824 to humble his own pride by such a devotion. Often when he would walk out with Edward Pusey, the newly elected Fellow of Oriel, they would fall to talking "of Henry Martyn and the missionaries," and Pusey would speak beautifully on the question, "Who are to go?" [18] Who, indeed? That was Newman's problem. Was he called to serve God in foreign lands or in a country parish or within the graying walls of his own college? He did not know, and time alone would give him the answer.

But why should Newman consider the office of college tutor to be the equivalent of missionary or priest? The answer to this question lies not merely in the fact that the colleges were religious foundations and normally required that their fellows (from among whom the tutors were chosen) should proceed to orders, but also that historically the role of tutor was less closely associated with secular instruction than with a species of pastoral care. In the days of Elizabeth and James, when undergraduates came up to the university at a very early age, the tutor was supposed to exercise a kind of parental control over his charges, regulating their expenses, forming their moral character, and even administering to their religious needs, and he was not supposed to be primarily a teacher. During the next two centuries, however, as the tutor partly relaxed into indolence and partly was required to supersede the professor in the actual instruction of the undergraduates, these duties went largely unperformed, and they were not taken up again until the appearance of the private tutor or cram coach in the early nineteenth century. By that time the college tutor had become something between a real tutor and a professor, but enough of the old idea still survived so that it was widely held, at least within the universities themselves, that there were some duties which a tutor had to perform, even if it were only to infuse a religious spirit into the secular subjects which he taught, that could properly be undertaken only by a clergyman of the Church of England.

On the other hand, if most people agreed that tutors ought to be clergymen, there was a genuine difficulty among religious men as to whether clergymen ought to be tutors. At their ordination they took a vow which gave them the charge of souls from that time until their death, and it was difficult to see how the teaching of mathematics or a heathen system of ethics, no matter how much they might infuse the spirit of religion into these subjects, could be reconciled with the plain meaning of their vow. The Rev. Walter Mayers felt the incompatibility so keenly that he continued in his employment of schoolmaster no longer than sheer necessity forced him to do so. Keble, too, though no evangelical, felt distinctly uneasy when he gave up his cure in 1818 to become an academic again, and he tried to reconcile himself to it by taking a religious view of the tutorship. "You consider Tuition," he wrote his friend J. T. Coleridge, "as a species of pastoral care, do you not? otherwise it might seem questionable, whether a clergyman ought to leave a cure of souls for it. And yet there are some people at Oxford who seem to imagine that College Tutors have nothing to do with the morale. If I thought so, I would never undertake the office." [19] In practice most tutors drifted away after a few years to the dignified leisure of a college living, but there was still the question whether they might not have deferred their ordination until the years which it seemed desirable to give to teaching had passed.

This was the problem with which Newman was confronted as he approached the canonical age of twenty-three. "I have been lately considering," he wrote in his journal, "whether I had better take orders soon or not. Scott [Thomas Scott of Aston Sandford], as a general rule, says Not soon. Hawkins says the same—Why bind yourself with a vow, when there is no necessity, and which *may* mean something incompatible with staying at College and taking pupils. R. [Samuel Rickards?] doubts the propriety of College Tutors being clergymen. Mr. Mayers, and he has been consulting Marsh of Colchester, advises immediate entrance into the Church by all means"—but not, of course, for the sake of teaching. Rather to become one of those free-lance clergymen, so much needed by the church, "who, without the tie of regular duty, can make progresses among their brethren and relieve them at certain seasons." [20]

So Newman wrote in June, 1823. But a year later, against all the weight of this advice and less than four months after his twenty-third birthday, he went ahead and was ordained deacon of the Church of England. "It is over," he wrote, "I am Thine, O Lord; I seem quite dizzy, and cannot altogether believe and understand it. At first, after the hands were laid on me, my heart shuddered within me; the words 'for ever' are so terrible. It was hardly a godly feeling which made me feel melancholy at the idea of giving up all for God. . . . I feel as a man thrown suddenly into deep water." And the next day, June 14, he added, " 'For ever,' words never to be recalled. I have the responsibility of souls on me to the day of my death." [21]

The immediate occasion of Newman's taking this step was the offer to him of the curacy of St. Clement's Church in Oxford, but it is clear that in accepting this offer he had not rejected either the way of the missionary or that of the college tutor. Indeed, as he explained to his father, one reason for taking the curacy was to get used to parochial duty early, so that if, after some ten years' residence in an Oxford college he should wish to return to it again, he would not feel awkward among poor and ignorant people.[22] Moreover, on July 3, 1824, only one day before his first service at St. Clement's, he called at the Missionary Society to inquire what qualifications were necessary for foreign service.[23] Thus it rather appears that by accepting St. Clement's he was not really adopting that way of life but was rather eliminating it in favor of one of the two extremes. Part of his reason for doing so, it appears, was a deep imagination, which had possessed his mind ever since his conversion, that God intended him for a single life, and also that "my calling in life would require such a sacrifice as celibacy involved." [24] This would not be the case with parochial duty but would be with missionary work and the tutorship, and therefore by October of the same year, when he was prompted by the occasion of his father's death to wonder whether he would ever be followed to the grave by children of his own, he foresaw that he would not, that he would "either die within college walls, or as a missionary in a foreign land. No matter where," he added, "so that I die in Christ." [25] Gradually during the following winter the more heroic alternative seems to have faded from his mind, and in March, 1825, when he accepted the vice-principalship of Alban Hall, he declared, "I have all along thought that it was more my duty to engage in College offices than in parochial duty," [26] and the the way of the missionary is left unmentioned.

By 1824 or 1825, then, Newman had come to believe that his ordination vow, though he had as deep a sense of its solemnity as anyone could have, might be fulfilled through the office of college tutor if that office were interpreted in its primitive, religious sense.[27] Therefore, when a vacancy arose at Oriel in January, 1826 and Newman was given the opportunity of filling it, he had no hesitation in resigning not only his academic appointment at Alban Hall but also his curacy at St. Clement's. In his journal he noted explicitly that "the succeeding to the Tutorship at Oriel has occasioned my relinquishing my curacy," [28] and he took the occasion of his next birthday, always a day of self-examination with him, to remind himself that if he was regarding the two offices as morally equivalent he must make them equivalent in fact. "And now, O Lord," he wrote, "I am entering with the new year into a fresh course of duties, viz. the Tutorship. May I engage in them in the strength of Christ, remembering I am a minister of God, and have a commission to preach the Gospel, remembering the worth of souls, and that I shall have to answer for the opportunities given me of benefitting those who are under my care." [29]

It is possible, of course, to suppose that in evolving this view of the tutor's office Newman was merely rationalizing his desire to hold it, but the evidence shows that he was quite conscious of such a danger and was continually watchful lest it should arise. "I have a great undertaking before me in the Tutorship here," he wrote to his sister Harriett in March. "I trust God may give me grace to undertake it in a proper spirit, and to keep steadily in view that I have set myself apart for His service for ever. There is always the danger of the love of literary pursuits assuming too prominent a place in the thoughts of a College Tutor, or his viewing his situation merely as a secular office, a means of a future provision when he leaves College." [30] And a short time later he made another report, not to Harriett, but to his own book of memoranda, "personal and *most* private."

> I have now been engaged in the Oriel Tuition four weeks. The College is filled principally with men of family, in many cases, of fortune. I fear there exists very considerable profligacy among them. There is much too in the system which I think wrong. I hardly acquiesce in the general reception of the Sacraments, which is expected, or even in the practice of having evening chapel. I think the Tutors see too little of the men, and that there is not enough of direct religious instruction. It is my wish to consider myself as the minister of Christ. May I most seriously reflect, that, *unless* I find that opportunities occur of doing spiritual good to those over whom I am placed, it will become a grave question whether I *ought* to continue in the Tuition.[31]

In the riotous state of undergraduate life in those days there was no lack of opportunity for doing good. The real question was whether an inexperienced tutor could hold his own, as witness, for example, the account of James Fraser, who was a tutor of Oriel in the early forties. When Fraser entered the tuition he found that ten of the fifty undergraduates were gentlemen-commoners whose sole passion was dressing, wining, and hunting, and that the remainder were mostly athletes, with whom boating and cricket were all the rage. Boxing matches were held in the rooms two or three nights a week, and Oriel "almost supported a retired prize fighter, who had been known in the ring as 'the Flying Tailor.'" [32] In his classes Fraser found himself studiously insulted, and he finally won the boys over only by the dazzling elegance of his dress, by his prowess in driving tandem around North Wales, and by wrestling and overcoming an undergraduate who was known as "the Bear" from the closeness of his hugs.

This was all very well for those who could do it—but it was not the method for Newman. And yet in his time the problem was hardly less serious than it was in Fraser's. In 1826, the year in which Newman entered the tuition, there was a group of undergraduates in Oriel, chiefly gentlemen-commoners, who were notoriously rowdy, "perhaps as bad," wrote Tom Mozley, " as any in the University." [33] Even over in Germany, Pusey heard rumors that the Oriel men "used to be famous for reading, but they are now tired of it, and were one of the most drinking sets in Oxford." [34] If such conduct had been disgusting to Newman as an undergraduate it was even more so now, for in the intervening years, and especially since his failure in the Schools, the austerity of his own personal life had greatly increased. Even the normal indulgence of the common room, slight as it was, was now a source of uneasiness to him. "I must explain myself in some way to the Fellows," he had written early in his association, "about my wish to keep Sunday Holy. Last Sunday I dined with the Provost; this morning I breakfasted with the Dean. I did not know what excuse to make. . . ." And again, "since October, I have, I may say uniformly declined invitations for Sunday evening among the Fellows - and, though I have sometimes dined with the Provost on Sunday, still, by intimating I wish to be alone, my friends have less perplexed me." [35] Playgoing, which he had once enjoyed, he no longer found innocent; newspapers were not to be read on Sundays; and in 1823 he buttressed these convictions by drawing up an argument for the strict observance of the Sabbath from St. Chrysostom and other Fathers. But he also noted that with every new strictness which he adopted for himself there was a tendency to be censorious of those who had not adopted it, and though he guarded against this tendency, it drove him more and more into silence where he could not criticize and into criticism where he could not be silent.[36]

Whatever might be necessary with his superiors, with the undergraduates, who were actually committed to his care, there was no need to be silent—indeed, it would have been wrong to be so. Therefore, with a fierceness born partly of principle and partly of inexperience, he set himself against this element in the college, and "like a new broom, began sweeping very vigorously, as far as my opportunities went." As might be expected, he again met with resistance, especially from the gentlemen-commoners, "who, relying on the claims of family and fortune, did their best to oppose me and to spread tales about me." [37] Indeed, his first year in office seems to have been almost continuous storm and tumult. In November, 1826 he wrote to his sister, "I have some trouble with my horses [college pupils], as you may imagine, for whenever they get a new coachman, they make an effort to get the reins slack. But I shall be very obstinate, though their curvettings and shyings are very teazing." [38] By May of the next year he had "hunted from the college two men," [39] and in June he wrote to his mother, "We are having rows as thick as black-berries. What a thing it is to be vigorous, J[emima], and dignified, H[arriett]. I am so dignified it is quite overpowering." [40]

It so happens that we know quite a bit about these rows, for two of the undergraduates involved later became prominent in public life and wrote memoirs of their college pranks. One was Sir Charles Murray, whose last year at Oriel coincided with Newman's first as a tutor, and who has left the following reminiscences of the future cardinal:

> He never inspired me, or my fellow-undergraduates, with any in-terest, much less respect: on the contrary, we disliked, or rather distrusted, him. He walked with his head bent, abstracted, but every now and then looking out of the corners of his eyes quickly, as though suspicious. . . .
>
> I well remember one trick we played him. I was up to him for Greek. At lecture he was quiet, and what I should call sheepish; stuck to the text, and never diverged into contemporary history or made the lecture interesting. He always struck me as the most pusillanimous of men—wanting in the knowledge of human nature; and I am always surprised, and indeed never can understand, how it was he became such a great man. I never heard him preach.
>
> We were a merry set of youngsters, fond of singing late into the night over suppers. The songs were not classical, but, I am ashamed to say, generally very noisy. They disturbed Newman, who liked quiet; but instead of coming himself and asking us to be earlier and quieter, he sent a porter, whom we sent to the devil. It showed either his cowardice or his want of humanity. If we were noisy, we were all of us gentlemen, and not one of us would have rebelled if he had spoken to us himself. As it was, he stuck up a big bell out-side his room, about twelve feet from the ground. At nine o'clock

or so, if we began to shout, he pealed this bell to summon the
porter to tell us to be quiet. This was too much. I said I'd have the
bell down; the others all chaffed me, and said I shouldn't. It was
impossible to do it alone, but not one of them would join me. At
last Lord Malmesbury's brother, Harris, a lieutenant in the navy,
who was up on a visit, volunteered, and we laid our plans. Next
night we brought a ladder and a pickaxe. The fellow had had the
bell fixed in with nails some five inches long, and we took it in turn
to hold the ladder and to pick at the nails. Of course Newman *must*
have heard us, and if he had been anything of a man, he would
have come out of his room and caught us red-handed; but he was
too pusillanimous for that, and we were allowed to finish our work
in peace, so far as he was concerned. Unluckily for me, though, as I
was coming down with the great bell and its fixtures in my arms my
foot slipped, and I fell, spraining my ankle. Of course next day
there was the devil of a row, but no one was sent down. . . . The
old Dean - Tyler - my tutor, and a great friend of mine, came and sat
by my bed where I was kept 'by an accident,' and I saw by the
twinkle in his eye that he knew all about it, but he kept his counsel,
and as it was the end of the term the thing blew over. But Newman
never put up his bell again.[41]

This same anecdote was repeated during Newman's lifetime by the
other undergraduate who was involved, James Howard Harris, later third
Earl of Malmesbury and Lord Privy Seal.

Of this last celebrated writer and divine, and now a cardinal, no
one at that time would have predicted the future career. He used to
allow his class to torment him with the most helpless resignation;
every kind of mischievous trick was, to our shame, played upon
him—such as cutting his bell-rope, and at lectures making the table
advance gradually till he was jammed into a corner. He remained
quite impassive, and painfully tolerant. I once saw him nearly
driven from Coplestone's table, when the Provost, who was an epi-
cure, upbraided him for what he called 'mutilating' a fine haunch
of venison, and shouting out, 'Mr. Newman, you are unconscious of
the mischief you have done.' [42]

This lively tale, which was first published in Lord Malmesbury's autobiography, was reprinted widely in the daily press in the autumn of 1884
and naturally gave great offense to Newman by its imputation of coward-
ice. After some hesitation he brought the matter to the attention of Lord
Blachford, a friend and former pupil, who immediately wrote to the

Daily News (as he had thought of doing before Newman's letter arrived) denying Malmesbury's statements. He himself, he said, had attended Mr. Newman's lectures for three years and he was sure that his contemporaries would agree that "Mr. Newman's conduct to the undergraduates and theirs to him was absolutely the reverse of what Lord Malmesbury describes. He was very kind and retiring, but perfectly determined (as might be expected from his subsequent history)—a tutor with whom men did not venture to take a liberty, and who was master of a formidable and speaking silence calculated to quell any ordinary impertinence." The table-jerking story, he went on, was in his day told of another tutor, William James, whose temperament it perfectly described, and "I cannot myself doubt that after half a century of active life he [Lord Malmesbury] has fastened on Mr. Newman his recollections of Mr. James." [43]

Newman hoped that this statement would elicit a retraction from Lord Malmesbury and so put an end to the matter, but when a fortnight had passed without a reply he felt that in justice to his own honor and to the truth of the case he must speak out for himself. He therefore wrote a short letter which was published in the *Daily News* on October 28, 1884, and which finally elicited a reply from Lord Malmesbury. This reply, while not withdrawing the original statements, did deny their offensive character and so was reluctantly accepted by Newman as a satisfactory apology. [44]

Of the various stories told against him Newman denied that of the table jerking, which apparently did belong to Tutor James, [45] but admitted that of the bell rope (or rather wire). It was done "at midnight," he said, "when I was in bed; but I suppose it was an insipid joke, for it was not done again," a remark which suggests that Newman did put his bell back up—if, indeed, the undergraduates ever actually got it down. As for the venison story, that was not a fact but "a mythical representation of what was the fact—viz. that I was not supported in my reforms by the high authorities of the college." [46]

If Newman was not supported by the college authorities then the real issue must have been much deeper than that of boyish escapades, and indeed it was. It was no less than a question of sacrilege. As ecclesiastical foundations, with their roots in the Middle Ages, all the colleges maintained religious observances which were rather more full than the taste of the age required. At Oriel, for example, there was morning and evening chapel and communion at the end of term, and as participation in all these services was expected, the sacred objects were thereby exposed to indifference and even contempt. The occasion of the Sacrament especially, coming as it did just at the end of classes, was often ushered in and out with a champagne feast; and although the liturgy said expressly that it was dangerous to partake unworthily, some who did partake were so obviously unworthy that they could hardly stand. To Newman, whose feelings about the communion were inexpressibly tender, such scenes were shocking beyond measure, and when he had first witnessed them at Trinity he had composed a youthful sermon on the subject and had also written a long letter to Mr. Mayers. Then, in 1822, on first coming to Oriel, he found that the problem had just been brought into the open by an anonymous pamphlet (the work of an Oriel undergraduate named Colquhoun) which argued that since the profanation of the Sacrament was really caused by the rule requiring communion, the rule itself should be abolished. It was unnecessary in the case of those who were worthy, for they would communicate anyway; and in the case of those who were not worthy it was sinful—and the authorities promoted the sin. "Be wise, Ye Presidents and Deans," wrote the poet Wordsworth,

> and, till the spirit
> Of ancient times revive, and youth be trained
> At home in pious service, to your bells
> Give seasonable rest.[47]

But the authorities would not be wise, and at Oriel the task of replying to Colquhoun's pamphlet fell to Hawkins. He admitted most of the facts but argued in favor of the rule on the grounds that if any were unfit for the Sacrament they were also unfit to be members of a society which was distinctly and formally Christian.[48] This was logical enough, but what Oxford head was going to rusticate a man for not being (what few could claim that they were) a good Christian? Certainly not Copleston, for when Newman asked the Provost in 1826 or 1827, "Are the men *expected* to take the Sacrament?" he was answered sharply, "I beg you will not put such an idea into their minds. I am persuaded the question never occurs to them"—though he knew very well that it did. And again when Newman said to Tyler, "Your men had a champagne breakfast the other day after the Sacrament," the latter answered, "I don't believe it, and if it were *true* I don't wish to know it." [49] Doubtless, after such an exchange, if Newman had shown some inexperience in carving a haunch of venison, he might well have been shouted at by a peevish head or dean.

Such was the story, then, of Newman's first year as a tutor of Oriel. "It gives me great pleasure," wrote his mother, "to see you appear so strong at the end of a troublesome term. I hope you will have effected a 'radical reform' by your vigorous measures, and that you are properly seconded." [50] Of course he had not been properly seconded nor was he really strong. Moreover, the troubles he had just been through were as nothing compared to those which lay before him in the winter of 1827–28. This winter, though he did not know it yet, was to mark a turning point in his life as significant as either his youthful conversion or his illness in Sicily, for it was the occasion of one of the "three great illnesses in my life." "The first keen, terrible one," as we have already learned, "[was] when I was a boy of 15, and it made me a Christian. . . . My second, not painful, but tedious and shattering was that which I had in 1827 when I was one of the Examining Masters, and it too broke me off from an incipient liberalism - and determined my religious course - The third was in 1833, when I was in Sicily, before the commencement of the Oxford movement." [51]

It is difficult to discover an incipient liberalism in Newman's position in 1827, but as he asserts several times that such was the case, we can only suppose that it came about as a reaction to the extreme conscientiousness of his first year as a tutor. Just as he came to feel at the end of his year at Alban Hall that he had been overly strict with the men there, so he may have recognized that there was some wisdom in the leniency of his colleagues at Oriel, and by continued association with men whose qualities he so much admired he may indeed have been drawn into something resembling the Noetic habit of mind. Certainly this process would have been furthered by his summer task, which was that of preparing himself to act as public examiner in the Classical Schools. In June, 1827, when he first learned that he would one day be required to serve, he wrote to his mother that he "must prepare for it, so I intend this Vacation once for all to read up some works which, learned as I am, are yet strangers to me. At one time I thought I should have to go into the Schools after the Vacation, but now that seems improbable, and I certainly won't go without a six months' notice." [52]

Actually he did go after the vacation and with only five months' notice, and therefore the summer was a period of intensive reading. It was like preparing for his own examination all over again, only in some ways it was worse. Indeed, if the undergraduates had only known it, it was really the examiner and not the examinee who was on trial, for in his case a dozen books would not do. He must master all the varying dozens which would be brought up during the entire year, and in the examination itself he must keep at it day after day before an audience which would be only too delighted to see him slip and fall. Moreover, the questions which a student has only to answer he must produce; and before a continuing audience and in the presence of his own colleagues he must produce them in some variety—otherwise he would be the laughing stock of the university. This was no idle fear. So great was the dread of exposure among the younger dons that there was a real difficulty, we are told, in finding six tutors a year who were willing to undertake the office.[53] Newman was not unwilling, but as the time for the ordeal approached he must have been keenly conscious of what had happened to him in those same Schools just seven years before.

He was to spend the summer partly at Brighton with his mother and sisters and partly at Hampstead, where he was doing duty for a friend; and at both places he would have one and sometimes two pupils reading with him. He took along an entire trunkful of books, some forty-five volumes of classics, lexicons, and histories to Brighton, two dozen others to Hampstead,[54] and he read in them an average of seven to eight hours a day from July 9 to September 15. He worked at Hebrew grammar, read all five volumes of Mitford's *Greece* and nearly two of Niebuhr's *Rome*, did some Homer and the *Clouds* of Aristophanes twice over, all of the *Fasti Hellenici*, twenty-seven "items" from the Greek orators plus eight speeches of Demosthenes, "F. Clinton on the Population of Greece" and "on Demosthenes," and then the work with his pupils as well. Afterward he admitted that he had read "too hard," that his mind had been "too much on the stretch, and had suffered from too intensely dwelling on the object, for which I was preparing myself." [55] Moreover there was a crisis in the affairs of his aunt, and the thought that she was in difficulty and that a large sum of money was sooner or later to be raised distressed him. Altogether the summer was "full of vexation and anxiety," and by late September he was very weak and showed symptoms of a low fever. He was still weak in November when he went into the Schools. Then, "several examinations of difficulty fell to me. . . . My dreams were full of the Schools and of examinations. To complete it, the news came of the promotion of the Provost [Copleston] to a Bishoprick, and we had the prospect of an immediate vacancy in the Headship of Oriel. This completed my incapacity. I heard of it on the Friday (Novr 23), when I was in the Schools—dreamed of it that night, and (I believe) the next - drooped during the Saturday, which was my leisure day - and on Sunday felt the blood collect in my head; on Monday found my memory and mind gone, when examining a candidate for the first class, and was obliged to leave the Schools in the middle of the day." On the doctor's advice he was leeched on the temples, but he got worse rather than better. "I was not in pain exactly; nothing acute, nothing like a rheumatic headache; but a confusion, an inability to think or recollect. Once or twice, indeed, when my head was on my pillow, I felt a throbbing so distressing, though it was not violent, [as] to make me sensible I had never experienced a real headache. It was not pain, but a twisting of the brain, of the eyes. I felt my head inside was made up of parts. I could

[59]

write verse pretty well, but I could not *count*. I once or twice tried to count my pulse, but found it quite impossible; before I had got to 30, my eyes turned round and inside out, all of a sudden." [56]

"And now," says Newman in this same memorandum, "how can I summon strength to recount the particulars of the heaviest affliction with which the good hand of God has ever visited me." He had been carried off to Highwood by his friend Robert Wilberforce, and after a few weeks, feeling somewhat rested, had rejoined his mother and sisters at Brighton. Christmas followed, and among the guests of the season was Maria Giberne, sister-in-law of the Rev. Walter Mayers. A letter of hers, written to Newman many years later, describes how at dinner on January 4 Mary Newman, John's youngest sister and the darling of the family, was seated next him, and how, "while eating a bit of turkey she turned her face towards me, her hand on her heart, so pale, and a dark ring round her eyes, and she said she felt ill, and should she go away? I asked you, and she went." [57] Spasms came on in the night but there seemed no danger, and the next morning Maria went out with a friend. When she returned rather late in the evening, she "felt a shock in entering the house, seeing no one but you—so pale and so calm, and yet so inwardly moved; and how, when I asked you to pray with us for her, you made a great effort to quiet your voice, sitting against the table, your eyes on the fire, and you answered, 'I must tell you the truth: she is dead already.' " [58]

Newman had lost his father three years before and was to lose his mother before many more years were past, but neither event affected him anything like the death of his sister Mary. On his following birthday, when he tried to write his usual memorandum, "personal and *most* private," of the year just past, he could only cry, "O my dearest sister Mary, O my sister, my sister, I do feel from the bottom of my heart that it is all right - I see, I know it to be, in God's good Providence, the best thing for all of us; I do not, I have not in the least repined - I would not have it otherwise - but I feel sick, I must cease writing." [59] He found it impossible for words to put down "those indefinite, vague, and withal subtle feelings which quite pierce the soul and make it sick," and which were always with him. "Not one half-hour passes but dear Mary's face is before my eyes." If he rode over to Cuddesdon, Mary seemed embodied in every tree and hid behind every hill. "What a veil and curtain this world of sense is! beautiful, but still a veil." He was distressed at the thought that her memory would gradually fade away, and urged his sisters "carefully [to] take down . . . all you can recollect that dear Mary said on every subject, both during the time of her short illness and the days before; we shall else forget it. Would it not, too, be desirable to write down some memoranda generally concerning her?—her general character, and all the delightful things we now recollect concerning her. Alas! memory does not remain vivid; the more minute these circumstances the better. To talk of her thus in the third person . . . is to me the most distressing circumstance, perhaps, attending our loss." [60]

The study which Newman is here proposing to his sisters is in striking contrast to that in which he had been engaged the summer before, in "F. Clinton on the Population of Greece." Both are a kind of research, but the one is that temporal research, or remembrance of things past, which is simply a renewal of what lies already at the center of one's being, whereas the other is an accession *to* one's being of what has hitherto lain beyond it. Personal and impersonal, unified and disparate, they are aspects of the One and the Many, and the gulf between them is but a measure of the change which had been wrought upon Newman's mind by his failure in the one research and the deep need of his nature for the other. The very form of his illness, which is precisely that of 1820 and 1822, symbolizes the fragmentation of his mind. His head inside is "made up of parts," "there is a twisting of the brain, of the eyes," and though he can handle poetry (or so it seems to him in his illness), he cannot handle the strict, successive order of mathematics. If he counts beyond thirty his eyes turn "round and inside out, all of a sudden," and this refusal of the eyes to encompass more is apparently validated by the sudden intelligence of Mary's death.

As Newman later assessed the significance of his illness, he was greatly impressed by the fact that it had come "when he was exercising his office of University examiner in the very same schools in which in 1820 he had failed as an examinee," and that it had come just "seven years later" and "on all but the same day (November 26, instead of November 25)." [61] To a mind so tenacious of anniversaries as Newman's was and for whom the seven-year period had ever a cyclical or terminal significance, this coincidence seemed almost preternatural. Not that he felt that he had again been guilty of an intellectual pride as gross as that which followed upon his winning the scholarship, but he was aware that pride and vanity were his besetting sin. In the year after his election to Oriel there had been an instance of this which had troubled him deeply. "In the beginning of this Term," he confessed, "I had to speak an Oration in Hall. The Provost said it was spirited. Well, I have been brooding on this, and repeating the composition again and again to myself. Wherever I go, I fancy people are looking at me and thinking of me." [62] Doubtless fancies of this sort were repeated as he approached the Schools. Daydreaming idly, as we all do, he may have seen himself as the intellectual hero of the hour, putting questions which astonished the spectators by their penetration and learning, being gracious to the timid and severe with the presumptuous, leading even the most brilliant candidates through their books with an ease and mastery which set the whole university buzzing with excitement. That he could have done such things is perfectly certain—but not after dreaming about them for weeks in advance; and therefore, when the event turned out so very differently from what he had hoped, when he was ironically deprived of his powers at the very moment that he hoped to display them, he must have felt like the prodigal who had suddenly come to himself. And what is more, he must have realized that he was being false to the promise he had made to himself that he would use the office of tutor as a fulfillment of his pastoral vow. Certainly the effect which his illness had upon him was to renew and deepen that promise in his own mind. "The truth is," he wrote in the *Apologia*, "I was beginning to prefer intellectual excellence to moral; I was drifting in the direction of the liberalism of the day. I was rudely awakened from my dream at the end of 1827 by two great blows—illness and bereavement." [63]

But what "completed my incapacity," said Newman, was the news that Copleston had got a bishopric and Oriel would need a new head. Why this should make him dream for two nights and send the blood into his brain one may well wonder, but the truth is that Newman's disposition was often sanguine beyond all restraint. When some new fact would fall idly into the cistern of things, Newman would seize paper and pen and let his mind race down avenues of speculation, noting advantages to be gained here, possibilities to be proved there, drawing them up, listing them, and numbering the lists until, as he wryly observed, he was eating fricassee of chicken before the egg was fairly hatched. The fricassee, in this instance, was not the picture of himself as provost of Oriel —that might be hard to keep out of the dreams, but it would never get into the lists—rather it was the picture of himself and the new provost remaking Oriel as he wished it to be. For to this work he had in a sense dedicated himself. His best wish was "to live and die a Fellow of Oriel," and he had abandoned St. Clement's and the work of a missionary for this purpose. It was no part of his purpose, however, to live and die in the Oriel of Copleston's creation, for although he was "proud" of his college as it then existed, he "was not at home there." [64] It had blocked his reforms and winked at disorders he could not tolerate, and therefore in the news of Copleston's resignation he saw a field of promise suddenly opening before him and he dreamed about it for two nights in a row.

The story of the Oriel election has often been told, but it is not certain that it has ever been told correctly. For historians and biographers, writing with their eye upon the Tractarian movement, are inclined to burden the event with all the consequences to which it unwittingly gave rise. It is true that one of the candidates, Hawkins, was later to become the most formidable opponent of the movement, and that the other, Keble, was to be its "true and primary author." [65] And it is also true that Newman, with what now seems like a perverse and tragic blindness, threw in his weight with the former and secured his election. But it is not true that the issues, as the college actually saw them in 1828, were the issues of Tractarianism or that they were in any way theological. They were the practical, moral, and educational issues that naturally would be involved in choosing a college head, and these too were the grounds—admittedly the mistaken grounds—of Newman's preference for Hawkins. "Let me add," wrote Newman in 1884, "what I have never yet brought out, that it was a longing on my part for some stricter discipline which was the direct cause of Hawkins' election. He had the reputation of even sternness. 'He was just the man we wanted,' I said. When Froude pleaded for Keble, I said to myself 'He cannot cope with the evil.' " [66]

For all that Newman might say, however, it remains true that the shift from Copleston to Hawkins did not at all keep pace with the real changes which were going on within the college from 1826 to 1828. The former year is considered by the college historian to be the highest point in Oriel's fame, and this fact may be symbolized by the great festivity which was held on June 15 of that year commemorating the five hundredth anniversary of the founding of the college by Adam de Brome. There was a service in St. Mary's with Copleston preaching and a great dinner in the college library with a hundred and forty guests attending. "The Society," wrote Copleston afterward, "in a very flourishing state, and in excellent discipline. The Fellows united, and the most cordial harmony subsisting." [67]

Copleston was unaware, however, that in this very gathering there were present the elements of a discord which would one day shake the college in an open quarrel and send it into a decline from which it never afterward recovered. For if that day was a triumph it was a peculiarly Noetic one, and the Noetic phase was past or just then passing. Within the year Tyler, who was Copleston's right-hand man, was to accept a living and depart, and within two years the Provost himself would leave Oriel for the See of Llandaff. Moreover, the spring of that year had brought in two new fellows, Richard Hurrell Froude and Robert Isaac Wilberforce, and it had brought Newman into the tuition. Newman was the pivot on which the change was made. For four years the admiring disciple of Hawkins, Copleston, and Whately, he was just beginning to discover that he really belonged with Froude, Wilberforce, and Keble. His estrangement from the former group was adumbrated by an Easter Day sermon which he had preached in Oriel Chapel in 1827. Hawkins, Whately, and Blanco White had asked to read it afterward, and "none liked it." [68] Newman studied their penciled comments and noted that he was "sure [he] must be more or less wrong," [69] since they said so, but that he had been led to the view as the result of much prayer and study. On the other hand, the estrangement which he suffered here was almost immediately repaired by his growing intimacy with the two new fellows, for they were just coming into residence in the autumn of that year. Froude was replacing Tyler in the tuition, beginning in Michaelmas Term, and Wilberforce followed soon after, when Hawkins became provost. Through them Newman was led to visit Keble in August, 1828, the "1st symptom of our intimacy," [70] and perhaps he then discovered (what he later recognized to be the case) that Keble's views on the mode of administering a college coincided much more closely with his own than did those of Hawkins. Indeed, so complete was his realignment by this time and so rapidly was it accomplished that if the resignation of Copleston had been deferred for a single year, Newman might well have thrown his weight the other way, and the whole history of his college and of the movement would have been changed.

Even as it was, however, Newman's position in the college had been completely altered. From being junior tutor in a group which was devoted to the Noetic way, he had become next to the senior in a group which was increasingly devoted to his own ideals. Obviously, if he had reforms to propose now was the time to propose them, and with characteristic energy he set about the matter at once. He held discussions during the following summer with Froude and Wilberforce, and perhaps also with Dornford, the senior tutor, about some of the measures which he hoped to enact. One of these concerned an evil which was apparently of present moment, for it was noticed only a year later in a pamphlet published by Thomas Vowler Short, a tutor of Christ Church. "The several members of each college," wrote Short, "are admitted three times in the year, sometimes oftener, so that any course must begin at least three times a year, or the system must be broken in upon, and young men of different standing mingled in the same lecture." [71] In a small college like Oriel it was the latter course that was taken, and the obvious remedy was that some one period should be appointed when the freshmen of each year should come into residence. This was what New-

[64]

man proposed, and in a letter to Wilberforce he envisioned great advantages, both to tutor and pupil, from having every man classed with those of his own standing.[72] The thing seems obvious enough, but at Oxford it had never been done.

This particular reform could not be put into operation at once, but other reforms could be and indeed were. In a letter to the Rev. Samuel Rickards written in Hilary Term, 1829, Newman detailed the accomplishments of the preceding year:

> We have gone through the year famously; packed off our lumber, parted with spoilt goods, washed and darned where we could, and imported several new articles of approved quality. Indeed, the College is so altered that you would hardly know it again. The tangible improvements of system have been, first, the diminishing the Gentlemen Commoners from twenty to eight or nine; then the dismissal of the Incurables; then the rejecting unprepared candidates for admission—the number is awful, some twice; then the giving chance vacancies to well-recommended and picked men; then the introduction of paper work into the Collections examinations; then the refusing testimonials to unworthy applicants; then the revival of a Chapel sermon at the Sacrament; then the announcement of a prize for Greek composition. The most important and far-reaching improvement has been commenced this term - a radical alteration (not apparent on the published list) of the lecture system. The bad men are thrown into large classes, and thus time saved for the better sort, who are put into very small lectures, and principally with their own tutors quite familiarly and chattingly. And, besides, a regular system for *the year* has been devised. But we do not wish this to be talked about. We hope soon to give some Exhibitions or Scholarships. All these alterations are, you observe, additional to that grand act at the election, of throwing open two Fellowships. Pretty well, we hope, for a year. . . . [Hawkins] has not (nor should a Head) taken the initiative in these innovations, but has always approved—sometimes kept abreast with us—and at Collections has slain the bad men manfully. It is said in College by the undergraduates that, 'Now, alas! the Provost was as bad as a Tutor.' Whereas, at Collections they used to hope the Provost would retaliate on the Tutors the blows they received from the latter.[73]

The reform which Newman describes as "the most important and far-reaching" must be discussed in some detail, for it was the immediate cause of the college quarrel. It involved, says Newman, "a radical alteration . . . of the lecture system," and it will be observed that this system, as established in the days of Copleston and Hawkins, placed very little emphasis upon the personal relation between a tutor and his pupil. It is true that every undergraduate upon matriculation was assigned to a particular tutor, for this much was required by the statutes of the university, but his actual instruction was borne by all the tutors in common. Prior to 1829 the matter was arranged in this way: On the first day of each term the tutors met together and formed classes in the various subjects of study, assigning students to these classes according to their needs and the exigencies of the weekly schedule. This done, they chose in rotation the particular classes which they wished to teach, and it goes without saying that these classes were not composed, or only to a small degree, of the undergraduates who had been assigned to them on matriculation.[74] Beyond this, of course, they did have a special obligation to their own pupils which was defined by Copleston in this way. "My beau-ideal was that a tutor should see all his own pupil's exercises, and remark upon them; that he should talk to him about the lectures he was attending, whether in his own classes or not; be ready to assist his difficulties, observe his conduct, and see more especially that his religious instruction went on." [75] This was the beau-ideal but, as Hawkins admitted, few tutors came up to it in practice, and in any case, of the two relations in which they stood to the undergraduates, that to their class was primary and official and that to their pupils was secondary and more or less undefined.

The result was that the normal relation between tutor and undergraduate was distant and even perfunctory. Newman had seen this on first entering the tuition—"I think the Tutors see too little of the men," he had written—and in 1854 in an article for the *Catholic University Gazette* he drew a picture of the Oriel of his day which, though he did not identify it, was not very deeply disguised.

I have experienced a state of things in which teachers were cut off from the taught as by an insurmountable barrier; when neither party entered into the thoughts of the other; when each lived by and in itself; when the tutor was supposed to fulfil his duty, if he trotted on like a squirrel in his cage, if at a certain hour he was in a certain room, or in hall, or in chapel, as it might be; and the pupil did his duty too, if he was careful to meet his tutor in that same room, or hall, or chapel, at the same certain hour; and when neither the one nor the other dreamed of seeing each other out of lecture, out of chapel, out of academical gown. I have known places where a stiff manner, a pompous voice, coldness and condescension, were the teacher's attributes, and where he neither knew, nor wished to know, and avowed he did not wish to know, the private irregularities of the youths committed to his charge.[76]

Newman himself had tried to do things differently, but when he had run up against the hard facts of young Malmesbury and Charles Murray, he had "turned for relief to his own special pupils, and primarily to the orderly and promising among them." To them he offered "his sympathy and help in college work," [77] and by 1828 he had acquired "such a devoted body of pupils as Oxford had never seen"—never, says Tom Mozley, since the Middle Ages.[78] He read, walked, and breakfasted with them, took exercises with them ("which is a larking thing for a don" [79]), and saw them in off hours and in the Long Vacation. In other words, he was being a public tutor and private combined, and that not merely in effect but by deliberate intention. He formally set himself against the system of private tutors, declaring that it inflicted upon the pupil an unnecessary expense and upon the tutor a loss of legitimate influence, and he undertook to combine both offices in his own person. He laid it down as his rule that to such of his pupils as wished to attempt the Honors he would give without charge the additional instruction which was necessary, and in great measure he was able to carry out this rule.[80] He saw, however, that he could not continue to carry it out alone. He could not forever give full instruction to his own pupils if he had to give partial instruction to the pupils of others as well, and therefore he devised the "far-reaching improvement" which was mentioned in the letter to Rickards. In effect, it was simply an extension to the entire college of the system which he had already been acting upon for the past year.

The essential purpose of Newman's scheme was to foster the personal relation between pupil and tutor by making each tutor responsible for the entire instruction of his own men. If he had devised this scheme on first coming into Oriel, as a pure expression of the pastoral idea, doubtless it would have taken the extreme form which that idea suggests. But from his two years' experience he had learned that some pupils do not desire a personal relation, and therefore his plan as actually formulated provided for grouping some men in small private classes under their own tutor, "quite familiarly and chattingly," while throwing the others into larger public classes which would be distributed among all the tutors according to the established system. The plan also provided for distinguishing between those subjects in the teaching of which an intimate, personal relation was especially desirable and those in which it was less desirable or not worth the trouble. Only in the former were private classes to be formed even for the better men, and these classes were defined by Newman as "either 1. in Moral subjects - e.g. Divinity - Ethics. or 2. in books continued term after term; e.g. history or 3. in order to prepare pupils for the public lectures, and therefore in all the subjects which are read in the public lectures - e.g. algebraical arithmetic, Euclid, Latin Composition, etc." The subjects in which it was not worth the trouble to form small classes were those "which are *necessarily* read, (Euclid, Articles, Logic,) or *generally*, (Greek Plays, Greek and Latin authors - or *often* (Mathematics, Rhetoric.)" [81] This system could also be modified, if the tutors agreed to do so, by exchanging pupils even in their private classes. On the other hand, the final principle of the system was that every tutor had the ultimate disposition of his own men and could, if he so desired, keep all of them (even the bad ones) exclusively for himself.

Newman admits that he was the "chief mover" in this reform, but he declares that Froude and Wilberforce "entered entirely into the views" on which he desired it and that it became the "unanimous act" of them all.[82] During the Christmas vacation in 1828 the three of them broached the idea to Dornford, whose reaction seems to have been skeptical but acquiescent. He noted, as making against the plan, that by having several tutors do separately what one might do for all they were reversing the principle of the division of labor and adding greatly to their own burdens. Apart from that, however, he found much in the plan to like and thought that if the others felt strongly about it they might make the experiment; and he agreed with Newman that there was no necessity to consult Hawkins before they began.[83]

Why did Newman wish to begin without consulting Hawkins? Only a twelvemonth before he had favored Hawkins for the provostship largely because of his views on college reform,[84] and only six weeks later he was still praising him for the manly way in which he had carried out these reforms. Nevertheless he apparently sensed that this particular reform was one which Hawkins would not approve and therefore never tolerate. For if Hawkins had been punctilious and unyielding before his election, he was even more so now that he was in power, and the truth is that those who had put him there were beginning to feel that he had kicked the ladder from under his feet. In repudiation of his former opinions he had traitorously aligned himself with the Hebdomadal Board instead of his own college, and he also assumed a donnishness of manner which irritated and annoyed the tutors. He began to speak of his "House" instead of his "lodgings," assumed the royal "we," and gave himself such an institutional character that he was mischievously referred to as "the College" by some of the younger Fellows.[85] Chafing under these rubs, the tutors decided that although they would not conceal from the Provost what they were doing, neither would they go out of their way to bring it to his attention. They would simply send him, as they normally did, the regular Table of Lectures which they drew up at the beginning of the term, and since this table did not of itself reveal the change which had been made, Hawkins did not actually learn of it for some months. The new system was instituted on January 14, 1829 at the beginning of Hilary Term, and it was in Easter Term that the matter accidentally came out. At that time the intelligence was received by Hawkins in what seemed to Newman a rude and inconsiderate way, and on a second occasion the tutors were told pointedly that they "must alter this next Term." [86]

This was the beginning of the college quarrel. It is not necessary to go into all the personal bitterness which the quarrel aroused (the latter part was conducted entirely by letter although the parties involved were living side by side in the same college) or to expound the various technicalities and stratagems by which each side hoped to maintain its position. In later years Newman conceded that it would have been much better to have told Hawkins from the beginning, and he also conceded that his part in the quarrel was conducted with an unbecoming truculence and insubordination.[87] On the other hand he was under great provocation, for not only was Hawkins stiff and authoritarian to a degree but also he infuriated Newman by assuming that his views, which were based on a deep religious principle, were simply the result of overwork and ill health and would pass away with a little relaxation on the sands of Brighton.

One incident must be noted for its bearing not only on the quarrel but also on Newman's intellectual development, and this is the contest over the re-election of Sir Robert Peel.[88] Peel, who was the representative of the university in Parliament, had recently reversed his stand on the question of Catholic emancipation and so had felt it proper to resign his seat, although in the end he was persuaded to offer himself for re-election. Newman had no particular views on the Catholic claims, but he felt that it was a deep affront to the university to ask it to veer and tack with all the winds of political expediency. A great academical institution such as Oxford was and ought to be independent of the state. Essentially it was an ecclesiastical body, and the issue here was "far more than a question of politics and political expediency; it was a moral, an academical, an ecclesiastical, nay a religious question," [89] for it involved nothing less than the independence and integrity of the church itself.

Thus Newman was violently aroused, and his excitement is interesting not merely because it embodies the spirit and issues of Tractarianism four years before the movement began, but also because it illustrates one kind of experience which Newman had in mind when he spoke of the integrity of the intellect. Heretofore his ideas had been reasonably well ordered, but now they were simply fused by the excitement of partisan conflict. The significance of the election flooded upon him like a great light and illuminated all the landscape round about. He felt that he understood, with a clarity he had never known before, the entire nature of the times in which he lived, and it seemed as though every observation, every fact and principle that he had ever learned fell now into its own place, perfectly and as though by prearrangement. In the excitement over his new views he wrote thirty letters on one day and seventy or eighty on the day after.[90] "What a scribbler I am become! But the fact is my mind is so full of ideas in consequence of this important event, and my views have so much enlarged and expanded, that in justice to myself I ought to write a volume."

"We live in a novel era," he went on, "one in which there is an advance toward universal education. Men have hitherto depended on others, and especially on the clergy, for religious truth; now each man attempts to judge for himself. Now, without meaning of course that Christianity is in itself opposed to free inquiry, still I think it *in fact* at the present time opposed to the particular form which that liberty of thought has now assumed. Christianity is of faith, modesty, lowliness, subordination; but the spirit at work against it is one of latitudinarianism, indifferentism, and schism." Hence, "the talent of the day is against the Church," [91] and this may be seen very strikingly in the present contest. Those supporting Peel "have everywhere styled themselves the 'talent' of the University," and Newman admitted that on his own side there were only "the inferior colleges and the humbler style of men." [92] There was, then, a real antagonism between reason and faith, and Newman developed a theory to explain its operation both in the individual and in the world at large. Each individual has certain instincts of right and wrong, antecedently to reasoning, on which he acts—and rightly so. But these instincts perverse reasoning may supplant, and if so they can be regained only with difficulty and from the same source by which they were perverted, that is, not from nature but from reason rightly conducted. The task of stemming infidelity, then, is twofold, to infuse into the reason that religious spirit which will ensure its right conduct and, where it has already gone astray, to bring it back by means which lie within its own nature. Thus the task is intellectual rather than political, and the victory over Peel, satisfactory as that was when it came, was only a temporary victory in a contest which eventually would be decided, not at the hustings, but in the colleges and universities of England.

Seen against this background, the reform of the college tuition took on a new importance in Newman's eyes. It was an essential measure in the major contest of the day. Moreover, the Peel affair had lent bitterness to the quarrel which arose out of the reform, for Hawkins had been on one side and his four tutors on the other; and in Newman's opinion Hawkins had acted in a way that was peremptory and out of line. Hence, whereas in a letter of February 6, before the matter broke, Newman had praised Hawkins for his part in the college reforms, on February 17, five days after it broke, he spoke of him as "our meddling Provost," [93] and from that time on all real harmony was at an end.

Since the quarrel was kept within the family as much as possible, the reports which got abroad were often garbled and make it difficult to give the proper weight to the various issues which were involved. Both Dean Burgon and Tom Mozley, for example, say that the tutors' desire to introduce "new books" into the curriculum was an important issue.[94] Mozley adds that Newman, Wilberforce, and Froude were already lecturing on the minor Latin poets, and that they wished to introduce "modern classics for illustration and comparison with the old," Butler's *Analogy*, for example, to be read by the side of Lucretius. It seems unlikely that Newman (although one feels less certain about the others) desired any striking revolution in this respect, but certainly Mozley, who was Newman's pupil at this time, was in a good position to know. Moreover, it is true that some changes in the books would naturally follow from the fact that the curriculum was no longer the joint work of all tutors but was arranged by each one individually for his own men. Naturally, too, Hawkins would oppose such changes, not necessarily out of conservatism but merely because the curriculum of studies would in this way pass from his own hands into the hands of the tutors. The only real control which he exercised over the tuition lay in the fact that he presided over the terminal examination of Collections. But if the tutors were continually introducing new books, each one a different set, he would be hard put to it to get them up and in the end would have to take a lesser part in the examination.

Another interpretation holds that the real meaning of this dispute was a wish on Newman's part to favor the good students at the expense of the less able. Certainly this is the impression given by Newman's account to Rickards that "the bad men are thrown into large classes, and thus time saved for the better sort," but actually it does not appear that the bad men were given less time than under the old system but only that the good men were given more. Further, by "bad" men Newman did not mean those who were less able so much as those who were willfully idle, and if they were sacrificed one can only say that it was a sacrifice to which they submitted with some alacrity. Indeed, in providing for two distinct grades of education Newman was simply extending into the tuition a principle already recognized in the Pass and Honors degrees, and the real element of change in his system, as Tom Mozley pointed out, was that he gave to the Honors men, free of charge, "as much time and trouble as is usually only expected from very good private tutors." [95]

All these issues, however, were merely subsidiary to the main one, which was that Newman regarded his office as a pastoral one and believed its pastoral character would be largely destroyed if he were made into a lecturer on books rather than a teacher of men.[96] Nor can we say that his stubbornness on this point was merely a scruple over fulfilling his ordination vow. Long before the quarrel began he had succeeded Hawkins as vicar of St. Mary's and so could be quite easy on this point. It was rather that he had a scruple over the nature of education, to wit, that its scope must be religious and its method personal or else it was not a work which he was interested in doing. Many years later, when he was a cardinal of the Catholic church, he recollected and reiterated this view. "When I was Public Tutor of my College at Oxford," he wrote, "I maintained, even fiercely, that my employment was distinctly pastoral. I considered that, by the Statutes of the University, a Tutor's profession was of a religious nature. I never would allow that, in teaching the classics, I was absolved from carrying on, by means of them, in the minds of my pupils, an ethical training. I considered a College Tutor to have the care of souls, and before I accepted the office I wrote down a private memorandum, that, supposing I could not carry out this view of it, the question would arise whether I could continue to hold it. To this principle I have been faithful through my life." [97]

What was Hawkins' position in this controversy? It was not, certainly, that he saw anything wrong about the pastoral conception of the tutor's office, although he did believe that all needful religious instruction could be given under the traditional system. His main objection was simply administrative.[98] He saw that Newman's proposal, although it might work superbly well with the tutors then in office, was not adequate as a permanent arrangement in the college, for if one tutor were of unequal attainments his pupils would bear the entire brunt of his incapacity, and if the various tutors were not personally in harmony there would be no harmony at all in the teaching of the college. The college would be at the mercy of the individual tutors. Its course would be brilliant but erratic. It would live under the rule of personal influence, with none of the steadying effect of system or law; and Hawkins, as the representative of law, would find his part reduced to little or nothing. As the one finally responsible for the welfare of the college he obviously could not permit this, and therefore the deadlock was complete.

The actual course of the quarrel can be briefly told. The new system was put into effect at the beginning of Hilary Term, January 14, 1829 but was not discovered by Hawkins until Easter, and even then he did not fully realize the extent of the change. At that time he told the tutors to go back to the old system, but through various misunderstandings this was not done and the matter did not come into the open until Dornford, who was unwilling to persist in the scheme against the Provost's wishes, raised the whole issue in a college meeting of April 24, 1830. Both sides were adamant. The position adopted by the tutors was that their office, as defined by the statutes, was a university rather than a college position, and that although the provost had the appointment of them and might remove them at pleasure, their responsibilities in the conduct of the office were to the vice-chancellor and not to him. To this Hawkins replied that Oriel had only one tutor in the university sense (the senior tutor) and that the rest were merely "assistant[s] to the Senior for the time being and . . . Lecturer[s] to the men generally." [99] At first Newman was inclined to accept this interpretation and resign, but Froude suggested that they ought to require such formal confirmation of the fact as would be implied by listing Oriel in the university calendar as having only one tutor. This Hawkins was naturally unwilling to do, and so at length, on the advice of Copleston [100] and with genuine reluctance, he determined gradually to exclude Newman, Wilberforce, and Froude from the tuition by the simple expedient of not assigning them any more pupils. He wrote Newman of his intention on June 9, 1830, and a year and two days later Newman noted in his diary, "second day of collections—finished *my* men—and so ends my Tutor's work!" [101]

The year in which Newman ended his work was taken by Mark Pattison as "the turning-point in the fortunes of Oriel. From this date the college began to go downhill, both in the calibre of the men who obtained fellowships and in the style and tone of the undergraduates. In the race for University honours Balliol rapidly shot ahead, and still (1883) maintains the first place among the colleges." [102] This view is corroborated by the official college historian, who agrees that the quarrel "dealt a blow to the intellectual prestige of the college, from which it never recovered during Hawkins' long reign." [103] Naturally Newman was quick to attribute this decline to the defects of the old system. One of the arguments which Hawkins had given in its favor was that it had achieved such brilliant results in the past, gaining Oriel fifteen Firsts in the eight years before 1828, a number which, though Oriel was not the largest of colleges, was exceeded only by Christ Church and approached only by Balliol. But Newman pointed out that these Firsts were really due to the private tuition which supplemented the public, and that as his system was simply private tuition made official and given free of charge the record was really a tribute to the correctness of his own views. A more accurate test, he said, could be had by comparing three four-year periods, that of 1825–29, when the old system appeared in its true form, the private tuition having largely ceased, that of 1829–33, when the outcome of the new system was felt, and that of 1833–37, when the old system was "partially restored." [104] The numbers of Firsts were respectively two, eleven, and five, which as far as figures go would seem to prove Newman's point.[105]

Newman's point, however, was not simply that of individual tuition. As one looks back upon the episode it can be seen that the entire quarrel was simply the first ground swell in the rising Tractarian feeling, and that it took an educational form because the persons involved happened to be engaged in the work of education. What they later tried to do for the office of priest they were now doing for the office of tutor, namely returning it to its original Laudian form. That Newman's conception of the tutor's office was the ancient and original one there is no question, but there is also no question that it was not the conception of the future. The future had no place for either of the two ideas which Newman's system involved: on the one hand the mingling of religious superintendence with secular instruction, and on the other the entrusting of a student to the exclusive care of a single man. During the years of the movement these ideas would continue to be championed,[106] but after the condemnation of Tract 90 they quickly sank back and were simply lost to view. They could not stand, on the one hand, against the rapid secularization of the university or, on the other, against the extension of the curriculum to the point where no teacher, be he religious or not, could possibly achieve competence in all the subjects in which a pupil has to be taught.

Mark Pattison always held that if Newman had had his way he would have transformed Oriel into a theological seminary, and something like this must be the impression which the preceding narrative has given. Really, however, it is a false impression. The pastoral conception of the tutor's office is the most distinctive feature of Newman's work and so comes out most prominently in an external history of these years. But a little reflection will tell us that the great bulk of Newman's time must have been spent not in religious superintendence but in the daily round of secular instruction, and the question arises, how well did he manage in this ordinary kind of instruction?

In the first place, he would not have had to be very good to be better than the run of his fellows, for the general standard of teaching was still not high, even in the better colleges. When Mark Pattison went up to Oriel in 1832 he found that a college lecture meant nothing more than "the class construing, in turns, some twenty lines of a classical text to the tutor, who corrected you when you were wrong." [107] One of his tutors (G. A. Denison) had some reputation as a scholar, but Pattison declares, "I do not remember in the whole course of the term that [he] made a single remark on the two plays, *Alcestis* and *Hippolytus*, that did not come from Monk's notes," [108] and in less than a week he was completely disillusioned as to what might be learned in an Oxford lecture room. ⌐m Mozley gives the same testimony. In 1835 he refused the offer of an Oriel tutorship for the novel reason that he was unfit. "I could certainly keep ahead of my pupils," he wrote, "which was all that many tutors ever did. I could come round my class by questions they were not prepared for. I was sure always to hear mistakes which it would be easy to correct. In matter of fact a tutor often did no more than half the class could have done quite as well." [109]

Newman had in view something different. A really good tutor, in his conception, was one who had so thoroughly mastered his subject that it was part of the very fabric of his mind. In 1828, when it was proposed to bring W. J. Copleston, nephew of the former provost, into the tuition, Newman opposed him as being "a jogtrot man" who lacked "the power of making the thoughts of others his own," who always spoke "by rote and rule, not as if his mind worked upon a subject, but as if he recollected what he had learned." [110] A "capital tutor," on the other hand, was Upton in *Loss and Gain*—"he knew his subject so thoroughly." "His lecture in the Agricola . . . was a masterly, minute running comment on the text, quite exhausting it. . . . yet he never loaded his lectures; everything he said had a meaning, and was wanted." [111]

That this was nearly the method of Newman himself is clear not only from Sir Charles Murray's charge of "sticking to the text" but also from the evidence of the editions which Newman used in the lecture room. His *Ethics* is a fat interleaved copy in which, among other notes elucidating the work, are passages in light blue ink made up of questions apparently intended to serve as the basis for class discussion. "Do men agree in the *name* of the agathon?" he asks; "what general and vague definition do they agree in? - but when we come to ask persons what they understand by eudaimonia they do not agree - very well - now in what class of things do some place it?" [112] Or again, in the discussion of moral virtue: "How can we say that a person by doing just actions *becomes* just, is he not just already—a person who performs grammatical or musical actions is a grammarian or musician—? Your second answer declares the arts not to be analogous to the moral virtues; as long as it suited your purpose they were so, vid chs. 1, 2 - how do you reconcile this? What three things are tests of a virtuous action? What thing *alone* is requisite for the possession of one of the arts? Is this same thing of *much* avail in the moral virtues?" [113] And so on. We are told that Whately's method of teaching Aristotle was to present the student in advance with questions on the matter of each chapter, getting him to puzzle out the answers for himself and then, when he had done as much as he could, sending him on to the text for the solution of his difficulties.[114] Perhaps Newman did this as well, but in any case the purpose of his questions was the same as Whately's—to challenge the student and make him think for himself. He wanted him really to understand what he was reading, and in order to do this the student must draw out the implications of the work and discover its underlying assumptions. He must compare and systematize, challenge and contradict; he must reduce the argument to its logical form and test it by historical examples; and then, if he could reproduce it in his own words or apply the method to a present occasion or imitate its style upon another topic, he would know that he had really entered into the book in the manner that Newman desired.

Something like this is the burden of all Newman's advice to his pupils. If it is a young man inquiring about a translation of Homer, Newman urges that he consult it only after he has made every use that he can of grammar and lexicon, and he even suggests that he place the translation in other hands than his own if that will be a relief to him and assist him to be sparing.[115] To another lad he writes a long letter on how to read Euripides. Go through the plays attentively, he says, "marking every passage which presents a difficulty - and satisfying your mind about every construction, as far as you can, from Matthiae's grammar. Read also . . . what the Greek Theatre says about the Iambic Trochaic and Anapaestic Measures - and perfect yourself in them by applying the rules to different passages. . . . Mark the most important notes, and refer as far as you can to the passages from other plays cited." [116] Abstracts and analyses are a great help in forcing the mind to be active. The best way to read Livy, for example, is for the student to "have a sheet of paper by his side, as he reads, and, whenever a Law is stated to have passed, write it carefully down in printing [roman] letters with the date annexed - the lesser events may be put in smaller letters on each side of this Law. . . .

Pursuing this plan, he may get the first Decade into one page of a letter-sheet of paper - and it should not be longer. On the opposite side of this page, let him put down, as they occur, a list of odd phrases, which he has not met with in another author." [117] It will be remembered that Newman himself had done something like this in preparing for the Schools, though on the whole he tended to condemn his own reading as "superficial." [118]

Newman's method, with its emphasis on activity of mind, evidently derived from the practice of the Noetics, and it carried with it the marks of the classroom drill which is so well suited to logical, mathematical, and grammatical studies in their elementary form. The trouble was that without the genius of Copleston and Whately this method had degenerated into the mere construing deplored by Pattison and Mozley, and Newman's contribution certainly was not to bring the old method alive again, which he could never have done, but rather to extend it from the language of the books to their subject matter. According to Mozley, one of the issues in the college quarrel was that Newman "asked for subjects, rather than particular books," [119] and although there is nothing in Newman's papers to indicate that this was a formal point of controversy, the introduction of modern books to be read along with the old does suggest that the latter were to be studied less for the language than for what they had to say.

If this were to be so, a new type of examination was then in order, for the old viva voce, which was so admirably adapted for testing the student on points of grammar, was "more or less technical, narrow, partial, and unphilosophical" when applied to a subject, whether science or history. So wrote Newman in a paper of "Proposals" which he drew up in 1828 and sent about to the eight men who were serving with him as examining masters in the Schools.[120] His suggestion was that the viva voce should be retained to test a man's knowledge of his books but that the subjects of those books should be treated in a written examination. It is interesting to note that this reform was actually accomplished, though presumably not solely at Newman's instance, when the Examination Statute was revised in 1830.[121]

In making this proposal Newman was attempting to do for the university examination what he had already done for the college examination of Collections. Under Copleston Collections had always been conducted in the tower as a viva voce, but on June 9, 1828, the spring after Hawkins became provost, Newman set the questions for a "paper examination according to [a] new system." [122] This examination was held in hall during the two days immediately preceding the regular tower Collections, and once again its purpose was to provide the sort of comprehensive essay question which requires organized knowledge and original thought rather than mere points of information.

Even within the framework of the viva voce, however, Newman continually tried, during the one term and part of another when he was public examiner in the Schools, to steer the student into these larger and more thoughtful concerns. He has left behind him a bundle of twenty-six loose sheets, "the papers of notes which I used to examine by in the Schools," [123] which show the kind of question he was inclined to ask. Some of them, such as the terse bidding to discourse "On καί" or on "Grecisms in Virgil and Horace," are sufficiently cut and dried, but the others show his passion for the connected view of a large subject which was to him the hallmark of an educated mind. "How are matters of fact proved?" he asks, a question which carries us forward to the *Grammar of Assent;* and there are other questions which show him already occupied with problems later raised in the *Idea of a University.* "What is the practical utility of the first part of logic viewed apart from the third?" "The analogy between φρόνησις in moral action and correct taste in the fine arts." "On the connexion and difference between habits of art and habits of moral virtue." "Plato's view of the philosopher as ὕπακρος τὰ δευτερεῖα δ' ἔχων - illustrated with reference to modern times - e.g. the contrast between the cultivation of the useful arts and a liberal education. &c. &c." Some of the papers are not in the form of questions but of notes for an argument, a kind of skeletal Socratic dialogue, moving from point to point, raising apparent difficulties to see if the student will be caught by them and real ones to see if he can solve them. A discussion of the kind of pleasure afforded by poetry is one example of these.

Newman was not content, however, with simply leading the student into general views. What he wanted above all was to make the student see that a general view of these questions was of vital importance for his own life. He complained bitterly of those students who in preparing their Aristotle stored its sentences in their memory "with little regard to their truth or reasonableness, technically and abstractedly, as a mathematical theorem, or *a* mode of viewing things, or a charm which superstitious men repeat without understanding." [124] The *Ethics* was not to be read because it was by Aristotle or, as Fielding says, by somebody who will be equally famous when he has been dead as long, but because "the great Master does but analyze the thoughts, feelings, views, and opinions of human kind. He has told us the meaning of our own words and ideas, before we were born." [125] And therefore Newman's whole effort, as is clear from the lecture notes quoted above, was not merely to bring out what Aristotle had said but, by means of what he had said, to bring home to the student the real nature of justice and of the mean and of the relation of intellectual to moral virtue.

And this was what his pupils chiefly admired him for—the wonderful sense of reality which he gave to all aspects of their studies. Nothing was a mere exercise. Even the themes and disputations, which had fallen so generally into contempt that, according to Mozley, "not more than a dozen of the undergraduates [at Oriel] took pains" [126] with them, Newman restored to life. He did this by assuring his students that they were not obliged by law to be dull or grave—they did not need to "aim at a style"—they could simply say in their themes what they normally would say if they were talking to sensible people about a serious subject. In a word, they should "endeavour to be in *earnest*." [127] "His first care," according to Tom Mozley, "was that the pupil should know what he intended to say, and what his words stood for." [128] If he came on the expression "principle of evil" in a composition, he pressed the writer for an explanation of what evil was and whether by "principle" he meant a person or a thing. He never flattered. He reminded his pupils that what they considered their best things were generally their worst, and he wrote long and probing criticisms of their work, some of which still survive. At least one pupil kept these criticisms for many years, and he says he never looked at them "without being deeply impressed with the truth of Newman's comments." [129]

On October 24, 1831, the first term after Newman had ceased to be tutor, he received from his former pupils "a very valuable present of books . . . consisting of thirty six volumes of the Fathers. . . . They are so fine in their outside," he wrote to his mother, "as to put my former ones to shame - and the editions are the best." [130] It was the tribute of those into whose lives Newman had intruded in so insistent a way. He had insisted that the teacher, where he was welcome at all, should not merely betake himself bodily into the presence of his pupils, but should live with them as intimately as he could, should walk, read, and study with them, should vacation with them, breakfast with them, meditate and worship with them day in and day out. His notebooks are full of the evidences of this concern—lists of undergraduates invited to breakfast, memoranda that in meeting with the freshmen he should not only "explain to them the reason of paying tuition in absent terms" but should also "talk to them about the Sacrament." [131] In short, whereas, says Mozley, "there were plenty of college tutors in those days whose relation to the undergraduates about them was simply official and nominal," Newman "stood in the place of a father, or an elder and affectionate brother." [132]

CHAPTER 4

Sicily and Adam de Brome

So far as I can remember, from my election at Easter 1829 to Newman's return from the Mediterranean at Midsummer 1833, his main idea, still rather a dream than a purpose, was the reconstitution of the college in the old statutory lines. . . . For several years the notion of a large body of resident Fellows, occupying their own college rooms, and engaged in religious studies, was steadily maintained as the *beau ideal* and true purpose of a college.
—Tom Mozley, *Reminiscences*

EVER since his breakdown in the Schools in December, 1827, the movement of Newman's mind had been inward. It was a centripetal movement, swirling in upon itself, concentrating its materials more closely, directing them more fiercely upon the religious issues which lay at the center of his thought. This movement culminated in the college quarrel, and it was only natural that after the resolution of that quarrel Newman should have relaxed again and turned his thoughts outward upon the world of secular learning. Thus within two weeks after his dismissal he began a course of study in the more advanced branches of mathematics, which he had not attempted as an undergraduate. Mathematics, indeed, which had been so long neglected at Oxford, was just beginning to look up at this time,[1] and Newman was personally involved in its revival. Doubtless his ideas were reflected in a pamphlet published by Froude, *Considerations Respecting the Most Effectual Means of Encouraging Mathematics in Oxford* (1830), which urged re-establishing the "ancient" mathematics (Euclid, Newton, and so forth) as part of the School of Literae Humaniores and encouraging the modern branches by scholarships and prizes. Newman himself subscribed £20 in June, 1830 to the three scholarships which were actually founded in March of the following year.[2] It was also his wish, however, to qualify himself in the disciplines which they were designed to encourage. Previously he had been "more accustomed to geometrical proof, fluxions, Newton &c.," but now he wished to learn "analytics and differentials."[3] To this end he was told by Robert Wilberforce that he must "*work problems*," as no reading would do; and Robert sent him a list of books on trigonometry, the integral calculus, mechanics, hydrostatics, and optics.[4] How far he got in these we do not know. In the summer he "made a bold inroad into Trigonometry" by means of the *Encyclopaedia Metropolitana* and studied Hamilton's *Conics*, and the next January he "began Newton's *Principia* in earnest [I had got it up carefully (3 sections) as an undergraduate]."[5] But by March or April his thoughts had turned quite away from all these subjects. Rivington, the publisher, had written proposing a book on the councils of the church, and this work, which was to become the *Arians of the Fourth Century*, occupied him fully for the next year and a half.

By the time he had finished the first draft it was the year of reform, 1832, and Newman was deeply alarmed at the spirit which was abroad in the country. Men were simply intoxicated, he felt, with the idea of progress. The advances they had made in the useful arts and experimental sciences had led them to ignore the thought and practice of their duty as immortal beings. "The country seems to me to be in a dream, - " he wrote to a former pupil, "being drugged with this fallacious notion of its superiority to other countries and times. And I think from this another mistake follows. Men see that those parts of the national system, (and those, of course, far the most important and comprehensive) which really depend on personal and private virtue do not work well—and, not seeing [where] the deficiency lies, viz. in want of personal virtue, they imagine they can put things right by applying their scientific knowledge to the improvement of the existing system." He does not deny that the system needs improvement, "but still, in spite of all this, I will state a principle, which seems to me most important and most neglected - that the difference between this or that system is *as nothing* compared with the effects of the human will upon them, that till the will be changed from evil to good, the difference of the results between two given systems will be imperceptible."[6] It was the fashion of the day, however, to neglect the will and put all trust in the intellect. The intellect, by the aid of the new sciences, could devise mechanisms which, without reforming the will, would channel its existing drives into socially acceptable forms, and in this way it could create the good society without going to the trouble of creating good individuals to compose it. Needless to say, this was a delightful prospect, being simply the Socratean thesis that knowledge is virtue made true in a practical form. But to Newman it was a pure delusion, and it was the more dangerous in that the new sciences did seem to promise something of the kind and, quite apart from those promises, were so novel and attractive in themselves that they led the mind by a kind of enchantment away from the problems which were its first and proper concern. Those problems did not deal with the laws of human wealth or the secrets of the rocks but with the rectification of the human will. That was the main point, the first duty of man. But it was also true that one could follow this duty into an opposite danger, that of neglecting the human aids which the new sciences provided and so becoming narrow and bigoted in mind; and although this was not a danger to the nation at large, it was a danger, so Newman considered, to himself.

It was this very problem, indeed, that Newman was pondering in the autumn of 1832 when he received a proposal from Hurrell Froude and his father to accompany them on a voyage to the Mediterranean. The proposal was unexpected and threw Newman into a flurry of excitement which was disconcerting, for it showed how little "real stability of mind" he had yet achieved. Only the year before, while sailing with Froude off the Devonshire coast, he had marveled at the brilliant colors and sharp forms of the Torbay rocks, and then had been provoked at himself for gaping at what others knew and accepted as a matter of course. Was he not in real need of that enlargement of mind which travel is said to convey? "I am suspicious of becoming narrow-minded," he wrote to Hurrell, "and at least I wish to experience the feeling and the trial of expansiveness of views, if it were but to be able to *say* I had, and to know how to meet it in the case of others." [7] And with this strange explanation—that if he were going on a Mediterranean cruise it was not for pleasure or health or even for education in the ordinary sense, but in order to weigh the effect which foreign travel would have in enlarging, and perhaps unsettling, his mind—he went on board the *Hermes* on December 8 bound for Malta.

His first observation was of the sailors who were his companions on shipboard, the very type of the well-traveled man, but how far from the ideal of true philosophic enlargement: "They . . . have seen a great deal of all parts of the world," he wrote to his mother, "have much interesting information, and are very gentlemanlike." And yet, "they have (most of them) made very few inductions, and are not in the habit of investigating causes—the very reverse of philosophers." [8] Twenty years later these "sea-faring men" were to reappear in the *Idea of a University*, where they would reinforce the view that travel may as easily load the mind with random facts as give it that true enlargement which embodies new facts with old in a synthetic view.[9] And on the whole this was Newman's final judgment. As education, the voyage had failed. "I have learned . . . ," he wrote at the end of his tour, "to think all places about the same, which I had no notion of before. . . . All this is gain, and I suppose is part of that *nil admirari* which one gets by travelling. . . ." But on the other hand, "I have (alas!) experienced none of that largeness and expansion of mind which one of my friends privately told me I should get." [10]

The manifest reason for this failure was that Newman was traveling among things he did not know and could not hope or care to understand. To him the world of cities was little more than a busy and fretful dream, and the only true voyage was that which he took in the silence of his own heart or among the works of his beloved Fathers. Like Thoreau, he had traveled a good deal in Oriel, and further afield was simply farther from home. Such travel should be left to another young Englishman who, by an odd coincidence, was at that moment on another admiralty vessel somewhat farther south in the Atlantic. His observations were also random and disparate at first, but unlike the seafaring men he did have the habit of making inductions and of investigating causes, and so he finally produced the greatest synthetic view of the nineteenth century, the theory of evolution by natural selection. For Charles Darwin such a voyage made sense, but for Newman, who had his eye on another world, it was like viewing the tapestry of life from the wrong side, and it told no story.

But Newman was even more concerned lest travel, while giving the illusion if not the reality of mental enlargement, should actually intoxicate and unsettle the mind after the manner of the new sciences. This was the danger which he wished to be able to meet in the case of others by first feeling and meeting it in himself. For Newman was keenly alive to the beauty and interest of all he saw, and his letters home are almost Ruskinian or Proustian in their attempt to define the exact contour of the coastline, the richly subdued hues of the rocks and their clinging vegetation, the colors of the sea, now deep indigo, now transparent green, white, white-green, changing in the darkness off Gibraltar to a wonderful phosphorescence, rising in sparkling showers of liquid fire from the splash of the oar, the sight of Algiers in the distance and the lithe grace of the Saracenic boatmen who rowed out to meet them and lounged about in groups the most harmonious one could imagine, the overwhelming thought that one was passing the site of ancient Carthage or coasting rock-bound Ithaca, the strange aromatic flavor of Turkish coffee, the paradox of Rome, the horror of Naples, the weird, sulphurous interior of Vesuvius, the elusive, indefinable flavor of an orange picked up by the wayside in central Sicily. All these things fascinated and interested him intensely, but he felt them as a danger. He had never been tempted by the ordinary pleasures of the world, as balls or parties, but he thought it did require "strength of mind to keep the thoughts where they should be while the variety of strange sights—political, moral, and physical—are passed before the eyes, as in a tour like this." [11]

Nonetheless he did find the requisite strength. At no time, he says (except possibly when he first saw Cadiz with the hopes of landing there), did he not feel willing, even eager, to be transported in that very instant back to his room at Oriel and to resume the simple duties and pleasures which were his lot as a Christian priest. He declared of the various novelties which passed before him that he was pleased at what he saw without being interested in them, without being involved or in any sense drawn out of his way. Thus he could see countries which were pagan merely to understand what they were and would not be harmed by them if he did not become involved in their spirit. And he could go to the opera at Naples, which he did with great repugnance, if he went merely out of curiosity to see what the opera was, and not to participate in the pleasure which it afforded. But perhaps the best way to secure detachment was to regard the trip itself as a kind of dream or even a torment suffered only for the sake of reliving it later on in the memory, where the pleasures would be purified and tranquilized, less violent and less intense. Indeed, under the weariness of travel and the multiplicity of sights Newman began to feel the same exhaustion of mind which he had felt when reading for the Schools, as if his mind "were literally pulled about, and had now a leg twitched and now one's head turned"; [12] and therefore he was genuinely glad, on returning a second time to Malta, to be for a while off the sea, "that restless element which is the type of human life," [13] and to be imprisoned for twelve days' quarantine in the lazaretto. What if he did hear a ghost there and catch a cold while waiting for it with the bedclothes off? The confinement was at least a tranquilizing experience, and the bad cold enabled him to avoid the sights of Malta.

There was one sight, however, which he could not and would not avoid—Sicily. He had caught just a glimpse of it in traveling from Malta to Naples and had been entranced by what he saw. The mountains were open, mild, and lovely, not huddled like those of Greece. It was the meeting place of Greek and Roman civilization, and above all it was the land of Thucydides. In passing he had seen Egesta, its ruins with its temple. "O wonderful sight! full of the most strange pleasure. . . . It has been a day in my life to have seen Egesta. From the moment I saw Sicily I kept saying to myself, 'This is that Sicily,' " and he admits he is "drawn to it as by a loadstone," that his mind goes back to the recollection of it "as one smells again and again at a sweet flower." [14] He felt he had to return, but his companions were unwilling and so he determined to go it alone. They tried to dissuade him. Wilberforce, whom they met in Rome, tried to dissuade him, but the thought drew him on like the odor of forbidden fruit. "Spring in Sicily! It is the nearest approach to Paradise of which sinful man is capable. I set out on Easter Monday." [15] Unluckily, however, his boat was delayed, and he actually arrived at Messina on a Sunday morning; and what was even more disquieting, his efforts to get up a service proved unsuccessful.

The trip from Catania to Syracuse and return involved a series of physical discomforts which made Newman seriously reflect on the wisdom of his lonely journey, but on the whole he thought he had not been injudicious, only unfortunate. "The only question is: whether I was right in going on a Sunday, and whether this wrong step has not brought all this upon me?" [16] "All this," of course, was very little compared with the trials which were yet to come. The island was fever ridden, and by May 2 Newman was lying ill in the inn at Leonforte, alone except for his servant and with people dying all about him. He was soon delirious and in his fever received impressions, which never faded altogether from his mind, that this illness, though doubtless having its physical cause, was in a deeper sense a judgment for past sins and a preparation for the work he was yet to do. It haunted his mind that the last university sermon he had preached before leaving Oxford was on the "wilfulness of Saul," and that willfulness, in thus coming to Sicily against the wishes of his friends, was likewise his own sin. Nevertheless he was profoundly convinced that he was not destined to die at this time. "I told my Servant so, and gave as a reason (even when semi-delirious and engaged in giving him my friends' direction at home and so preparing externally for death,) that 'I thought God had some work for me'—these I believe were exactly my words." [17] But this interpretation of the event, though obscurely present in Newman's mind from the first, was not really developed until after the course of the Oxford movement had seemed to bear it out. At the time it was less the work of the future than the sins of the past that interpreted the "strange meaning" of this illness to him.

At the time I was deeply impressed with a feeling that it was a judgment for profaning the Lord's Supper, in having cherished some resentment against the Provost for putting me out of the Tutorship; though this impression has now faded away. Again I felt it was a punishment for my wilfulness, in going to Sicily by myself. . . .

As I lay in bed the first day many thoughts came over me. I felt God was fighting against me - I felt at last I knew why - it was for selfwill. I felt I had been very selfwilled - that the Froudes had been against my coming - so also the Wilberforces - perhaps the Neates and Andersons. . . . Yet I felt I kept saying to myself 'I have not sinned against light.' And at one time I had a most consoling overpowering thought of God's electing love, and seemed to feel I was His. But I believe all my feelings, painful and pleasant, were heightened by somewhat of delirium, tho' they still are from God in the way of Providence. Next day the selfreproaching feelings increased - I seemed to see more and more my utter hollowness. I began to think of all my apparent principles, and felt they were mere intellectual deductions from one or two admitted truths. I compared myself with Keble, and felt that I was merely developing his, not my convictions. I know I had *very* clear thoughts about this then; and I believe in the main true ones. . . . Still more serious thoughts came over me. I thought I had been very selfwilled about the Tutorship affair - and now I viewed my whole course as one of presumption - It struck me that the 5th of May was just at hand, which was a memorable day, as being that on which (what we called) my Ultimatum was sent in [to the Provost]. On the [3rd] anniversary I should be lying on a sick bed in a strange country. Then I bitterly blamed myself as disrespectful and insulting to the Provost, my superior. So keenly did I feel this, that I dictated to myself (as it were) a letter which I was to send to (I fixed upon) James, (the late Fellow) on my getting to England, stating in strong terms my selfreproach; and I was not to preach at St. Mary's or any where for a length of time as a penitent unworthy to show himself. . . . I thought strongly, and retained the thought, that my illness came upon me as having come to the Sacrament in malice and resentment.[18]

A few weeks later Newman was well again and sailing on the orange-boat to Marseilles. There, becalmed in the Straits of Bonifacio, he wrote the famous hymn which is a submission of his will to the Kindly Light of which he had been conscious even in illness.

> I was not ever thus, nor prayed that Thou
> Shouldst lead me on.
> I loved to choose and see my path; but now
> Lead Thou me on!
> I loved the garish day, and, spite of fears,
> Pride ruled my will: remember not past years.

The willfulness of the past, associated as it was with his thirst for the scenery and antiquities of Sicily, with the intellectual character of his own religious system as contrasted with Keble's, and with his presumption in the tutorship affair, was largely the willfulness of intellectual pride, of the curious and far-ranging spirit which had led him again and again to attempt more than he was able or more than was right, until at last he broke down and then saw in that breakdown a judgment upon his own pretensions. This illness he ever regarded as a major crisis in his life,[19] and it is the most famous of all the various illnesses he experienced. Its fame is easily understood: there is the wild and romantic setting, the striking phrases snatched from the delirium, the association with "Lead, Kindly Light," and the sense that a great historical movement is here beginning. And yet the importance of the crisis in Newman's spiritual development was not so great as its later fame. Its cause, for one thing, was more purely physical. Indeed, it was not a spiritual crisis at all except as it became such when seen through the mists of fever and in retrospect. Moreover, it introduced nothing new into Newman's thought. The turning away from liberalism, which was the fundamental change, had come five years before in the crisis of December, 1827, and the Sicilian crisis was merely a deepening and re-affirming of a purpose held rather steadily in view ever since that time. It was not a repudiation of the past, for if Newman had sinned he had not "sinned against light." And neither was it an anticipation of the future, for if Newman "had a work to do," what could that phrase mean in his own mind, at a time when the Oxford movement had not yet taken form, but a work of the same kind as he had been trying to do in the years just gone by? It would be a larger work, perhaps, spiritualized and transferred to a new and different scene, but it would be essentially the same work as before, that which he had seen as necessary in the Peel affair and which he had tried to accomplish in a small way in his own college.

In his college he had failed, and one might say that the Oxford movement was simply an attempt to by-pass the college and to capture the university and indeed the nation at large. In its national aspect, of course, it became a purely religious movement and so goes beyond the limits of this study; but in its university aspect it had an educational as well as a religious side, and was, indeed, simply an extension into a larger sphere of the principles which had already been at issue in the college quarrel.

That quarrel, however, was not yet over. Newman was no longer a tutor, but he was still a Fellow and on his return from the Mediterranean he was elected dean.[20] This was simply the deferment of an office he was to have had the previous year,[21] but it comes rather strangely at either time, for the dean was a representative of the provost in charge of discipline, and Newman thought it "very doubtful whether my views of administering the Law would have been considered by the College as compatible with the Pr[ovost]'s." [22] In the end, of course, they were not, but the differences cannot be followed in detail, for in 1860 Newman destroyed a parcel of Hawkins' letters which covered the period 1830–34. They reminded him, he said, of "the painful state of our relations between 1829 (Feb^y) and 1845 . . . a state of constant bickerings, of coldness, dryness, and donnishness on his part, and of provoking insubordination and petulance on mine." The destroyed letters related to two subjects: "1. the matter of testimonials for Orders, in which I naturally took the severer, he the laxer side, and 2. the custom of Gentleman Commoners dining with the Fellows, which he maintained was one of the *laudabiles consuetudines* to which we all were bound, but which I and others wished to dispense with." Evidently the Dean was still a "new broom." William Lockhart, for example, tells of an undergraduate who was called up before him for a breach of discipline and who, on being asked later what Newman had said to him, replied, "I don't know, but he looked at me." [23]

Beside being in charge of college discipline, the dean assigned the subjects for declamations and weekly themes, which all undergraduates were required to write, and also looked them over and selected the best to be read in hall. On one occasion he selected Mark Pattison's and suggested revision. Pattison, however, patched it instead of rewriting, and he says that when he next met Newman, who was burning with indignation at his negligence, he learned to fear the new Dean's watchfulness.[24] That he was not the only one is indicated by a notebook with a list of "Points noticed in Hall," that is, errors of Latinity, each of them checked off, apparently as Newman called it to the author's attention, whether publicly or in private. The notebook also contains a list of the subjects which Newman set for the declamations and themes from Michaelmas, 1833, to Easter and Act Term, 1835. Some of these are merely traditional, as "Ne quid nimis" or "finitima sunt falsa veris," but others show an effort to get the men thinking about the problems of their own education: "Whether poetry is useful in the formation of the citizen," "Whether the study of what are called the physical sciences is useful in forming manners," [25] both of them questions which would be raised again in the *Idea of a University*.

The deanship was a yearly tenure, and Newman was elected twice. Thus by 1835 his last official relation with the undergraduates of his college had ceased. This did not mean, however, that he had given up hope of reforming the college in accordance with his ideal. As his views enlarged beyond the circle of his own pupils, he saw that the issue of the tutorship, on which he had been defeated, was simply one aspect of a larger problem which could be approached in many ways. He had begun there because that was where the problem had touched him personally, but as he studied the matter further he perceived that what he really wanted was a return, not to the Laudian conception of the tutor, but rather to the medieval conception of the college.[26] It was not one office in the college but the college as a whole which ought to be reformed, and it ought to be reformed in the image of its founder's intent. What Adam de Brome had conceived when he established the college in the fourteenth century was a body in which there were no tutors for the simple reason that there were no students. Or rather, all were students and tutors together, all learning from each other and all using their learning in the service of God.

Newman was entranced by the thought of that small society which had lived five hundred years ago on the very spot where he was now living and whose lives he could read in the medieval Latin statutes which still regulated, but much less stringently, his own. They were a head and ten scholars, living together in brotherhood, eating at a common table, and being read to aloud while they ate and listened in "attentive silence." [27] The books in their library were so few that each scholar was allotted only one, which he kept for the entire year, returning it on All Souls' Day to exchange for another. Their poverty was ensured by the conditions of their fellowship, and they did not go abroad without the permission of their provost. Thus far the manner of their living was nearly monastic, but they differed from the religious orders, which they were not permitted to join, in having as their end neither contemplation nor preaching but simply study. They were concerned not with the salvation of souls but with the pursuit of learning, and they interpreted this pursuit about as broadly as the age of faith would admit. True, their principal study was theology, but five or six of their number were also to study canon and perhaps civil law, and each new member was required upon admission to devote himself to the liberal arts and philosophy until, in the judgment of the entire body, he was fit to proceed to his theological studies.

The learning they were concerned with was exclusively the higher learning. Of the twenty years or more which the medieval course of study prescribed, they had already spent seven in the Schools of the university "determining" as a Bachelor, for only Bachelors were eligible for admission to the college. Even then, though some of the younger masters might engage in elementary teaching in the university, they did not normally do so, for the very purpose of their endowment was to free them from this need, not only for the dozen or fourteen years which would make them a Doctor, but also, if they wished, for all the fruitful years which remained. Thus the College of St. Mary, as Oriel was called in its first years, was a body of advanced scholars engaged in individual study but helping and stimulating each other by the community of their interests. It contained no undergraduate members, and it was not formally divided into the teachers and the taught but was a hierarchy of those more or less advanced in the prosecution of their studies.

Gradually, however, the character of the college had changed. Already in the fifteenth and even the fourteenth century the Fellows would occasionally admit to the privileges of residence and the common table some well-born youth who was pursuing his studies in the Schools of the university. He was called a *commensalis* (Fellow-commoner) and as such was not on the endowment but paid for the privilege. Later *communarii* (commoners) were admitted as well, but neither the one sort nor the other became frequent until by Lord Leicester's statute of 1581 membership in a college or hall was made essential to membership in the university. This act did two things: it made the university exclusively Anglican, since the colleges were all religious foundations, and it made the colleges into undergraduate teaching bodies instead of societies for advanced study. For where youths had previously gone direct to the university for their degrees, they now clamored for admission to the colleges, and the latter had soon to provide them with tutors, first for their moral supervision and later on for their instruction. In the end, the pressure to house these young men drove the Fellows right out of their rooms, so that by Newman's day, although every Fellow was technically entitled to college quarters, he never laid claim to these quarters unless he was actively engaged in the tuition.

Exactly in what form Newman proposed to revive the college of Adam de Brome is not certain. Obviously he could not turn out of doors some ninety undergraduates and appropriate their rooms for the nonresident Fellows. What two and a half centuries had done could not be undone now even if that had been his wish, and we may be certain that it was not. But he did wish to restore that portion of the ancient college which had fallen away, namely the idea of a resident body of Fellows engaged not in teaching but in advanced theological study. He went carefully over the statutes making a copy for his own use, and, according to Keble, found "only two things which are not in substance (he thinks) observed; the Provost living with the Fellows, and the Fellows residing. This excepts of course the great deviation common to all the Catholic Foundations: the cessation, i.e. of Prayer for the Founders." [28] The first was doubtless a minor point, and as to the last, Newman had already remedied that for himself. For several years now he had said prayers for "The Universities as schools of the Church" and for "All my benefactors," including Edward II and Adam de Brome, the two founders of Oriel; Bishop Carpenter and Archdeacon Franck, who had endowed fellowships in the fifteenth century; and Edward Lord Leigh, who had bequeathed all his books to the college library.[29]

The great problem was the Fellows' not residing. Unless they held official positions they usually left Oxford after their year's probation, and within a few years more resigned their Fellowships upon securing a living or getting married. Newman's plan was that they should remain in residence and make the advance of knowledge the primary object of their lives, not necessarily engaged in tuition but assisting and encouraging all the members of the society in their own line of study. Actually he created some sentiment in favor of this plan, and for a while men who left at the end of their probation were looked on as deserters and rallied accordingly.[30] But to carry it through he needed a body of like-minded men about him, and thus for nearly a decade there was a silent struggle between himself and Hawkins over the election of Fellows, Newman (says Pattison) looking not for promise or originality but for congeniality, and Hawkins "endeavouring, upon no principle, merely to resist Newman's lead." As a result many inferior elections were made, but even Pattison admits that the blame of the worst elections lay with the party of Hawkins, for they possessed no one with Newman's "keen instinct . . . for recognizing, through an examination paper, the kind of merit and character which he wanted." [31] Mozley goes even further. "The college made some very indifferent or useless elections," he says, "in an excessive anxiety to resist Newman's lead, while every single election made in accordance with that lead justified itself by its results." [32]

In the end Newman was defeated less by the opposition of the Provost than by the simple impossibility of turning nineteenth-century undergraduates into medieval cenobites. Nevertheless he did not renounce his plan completely—rather he resigned himself to achieving it in a smaller and more personal way. An example had already been set him by Pusey, who, feeling that his house and income as canon of Christ Church had not originally been intended merely for the convenience of the occupant, resolved to take in three or four young graduates, giving them rooms and the free use of his library on the condition that they study theology or subjects connected with it.[33] On Newman's suggestion James Mozley, the younger brother of Tom, availed himself of this privilege in April, 1836, and in Michaelmas Term he was joined by three others. The arrangement lasted for two years until Mrs. Pusey's health made it impractical to continue, but Newman thought it far too good an idea to be allowed to lapse. Thus in the winter of 1837 he decided to take a house of his own, which he did the following April in St. Aldate's, directly across from Pusey's. He furnished it "very plainly," no sofas or armchairs being permitted, and he would have had deal in the bedrooms, but this was vetoed by James Mozley as being ostentatious. Mozley was to be "a leading member—though whether principal or vice-principal I cannot tell," but when the house opened in November, 1838 there were only two inmates, and so, he says, "I must either be one or the other." [34] The plan was that the occupants should not be entirely free in their choice of study as they had been at Pusey's, but should collaborate in the *Library of the Fathers* and other projects of Pusey and Newman. They were to be "a reading and collating establishment," and thus when Mark Pattison joined the group, he collated manuscripts of Cyprian in the Bodleian and translated the *Catena Aurea* of St. Thomas Aquinas on St. Matthew.[35]

Nevertheless the house did not flourish. Men who wanted to stay up at Oxford wanted to stay as Fellows of a college, and as soon as they were elected they of course left St. Aldate's. But what was worse, they found that if they did join St. Aldate's they were not elected, for Tractarianism was becoming a bar to a college and they were marked men.[36] Both Mozley and Pattison experienced such difficulty that others were reluctant to join them, and thus when they finally did secure fellowships, the last in July, 1840, Newman decided to close the house. "The house in St. Aldate's has ended well," he wrote, "in spite of men's backwardness to enter it. Pattison, Christie, and Mozley all Fellows." [37]

Just at this time another opportunity presented itself to Newman for urging his views on collegiate reform. In January, 1840 G. R. M. Ward, late Fellow of Trinity, published a translation of the statutes of Magdalen College, and on the 29th Newman wrote to his young friend James Hope (later Hope-Scott) informing him that the Magdalen men intended "to set about reforms. But 1. how are they to make them? 2. will not the Edinburgh be at them first?

"Now it has been suggested to me, that a review of them [i.e. the statutes] in the British Critic with these two objects in view would be very important, 1st, and the lesser, to ward off the adverse reviews &c. 2nd and the greater, to instruct them practically what they shall do—else, with the best intentions they will be doing wrong. Now can you throw light upon this subject yourself?" [38]

Hope wrote the review at once and sent it to Newman, who found it "very good and interesting." [39] It was published in the *British Critic* for April and gives the most extensive account we have of the sort of

reform that Newman would have espoused. It describes the college
founded by William of Waynflete in the fifteenth century as devoted to
"the exaltation of the Christian faith, the advancement of the Church,
and the increase of divine worship, and the liberal arts, sciences, and
faculties." [40] Unlike Oriel, it had a class of poor boys called "demyes,"
"who were diligently to learn grammar, logic, and sophistry," but its forty
scholars were normally Bachelors or Masters of Arts who became Fellows
after two probationary years and whose "bounden duty" it was to study
in their appointed faculty. In the case of two or three this might be law
and in the case of two or three more medicine, but all the rest were to
proceed through arts and then "forthwith to turn aside to the faculty
of divinity, to which they were constantly and diligently to apply themselves, and not to meddle with the other faculties, saving only in the
vacations." [41] They were to live under a common discipline and were
animated by a common cause, which was the honor of the college, the
advancement of the church, and the glory of God. "And therefore, when
men once became members of the college, they were to be as persons
professed under a rule, and incapable of passing to another foundation.
Its secrets they were faithfully to keep, its privileges to defend; its offices
they durst not refuse, and for its business they were to be ever at command. The hall and chapel, which were the types of their collective life,
were to be maintained in splendour. . . . They were to escort their
brethren upon solemn academical occasions; they were to instruct and
advise each other, and to wear a common dress; . . . they were to remember [their] founder and benefactors with continual prayers." Such,
then, says the reviewer, was this institution of the fifteenth century, and
he raises the question of "the possibility or the advantage of carrying out
in these days such a design." [42] He notes that we live amidst the same
evils as Waynflete hoped to remedy, and he suggests that they can be
remedied in the same way, by "the institution of a school of the Church
which should afford the means of instruction to her clergy from the age
of twelve years upwards." Residence would be mandatory, and with it a
minute discipline extending to the distribution of time, the mode of
dress, the speaking of Latin, and the degree of subordination. Not all
these changes, of course, could be effected at once, but "if due care be
taken in the election of fresh members, indigence being considered as
well as talent, a docile Christian temper as well as scholastic attainments,
we may yet see [our colleges] filled with both 'young towarde scholars
and old fatherlye doctors.' " [43]

Newman, whether or not he was so sanguine as his young friend, certainly approved. "I like [your paper] so very much," he wrote, "or rather,

like is a poor word, that I cannot criticize it. It has carried me away." [44]

One might say that it carried him away to Littlemore, for it was during the very days when he was so moved by Hope's article that there "revived" in his mind a plan which he had often discussed with Pusey, that of building a μονή or monastic house at Littlemore and going there to live himself. [45] As he considered the plan, he hesitated between merely two rooms for himself and his books, something which would look like a parsonage but really be a cell, and the bolder plan of a regular monastic building. In any case, what he wanted was not merely the opportunity for a personal religious retreat and a closer attention to his parishioners—he also wanted to realize, in "a complete type or specimen," the institution which he and his friends had contemplated for so many years. As far back as 1833 Froude had proposed establishing colleges of unmarried priests as the cheapest way of meeting the spiritual needs of the great towns, and Pusey in 1838 was ready to found a network of such colleges all over the island with an endowment of £12,000 apiece. [46] Newman, with his characteristic distrust of system, had thought it better to begin with one and let it preach to others and train up men to serve them. Moreover, he did not want to begin in the great towns. Littlemore, being attached to a university and yet separated from it by open fields, would suggest the very character he wished his house to have, neither purely evangelical on the one hand nor properly academic on the other. It would be neither a mission nor yet a college but rather a hall, a body dependent on a college but with a life and purpose of its own. For this he had a precedent in the fourteenth-century Hall of St. Mary's, which had been attached to Oriel and had received its principal from among the number of the college Fellows. Now, through his own position as Fellow, perhaps the house at Littlemore might be given a similar dependence on the Oriel of today. It could be called St. Gregory's Hall or St. Mary's at Littlemore and would then realize what Newman now acknowledged could never be realized at Oxford, the ideal of a life immersed in the world of learning and yet free from its stubbornly secular spirit. [47]

The importance to Newman of this ideal can scarcely be overestimated. For twelve years he had been laboring to revive, now in one form and now in another, the ancient academical institutions which he believed were most fitted to serve it, and if Littlemore was simply a continuation of this labor, so too, once he became a Catholic, was the Oratory of St. Philip Neri, which he chose as his vocation. There he was unfortunately settled in one of the "great towns," and so in 1864 he tried once again to remove to Oxford in order to give his house that connection with a university which, in the perfection of its type, he thought that it ought to have. He had said, when he first became Fellow of Oriel, that he had no wish except to live and die within college walls, and if one gives to the word "college" the sense which it soon acquired in his own mind, then this wish was not frustrate when he resigned his Fellowship and left Oxford but was rather more perfectly and fully achieved.

CHAPTER 5

Tractarian Education

They think Education consists in knowledge; we do not. . . .
　　　　　—H. A. Woodgate to Newman, April 23, 1834

THE same principles which Newman applied to the reform of the college he also applied during these years to the reform of the university. Actually the questions raised were of two sorts, one as they touched the professoriate and another as they touched the undergraduate body; but in both cases they concerned the role of religion in the life and studies of the university.

The question about the professors was put most clearly and most amusingly in the contest over the Sanskrit professorship in 1832. This chair had been endowed, according to Newman, *"for the purpose of* extending the knowledge of Christianity in India," [1] not, as one might expect, for the purpose of extending the knowledge of Sanskrit in England. Thus, with the founder's will itself leaving some doubt as to whether Oxford was electing a professor or a missionary, it is not wonderful that there was some disagreement about the man. The candidates were two, Horace H. Wilson, a surgeon, and William H. Mill, a clergyman, both of them resident in India. Newman was for Mill because, although "Mr. Wilson, I believe, is a better Sanscrit scholar . . . , this is all that is known of him. His fitness for the peculiar purpose which the will directs should be kept in view, is quite unknown to us. Not only not a clergyman or a University man, there is nothing [even] to show he is a classical scholar, or a Hebraist, or a divine, or a literary man in any sense, or that he has any formed religious opinions, or that he is a gentleman, or that he has the temper and judgment necessary for an academical man, or that his moral qualifications are such as to admit him into Oxford society. We know nothing except that he is the best Sanscrit scholar." There is no irony in Newman's remark, for what follows is too disquieting to permit it. It is even possible, he adds, that Wilson "may be a mere liberal, and consider the Sanscrit theology not inferior to the Christian." Admittedly this would be an "extreme supposition, but one which at the present day we must guard against," [2] and all Newman's friends were agreed that indeed they must. R. I. Wilberforce was "glad" to hear that their candidate was a distinguished orientalist, but "what . . . makes me most anxious to support him is, that I believe he is a thoroughly good Churchman and a clever man." [3] Rickards had heard differently. He had no enthusiasm for bringing in Mill "except for the purpose of keeping out a scandalous person like [Wilson]," [4] but Bowden even rejoiced in the fact that Mill was so weak. "I think that Wilson's acknowledged (is it not?) superiority . . . happens rather conveniently, as it brings . . . the real issue, openly before us." That issue is "whether we are to look for Sanscrit literature alone, or for that and religious character jointly"; [5] and obviously if the best churchman had also been the best scholar the issue would have been unhappily obscured. In the end it might have been better if it had, for on March 15 the man who had nothing to recommend him except that he was "the best Sanscrit scholar" was elected professor of that subject by 207 votes to 200, and perhaps never again was this particular issue put so nicely. [6]

It was put in a way more personal to Newman, however, in the autumn of 1833, when the moral philosophy professorship fell vacant and Newman decided to stand. "Don't you think I should make a good Professor?" he wrote to Froude. "At all events let us look out for one. I do not see any one we could so well put forward. (!) But if you think that you would do as well yourself, n'importe. You shall be the man." [7] For a time he affected great diffidence about his own candidacy. There was no emolument to the office and he had "quite enough to do without mastering Hobbes and Epictetus." [8] On the other hand, "it might be the means of giving me influence with the Undergraduates; and there is no situation which combines respectability with lightness of responsibility and labour, so happily as the office of a Professor." [9] He had a "fair" chance of getting it, he thought, "because no one else is standing," [10] but alas! on the very last day R. D. Hampden, the principal of St. Mary's Hall, also put in, and "being a Bampton Lecturer," says young Mozley, "and an Aristotelian, and a Head of a House, and a Liberal, and, moreover, a stupid man in his way, he was of course the successful candidate." [11] Newman was "floored." So confident had he been of election that he had advised his publishers to put the new flourish on the title page of his forthcoming volume of sermons. Luckily, however, the printing had advanced too far for this to be possible, and so Newman was spared the humiliation of having publicly counted his chickens before they were hatched. [12]

A much more famous election which Newman lost, and again to Hampden, was that to the Regius Professorship of Divinity in 1836, but in the so-called "Hampden controversy" the issue was not educational but theological. It was not whether religion should enter into the teaching of a secular subject but simply what view of religion should be expounded by the official professor of that subject. Even the contest over the poetry professorship in 1841, in which Isaac Williams was defeated by the liberal candidate, does not represent the university's determination to keep religion out of the teaching of literature but simply its determination to keep a Tractarian out of any position whatsoever. By this date, indeed, the lesser question of whether the university was a school of the church had been lost in questions about the nature of the church itself, and although Newman himself was primarily engrossed in the latter he never lost interest in the earlier problem of the university. In 1840, when the Duke of Wellington was ill and it appeared that the university might soon be electing a new chancellor, James Hope wrote to Newman about putting forward the Bishop of Salisbury, and Newman replied that long ago he and many of his friends had been desirous of a clerical chancellor. In 1834, when the Duke was first elected, Newman and Keble had privately put forward the name of the Archbishop of Canterbury, but it had been coldly received and the Archbishop himself would not allow it, and so the ideal that the head of the church should be the titular head of the school of the church was not to be accomplished at that time.[13]

Matthew Arnold has called Oxford the home of "lost causes and . . . impossible loyalties." But for Arnold's father and for Stanley and Tait and Hawkins and Jowett it was not the home of lost causes, and it was the home of impossible loyalties only because for a considerable period of years it was the home of Newman. All Newman's loyalties were impossible, if only because they ran counter, directly and advisedly counter, to the spirit of the age. This was true in religion and it was true in education. The age was agog with educational projects, but they were all directed toward a knowledge which was secular and utilitarian. The Society for the Diffusion of Useful Knowledge, which poured forth cheap publications from 1826 to 1846, proclaimed by its very name a hostility to the Society for Promoting Christian Knowledge. "As numerous Societies already exist," said one of its prospectuses, "for the dissemination of Religious Instruction . . . , no Treatise published with the sanction of the Committee shall contain any matter of Controversial Divinity, or interfere with the principles of revealed Religion." [14] What their treatises did contain was chiefly natural philosophy and the inspiring lives of "self-exalted men" like Benjamin Franklin and James Watt. Newman speaks of the "religion" which this philosophy provided for some people, and if so, the biographies of Franklin and Watt were the gospels of this religion, and "self-help," in the phrase of Samuel Smiles, replaced the help afforded by God. Nor was the religion without its organized congregations. They were the Mechanics' Institutes, which had been started in London in 1823, had spread to Manchester in 1824, to Birmingham and Liverpool in 1825, and by mid-century had seven hundred branches and over 100,000 members throughout the country. Their organ was the *Penny Magazine* (1832), which had achieved 200,000 purchasers and perhaps a million readers in the first year of its publication. Such a work, the editors declared, could be produced only in a country "where civilization is carried forward to very high degrees of perfection," but presumably this was not because of its contents, which consisted largely of anecdotes on "The Crocodile—Method of Killing" and "Singular Dexterity of a Goat," but because of the amazing system of production and distribution which, within two weeks' time, could manufacture and carry the sheet all over the kingdom for only a penny. "This is a striking illustration," said the editors, "of the civilization of our country." [15]

The society and the institutes were organs of popular education, but on the higher level their spirit was embodied in the newly formed "London University." It was in 1825, the year before Newman became tutor of Oriel, that Thomas Campbell, the poet, addressed a public letter to Lord Brougham, the apostle of the popular education movement, urging the foundation in London of a university for the higher education of the middling classes. It was to be modeled not on Oxford and Cambridge but on the universities of Germany, that of Edinburgh, and the University of Virginia in America. It would be nonresidential, which would make it cheaper; it would be professorial rather than tutorial in the mode of its teaching; and it would not be confined to the members of any particular religious body.

Campbell's proposal was widely canvassed in the public prints and of course was "much talked of" at Oriel. The freshman who reports this fact adds succinctly, "The liberals like it. The others don't," and we may be sure that among the latter was the "new tutor [who] has just come into our college, of great credit for scholarship." [16] Newman's ideas were not yet fully formed, but he must have recognized in the new university a violation of the two principles which were to be central to his own conception. By its nonresidential and professorial character it seemed to emphasize the imparting of information rather than the forming of minds, and by its nonresidential, as well as its nonsectarian, character it gave up that religious instruction which to Newman was the soul of all the rest.[17]

The latter defect, which was much the greater of the two, was noticed in the formal statement issued by Brougham, Campbell, George Grote, James Mill, and the other members of the University Council. After dividing the subjects of study into liberal, ornamental, and professional, the committee at last observed, "One great and important branch—Theology, yet remains; and it is necessary to explain why that is not provided for." The reason is that Oxford and Cambridge take care of the clergy of the Established Church, and whereas "it is a fundamental principle of the University of London, that it shall be open to persons of all religious denominations, . . . it was manifestly impossible to provide a course of professional education for the ministers of religion of those congregations who do not belong to the Established Church. It was equally impossible to institute any theological lectures for the instruction of lay students of different religious persuasions, which would not have been liable to grave objections; still less was it practicable to introduce any religious observances that could be generally complied with." Therefore, the religious education of the pupils will be left to "domestic superintendence." [18]

The threat to religion which was posed by such a plan naturally aroused widespread opposition, and in February, 1828 the rector of Lambeth, George D'Oyly, addressed an open letter to Sir Robert Peel in which he analyzed this danger and called for the establishment of a rival institution on opposite principles.[19] The suggestion was well received, and the following June, at a public meeting presided over by the Duke of Wellington and attended by a distinguished assemblage of prelates and peers, it was resolved "that a college for general education be founded in the metropolis; in which, while the various branches of literature and science are made the subjects of instruction, it shall be an essential part of the system to imbue the minds of youth with a knowledge of the doctrine and duties of Christianity as inculcated by the United Church of England and Ireland." [20] Under the patronage of the king, this institution was to be called King's College, London, and it actually opened its doors in October, 1831, three years after its rival had done so in a new building on Gower Street.

It will be noted that the one institution called itself a "college" and the other a "university," but in the eyes of most persons at Oxford and Cambridge these designations might more properly have been reversed. "When London University (College) rose, about the year 1828," wrote Newman's brother Francis, "a most popular objection to it at the old Universities, was, that, 'not teaching Theology, it did not teach *all* sciences, and therefore was not a University.' " [21] For this reason, argued its opponents, it ought not to have the power of granting degrees, at least degrees which bore the same titles and carried the same privileges as those of Oxford and Cambridge; and for over a decade the two older universities did everything in their power to prevent its receiving a charter. King's College had received its charter (though not for conferring degrees) within a year after its application; but the petition of the "London University" was delayed until 1836, and even then the title of "University" was reserved for a newly created examining board, and the institution at Gower Street was assigned the compromise designation of University College, London.

In the end the effect of this strategy was more grievous to the older universities than it was to the institution at London, for it involved them in a controversy which raged actively for two years and did not altogether cease for nearly forty. Where there was controversy Newman was sure to be found, and since this particular controversy was one of the two great debates which provided Newman with materials for the *Idea of a University*, not only his part in it but also its general bearing must be recited somewhat in detail.

For over two centuries Oxford and Cambridge had been almost the private preserve of the Anglican church: the university and college officials were nearly all in orders, and most of the undergraduates were drawn from Anglican families. This condition was secured largely by means of religious tests, which at Oxford were slightly more stringent than they were at Cambridge. At Oxford the student was required by university statute to subscribe the Thirty-Nine Articles on two occasions, when he first entered the university and again when he presented himself for his degree. At Cambridge the former act was omitted, and on the latter occasion the candidate was required, again by university statute, either to declare himself a member of the Church of England or to subscribe the three articles of the Canons of 1604. These articles asserted that the sovereign was the supreme governor of the church, that no foreign prince or prelate had any ecclesiastical or spiritual jurisdiction within the realm, and that the Prayer Book and Thirty-Nine Articles were in accordance with the Word of God. The Cambridge statute dated from 1613, the Oxford from 1581. Originally both statutes had been directed against Catholics and had had the approval of the country at large. Since that time, however, their object had shifted from this body, who now preferred to educate themselves, to Dissenters, and the number of Dissenters had vastly increased. As a result there was a real and growing discrepancy between the religious composition of the country and that of the universities, but although the tests had often been criticized and on one occasion, in 1772, had been sharply challenged, the challenge had not been effective, and in the early nineteenth century they still stood as a barrier to a large body of persons who wanted a higher education but were reluctant to travel north of the Tweed to get it.

By 1834 the time seemed ripe to remove this barrier. The repeal in 1828 of the Test and Corporation Acts, which excluded Dissenters from municipal and other offices, and the passing in 1829 of the Catholic Emancipation Act obviously weakened the case for religious tests in the universities. Then, when the Whigs were swept into office in 1831 and showed themselves able to carry the Reform Bill, the Dissenters who had supported them were encouraged to petition openly for a redress of their grievances, and of these, exclusion from the universities was the most important. Actually, when the matter broke it was due not to the Dissenters but to a small group of liberals in the Cambridge University Senate.[22] This group had twice moved the question of tests and twice seen it vetoed. Then, when the Senate also voted against the London University charter, they became convinced that it never would be brought either to reform itself or to permit reform elsewhere, and that there was no alternative except to go over the head of the university and appeal to Parliament itself. Thus on March 13, under the leadership of Adam Sedgwick, professor of geology, they drew up a petition signed by sixty-three members of the Senate (about one-third of all the residents), which was presented in the House of Lords on March 21 and in Commons on March 24. The reaction was instantaneous. A protest against the petition was quickly signed by 110 residents, including eleven heads of houses and the three divinity professors, and this with a general Senate petition and a petition of 755 undergraduates was debated in both houses on April 21. On the same day G. W. Wood, a Dissenter, who was apparently not acting for the Cambridge group but on his own behalf, brought in a bill which would make it "lawful for all His Majesty's Subjects to enter and matriculate in the Universities of England, and to receive and enjoy all Degrees in Learning conferred therein (Degrees in Divinity alone excepted) without being required to subscribe any Articles of Religion, or to make any declaration of religious opinions respecting particular modes of Faith and Worship, provided such applicants be of unexceptionable moral character, and of competent knowledge, and willing to conform to such rules of discipline as are or shall be established by the authorities of the several Colleges or Halls." [23] With this bill the debate was really begun.

Newman was in on it from the very first. Early in March, H. J. Rose, editor of the *British Magazine*, had written to him asking if someone at Oxford would send an article, "*Short* and *strong*," on the Dissenter question, and on the 17th Newman dispatched "a scribble" of his own which was published on April 1.[24] It is a short, impassioned letter, urging Oxford not to retreat to the Cambridge position, declaring that the education she gives is so intimate, and religion so intimately involved in it, that to exclude religion would be to destroy the whole. "The students are required to attend chapel, morning and evening, (as the rule,) and the Lord's Supper terminally. Each tutor knows all his pupils personally, with more or less intimacy according to the disposition of each party, &c.; but still, in many cases, with an intimacy bordering on friendship. The tutor is often the means of forming his pupils' minds, of setting up a standard of thought and judgment in his society, and that, of course, in accordance with, or rather based upon, the doctrines of the church." [25] How is it possible, Newman asks, for the tutor to achieve this easy or sympathetic relation with one who does not recognize him as a minister of religion? And what is to be done about the lad's faith? Is he to go to chapel although dissenting, or to have a chapel of his own, or simply to stay away? Is he to be examined in divinity when he comes up for his degree, or is he to be excused? No, concludes Newman, one cannot conduct a religious body on the basis of two different religious principles. We can be Anglican *or* Dissenter, we cannot be both at once.

This brief letter and another to the *London Standard* are Newman's only contributions to the pamphlet warfare of 1834–35.[26] For some reason he left the writing to other men and busied himself with the practical work of organizing the resistance, but in this he was probably one of the three most active and powerful figures in the Oxford camp, the other two being Pusey and William Sewell of Exeter. Thus, on the day that Wood's bill was introduced into Parliament he attended a "splendid meeting" of professors, deans, and tutors at Magdalen College, and the following day was put on a committee along with Pusey and Sewell and the two professors of divinity, Edward Burton and Godfrey Faussett, to manage the defense.[27] His diary for April and May shows that he was "engaged all these days with Committees," and a later memorandum states that throughout the Easter Term he was "much concerned" with the resistance to the bill.[28] The chief work of the committee was to draft a declaration of principle and secure signatures to it from the various groups concerned. The first group canvassed were those "immediately connected with the instruction and discipline of the place," [29] that is, the professors, deans, and tutors; and their declaration came out on the 24th with eighty-two signatures. About six persons refused to sign, and with this encouragement Thomas Arnold, who was off at Rugby, set about a counterdeclaration, beginning, "We, the undersigned, &c. *many of whom* are engaged in Tuition in the University"—

"but I cannot learn," wrote Newman, "of one signature being attached to it." In the end all but two of the recusants came in, the final figure standing at ninety or ninety-two.[30]

The Declaration of Professors, Deans, and Tutors was probably the most important document in the early phase of the controversy. It was reprinted in half a dozen forms and circulated by the thousands over all the country. Newspapers and magazines republished it, and it was presented to both houses of Parliament as embodying the official view of the university. Although worded so as to apply only to those actually engaged in the tuition, it was used as the basis for declarations of agreement which were circulated widely among other interested bodies. In this form it was signed by twenty-five heads of houses and proctors, by forty-one private tutors, by more than 1,900 of the 2,519 members of Convocation,[31] by over 2,000 parents and guardians of undergraduates then in residence, by 1,050 to 1,200 of the undergraduates themselves, and by many thousands of parishioners in the nation at large.[32] It read, in its relevant paragraphs, as follows:

> They [the professors, deans, and tutors] wish to state in the first place, that the University of Oxford has always considered Religion to be the foundation of all education; and they cannot themselves be parties to any system of instruction, which does not rest upon this foundation.
>
> They also protest against the notion, that Religion can be taught on the vague and comprehensive principle of admitting persons of every creed. When they speak of Religion, they mean the doctrines of the Gospel, as revealed in the Bible, and as maintained by the Church of Christ in its best and purest times. They also believe in their consciences, that these doctrines are held by the Church of England. . . .
>
> In thus stating it to be their solemn duty to provide for a Christian education, they feel that uniformity of faith upon essential points is absolutely necessary; and that the admission of persons who dissent from the Church of England would lead to the most disastrous consequences; that it would unsettle the minds of the younger members of the University; would raise up and continue a spirit of controversy which is at present unknown; and would tend to reduce Religion to an empty and unmeaning name, or to supplant it by scepticism and infidelity.[33]

It is very possible that Newman composed this declaration himself;[34] certainly he helped to compose it and was a key figure in its distribution. In his own person he mailed out copies in large numbers and attended to a heavy correspondence on the subject. With H. J. Rose he tried to coordinate the resistance of Oxford and Cambridge, and in the case of the Parish Petitions he placed at the disposal of the committee the organization already employed for the distribution of the tracts. Indeed, the Declaration of Tutors is really a miniature tract on a specialized subject.

In the first half of the year there were over a score of pamphlets against the bill and only half a dozen in its favor. Nevertheless Newman was anxious. Bowden had written that the measure was "horrible," was no less than a "declaration of the Legislature, that Christianity should no longer form the basis of University Education." Oxford, he thought, was "destined to a fiery trial." [35] Keble was "fully prepared to refuse obedience" [36] if the bill were passed, and Sewell was "ready for martyrdom." Newman knew that it was wonderful, "nay supernatural," how Oxford had come forward in the last year, and yet, if the bill were passed, "I quite dread lest we should want pluck. . . . What a time it is! . . . Pusey is willing to give up house and lands rather than move a step - but many people are talking of going *as far as* Cambridge. . . . [i.e. to take off the subscription to the Articles at entrance &c.].—in the beginning of the year such a measure came before the Board of Heads, and there were 7 men among them who supported it - a fearful number - I am very desponding at this instant. But one must keep a face." [37] The test came at the end of July. On the 28th the bill was read for a third time in Commons and passed 164 to 75, but three days later it was defeated in the Lords.

This same month, as a kind of sideshow to the main event, Newman got involved in what he called the "Jubber scrape." A certain Miss Jubber, the daughter of a Dissenting pastry cook, asked him to officiate at her wedding, and of course one of the five complaints of the Dissenters, along with that of exclusion from the universities, was the fact that the law compelled them to be married by an Anglican priest. But as Newman saw it the priest had a complaint too, in being asked to administer a sacrament to a person who regarded it as no more than a human ceremony; and since in this case the party had not even been baptized, he decided to make it a point of conscience, and refused. The thing got into the papers, there was a great hullabaloo, and Rose inquired mischievously if this was "a scheme of yours for putting an end to the breed of Dissenters in general." [38]

The question was not entirely settled, of course, by the defeat of the bill (indeed, it was not until 1871 that the universities were entirely freed of religious tests),[39] but without following out the controversy in all its details, we may briefly notice what were the positions assumed and the arguments adopted by the two sides. On either part there was a technical or legal, and a general or educational, argument; and although it was only the latter with which Newman was really concerned, both arguments may be given briefly.

Technically, the position of the universities was that they were private corporations with every right to regulate their own internal affairs, including the conditions of membership, and that the legislature had no power to intervene. And if this were not true of the universities, they said, certainly it was true of the colleges. To this argument the liberals replied that whatever the original status of the universities, which was difficult to ascertain, they had in fact become national, not private, establishments, and the Dissenters, as part of the nation, were fully entitled to share the privileges they afforded. Degrees from Oxford and Cambridge, for example, conferred certain immunities on those entering the College of Physicians, Inns of Court, and other civil corporations; and it was clearly unjust that Dissenters, simply by reason of their religion, should be placed at a disadvantage in their chosen professions of medicine and law. To this the universities replied that the remedy lay equally with the College of Physicians and Inns of Court, and they further showed that university degrees were not merely symbols of attainment but also gave entrance to Fellowships and to the instruction and the government of the university. But it would be intolerable to have Dissenters in these positions, for whatever else the universities were or ought to become, they were also the schools for training the clergy of the Established Church, and so they must certainly be under the control of the church. And when the Dissenters protested that their claims did not go so far, the universities were inclined to be skeptical or at least to opine that these further claims would be only a matter of time.

The more general argument of the universities may be put in the form of a syllogism. The education given at Oxford and Cambridge has, and ought to have, a religious foundation. It is impossible to give such an education to persons of various religious persuasions. Therefore, to admit Dissenters into Oxford and Cambridge would be to destroy the peculiar type of education which they gave. The universities did not see that either premise was open to objection; the liberals declared that both were false.

In denying the first premise, the liberals did not attack religion itself but simply minimized the place which it actually held in the two universities, and much of the controversy was concerned with this matter of fact. A considerable episode was provided at Cambridge, for example, when Connop Thirlwall, Fellow of Trinity, published a letter declaring that the religious instruction in his university was very slight. This was denied in a statement signed by fifteen tutors and in several other pamphlets, but ultimately it did appear that there was less religious instruction at Cambridge than there was at Oxford. The best account of the Oxford practice was given by George Moberly, a tutor of Balliol. In his college the lectures for two days in the week, he asserted, were almost exclusively theological. During the first year and a half they covered the Four Gospels and Acts in Greek and Paley's *Horae Paulinae;* during one term either Paley's *Evidences* or Bishop Pearson on the Creed or Bishop Jewel's Apology; and in the last year the Thirty-Nine Articles. Further, a weekly lecture was given Sunday evening in chapel on the doctrines of the Church of England as contained in her formularies, and undergraduates of less than two years' standing were required to write answers to questions on these lectures. Also, in each term everyone wrote out an abridgment of one historical book of the Old Testament, so that in two years' time he went from Genesis to Nehemiah; and all these matters were included in the terminal examinations. There was an entrance examination in the contents of the Gospels and the doctrines of the Catechism, and a final examination in the history of the Old and New Testament, the contents of the Gospels, the evidences of Christianity, and the Articles. Every undergraduate attended daily prayers and appeared at the Sacrament three times a year.[40]

In truth, the main flaw of Wood's bill, which the author apparently did not understand himself, was its assumption that the universities were Anglican establishments solely by virtue of their religious tests, and that if only these tests could be removed then the universities would at once provide an education acceptable to Catholic, Dissenter, and Jew alike. Wood apparently did not consider that the tests were merely the formal notice of a difficulty which the non-Anglican would encounter at every step of his career, and that the universities could not be secularized by an act of Parliament until after they had been secularized in fact. This was a process which would take many years, and in the end Parliament was forced to wait upon its completion.

The second premise of the universities, that one cannot give a religious education to persons of various religious persuasions, was likewise denied by the liberals. They saw two means of doing this successfully. The first was to make separate arrangements, and this proposal was obviously feasible if it meant founding separate halls or colleges for those sects whose members might attend in some numbers, for there was a real sense in which religious instruction was less intimately associated with the university than it was with the colleges. True, the university examinations, which required the study of divinity, would have to be modified, but this would be a much less sweeping change than that of altering the collegial teaching and conceivably it could be accomplished. The other means certainly could not. It envisaged, not separate arrangements for the various sects, but a mode of teaching religion which would be acceptable to all. This might be done, it was suggested, either by teaching whatever books were used in a merely historical and factual way, without reference to whether they were true or anyone believed them, or else by teaching only that part of Christianity which all sects held in common. It was not difficult, of course, for the universities to make game of these two notions. They pointed out that the first ought to be as repulsive to a Dissenter as it was to them, since even a Dissenter presumably believed his religion and doubtless would want his children to do so too, certainly would not want them to regard it in a cold and impersonal way. And as to "our common Christianity," they feared that this would turn out to be not a very extensive subject of study, or at least that it would be rather vague and misty, for when one teaches the truths of religion, as of any other subject, he has to teach some particular truths and not just religion in general. He teaches it this way or that, Anglican or Socinian, and not all ways together.[41]

From this it followed, in the view of the conservatives, that to admit Dissenters was simply to secularize the university. The universities were called "exclusive," but was it more exclusive to bar a body of persons or to bar the study of a great and important subject such as religion? For this would be the result of the proposed measure. Broad and reasonable as it appeared, it would not merely disestablish the church in the very centers where its leaders were formed and so lead to disestablishment in the country at large, but would also disestablish Christianity as a subject about which anything could certainly be known. The maxim of the bill, wrote Sewell, was "Education without Religion; and Religion without distinction. In plain and simple words, No Christianity." [42]

During the first phase of the controversy great emphasis was laid by several speakers in Parliament upon the discrepancy between the Oxford and the Cambridge systems of exacting subscription, and upon the apparent anomaly involved in the former. Oxford required subscription at matriculation, but to require that a young man declare his belief in articles of religion which he possibly had never read and very probably did not understand seemed absurd and even immoral. The very fact that the university subsequently gave instruction in these articles showed that they did not expect the young man to understand them at the moment that they required him to believe them. He was to believe them first and understand them later, and some persons wondered whether this was generally the way that Oxford went about that famed "cultivation of the intellect" to which she was so deeply attached. Even her defenders in Parliament, among them the Duke of Wellington, found themselves embarrassed to explain this practice; and it was intimated to the university that she could more easily be defended if she would render her position more intelligible, either by dispensing with the first subscription, as Cambridge did, or by substituting some other form that would be less offensive.

Newman had been apprehensive even early in the spring that something like this would come, but it was not until the Long Vacation that the groundwork for it was laid by the publication of R. D. Hampden's *Observations on Religious Dissent*. "Hampden," wrote Newman to Rose, "has just published a pamphlet which, I fear, destroys our glory. . . . I fear he calls all articles impositions of human authority, and advocates their removal as a test on matriculations—and assures his reader that all this is in no wise inconsistent with his being partner to the Declaration of May last. Do not take my word for it, since I have not read his effusion." [43] What Newman had learned on hearsay was perfectly true. Hampden's thesis was that Christians differ very little in their acceptance of revelation but very largely in the conclusions they draw from it. "It is chiefly the introduction of human opinion into the matter of Revelation that occasions a difference of professions," and we should remember that "no conclusions of human reasoning, however correctly deduced, however logically sound, are properly religious truths." Even the Scriptures themselves are not properly revelation, for revelation "consists of matter of fact" and is "independent of any peculiar wording of it." The revelation in St. Paul's Epistles, for example, is simply "the collection of facts involved in that general expression, 'Christ crucified,' which is the sum and substance of his writings. The rest is enforcement of this on the minds and hearts" of his hearers. If this be true, then *a fortiori* "no speculative deductions from the language of Scripture carry with them the force of divine truth," and this applies to all our theological formularies. Thus he sees no objection to the admission of Dissenters, from whom we do not "really differ," and would urge the removal of all tests, though he insists that this should be done by the university itself and not by the legislature. [44]

Hampden sent Newman the second, corrected edition of his pamphlet, which Newman acknowledged in the following classic terms: "The kindness which has led you to presenting me with your pamphlet encourages me to hope that you will forgive me, if I take the opportunity it affords to express to you my very sincere and deep regret that it has been published. . . . I feel [an utter aversion] to the principles it professes, as (in my opinion) legitimately leading to formal Socinianism." "This letter," comments Newman, "was the beginning of hostilities in the University," [45] but he of course means in the Hampden controversy, for hostilities over subscription had already begun. On November 10 the Hebdomadal Board decided by a majority of one to introduce a measure into Convocation replacing undergraduate subscription by a simple declaration of conformity to the discipline and worship of the place.[46] Within a week, however, they had been frightened back by the intense activity of Newman and Pusey. Overnight the latter drew up a paper of twenty-three queries which were printed and circulated in the common rooms,[47] and three days later Newman wrote a protest which was signed at once by fifty M.A.'s. This was sent into the board for its information,[48] and on the 17th the board voted to drop the matter. "The Queries," wrote Pusey, "especially one of yours, seems to have done the work." [49]

The work was done only for a time, however, for on April 1, 1835, the Vice-Chancellor formally gave notice that during the ensuing term a new statute would be submitted to Convocation which would replace undergraduate subscription by a declaration in the following form: "I A.B. declare that I do, so far as my knowledge extends, assent to the Doctrines of the United Church of England and Ireland as set forth in her Thirty-nine Articles; that I will conform to her Liturgy and Discipline; and that I am ready and willing to be instructed in her Articles of Religion, as required by the Statutes of this University." [50] It was felt by the board that such a declaration would be the exact equivalent of subscription, so far as exclusiveness was concerned, and that it would be free from the objections involved in an act of uninstructed assent.

With this the battle of the university was really joined, and in some ways it was a more bitter controversy than that of the previous spring. Then the attack had been made by outsiders and the university was almost united in its defense; but now it was a family quarrel, between on the one hand the liberals of the university, and on the other a group whose nucleus was formed by the rising Tractarian party. Moreover, the issue, which in the contest over the admission of Dissenters had been clouded by misunderstanding and misinformation, was now more clearly and sharply drawn. Each side knew what it believed, and its beliefs, which concerned the whole spirit and method of education, were simply irreconcilable with those of the other party.

The liberal position was clear enough. For the most part they had no desire to admit Dissenters or to alter the instruction of the university. They simply wished to be clear of the anomalies involved in asking a youth of sixteen to write his name in a large vellum book which also contained a copy of the Thirty-Nine Articles. They felt either that this was immoral, if it implied an act of assent to propositions which the youth did not understand, or that it was indecent, in bringing what ought to be a solemn act into disrepute by the perfunctory manner in which it was performed, or at least that it was useless and if it brought odium upon the university, could very well be dispensed with. The first of these was the more characteristic and important position.

Those who resisted the change were not so united in their views. The official apology, which had been developed as early at 1757 and was expressed in Parliament by the Bishop of Exeter, was that the first subscription meant simply that the undergraduates acknowledge a belief in the Articles "grounded *on the authority of others*. And nothing farther, I suppose, does any man conceive to be meant by their subscriptions." [51] The difficulty with this view was that the statutes, which were framed at a time when students came to the university at a very early age, did not exact subscription from those who were under twelve, and there seemed no reason for this distinction except a belief that those over twelve were capable of understanding the meaning of what they subscribed. For this reason, then, and also because the explanation was rather high and dry, it was not accepted by the party of Newman and Pusey.

A second and very interesting view was developed by F. D. Maurice in a lengthy pamphlet entitled *Subscription No Bondage*. Maurice was peculiarly qualified to enter this controversy, for he had studied at Cambridge as a Dissenter and then at Oxford as a member of the Church of England, and thus was a kind of Tiresias in the educational world. He held that there was no point in arguing over the grounds on which an undergraduate believed the Articles, for he did not *believe* them at all. They were not meant to be believed. In form they were not a confession of faith but a statement of propositions, and so were more like Bacon's *Novum organum* than the Apostles' Creed. They were not intended as a test but rather as a declaration of the terms on which the university proposed to teach and the pupils agreed to learn. They did not bind the student to conclusions beyond which he might not advance but rather warned him against superstitions which he would encounter on the way. This explains the "object which the University proposes to itself in imposing Articles. These are our *conditions of thought*; by these the teachers engage to teach; by these the learners engage to learn." [52] One may object to the imposing of any conditions of thought, but every university does impose them, and Oxford differs from the others only in making hers explicit.

Newman and Pusey were shown this pamphlet in proof and accepted it as one contribution to the cause.[53] It was obviously not the contribution they would have made, for they could hardly agree that the Articles were a mere hypothesis or simply a *caveat* against Rome. Their own view was expressed in a number of pamphlets published during the spring months. Pusey revived the method he had used in the Queries and wrote twenty-seven *Questions Respectfully addressed to Members of Convocation*, which were widely circulated, first in their original form, then with Answers by Hawkins and another opponent, and finally with Notes on the Answers by Pusey. Newman wrote nothing himself, but he encouraged his young followers to write and so elicited from J. W. Bowden, Benjamin Harrison, C. P. Eden, Charles Marriott, H. W. Wilberforce, J. F. Christie, and Frederick Oakeley pamphlets which clearly reflect his own ideas.[54] Out of these pamphlets one can reconstruct the position which Newman held.

In the first place, he felt that the Declaration of Conformity did not answer the purpose of subscription because the former was purely a religious *test*, whereas the latter was an element in the university's *teaching* of religion. The very fact that the Articles were difficult to understand encouraged the student to prepare himself beforehand or to follow up his act with subsequent study, whereas the declaration that I do assent "so far as my knowledge extends" not only allowed the student to rest in ignorance but even encouraged willful ignorance and was likely to turn the action into a standing jest. Furthermore, the promise to "conform" to the liturgy and discipline of the church emphasized outward compliance rather than inward assent and was actually too severe, for it turned every omitted service into a broken promise. In sum, an act of assent, although obviously the student could not rise to the full meaning of the Articles, at least encouraged him to rise as high as he could, whereas the Declaration of Conformity encouraged him to take them in the lowest and most trivial sense.

As to the objection that subscription means assent "beforehand to what the Students are afterwards to learn," [55] Newman and Pusey thought this was simply the normal method of education and the method it ought to pursue. Continually we predispose the minds of children toward those values which they will later be in a position to understand, and if we did not, contrary habits would spring up which would make them lose the values forever. So it was that Coleridge, when he was told by his friend Thelwall that it was wrong to do this, took him out into his garden and explained that it was choked with weeds because he did not think it right to predispose the soil toward roses. The soil must make its own choice. And so the student was to say, "I assent," "I conform," "I am willing to be instructed," as though, having coolly examined the alternatives, he was now ready to confer this favor upon the church, and private judgment would reign supreme.

Newman and Pusey thought that sensible men proceeded on a different plan. They made their children memorize the creed that their minds might have wholesome truths upon which to work. They baptized them in the church of their own belief that they might live within its fostering influence and gradually come to understand those doctrines which they certainly did not understand at the moment of acceptance. It was an "evil maxim of the day, that 'one cannot believe that which one does not fully understand,' " [56] for the reverse of this is constantly seen to be true. When humble or immature people join a church they give their assent to innumerable propositions with which they will never have any acquaintance, and theologians call this an act of implicit faith. An implicit truth is one contained, or perhaps concealed, in some other clear or definite truth, and an explicit belief in the latter involves a belief in the former which is called "implicit." "Subscription," in Newman's view, "was an act of fides implicita in the Church, exacted *when youths came for encyclopaedic instruction*." [57] Its original purpose was not merely to keep out Roman Catholics but also to provide a basis for theological study, and now it provided a similar basis for general education.[58] One purpose, therefore, of a youth in coming to the university was to transform his implicit faith in such truths as the Articles contained into an explicit faith, and subscription, far from doing violence to his intention, was simply the first step in its fulfillment. When the Declaration was first proposed in November, 1834, Pusey and Newman were willing to go so far as to allow an additional sentence in the statute "explanatory of our meaning in imposing the subscription," and the form which Pusey proposed was as follows: "The University supposes that those who, coming for her instruction, subscribe the Articles, thereby profess according to their different attainments, that they receive these articles as believing them to be true either from their own conviction or at least upon the authority of the Church. She would not however wish altogether to exclude those of a scrupulous conscience who might hesitate to state this of themselves, and yet knew of no opinion which they held opposed either to the discipline or doctrine of the Church of England." [59] Moreover, by asking to have unfolded to his understanding the truths which, by the rightness of his will, he is able dimly to apprehend, the youth further confirms himself in a habit which will make him truly docible, and docible of those particular truths which he wishes to learn. The principles which he has accepted will guide him among the circumstance which he wishes to explore, and without these principles he would be lost. His own imagination would lead him astray. If we ask ourselves, therefore, what the real benefit is that we receive from subscription to the Articles, we have to reply that it is "the benefit of SELF-PROTECTION; protection of self against self; protection for your proper self against the thousand extravagant fancies which will run away with you if they can." [60]

Such was the nature of the controversy which formally opened on April 1 with the proposal of a Declaration of Conformity in the place of subscription to the Articles. The course which the controversy followed was about the same as the spring before. Again there was the protest signed by resident members of Convocation, and again the committee of defense with Newman and Pusey involved. This time the work of the committee was not to secure signatures for Parliament but to win over the votes in Convocation, and therefore all through April and early May Newman was writing out to absent members urging them to come up on the stated day. [61] That day arrived on May 20, 1835, and what happened has been graphically described by Frederic Rogers, who witnessed the event from the gallery of the Sheldonian Theatre.

All the Convocation affair went off most triumphantly for the party who wished no change, the numbers being 459 to 57; rather more than eight to one against the Declaration. The only unpleasant part is that the beaten party are excessively angry, and it must be confessed that what happened to them was a trial of temper. The division was in the Theatre (N.B. not the playhouse), and undergraduates were admitted to the gallery, who took the liberty of expressing their opinion by shouts &c. pretty freely. The voters (the M.A.s) were in the area . . . , and just as they were beginning to give their votes, which they usually do by going up one by one to the Proctor and whispering in his ear, one of the anti-reformers cried out "Non placet" (the form of negativing) and walked to one side of the Theatre. It seemed from the gallery, where I was, as if the whole crowd were following him. You just saw a few spots here and there stationary, in the midst of the great current, and rather struggling not to be carried away in it, as little bits of dirt do when you are pouring water out of a basin; and after a short settling we saw about forty gentlemen left "alone with their glory" in the middle of the room, looking very foolish, and hardly knowing whether to stand boldly forth or not, to bear as best they might the shoutings of the opposite party and the undergraduates. However, the others soon took compassion on them and spread themselves again over the whole area, and their only penance after that was to listen to the expression of the undergraduate feelings, till the Proctor had done counting the votes. It is rather curious that these very young gentlemen whom people are so anxious to liberate from the yoke of subscription are the most vehement and noisy opponents of any "relief bill" that are to be found. I only wish they had confined themselves to applause, whereas they took the liberty of hissing our respectable Provost [Hawkins], who is the great patron of change. Of course we have been inundated with pamphlets, with and without names.[62]

There is no need to follow Newman's course in detail through the last ten years before his conversion to Rome. More and more his thoughts were given to religious rather than educational concerns, and therefore, rather than continue the narrative, we shall pause briefly at this point to give an estimate of what we have called "Tractarian education." For the usual view of such a phrase is that it is almost a contradiction in terms, that Oxford, during the years of the movement, was so deeply involved in theological controversy that it had no time for its proper work of education. Reform at Oxford, say the proponents of this view, began in 1800, continued for about thirty years, received a severe check from the Oxford movement, and then revived again after 1845. J. A. Froude, for example, says that "famous as the Tractarian leaders were to become, their names are not connected with a single effort to improve the teaching at Oxford or to mend its manners." [63] And Mark Pattison has made the same charge. "Probably there was no period of our history," he says, "during which, I do not say science and learning, but the ordinary study of the classics was so profitless or at so low an ebb as during the period of the Tractarian controversy." [64] Goldwin Smith also notes that "only clerical studies and interests could find a place in the education [of Oxford], and that in times of religious controversy the University became an ecclesiastical cockpit." [65] To such a charge one may immediately concede that certainly there was no time in the nineteenth century when Oxford was more agitated by religious debate than during the years 1832–45, and further, that the great periods of university reform were certainly those of 1800–09, 1850–58, and 1871–82, with which Newman and his friends had nothing to do. But beyond this what do the charges mean?—a question the more necessary to ask because they have been contradicted by the very men who made them. Pattison, for instance, on receiving in 1856 a copy of Newman's "book on Universities" (probably the *Office and Work of Universities*), asked that he might be "allowed to take this opportunity of saying that I can never forget the great obligations I am under to you. I do not exaggerate in saying that to the mental and moral influence derived from you I owe the formation of my mind." And fourteen years later he wrote again of "that old time when in Oriel Common Room, I was for the first time introduced to ideas and to men who would utter them - an introduction which I owed to you." [66] Froude gives the same testimony.

The very essay which says that the Tractarian leaders did nothing to improve the teaching at Oxford contains one of the most striking tributes ever written to an Oxford teacher. "Newman's mind," says Froude, "was world-wide. He was interested in everything which was going on in science, in politics, in literature. Nothing was too large for him, nothing too trivial, if it threw light upon the central question, what man really was, and what was his destiny. . . . Keble had looked into no lines of thought but his own. Newman had read omnivorously; he had studied modern thought and modern life in all its forms, and with all its many-colored passions." For this reason Froude and the other undergraduates, "who had never seen such another man, and to whom he appeared, perhaps, at special advantage in contrast with the normal college don, came to regard Newman with the affection of pupils . . . for an idolised master. The simplest word which dropped from him was treasured as if it had been an intellectual diamond. For hundreds of young men *Credo in Newmannuum* was the genuine symbol of faith." [67]

If the matter is examined more carefully we are inclined to make several distinctions. The first is that, although Newman was determined to infuse a religious spirit into education, he in no sense wished to turn Oxford into a seminary or to distract boys from their studies by the excitement of religious debate. At Oxford boys were always being distracted from their studies by one thing or another, and if Newman had done it with religion instead of with rowing or prizefighting, that sport would doubtless have been no rougher or more mischievous than any other. But he did not much distract them. The great crises of the movement were few and brief, and even those persons who were most deeply involved continued to read, to attend lectures, to take examinations, and even to pass them. Newman, indeed, would have nothing else. When he wrote to Pattison about the possibility of coming back to Oxford in the 1860's, he said he would not think of addressing himself to the undergraduates because their business was study. Moreover, this had always been his view. "With us undergraduates," said Froude, "Newman . . . did not enter on such important [i.e. religious] questions, although they were in the air and we talked about them among ourselves. He, when we met him, spoke to us about subjects of the day, of literature, of public persons and incidents, of everything which was generally interesting." [68] For the most part undergraduates now met him only at the teas which he gave every Monday evening during term from 1837 to 1841, but he never used these occasions to press upon them his own religious views.[69] This is supported by an anecdote of Miss Mitford, who discovered much to her alarm that a young relation of hers, an undergraduate, had been invited to breakfast with Newman once a week. She anxiously questioned him about the subjects which they discussed and was told, "He talks to me of every sort of subject, except what is called Tractarianism, and that he has never mentioned." "Now this seemed to me most honourable," was Miss Mitford's comment.[70]

In the second place, the religious spirit which Newman infused into the university, although it was strongly anti-rationalistic, was in no sense anti-intellectual. Even the enemies of Tractarianism were constrained to admit that it was a learned movement, and indeed, according to Pattison, "the very earliest objection urged home against the new 'doctors' was, that in their system the road to truth seemed to be laid through learning, and by consequence the plain and unlettered man was excluded from salvation." The High Church leaders presumably had other recommendations above their learning, but the Tractarian school was felt from the first to be "a revival of the spirit of learned research" and its leaders to be direct descendants from the seventeenth-century divines.[71] Indeed, in one aspect the Oxford movement was simply a part of that great recovery of the past which was the general work of ninteenth-century thought, and in learning and power of analysis and even in scholarly method its leaders do not compare unfavorably with the historians of the rationalistic or liberal Anglican schools.

Moreover, it was not merely that the movement was learned in character but also that it distinguished more sharply than did the liberal school between the provinces of religion, morality, and intellectual excellence. The last could never be a substitute for the first or second, but neither could the first or second be a substitute for the last. The end of a university, therefore, was the cultivation of the intellect: it could do little more than that, and nothing less than that would serve. Religion and morals might be infused into the university, but not with such unction as to weaken or sentimentalize its studies, which remained as before the principal object of the place. Thus in 1829 or 1830 the Hebdomadal Board sent about a questionnaire to determine, among other things, what was "the leading and direct object" of the final examination. Is it, they asked, "to ascertain *Intellectual* qualifications?" and Newman replied that it was. "The decision of the Examiners should [not] depend in any measure," he wrote, "on the moral qualities of the Candidates, in respect of their industry or idleness . . . [but] solely on the actual attainments . . . produced." [72]

The third distinction which ought to be made is that although Newman certainly did little to alter the *system* of an Oxford education, this does not mean that he did little to improve its teaching. Even as regards the system he was not invariably opposed to reform, for he voted in favor of the new examination statute which was proposed in 1830 and which was lost, says Cox, "by aiming at too much." [72] Moreover, his answers to the questionnaire mentioned above show him as pressing for many changes which the liberals would also have approved. He would like Responsions to come earlier and be given a higher standard so as to secure the advantages of a matriculation examination without the difficulties which it involved. He would like an examination for the M.A. degree, but since this is impossible he suggests requiring testimonials of attendance on lectures in Hebrew, chemistry, anatomy, natural philosophy, or modern history.[74] His desire to restore Euclid to the School of Literae Humaniores was doubtless a conservative move, but the proposal to encourage the more modern branches of mathematics by scholarships and prizes certainly was not. Moreover, his attempts to enlarge the written part of the final examination, to make it deal with subjects as well as "books," to have a single time of the year for matriculation, and to dethrone the gentlemen-commoners from their privileged place were all progressive projects of reform. But perhaps the most far-reaching change proposed in the Oxford of Newman's day was the attempt of the Hebdomadal Board in 1839–40 to bring back into operation the decayed professorial system. The measure was lost in Convocation, and we do not know how Newman voted, but in advance he did not "see why one should be averse" to it. It was "a most immense change or rather revolution," and he thought the Board had not gone about it legally, but on the other hand, "College Tutors are overworked. And Professors could take from them advantageously many departments of general education - and then the Tutors would be more strictly guardians and formers of the Pupil's minds." [75] In this way the old could be combined with the new.

Nevertheless, it remains true that Newman did very little to reform the system of Oxford education, and this was because "system" was not the method by which he worked. His method was that of personal intercourse—*cor ad cor loquitur*—and within that method he was certainly one of the greatest intellectual forces Oxford has ever known. Estimates vary as to how deeply he penetrated the university. A young American who visited Oxford and asked about the movement was told, "We leave all that to the M.A.s," [76] but others have given a different and more considered judgment. According to Principal Shairp, the older dons and the younger undergraduates were largely unaffected by the movement, but the great body that lay between, the younger dons and the older undergraduates, were in one way or another stimulated by the new questions and by the mind that raised them. "There was not, in Oxford at least, a reading man who was not more or less indirectly influenced" by the movement, and Newman was "the centre and soul from which so mighty a power emanated." [77] Dean Lake also says that Newman's influence extended "over nearly all the more thoughtful of the undergraduates," and that in the 1830's he rapidly became "the greatest force both morally and intellectually in the University." [78]

The seat of his influence was of course the pulpit at St. Mary's, but his sermons there were seldom directly theological and his influence was not exclusively religious. He was concerned with transforming the whole man, and he did this by speaking of all those things which most deeply affected the undergraduates and by being himself a person whom they could unreservedly admire.

> He seemed always to be better informed on common topics of conversation than any one else who was present. He was never condescending with us, never didactic or authoritative; but what he said carried conviction along with it. When we were wrong he knew why we were wrong, and excused our mistakes to ourselves while he set us right. Perhaps his supreme merit as a talker was that he never tried to be witty or to say striking things. Ironical he could be, but not ill-natured. Not a malicious anecdote was ever heard from him. Prosy he could not be. He was lightness itself—the lightness of elastic strength—and he was interesting because . . . he had something real to say. . . . He seemed to be addressing the most secret consciousness of each of us—as the eyes of a portrait appear to look at every person in a room.[79]

This is the tribute of that same Froude who wrote that Newman's name was "not connected with a single effort to improve the teaching at Oxford or to mend its manners." The paradox can be resolved only by supposing that Newman's method was so informal that often people did not realize, when they sat under him, that this was the moment in which their education occurred. Matthew Arnold was more perceptive. Though he had less direct contact with Newman than either Pattison or Froude, he nevertheless realized that Newman was one of the four persons (the other three being Wordsworth, Goethe, and Sainte-Beuve) from whom he had really learned—"a very different thing from merely receiving a strong impression"—learned "habits, methods, ruling ideas." [80] The effect produced on him by Newman he describes as consisting in "a general disposition of mind rather than in a particular set of ideas," [81] and was so mixed up with all that was most essential in what he did and said that he could never cease to be conscious that it was there.

After the crisis of Newman's secession in 1845 it was wonderful, says Pattison, how quickly the university returned to normal and set about its proper business of education.[82] Almost overnight it was transformed from a place of ecclesiastical contention into an efficient, modern university dedicated to science and learning. Once again, however, although the fact of the change can hardly be doubted, its meaning is not so simple as Pattison implies. It is not that religious controversy diverted Oxford from education and once the controversy was over the education could proceed, but rather that, mingled with the religious views of the movement, there were very definite views on education, and Oxford, in repudiating the former, repudiated the latter as well. Naturally, then, in a very few years all was changed. In 1850 the Royal Commission moved in, and by the bill which followed four years later the educational world not only of Newman but also of Copleston and Whately was largely swept away. Newman might write to Isaac Williams that "of all human things, perhaps Oxford is nearest my heart," [83] but after his conversion to Catholicism he was no more alien to the faith of Oxford than, after the conversion of Oxford by the Royal Commission, he was to its educational philosophy. Already in the autumn of 1844 he sensed the strangeness which was coming on. John Bowden, the first friend he had ever had at Oxford, was dying, and this seemed to cut him off from the home that they had had in common. "I do fancy I am getting changed," he wrote to his sister. "I go into Oxford, and find myself out of place. Every thing seems to say to me, 'This is not your home.' The college seems strange to me, and even the college servants seem to look as if I were getting strange to them." [84] The snapdragon growing on the walls opposite to his freshman rooms at Trinity he had for years taken as "the emblem of my own perpetual residence even unto death in my University," [85] but this was not to be. In June, 1845 he asked his sister to meet him in Oxford, saying that he should use the meeting "to take a last look at the Common Room," [86] which had been the *locus* of his intellectual ideal. Then, on October 3, six days before his conversion, he wrote Hawkins a letter whose very coldness betrays the deep anguish which it surely involved.

> Mr. Provost,
>   I hope you will find the inclosed form correct.
>   I shall be obliged if you will remove my name from the books of the College and the University.
>
>   I am, Mr. Provost,
>   Yours truly,
>   John H. Newman

To which Hawkins replied on the 6th: "The form of Resignation is quite correct; and, if I hear nothing further from you to the contrary, I must of course comply with your desires. . . ." [87]

Dublin

CHAPTER **6**

The Irish University Question

Now for our Irish wars. . . .
—*Richard II*

S IX years after his withdrawal from Oxford, Newman, now a priest at the Oratory at Birmingham, was called to assist in the founding of a Catholic university in Ireland. "Curious it will be," he wrote to the wife of a friend, "if Oxford is imported into Ireland, not in its members only, but in its principles, methods, ways, and arguments. The battle there will be what it was in Oxford twenty years ago. Curious too that there I shall be opposed to the Whigs, having Lord Clarendon instead of Lord Melbourne,—that Whately [now Archbishop of Dublin] will be there *in propria persona*, and that while I found my tools breaking under me in Oxford, for Protestantism is not susceptible of so high a temper, I am renewing the struggle in Dublin with the Catholic Church to support me. It is very wonderful,—Keble, Pusey, Maurice, Sewell, &c., who have been able to do so little against Liberalism in Oxford will be renewing the fight, although not in their persons, in Ireland." [1]

The battle was indeed the same as before, but as Newman noticed elsewhere, [2] the forces in the battle were curiously and ironically reversed. For the very persons who in England had maintained against the government the principle that secular instruction should not be separated from religious were now unwilling to grant that principle to the Catholics in Ireland. The anomaly arose, of course, from the fact that the religion established in Ireland, unlike that in England, was not the religion of the people. The population of Ireland in 1845 was eight and a half millions, of which seven million were Catholics and three-quarters of a million belonged to the Established Church. Nevertheless, it was only for this minority that a system of higher education was provided. The only university in Ireland was the University of Dublin, and the only college which it contained was that of the Holy and Undivided Trinity. Although the university and the college were distinct legal entities, entrance to the university was only through the college, and the latter, which had been founded by Elizabeth in 1592, presupposed, although it did not legally require, that its members should belong to the Anglican faith. By a statute of 1637 and another of about the same date "all the Students" were required to attend divine service and receive the holy communion according to the Anglican rite, and on presenting themselves for a degree they were further required to take an oath against transubstantiation, invocation and adoration of the Virgin Mary, and the sacrifice of the Mass.[3] An oath was also imposed upon all Fellows, and thus the situation in Trinity up to the end of the eighteenth century was almost exactly the same as that in the older universities of England.

The Catholic Relief Act of 1793 was an attempt to ease the problem, but it took the method, not of throwing Trinity College open to all comers, but of making it lawful for Catholics to take degrees and hold offices in any college thereafter to be founded within the University of Dublin. Until such time, a Royal Letter of 1794 made it possible, by a partial abolition of religious tests, for Catholics to proceed to degrees in Trinity College but not to accept any position of trust or emolument; and as no steps were taken to found another college, this was the situation which obtained for another half century.[4] Obviously it was not very satisfactory. It placed a peculiar strain upon the faith of a young man to be allowed to compete for a scholarship or fellowship and then, if he was successful, to be allowed to claim his reward only through an act of formal apostasy. Such acts, or at least instances of a temporary estrangement from the church, were not rare, and although the situation was of course protested, it was not until 1843 that any measure of publicity was given it. In that year a Catholic undergraduate of Trinity, Denis Caulfield Heron, came out fifth in an examination on the results of which sixteen scholarships were to be presented, and he determined to contest his right. On the two following Sundays he deliberately failed to present himself for communion, and on being questioned by the authorities, he declared he was a Catholic. On that count he was disqualified, and though he appealed to the College Visitors, they ruled against him in the end. Nevertheless the question had been raised in a highly acute form.[5]

It was to be answered by forces which went far beyond the problem of an Irish university, for the situation throughout the country was rapidly becoming critical. In 1840 O'Connell had founded the Repeal Association for repeal of the Union, and with the accession of the Young Ireland Party the movement had gained a strength which the government could no longer ignore. Monster meetings, attended by hundreds of thousands, were held all over the country, and though O'Connell himself was pacific in policy, Gavan Duffy in the *Nation*, the organ of the Young Irelanders, did not hesitate to adopt a menacing tone. The crisis came on October 8, 1843, when the last meeting of the year, scheduled for Clontarf on Dublin Bay, was banned by the government and troops were held ready to enforce the order. O'Connell capitulated, was charged with conspiracy, and received a heavy sentence which was immediately quashed by the House of Lords. Once again he put himself at the head of the movement and just at this juncture was aided by events from across the sea. The dispute over the Oregon boundary in America was bringing England and the United States to the verge of war, and the American claims were received sympathetically in a land that was already aroused. Obviously an outbreak in Ireland at this moment would have been disastrous, and Peel attempted to forestall the danger by a policy of conciliation. In the spring of 1845 he proposed three measures by which he hoped to redress the Irish grievances. The first was a Land Bill, which would compensate evicted tenants for improvements made by them in their holdings; the second was a bill tripling the annual grant to Maynooth College, the Catholic seminary for the training of priests; and the third was the so-called Queen's College Scheme. The first bill was lost, the second was passed, the third also passed but was hardly the measure that the Irish desired.[6]

The Queen's College Scheme boldly embraced a principle of education which had been developed on the Continent during the revolutionary era, had made rapid progress in France and Germany, and had recently been popularized in England through the writings of Joseph Lancaster and Lord Brougham.[7] This principle held that education was the prerogative of the state and hence that it must transcend the views of particular private societies, including those of the various religious denominations. Peel himself did not like the principle; he had fought against it when applied to Oxford, but he believed that in the particular situation it was the only one that could be adopted. Moreover, he felt that he had a precedent for it in the National Education Act of 1831. This act had established in Ireland a state system of primary education under which Catholic and Protestant children received common secular education but separate religious instruction. At the time it was regarded by most of the Irish as an advance upon anything previously offered, but in the following years the attitude of the hierarchy had begun to change. In the first place, "mixed education," as the practice of mingling pupils of various faiths was called, was a relatively new thing in Ireland, and it required time for the authorities to realize that a system which was objectionable in theory could not be made tolerable in practice, even as a temporary expedient. Thus in the beginning they were eager to make the best of it, and it was only later, when the impartiality of the system was gradually lost and it appeared that some members of the administering board, including Archbishop Whately, were using it as an instrument of proselytism, that a conflict developed among the Catholic bishops as to whether they should continue to cooperate at all. Some, such as John MacHale, archbishop of Tuam, said not; but a larger group, under Daniel Murray, archbishop of Dublin, were willing to compromise. In the end they were unable to agree among themselves and referred the matter to Rome, but the answer which they received in 1841 was cautious and indecisive.[8]

So doubtful, then, was the reception of the principle which Peel had now determined to extend to university education. Briefly, his proposal was to establish in Belfast, Cork, and either Limerick or Galway, colleges of university standing which should not become part of the University of Dublin but should constitute a new university, the Queen's University of Ireland. Both the colleges and the university would be strictly nonsectarian, and elaborate safeguards would be provided to keep them so. No religious tests would be permitted either at entrance or on admission to degrees, and no religious instruction except what the various sects might provide at their own expense. No topic of a religious nature was to be introduced into the lecture rooms, and religious considerations were not to weigh in the appointment or dismissal of professors. Trinity College, on the other hand, was to remain "entirely a Protestant foundation."[9]

In the course of the Parliamentary debate the measure was vigorously attacked by Sir Robert Inglis, the member from Oxford, as a "gigantic scheme of Godless education,"[10] and this phrase was taken up by O'Connell and used with such effect that "the Godless Colleges" became the common name for the new institutions among those who opposed them. There were many, of course, who welcomed the plan. The Young Irelanders, in particular, favored the bill, not because they were indifferent to religion but because they thought its interests could be adequately safeguarded at the same time that the urgent need for higher education was met. Also, the bringing together of Irishmen of all faiths was obviously congenial to their nationalist aspirations. O'Connell too had once favored mixed education, but gradually and with some indecision he had altered his views; and now, in the face of Peel's plan, he proposed an alternative arrangement whereby the college in Belfast would be controlled by the Presbyterians and those in Cork and Galway by the Catholic bishop of the diocese. "We feel," he said, "that the Presbyterian, the Protestant, the Dissenter, the Catholic, should be freely and separately educated. That is what we desire."

The Catholic bishops were similarly split and because of this were indecisive in their action. On May 23, a fortnight after the bill had been introduced, they issued a memorial proposing that a fair proportion of the professors in the new colleges should be Catholics, that dual chairs should be established in subjects which were controversial, and that provision should be made for dismissing any official who attempted to undermine the faith or injure the morals of the students.[11] On this they could agree, but on whether this meant that they were accepting or rejecting the principle of mixed education they could not agree. Toward the end of June they divided seventeen to eight against the Colleges Bill as it then stood, and on November 18, after the bill had become law, they decided unanimously to refer the matter to the Holy See.[12]

"Both her enemies and her admirers," writes Father McGrath, "are at one in claiming that Rome acts slowly, and it was just two years before an authoritative reply was received." [13] In the meantime several events had occurred which were destined to affect the future of the new colleges. The great potato famine of 1845 and the years following swept off a million persons, and the way in which the emergency was met deeply intensified the bitterness of the Irish toward any project which emanated from across St. George's Channel. At the same time the death of Gregory XVI in Rome brought into the papal chair a man whose hostility to mixed education was well known. Pius IX, while still cardinal bishop of Imola, had had circulated in his diocese a pastoral by Cardinal de Bonald, archbishop of Lyons, denouncing indifferentist education in the University of France; and after his succession to the papacy he complimented De Bonald upon his stand.[14] It was not surprising, then, that the same views were found to be embodied in the Rescript which finally was released by the Sacred Congregation of Propaganda on October 9, 1847. "Grave danger to the Catholic faith," said the Rescript, may be feared from the Queen's Colleges, and it admonished the Irish prelates "to take no part in them." [15]

The admonition was not regarded as final, however, and both sides in the controversy took steps to represent their views more fully at Rome. The minority, under Dr. Murray, were acting on the basis of certain changes which had been introduced into the bill before passage and which, on the assurance of Lord Clarendon, the Irish viceroy, would be embodied in the actual working statutes of the colleges. Before passage the bill had provided for loans to private religious bodies for the erection of residential halls where theological lectures might be given, and it was now proposed that three further modifications should be made. Each college should have as its visitors the archbishop of the province and bishop of the diocese in which it was situated; Catholic students

[127]

should have separate houses of residence; and deans should be appointed to supervise these houses. Notice of the modifications was at once forwarded to Rome, but two members of the opposing party, Dr. MacHale and Bishop O'Higgins, were soon there to counter its effect. "Most Holy Father," they urged, "time Anglos et dona ferentes." [16]

On October 11, 1848 the second Rescript from Propaganda confirmed the decision of the previous year, and with this document it was at last clear that those for whom the colleges were primarily intended would never be able to support them.[17] Even with this prospect of failure, however, the government was not discouraged from proceeding with its plans. Already collegiate buildings in the Gothic style were being erected on ten-acre sites in Belfast, Cork, and Galway, and toward the end of the year it was announced that the colleges would be inaugurated in October, 1849. Each one was to be provided with a staff of twenty professors in addition to a principal, registrar, librarian, and bursar, and in August, 1849 an imposing list of appointments appeared in the papers. To get students, forty-five junior scholarships of thirty pounds a year were offered in each of the colleges, and senior scholarships of fifty pounds were to be available later. So successful were these measures that on the announced dates the colleges did open with 223 students, of whom eighty were Catholics; and in the following September the Queen's University, a body for awarding degrees in arts, medicine, and law, also came into being.

In the original list of appointments seven out of the sixty professors had been Catholic, but in April, 1850 a third Rescript from Propaganda prohibited the clergy from holding any office in the colleges and laid on the bishops the obligation of discouraging their subjects from entering.[18] In order to formulate a common policy a National Synod was convoked at Thurles on August 22, which implemented the Rescript in a series of stringent decrees. No bishop was to cooperate in the administration of the colleges; the laity were to shun them as involving grave and intrinsic dangers to faith and morals; and the clergy were prohibited, under pain of suspension to be incurred *ipso facto*, from holding any office in them, whether as professors or as deans of discipline.[19] Nevertheless, although so decreeing, the bishops were again divided, and again the minority appealed to Rome, but this time the Pope's reply declared that the question was closed.[20]

Such is the history of those "Godless Colleges" which, with their counterpart at London, are the very antithesis of Newman's idea of a university. In their early years they barely struggled along, and there is no question that their difficulties were due almost entirely to the opposition of the ecclesiastical authorities. The authorities felt, however, that they could not do otherwise. "The system," said the Synodical Address of the Synod of Thurles, "may have been devised in a spirit of generous and impartial policy; but the statesmen who framed it were not acquainted with the inflexible nature of our doctrines, and with the jealousy with which we are obliged to avoid everything opposed to the purity and integrity of our faith." [21] Whether, if the colleges had been supported, those in Cork and Galway would not have become as purely Catholic as the surrounding population is a question that cannot be answered now, but the majority of the bishops did not think it wise to take the risk.

If the Queen's Colleges were to be put aside, however, some alternative must be offered in their place, for the need for higher education among Catholic youths was clearly apparent. This need had been recognized in both the first and second Rescripts from Propaganda, and the recommendation had been made, perhaps at the suggestion of Pope Pius himself, that a Catholic university be established in Ireland. For a time, little could be done to carry out this recommendation because one of the most determined members of the liberal minority was Dr. Crolly, the Archbishop of Armagh and Primate of All Ireland. In 1849, however, Dr. Crolly died, and he was replaced by a person of the opposite school, Dr. Paul Cullen, rector of the Irish College in Rome. Dr. Cullen, who was a friend of Dr. MacHale, had already been very active in Rome against the Queen's Colleges, and it was to him that the task was now entrusted of bringing their alternative into being. Unfortunately it was a task for which he was not altogether qualified. Having lived in Rome for the past twenty-nine years, he was out of touch with his own country and people. He tended to see in the Young Irelanders merely a counterpart of the godless followers of Mazzini, and being autocratic by temper, he thought that his own role in the situation was to bring this rough country into order by stern, unbending, Roman ways. Nevertheless he was a person of genuine zeal and piety, and although sometimes devious in his ways and conspiratorial in his mentality, he was never ungenerous or selfish, and he really believed in the project of a Catholic university. Thus at the Synod of Thurles, over which he presided, the establishment of the university was made a principal object, and a Catholic University Committee, consisting of the four archbishops, four bishops, eight priests, and eight laymen, was appointed to prepare the way. Its first work was to draw up an *Address to the People of Ireland*, informing them of the need for a university and of the character it ought to assume. "Is it not of the utmost consequence," inquired the *Address*, "that the education of our youth be Catholic? One of the greatest calamities of modern times is the separation of religion from science, whereas the perfection of knowledge is the union of both." From science without religion has arisen a spurious philosophy which results in civil anarchy, for we see everywhere that the standard-bearers of anarchy are "students of colleges and universities in which, according to the modern fashion, everything is taught but religion." [22] Other addresses followed in the early part of 1851, and on March 16 a collection was made throughout Ireland which brought in contributions totaling £22,840. It actually seemed as though the university would soon be a tangible reality.

CHAPTER 7

The *Discourses:* Composition
and Rhetoric

A perfect poem like *Lycidas,* a perfect fiction like *Esmond,* the perfect handling of a theory like Newman's *Idea of a University.* . . .
—Walter Pater, *Appreciations* (1889)

IT was at this point, in the spring of 1851, that Newman
first became involved in the Irish university question. Previously he had
known Dr. Cullen at Rome, where the latter had done him good offices
and had acted as the theological censor of his four Latin dissertations;
and since then he had received (and declined) an invitation to preach
at the dedication of a church in Dr. Cullen's diocese.[1] But now, on
April 15, 1851, Dr. Cullen wrote to Newman about the plans for the
new university and asked his advice on the selection of a superior, a vice-
president, and professors. Also, he concluded, "Should you have any intention of coming to Ireland this season, your presence at the meeting
of our committee in Dublin would be most useful. Indeed if you could
spare time to give us a few lectures on education, you would be rendering
good service to religion in Ireland." [2]

This is the first mention to Newman of those lectures which were
delivered the next year as *Discourses on University Education* and which
later were known under the more famous title, *The Idea of a University.*
The credit for suggesting them apparently belongs to Robert Whitty,
a young Irish priest, later a Jesuit, who had become friendly with Newman after his conversion. In a letter written near the end of the century
Whitty declared, "In one sentence of [Dr. Cullen's] letter of 1851 you
have the origin of Newman's 'Lectures on University Education.' During
my holidays in Ireland that year people complained bitterly at not being
able to *get at* Newman. He would not dine out, he would not preach
Charity Sermons or any Sermons. And so talking one day to Lucas in
Kingstown we hit on the idea of his giving a course of lectures and I
knowing the weight of a Bishop's word and wish with Cardinal Newman,
there and then wrote to Archbishop Cullen." [3] The resulting invitation
was acknowledged by Newman on April 16. "There is nothing at all,"

he wrote, "which I can feel more interest in than the subject of Irish Education - yet I do not know how I can possibly promise myself the pleasure of the visit in question." [4] As to the appointments, a fortnight later he sent a list of ten persons who struck him as fit candidates for professorships, but he thought of no one, he said, who was qualified to be the superior.[5]

The matter was to be settled very soon. On July 8 Dr. Cullen called on Newman at Birmingham to discuss the university and then, going on to London to consult with James Hope, Manning, William Monsell, and others, wrote back requesting Newman to join them there.[6] Hope added his voice to that of Dr. Cullen, for "there is no one whom I have yet met," he wrote, "who has any *view* (an Oriel Term I think,) which one can either accept, or, by antagonism, make the parent of another. All seems insulated and partial, and so the strength of all is comparatively useless." [7] Newman, on the other hand, realized that "all things are parts of a whole and must be done on an idea," [8] and by virtue of his Oxford experience he possessed the idea of a university. Unhappily, Newman was still busy with his lectures on the *Present Position of Catholics* and so was unable to come to the London meeting, but Dr. Cullen called again on his way back to Ireland and reported what they had done.[9] They had agreed that the university should be started informally, without statutes, and that the rector and his assistants should govern it according to their discretion until experience had taught them how to establish it in a more regular way. "Our whole idea then depends on the *men* who start it," and it was the wish of the committee, which Dr. Cullen now formally expressed, that Newman should allow himself to be made the rector.[10]

Newman's first reaction was that prefect of studies would suit him better. It would commit him less, would interfere less with his duties at the Oratory, and if necessary would be a temporary office, whereas "a Rectorship was almost identified with the University itself." [11] No sooner had he settled this with Dr. Cullen, however, than his own people clamored that he should be rector. It was *infra dig*, they said, for one who was their superior to be a subordinate elsewhere, and besides he could do more good for the university if he were fully in charge. So Hope and Faber and others also advised,[12] and therefore on July 23 Newman wrote to Dr. Cullen that his only desire was "to do as much work for the University as possible with *as little absence as possible* from this place. This problem being satisfied, I do not care what you are pleased to make me." [13] From this point on it was pretty well agreed, though without any formal commitment on either side, that Newman would be rector of the new university.

For the time being he was simply one of a subcommittee of three appointed to report on the best mode of establishing the university. The other two members were the Rev. Patrick Leahy, later archbishop of Cashel, and Myles O'Reilly, a country gentleman educated at the London University.[14] The two of them arrived in Birmingham on August 27, bringing with them a list of questions which they had drawn up and which they proposed, in accordance with their instructions, to send to various Catholics eminent in the world of education. The questions, which Newman revised slightly before they were sent out, concerned all aspects of the structure and organization of the university, its mode of teaching and internal discipline, its site, the time of beginning, and the steps it should take to secure a charter for granting degrees.[15] Answers to the questions were slow in coming in, but on September 30 Newman and T. W. Allies, an Oxford convert who was serving as secretary to the subcommittee, proceeded to Thurles in Ireland to consult with Dr. Leahy and Mr. O'Reilly and to draw up their report.[16] This document, which runs to about ten pages, contains Newman's first thinking about the organization of the new university.[17]

Following the medieval tradition, the university was to consist of four faculties, arts, medicine, law, and theology, and the first of these would be subdivided into letters and science and would have as a subsidiary a school of engineering. Only the faculty of arts would be founded in the near future, however, and therefore it alone is described in detail. It will embody a four-year course leading to the B.A. degree with further years of study for the degree of Master. The branches of study will be "Latin; Greek; the Semitic and Modern Languages; History, Ancient and Modern, both National and Ecclesiastical; Archaeology, Christian and Profane; English Literature, and Criticism." In science the studies will be "Logic, Metaphysics, Ethics, including Economy and Politics; Philosophy of Religion; Mathematics; Natural Philosophy; Chemistry; Natural History; Mineralogy and Geology, etc., etc." [18] For the more important of these studies professors will be appointed; for the less important, such as the natural sciences and the modern foreign languages, lecturers; but both the one sort and the other will also work as tutors, for it is expected that the advantages of both systems of instruction will be combined.

The government of the university will be committed to a rector, nominated by the bishops, and he will be assisted by a vice-rector, deans of discipline, a secretary, and a bursar. The vice-rector (though this later became a touchy point with Newman) was to be nominated by the bishops, the other officials by the rector subject to the approval of the archbishops, and the professors by the archbishops on the nomination of the rector. The professors of each faculty were to have the power to elect their own dean and secretary and to draw up the sessional program of studies for the approbation of the rector. The deans of the various faculties together with the vice-rector will form the Rectorial Council, to be assembled by the rector when he deems it necessary; and the rector, vice-rector, secretary, and professors will form the Academic Senate, which shall be the legislating body of the university and which, after a period of ten years, shall be enriched by such a number of graduates as does not exceed one-fourth of the entire body. "All the Officers and Professors of the University," says the report, "shall be required upon entering into possession of their office to make a Profession of the Catholic Faith according to the form of Pope Pius IV," and they shall be bound, "not only not to teach anything contrary to Religion, but to take advantage of the occasion the subjects they treat of may offer, to point out that Religion is the basis of Science, and to inculcate the love of Religion and its duties." [19]

It is interesting to note that in the organization proposed for the university there is very little to suggest Oxford. The colleges, which form the most prominent feature of the English university, are simply missing, and although the Rectorial Council might at first suggest the Hebdomadal Board and the Senate the Oxford House of Convocation, there is really no resemblance between them. The Senate, indeed, is more nearly akin to the ancient House of Congregation, which had fallen into decay at Oxford and was not to be restored to its powers until the Oxford University Bill of 1854. Actually, however, the model for the government of the university was not Oxford but the University of Louvain, founded by the Belgian bishops in 1834. It had been specially pointed out in the first Rescript of Propaganda as an example for the Irish bishops to keep in view, and although its distinguished rector, Msgr. F. X. de Ram, did not reply to the subcommittee's questions in time to influence their report, the printed statutes and *Annuaire* of the university were available, and its organization was common knowledge among Catholic circles in Europe.[20] It, too, was governed by a rector who was ultimately responsible to the bishops, had a *Conseil rectoral* composed of the vice-rector and the deans of faculties, and of course had the traditional four faculties, but with an added faculty of science distinct from that of philosophy and letters.

Newman stayed in Ireland a week, drawing up the report, discussing it with Dr. Cullen at Drogheda, and talking with persons interested in the university. He came home a little dismayed—*Quot homines, tot fuere sententiae* [21]—but he was even more dismayed when the University Committee merely read the report at its October meeting and deferred approval until the following month. "Great matters *will* take time," he knew, "but this suspense is a great nuisance." [22] Nevertheless, at the next meeting on November 12, the committee adopted the report as the "fundamental rules" of the university, and it also requested Newman "to allow himself to be named the first President of the Catholic University of Ireland." [23] The request, wrote Dr. Cooper of the Pro-Cathedral, was passed "not only unanimously, but with an acclaim not loud, but most cordial." [24]

Newman's impatience at the delay was partly due to his desire to get on with the lectures which he had promised to Dr. Cullen and which he did not expect to deliver unless he were called to Ireland as rector. But the "damp and doubt" [25] which this uncertainty cast upon him was as nothing compared with the anxiety he was soon to suffer from the Achilli trial. There are many literary classics which have acquired an additional interest from the fact that they were written in prison, but the *Idea of a University* is not one of these. In many ways it might have been a better book if it were, for instead of being composed under the tranquil circumstances which prison affords, it was composed under the stress of the author's believing, and yet not knowing, that he might any day be sent to prison—and in these circumstances it seems wonderful that it was composed at all. The stages of its conception, its oral delivery, and its publication coincide in a remarkable way with the various stages of the unfolding of the trial, almost as if that affliction had been designed by some advocate of the Queen's Colleges to impede the production of the work which was preparing against them. Thus it was in July, 1851, the very month when the prospect of the rectorship was first opened by Dr. Cullen, that Newman delivered the lecture which was the basis of the libel suit that followed. The lectures on the *Present Position of Catholics*, it will be recalled, were designed to meet the "no-Popery" sentiment which had been aroused in England by the re-establishment of the hierarchy in 1850, and in the fifth of the series Newman took notice of Dr. Giacinto Achilli, a former Dominican friar who had become a popular hero in London by exposing the scandals of the Roman inquisition. He himself had already been exposed by Cardinal Wiseman in the *Dublin Review* as a person notorious in his own country for the crimes of rape and adultery; and Newman simply repeated in his lecture the detailed charges which Wiseman had made. He did not do this without taking counsel on the wisdom of the step, but his counsel misjudged the boldness of the enemy, and so in August, as Newman was conferring with Dr. Leahy about the university, there came rumors of Achilli's intended action. The rumors proved true, and throughout all the next year Newman was torn between thoughts about the university and thoughts for his own defense. As he wrote the serene prose of the opening discourses, he was wrestling with the problem, first of finding the various women whom Achilli had violated, then of transporting them from Italy and keeping them and their families happy through the interminable delays, and finally of somehow raising the money for all this and for his lawyers' fees. What with the uncertainty of the date, it was even difficult to know when he could deliver the lectures; but finally, between the various postponements of the trial, he managed to go over to Dublin, speak, and come back again in time to be present at his conviction on June 25. Then he must await judgment, and during this period he composed the last of his discourses, so that when he appeared in court on January 31, 1853, to be fined one hundred pounds and lectured by the judge on the deterioration of his character, he knew that two days later there would be published the first collected edition of a work which testifies to the contrary. On its opening page it bears a dedication to the Catholics all over the world who contributed the twelve thousand pounds which the trial had cost.

> In grateful never-dying remembrance
> Of his many friends and benefactors,
> Living and dead,
> At home and abroad,
> In Ireland, Great Britain, France,
> In Belgium, Germany, Poland, Italy, and Malta,
> In North America, and other countries,
> Who, by their resolute prayers and penances,
> And by their generous stubborn efforts,
> And by their munificent alms,
> Have broken for him the stress
> Of a great anxiety,
> THESE DISCOURSES,
> Offered to Our Lady and St. Philip on its rise,
> Composed under its pressure,
> Finished on the eve of its termination,
> Are respectfully and affectionately inscribed.

In asking Newman to deliver the lectures on university education, Dr. Cullen had not defined the precise subject, but it gradually became clear that he was not without an opinion on this matter. On September 15, in mentioning again the need for "a few lectures on education," he added that "it would be necessary to put many persons' ideas right on this subject." [26] Newman replied that he was most willing to give the lectures, but he considered he ought to know something about the state

[136]

of public opinion in Ireland on the subject of education, and also "your own ideas what [the] lectures ought to be about. . . . I do not see I could do them well," he added, "unless I did them with a good deal of thought. But, as a first condition, I should like to have the *definite* subjects to be treated of from your Grace." [27] Dr. Cullen's reply, which was written from Liverpool on September 20, may be given in full, for it has never been published before and it contains the instructions which Newman was supposed to follow in writing the first half of the *Idea of a University.*

I am very much obliged to you for your kindness in thinking of the subject for lectures which I mentioned. What we want in Ireland is to persuade the people that education should be religious. The whole tendency of our new system is to make it believed that education may be so conducted as to have nothing at all to do with religion. Moral philosophy, law, history are proposed to be taught in this way. The project is in itself absurd and impossible, but it is necessary to instruct us a little upon the matter. To do so however I suppose the whole question of education should be reviewed. The subjects or some of the subjects might be the advantages of educating the people and the sort of education they ought to receive - Mixed education - Examination of the education given to Catholics in Trinity College and its effects - education in the Queen's Colleges, or education without any religion - The sort of education which Catholics ought to seek for - I have thrown out these subjects without order and merely to give some little idea of what we want - You will easily understand what will suit us best - There is one fine subject which should not be omitted - the services rendered by the Catholic church and its Pontiffs to literature - But you will best know what points to select, and how to treat them. [28]

"My subjects . . . ," wrote Newman to a friend shortly before he was to deliver his first lectures, "will seem *dry* - but (in confidence) they were suggested by high authority." [29] Dr. Cullen was the "high authority," and if Newman's first few lectures do seem dry to some persons, one can only consider what they would have been if he had followed more closely the suggestions in this letter. Doubtless he foresaw the difficulty and so replied rather vaguely: "Thank you for the subjects you mention for Lectures. They are most important ones - but will take a long time thinking out." [30]

Nevertheless he promised to turn his mind to the subject at once, and on his return from meeting with the subcommittee at Thurles on October 9, 1851, he did actively begin work. [31] The great difficulty was that

"I ought to know something of the state of feeling of my audience before I actually do any thing." [32] His week in Ireland had shown him the complexity of these feelings but had done nothing to help him understand them, and he realized that he needed advisers. There were three persons whom he knew sufficiently well to turn to—Frederick Lucas, Robert Ornsby, and Henry Wilberforce—all of them Englishmen, converts to Catholicism, and now resident in Dublin. Lucas, who had been longest in Ireland, was editor of the *Tablet*, a weekly Catholic paper which he had founded in 1840, a year after his conversion. He was a personal friend of Dr. MacHale but, being strong for Repeal, bitterly at odds with Dr. Cullen. Newman also disliked his politics but thought him "an honest good man." [33] Ornsby, who was assistant editor of the *Tablet*, was better known to Newman, for he had been Fellow and Lecturer of Trinity College, Oxford; and Wilberforce, the brother of the Oriel tutor, was one of the dearest of Newman's friends, his pupil at Oxford, his follower to Rome, and now his harbinger to Ireland as secretary of the newly formed Catholic Defense Association.

The picture of Irish society which Newman received from these three friends, whether it was accurate or not, was that from which he worked in planning the rhetoric of his opening lectures. He was told, in the first place, that even among the educated classes in Ireland there was wanting the very conception of a university such as Oxford was and of the culture which a university gave. At Trinity College, Dublin, they read authors like Dugald Stewart and Thomas Brown, and at the Catholic colleges the whole emphasis was on "useful knowledge . . . , natural philosophy, mechanics, declamation, etc." Their Latin and Greek, correct as far as it went, was limited to a few authors, and they had no conception of how these might be used in forming the mind. Indeed, the very idea of the special studies of a university was wanting to their mind, and they "require[d] to be taught, and to have an idea imparted to them, what Oxford really was, and what it did for those who were educated there." [34]

Further, he was told that he would find very little instinctive Catholic feeling among his auditors. As one went farther down in the ranks of society, the instincts of Catholicity were more true, but among the upper classes people were almost imbued with Protestant ideas, and that without realizing it. They would read Carlyle, for instance, without *feeling* that he was hostile to the faith; and once when Ornsby had tried to give an Irish Catholic, a very intelligent man in his way, some notion of the ideals of the Tractarian movement—its admiration of the life of perfection, of fasting, and so forth—the man replied, "Well, all that would be totally new in this country." [35]

As to the question of mixed education, Newman was told that there was nothing about the education that was more "mixed" than the question itself. It was not merely that the bishops were divided—Dr. Cullen being for an education which was religious before all, Dr. MacHale for an education which was Irish before all, and Dr. Murray for an education which could be had only from a government that was neither Irish nor religious—but it was also that the bishops were divided from the more influential of the laity. The lower classes, of course, would follow Dr. Cullen or Dr. MacHale and contribute their pennies whenever they were told, but it was not from them that students would come or by their support that the university would live. It was the upper classes whose support was needed, and they, for the most part, were so far wanting in true Catholic instincts as to side with Dr. Murray in openly preferring the Queen's Colleges. There were several reasons for this. One was the matter of personal consistency. For years, under the liberal bishops of the twenties and thirties, equal rights in education—that is, mixed schools—had been all the cry, and now the persons who had joined in that cry suddenly found that they were required to put aside their seasoned opinions and adopt new ones. This they resented, so much so that Newman later found they would refuse even to allow their names to be inscribed on the books of the university, lest this be taken to imply "the abandonment of their opinions, and a compromise of their consistency." [36] A second reason was put to Lucas in this way: "The question is in a pretty state. Where is the line of demarcation to be drawn? . . . in the abstract, or if one could make a world of one's own, separate education would be the true thing. But in this island where people are mixed and society is mixed, education must be so." Indeed, to many people one of the advantages of mixed education was that it brought together persons of various faiths and so promised a solution of Irish discord. Add to this, wrote Lucas, "the further belief that Government aid is indispensable and can only be had for mixed education—you will have a notion of ¾ths of that part of the attachment to the Colleges which is honest." [37] By the "dishonest" part he meant all those Catholics who had recently been enabled to rise in the world by the relief legislation and who saw that advancement in their own profession and the further advancement of their children were closely linked with the success of the government scheme. Honest or dishonest, this was a highly important group.

From the letters of his friends it gradually became clear to Newman what a touchy and delicate situation it was that Dr. Cullen was getting him into. The Irish were having a quarrel over education, and he, as a distinguished Englishman, was being called in to settle it. He was to take it upon himself "to teach the Paddies what education was, what a University, and how it was their duty to have one with me for a Rector," [38] and he rightly feared that it would require all his rhetorical skill to do this. He sincerely believed in the cause which he had been called in to defend, but he was not willing to attack the Queen's Colleges, or Trinity College, in the open way that Dr. Cullen's letter had suggested. If Dr. Cullen had dirty work to do, he ought to do it himself or get an Irishman to do it; and therefore, as the Archbishop continued to write reminding him of the lectures, Newman began to prepare him for not finding in them exactly what he had hoped. "As to the subjects on which I propose to lecture," he wrote, "I have kept your paper of instructions in view - but I cannot tell how far I shall *advance* towards the fulfillment of them. I suspect that it will take a long while to lay the *foundations*. I suppose I shall almost confine myself to the great subject of the connection of religion with literature and science. What I think I shall do is this - to *get ready* some three or four lectures to start with - but, as to what is to follow, to be guided by what I hear said of the first three or four, by friends and enemies. I must *feel* my way." [39] This did not altogether please Dr. Cullen (although he said that it did), and he at once returned to the charge. "The system you propose to follow will answer perfectly well. It will be necessary however to make an effort to form a public opinion in Ireland on the necessity of uniting religion with education. The great mass of our people understand this very well - but those who have been educated in Trinity college and other protestant establishments such as our Lawyers, Doctors, etc. are very unsound in their opinions. All those also who are looking up to Lord Clarendon for promotion or otherwise depending on his government are obliged to be nearly protestant in their notions. Altogether it will not be easy to set us right - but your lectures will I am persuaded produce a most powerful effect." [40]

Newman, alas! was not so confident. How was he, a total stranger to the situation, to "set right" the persons who knew it so much better than himself? And as to "powerful effects," he had a notion that these were produced, not by hitting one's audience over the head, but rather by finding some point of agreement with them, and then, when a common feeling had been established, leading them quietly on to positions they would have shied at in the first instance. The problem, of course, was to find that point of agreement, and as Newman considered the matter, he felt that it might be found in his own experience at Oxford. "It struck me," he wrote Ornsby, "and my judgment was confirmed on consulting another, that, as I was addressing the English party, I mean, the Dublin Barristers &c &c, I was rhetorically safe in appealing to my antecedents. And then again I found the view variously brought out by old Catholics that 'the new University must be *as good as* Oxford—' And then again, why was I chosen except as having been connected with the English Universities - " [41] Surely Oxford was the point on which they could agree, and then, in subsequent lectures, he would gradually tell them about the controversy in which Oxford, although it was Protestant, had repudiated the principle of mixed education some twenty years before.

By adopting this strategy Newman was naturally led to review his life at Oxford, and he was assisted in this task by a happy accident. During the early months of 1852 the Oratorians were engaged in moving from their house in Alcester Street to the new building in Edgbaston, and as everyone knows, when one moves, his entire life passes before his eyes and even under his hands. So it was with Newman. It was on April 3 that he "finished getting in all my books and papers into my room at Edgbaston," [42] and only one who has seen that room, with the papers filling the cupboards from floor to ceiling of one entire wall and part of another, can appreciate what that means. For Newman was one of those persons who saved every scrap of paper which ever came into his hands, and thus, as he moved from his rooms at Oriel to the house at Littlemore and then to Maryvale and Alcester Street and Edgbaston, he was followed by a growing train of wooden boxes which contained the record, quite wonderful in extent, of all his outward and inward life. Obviously, if he now wished to review that life, he did not have to review it in memory, for he had before him the very papers in which it was recorded. He could take up and read his first exercises at Trinity, his themes, his Latin verses, his problems, and the book containing his hours of study in preparing for the Schools. He could see what questions he had been asked at Oriel and what questions he himself had thought proper to ask others. He could check over the account he had written in 1830 of his quarrel with Hawkins, and in the letters from Froude and Pusey and Keble he could reconstruct their efforts to revive the ancient form of college and university. He was the more inclined to do this because, as he put his papers in their places and felt how much of his past life they contained, he was "all this time thinking I might have to leave them for prison." [43] He sorted them out not merely as one does who is moving but also (so he wrote to Mrs. Bowden) "as if I were dying." [44] He tied them up in packets and labeled them, he wrote comments on them for some future biographer or literary executor, and all the time he did this he was simultaneously composing the first three discourses of the *Idea of a University*. Obviously, if these discourses contain so much that belongs to Oxford, if they delighted Isaac Williams because "he remembered so many of the allusions in them, and they recalled to his mind jokes between you and Hurrell," [45] it was partly because they were written in a period when Newman was steeping himself in the memories of his Oxford years.

Even after Newman had decided upon his rhetoric, however, the composition of the lectures gave him infinite difficulty. "My Lectures," he wrote to Ornsby, "have taken me more trouble than any one could by a stretch of fancy conceive - I have written almost reams of paper, - finished, set aside - then taken them up again, and plucked them—and so on. The truth is, I have the utmost difficulty of writing to people I do not know, and I commonly have failed when I have addressed strangers, as in the St Isidore's Oration at Rome." [46] The Irish were certainly strangers, but in this instance ignorance about them was more soothing than the knowledge which Newman was rapidly acquiring. Hardly a packet crossed the channel which did not bring him letters, from persons known to him and unknown, but all at one in the alarming picture which they presented of the Irish character. What was he to think when a reverend ecclesiastic, later an archbishop, wrote to him begging a place in the new university and warning him "not to heed as regards my humble self the opinion of *one particular person* in Ireland with whom you will certainly fall in" and who is "not very scrupulous in dealing with others." [47] Or what when he received a sixteen-page letter from an anonymous Catholic convert who offered to give him the information he would certainly need if he were to keep afloat in Irish society? As to the Protestant upper classes, wrote his informant, "I consider them the most despicable vermin on the face of the earth, they unite in their persons the vulgarity of the English and the brutality of the Irish . . . they have an innate and diabolical hatred of truth and justice in small and great matters. They do not blush for the avowal of sentiments which any respectable Englishman would be ashamed to entertain. . . . They are liars to an incredible degree, indeed I am sorry to say this vice is general to almost all the Irish especially in the neighborhood of Dublin. They would rather tell a lie than the truth on the most indifferent subjects. . . . Indeed Irish society might be described as a collection of vulgar unprincipled protestant bullies and Catholic slaves. As to the lower class of protestants, poor creatures, they are worse than the upper, having neither the promise of this life nor of that which is to come; they are either ferocious, brutal Orangemen, or drivelling [illegible] Methodists, and as a body fearfully immoral. . . . This is the dark side of the picture. . . ." The bright side was the Irish peasants—"faithful, affectionate, devoted Catholics, the most edifying spectacle I have witnessed. . . . their principal fault is a sad disposition to tell lies." [48]

Such letters were not very reassuring to Newman about the character of the people he was going to address, but it was even less reassuring to discover, as he gradually did, how set was the bitterness against his own race. When his friend Wilberforce had been appointed secretary of the Catholic Defense Association there had been a violent uproar against the choice of an Englishman, and now, in appointments to be made for the university, Newman found the same feelings at work. He realized that most of the positions would have to be filled by Irishmen, but since the beginning was to be informal and depend chiefly on the "men," he wanted to have two or three about him who were perfectly familiar with his own ideas and could work closely and easily with him. But every time he broached the subject of such an appointment he found that it was taboo, and Dr. Cullen would write darkly of "some ultra-zealous patriots," a set of newspaper editors, who were trying to "get up an agitation against every thing English" and might injure the university if once they were given a cause.[49]

This was provoking enough, but it was not until the middle of April, three weeks before the lectures were to begin, that Newman actually became alarmed. Ornsby had passed on the remark, dropped by Lucas, that it would be unwise of Newman to stay with his friend Wilberforce when he came to Dublin, because "there was already a strong feeling against the English party, and . . . any thing which would tend to make it appear a kind of set was being formed, would be liable to be laid hold of, if, as was very likely, an outcry on the subject were raised."[50] Newman was dismayed. If he could not even lodge with his own friend because he was an Englishman, what business had he in making Oxford the whole subject of his opening lecture? From ignorance of the situation his careful rhetoric was all wrong, and he saw now that he had much better have pretended he was from some other university, or from none at all, than thus to have advertised his connection with England. "I assure you," he wrote to Ornsby, "I have no security to myself that the Lectures will not be from beginning to end a failure - from my not knowing my audience."[51]

The reply that came back, from both Ornsby and Wilberforce, was reassuring. The former declared that the plan of beginning with Oxford was excellent, for "there is so much interest felt about you personally, and at the same time so much ignorance both about yourself and about Oxford, that the curiosity of your audience will be sure to drink in all that, and it will clear the way admirably for what follows."[52] Wilberforce sent a message from James O'Ferrall, a member of the University Committee, that "no such feeling really exists as you Englishmen fancy. . . . There are *very few* people who really feel it - chiefly Dr MacHale."[53] This was good news, and Newman wrote that it "relieves my difficulty in great measure about introducing Oxford - nevertheless it is the Archbishop of Tuam [Dr. MacHale] and his party I fear as much as any, so I shall merely feel my way in my first Lectures, and say little about the place." [54]

The lectures were originally planned for early in March but had to be postponed to the end of April because of the trial.[55] No sooner was this arranged, however, than the trial was changed to either April 20 or May 10, and so the lectures were again deferred till the first week in May. This time a hitch developed about the room,[56] and Newman, who had finished the first three lectures by April 10, took advantage of the delay to get through as much of the next two as he could.[57] Meanwhile, he thought it would be proper, things being as delicate as they were, to ask formal leave for the lectures of Dean Meyler, the vicar-general of the diocese in which they were to be given, but Dr. Cooper, to whom he sent the request, replied that it was unnecessary. "But as your intended letter for him is couched in such kind terms," he wrote, "I purpose reading it for him hoping it may exercise a soothing and conciliatory effect upon his mind." [58] By this time Newman may have felt that his own mind needed soothing too, for on May 2 he suddenly learned that the trial was again put off until June and that if he was going to lecture at all he had better do so at once. Immediately he wrote Ornsby to engage him a room—"and if I could have a low iron bed with a single hard mattress and no curtains, it would be the greatest boon you could do for me." [59] Then, at the last moment, a letter arrived from the secretary of the Irish Church Missions, a proselytizing body of the Established Church, speaking of "the intense interest which is felt by the Citizens of Dublin to learn the reasons which have induced you to abandon the Church of England for that of Rome" and begging him "to meet the Revd John O'Callaghan . . . (who is a convert from the Church of Rome) in the round room of the Rotunda, when by your respective statements, as to the reasons which induced you to abandon the churches of your fore-fathers, the public will be materially assisted in coming to a decision as to which church has the strongest claim upon their allegiance." [60] Happily Newman was already beyond the reach of this plea, for on Friday, May 7, he had taken the night boat to Dublin, and on the next Monday, at three in the afternoon, he appeared in the Exhibition Room of the Rotunda to deliver his first university discourse.[61]

Most readers today are familiar with this lecture only in the form which it took some twenty years later after two extensive revisions. In that form, with "much temporary, collateral, or superfluous matter" [62] removed, it has become a classic; but if one wishes to see how Newman met the problem of his original audience in 1852, one must return to the first edition. His problem, of course, was to come out strongly enough against mixed education so as to satisfy Dr. Cullen and yet to do it in such a way as not to alienate the party which favored the Colleges. Moreover, he must somehow, in the course of his remarks, contrive to render an Englishman who was a recent convert acceptable to Irishmen who were Catholics of long standing, and he must accomplish all these various tasks without sacrificing either the sincerity or the consistency of his views. In general, his method was to begin with an allusion to Protestant Oxford in his own day and end with Catholic Ireland in the time of her ancient greatness, for in these two places he found symbols of the opposing tempers to which he would have to appeal. Therefore, as he began, his tone was measured and dry, even harsh. The views on education which he had learned at Oxford were those of "an heretical seat of learning," and he would not have introduced them to this body except for the fact, not wonderful in itself, that they happened to be correct. Not wonderful, he had said, because the question was not one of theology but simply of practical wisdom and good sense, and that was the mode in which he proposed to treat it. He added, for the sake of the clergy, that he would not have presumed to treat it in any other way before an audience of which they formed a part, but his rationalistic approach was chiefly designed for the lawyers and doctors of Dublin. Many of them were already skeptical of the university as a project desired by the clergy for their own purposes, and therefore to be told that its principles were attainable simply by practical wisdom and good sense and that these principles had long been entertained by a university which was not even Catholic, though it was the greatest in the English-speaking world—this was as forceful an argument as any that could be devised, and certainly by the mid-point of his lecture Newman must have had the liberal party convinced of his absolute good faith. As he continued, he casually disassociated himself from the decision at Thurles which had rejected the Queen's Colleges, and he candidly admitted that he could not argue about the practical difficulties involved. Of these his hearers knew far better than he, but in the face of these difficulties he had one refuge, one only plea, which was that "Peter had spoken." And with the lovely passage which follows, where Newman vindicates the practical sagacity of the pope through all the ages, the rhetoric of the lecture entirely changes. The arid, argumentative manner is gone, and the language becomes warm and loving.

> After all, Peter has spoken. Peter is no recluse, no abstracted student, no dreamer about the past, no doter upon the dead and gone, no projector of the visionary. Peter for eighteen hundred years has lived in the world . . . he has shaped himself for all emergencies.

> . . . He came first upon an age of refinement and luxury like our
> own, and in spite of the persecutor fertile in the resources of his
> cruelty, he soon gathered, out of all classes of society, the slave, the
> soldier, the high-born lady, and the sophist, to form a people for
> his Master's honour. The savage hordes came down in torrents from
> the north, hideous even to look upon; and Peter went out with holy
> water and with benison, and by his very eye he sobered them and
> backed them in full career. They turned aside, and flooded the whole
> earth, but only to be more surely civilized by him, and to be made
> ten times more his children even than the older populations they
> had overwhelmed.[63]

So in all the ages the side of Peter is shown to be the winning side, and
if Newman later said of this passage that he was a "poor innocent" [64]
when he wrote it, nevertheless he believed it at the time, and it must
have dispelled from the minds of his hearers any lingering doubt that
this convert was not fully converted.

But it was the Archbishop of Tuam and his party that Newman
chiefly feared, and so in the end the lecture turns from Oxford and
Rome to ancient Ireland, and the listener is carried back, in a lyric
passage of historical evocation, to the period when his own nation was
the cradle of learning for all Europe and when the two sister islands
were one in their faith, and

> nothing passed between them, and no personal aims were theirs,
> save the interchange of kind offices and the rivalry of love. . . .
>
> The past never returns; the course of things, old in its texture, is
> ever new in its colouring and fashion. Ireland and England are not
> what they once were, but Rome is where it was; Peter is the same; his
> zeal, his charity, his mission, his gifts, are the same. He, of old time,
> made us one by making us joint teachers of the nations; and now,
> surely, he is giving us a like mission, and we shall become one again,
> while we zealously and lovingly fulfil it.[65]

"You are all expecting news," wrote Newman the next day to his
fellow Oratorians,

> and I have no one to be my trumpeter. . . .
>
> The Lecture, I suppose, thanks to our dear Lady, has been a hit,
> and now I am beginning to be anxious lest the others should not duly
> follow up the blow. The word "hit" is Dr. Cooper's word.
>
> The room is very good for my purpose, being very small. It is just
> the room I like, barring want of light; I cannot make myself heard to

many, and few care to hear me; paucorum hominum sum. The room holds, say 400 - and was nearly full. Mr Duffy whom I met in the train to Kingstown after it, said he had never seen so literary an assemblage - all the intellect, almost, of Dublin was there. There were 13 Trinity fellows &c. eight Jesuits, a great many clergy - and most intense attention. When I say that Dean Meyler was much pleased, I mean to express that I did not offend Dr Murray's friends. Surgeon O'Reilly, who is the representative perhaps of a class of laity, though too good a Catholic perhaps for my purpose, and who on Saturday had been half arguing with me against the University, said, when the Lecture was ended, that "the days of Mixed Education were numbered." Don't you suppose I am fool enough to think I have done any great things yet - it is only good as far as it goes. I trust it could not be better, as far as it goes - but it goes a very little way. . . .

Dr Moriarty, whom I made censor beforehand, was the first who gave me encouragement, for he seemed most pleased with the Lecture - and spoke of its prudence, and said it went with the Queen's College party just as far as it was possible.

I was heard most distinctly, or rather my voice so filled the room and I had such perfect command of it, that people *would not believe* I could not be heard in a great Church - but I know myself better. It was just the room I have ever coveted, and never had. The room will be fuller next week. There were a number of ladies, and I *fancied* a slight sensation in the room, when I said, not Ladies and Gentlemen, but Gentlemen.[66]

Only one slip had Newman made. In conceding to his opponents the practical difficulties of a Catholic university, he had said, "I cannot give a direct answer to their objections, nor do I pretend to do so." [67] Several of the clergy thought this was too strong,[68] and so in the proofs Newman altered the passage to read that, although he did not "mean here to give a direct answer to their objections," he did not say an answer could not be given, and indeed, he was confident it could.[69] Apart from this, the reaction was favorable. A long report of the lecture appeared in the papers [70] and was even published separately under the title, *Powerful Lecture of the very Rev. John Henry Newman, D.D. . . . on University Education.*[71] The editor of the *Dublin Evening Post*, a known advocate of mixed education, heard "the greater part [of the lecture] with approval, and almost every part with an acquiescence, somewhat qualified, we admit." [72] But for some listeners it seemed difficult to follow. Thus one person said that "The Doctor gave very good lectures, but rather *abstract*," and a Protestant paper accused him of "having too *many ideas.*" [73] "Never a truer word," wrote Newman, "than the Protestant's that I have too many ideas in Lecture 1. But if they were all to be developed, they would make the whole volume." In the same letter he added, "I am amused at the great cleverness of the Irish, which far surpasses any thing I ever saw elsewhere. The very ticket takers in the room followed my arguments, and gave me an analysis of the Discourse afterwards. The printer makes most judicious remarks and alterations in the proof - always clever and well meant, though generally wrong." [74] Among these, perhaps, was the printer of the *Freeman's Journal,* who had St. Peter going out against the barbarians "with holy water and with venison!" [75]

Newman's original plan had been to publish each lecture in the *Tablet* and also as a pamphlet at sixpence each, and before he had come over to Dublin he inquired about a good Irish publisher, for he realized it "would not be courteous going to an Englishman." [76] But now he found himself violently attacked as "anti-Irish" for giving Lucas a "monopoly" of the lectures, and so in disgust he withdrew them from the *Tablet* and simply presented the entire first edition of 2,500 copies to James Duffy, the official publisher to Archbishop Cullen. [77] He was immediately annoyed at himself for the loss of the money, but the Fathers agreed that he had done right. "You must teach the good folk manners," wrote Ambrose, "but I don't see why you should not take what he [Duffy] thinks fit to give you." [78] There is no record that Duffy ever thought fit to give Newman anything, but the lectures were nicely printed in octavo, each one about a week after delivery. [79]

Despite his initial success Newman became increasingly anxious as the time of the second lecture approached. He learned that he would not have the same room as before, for the ladies of the St. Vincent de Paul Charity were holding a Grand Bazaar there. His new room, moreover, would be "*much* larger and higher," and "so I am thrown upon the anxiety which I always feel before knowing how I shall be heard." [80] Indeed, by the day of the lecture he was nearly prostrate.

> 2. o'clock - [he wrote to Ambrose], the lecture at 4 the anniversary of my mother's death. . . .
>
> I have never been in such a state of confusion, as today, since the day when I was at Leonforte in Sicily, ill of the fever and hearing the whistling of a miserable beggar out of the window, who would not go, and looking and counting the squares of the patterns of the paper of the room, to keep [from] thinking of myself - or again that day, in Oriel Hall, when I was standing for the fellowship, and saw Pie repone te in the window.

And thank God, my nerves are not so acute as then - or where should I be? Yet I am dreadfully afraid of want of strength.

I have just discovered *how* I ought to have written my lectures - what would have been the true rhetoric - and how I have plunged into a maze of metaphysics, from which I may be unable to heave myself. When this broke on me, I quite thought of lecturing ex tempore quite a different lecture - but I am not equal to it.

A few hours later he added, "Lecture just over. - brass band playing good part of the time. HW [Wilberforce] liked it." [81]

As the letter indicates, Newman was concerned lest his argument was too philosophical for the purpose it was intended to serve, and despite the assurance of his friends that he was "*writing* for the world and for posterity" as well as "*speaking* to an audience," [82] he continued to feel some doubt. Part of the trouble was that he had not been able to deliver his lectures in the way he had planned. The first three he had written as a unit, to be delivered "close together," that is, within a single week. Their subjects, as he had described them on April 18, were "1 - The position of the question. 2. Theology as a branch of knowledge. 3. Bearing of theology on other branches of knowledge," [83] and he wished them to follow each other closely "because I shall not be able to finish one subject in less than three - and if they were at considerable intervals the effect would be lost, or the idea not brought out." [84] But when the difficulty developed about the room, he found that he would have to schedule them a week apart, on successive Mondays,[85] and so if his hearers were not to lose the thread of the argument he would have to recapitulate more than he had planned. Moreover, with the extra delay he now had time to compose two additional discourses, and whereas he had originally intended, after the first unit of three, to "go on to give the normal idea of a University" [86] (what is today contained in Discourses VI to VIII), he now felt that he neither had time to begin a new subject nor would be wise to abandon the old without developing it more fully. Hence he wrote a fourth lecture, "The Bearing of Other Branches of Knowledge on Theology," which, despite its title, does not really differ in subject matter from the third, "The Bearing of Theology on Other Branches of Knowledge." And he also wrote a fifth discourse to sum up and conclude the whole.

To the very end the composition and delivery of the lectures caused Newman such trouble as almost to achieve high comedy. At the end of his second week he had moved into rooms in a boarding school run by Dr. James Quinn in Harcourt Street, and there, when he came to compose his final lecture, he found that "the housekeeper . . . had

THE IMPERIAL INTELLECT

arranged, not only my clothes, but all my papers for me. I had put my letters in various compartments according to my relation towards them - and my Discourse papers, according as I had done with them or not. She had mixed every thing, laying them most neatly according to their *size*. To this moment I have not had courage to attempt to set them right - and one bit, which was to have come in, I have from despair not even looked for." [87] No wonder, as he wrote to Ambrose the same day, that he was "worried by and nervous about my Lectures. Here is the third Thursday I have been quite overthrown by the difficulty." [88]

On the whole, however, the lectures were well received by every-body,[89] and at the end of the course even Newman had to admit, "I have been prospered here in my lectures beyond my most sanguine ex-pectations." [90] It was a prosperity, however, for which he had paid by the most fearful toil. "These lectures," he wrote to F. W. Faber, "have oppressed me more than any thing else of the kind in my life, though, when I finished my previous [*The Present Position of Catholics*], I was in a state of fainting for days." [91] At the moment he was quite well, but the question arose how long he could, or ought to, continue. The fifth lecture, which he had delivered on June 7, had not been announced as the last, but neither had any definite number ever been promised, and now his trial was only a fortnight off.[92] In reason he thought he could do no more, and so on June 9 he broke off the series and took the packet for England. A few days later he wrote to Dr. Newsham, the president of Ushaw, explaining the reason why. "As to my Lectures, they have cost me, no one knows how much thought and anxiety - and again and again I stopped, utterly unable to get on with my subject, and nothing but the intercession of the Blessed Virgin kept me up to my work. At length I have intermitted the course, merely because I could not proceed to my satisfaction. For three days I sat at my desk nearly from morning to night, and put aside as worthless at night what I had been doing all day. Then I gave it up, and came here [to Edgbaston] - hoping that I shall be strengthened to begin again." [93] To this end he begs his friend to remember him in his prayers and "gain for me the light of Divine Grace, that I may say what is profitable and true, and nothing else." Ironically enough, nine days later he was convicted of libel, in a decision which the *Times* described as "little calculated to increase the respect of the people for the administration of justice." [94]

Only the first five of Newman's discourses were ever delivered. Why he decided to send out the others merely as "closet lectures" is uncertain. Doubtless it was partly the press of conflicting duties, partly that the summer was a bad time for lectures, and partly disinclination and simple want of strength. Moreover he had a feeling, despite the acclaim he had

[150]

received thus far, that he could not sail forever in these troubled waters without running into storms, and he had no taste for controversy now. Even his fellow Oratorians, whom he of course asked for criticisms, were sometimes too willing to oblige; and he foresaw that, as he left the problem of mixed education for that of "the normal idea of a University," this complaisance might easily spread. Indeed, he was not wrong. The sixth discourse, presumably the one he had been unable to complete in Ireland, was in proof by mid-July, and when he gave it to Father Joseph Gordon to read, the latter wrote four pages of objections. They were directed against the thesis, which Newman was there expounding, that the end of a university is not moral or religious but simply intellectual—it is the cultivation of the intellect for its own sake. Father Gordon was willing to admit that one subordinate end of a university might be so described, but he thought that its chief end was that of "making men Catholics or making Catholics *good* Catholics." [95] In this statement Newman recognized a type of criticism which he was likely to receive from many quarters, and although he was not disturbed in his own conception, he was disturbed lest his conception be misunderstood. What he was doing in this discourse was simply making a distinction in logic which could never be made in fact, and saying that a university, considered abstractly and in its idea, has as its end the cultivation of the intellect. True, the university may then be *used by* the church for the further end of making men Catholics or making Catholics good Catholics, and presumably no real university could ever exist, at least within the Catholic pale, which did not provide for the souls of its students as well as their minds. But in itself and simply *as* a university, its proper function was to provide for their minds.

On this Newman was perfectly clear. The difficulty was that in the serial mode of publication which he had adopted a storm could easily be aroused by one side of his conception before he had time to develop the other side, which would safeguard and correct it. Therefore he wrote, and had Duffy put into type, a four-page Introduction which would anticipate the objections that Father Gordon had made, and he sent it to various persons to tell him whether it was needed. [96] Father Bernard Dalgairns of the London Oratory said not. He had read the lecture without disagreement, and on reading Father Gordon's objections he gave the same answer as Newman, namely that "the end of . . . a Catholic University or of any university is 'liberal education'; though its ultimate end may be Catholicism." [97] Newman thanked him, but was not satisfied and so wrote a second Introduction, which he liked less than the first although it had the advantage of being simpler. "I so fear perplexing men, and making them suspect something by a laboured Introduction." [98] This fear evidently triumphed in the end, for when the discourse was finally published, on August 18, the Introduction appeared in a third version, even briefer than the second.[99]

Newman was engaged on the last half of his volume from June until mid-December. Part of it he wrote at Edgbaston, part in the summer house of the Oratory at Rednal, and part at Tervoe, the Irish estate of his friend Monsell. It was a wretched time. The Achilli affair still hung over him, and in July his sister Harriett had died. Moreover, he now began to learn how baffled and teased the rector of an Irish university could be. He was rector, but as yet he had no university, and he found that all his efforts to get one started were met by long periods of inexplicable silence followed by sudden decisions which he would never have taken himself and on which he certainly ought to have been consulted. Later, he called this experience "my campaign in Ireland," but at the moment he simply foresaw either that the university never would get started at all or at least that it would start all wrong, and it is no wonder if he sometimes hoped it would be the former.

But his chief burden was simply the discourses themselves. "These lectures lie like a tremendous load on me," he wrote to Dalgairns in July. "I cannot suspend them, they will fidget me till they are done. I am out on the ocean with them, out of sight of land, with nothing but the stars, and I so dread controversy." [100] At this point he was working on number seven, having decided to write ten, two less than he had thought of when he first began.[101] By August 4 he was trying to finish that and the eighth,[102] and by September he was working on the ninth. The ninth was an "anxious" one, for it dealt with "Philosophical Knowledge viewed in relation to Religion," and again he wrote to Dalgairns begging him to come down from London to discuss it. "Seriously, I *want* you," he said, "for my ninth lecture . . . is half in the Press, and I want you to revise it, and I shall willingly pay your journey for your criticisms." [103] Dalgairns came, but ordinary visitors were shooed away, "for I am pulled down by my Discourses, which hang on me like a millstone - and I feel very old." [104] On September 29 he broke down in the midst of an ordinary lecture,[105] and shortly after, when he consulted a doctor (partly for a testimonial that prison would shorten his life), he was told distinctly that he should have "a premature old age, and an early death." "I feel the truth of what he says," wrote Newman. "The first book I wrote, my 'Arians,' I was almost fainting daily, when I was finishing it - and (except my Parochial Sermons) every book I have written, before and since I was a Catholic, has been a sort of *operation*, the distress has been so great. The Discourses, now (thank God) all but finished, have been the most painful of all." [106]

On February 2, 1853, the fifth anniversary of the founding of the Oratory and the fourth of its settling in Birmingham, the completed volume was published. Duffy had advertised it "in a fancy cover," but by Newman's insistence it appeared in "a plain dark purple, like my volume of last year," and with "no gold, but a printed label on the back." [107] Presentation copies were sent to Newman's friends and to persons officially concerned with the university, and within a fortnight Duffy wrote that the work was commanding "an extensive sale." Among others he had just sold 150 copies to "an Australian Bookseller who is now in Dublin purchasing books for Australia!" [108]

Newman may have wondered what the Australians would make of the problem of mixed education in Ireland, and doubtless he already recognized that some day it would be necessary to free his lectures from the marks of their original occasion and adapt them for a wider reading public in England and America. Gradually, as the years passed, he saw how he wished to do this. In his position as rector he had been writing and speaking continuously on the subject of education, and in 1854–55 he had printed many of these pieces in the small monthly bulletin which he had started, the *Catholic University Gazette*. It now seemed desirable to bring all these educational writings together in a series of volumes uniform in appearance, and so in 1856 he selected a group dealing with universities in their historical and institutional character and published them with the English firm of Longman under the title *The Office and Work of Universities*. At the same time he thought of preparing a second edition of the *Discourses*, to be called "The Genius, Scope, and Method of Universities," [109] and in February, 1857 he worked out a plan for reducing it to the size appropriate for a companion volume. The plan entailed the contraction of the first five lectures into two, chiefly by the omission of "all local and temporary matter," [110] all matter which was predominantly theological rather than educational, and all superfluous illustrations. In this way the introductory discourse could be reduced to a few pages; the second discourse, which established theology as a branch of knowledge, would be omitted entirely; and the next three would be pared to the bare argument. The last five discourses were to be given entire. As it turned out, however, the second edition was not published until 1859, by which time another volume of educational writings, the *Lectures and Essays on University Subjects*, had also appeared. Thus the *Scope and Nature of University Education* (which was the title finally adopted) formed the third volume of this series, but the revision actually made was not so severe as that originally planned. The first discourse was compressed and made a part of the second, and the fifth was omitted entirely; but the remaining lectures, though improved in language and logical arrangement, were not substantially altered. A dozen years later, when Newman was preparing a uniform edition of all his works, he subjected the discourses to one final revision, expanding them again to nine by separating the first and second and joining them with the *Lectures and Essays* under the general title *The Idea of a University*. If, as Walter Pater has said, the resulting work is "the perfect handling of a theory," one must admit that it achieved perfection under painful circumstances and by slow degrees.

It is often said that Newman himself had a low opinion of his university discourses, and it is true that on two occasions he did convey such an impression. In the advertisement to the second edition he said that the lectures "required a greater effort to write, and gave him less satisfaction when written, than any of his Volumes," and in 1870, in his memorandum about the Catholic University, he described them as "a flash in the pan." [111] In that memorandum, however, he was speaking of the delay in commencing the university, and it is clear from the context that he did not mean by the phrase that the lectures were a failure, but rather that their effect, though brilliant at the time, was not lasting. As lectures they were a success, but they could not of themselves create the university, and this is all that he meant. Likewise his earlier statement, that the lectures gave him less satisfaction when written than anything else he had ever done, is rather nullified by a letter he wrote to Henry Wilberforce at the time that the lectures were completed. "My two most perfect works, artistically," he said, "are my two last," and he was of course referring to the *Present Position of Catholics* and the *Discourses on University Education*. "The former of them put me to less trouble than any I ever wrote - the latter to the greatest of all." [112] The discrepancy between this statement and that in the advertisement of 1859 can be reconciled only by supposing that Newman's dissatisfaction with the lectures dated not from 1852 but from some time later, and hence that it was really directed less against the lectures themselves than against the whole Irish "campaign" of which they were the product and the bitter reminder. This surmise is supported by the fact that the most severe excisions which Newman proposed were in 1857, when the "campaign" was at its height; whereas the two later revisions, made as the bitterness faded, were actually a process of restoration. Moreover, in restoring the text of the discourses he was also restoring them to their rightful owner. In the dedication of the first two editions, where he thanked those Catholics all over the world who had helped him in the Achilli trial, he had mentioned Ireland first and Great Britain second, but in the edition of 1873 he reversed the order. It was as if he were putting Ireland and the Irish episode behind him, and one may say that it was only after he had done this that he was again able to estimate at their true worth the lectures which had taken their rise on Irish soil. His final opinion, expressed in 1870, was that in his lifetime he had written five constructive works: the *Prophetical Office of the Church*, the *Lectures on Justification*, the *Development of Christian Doctrine*, the *Grammar of Assent*, and the *Idea of a University*.[113]

CHAPTER 8

The Catholic University
of Ireland

Between the idea
And the reality. . . .
—T. S. Eliot

NEWMAN was rector of the Catholic University of Ireland for precisely seven years, from November 12, 1851 to November 12, 1858. During the first three years he was rector without a university, but during the last four he organized and brought into shape an institution which continued to receive students throughout the nineteenth century and was finally incorporated into the present National University of Ireland. The history of his connection with this institution has been told elsewhere [1] and forms no part of the present study. It is a tale of misunderstandings, dissensions, and delays, and was as much the frustration as the fulfillment of Newman's idea of a university. Nevertheless, a portrait of the actual, working institution which Newman hoped to achieve and did achieve in part provides a kind of realistic commentary upon the *Idea of a University*—the kind of commentary which the acts of a political party in power provide upon the manifestoes which it issued when it was out of power—and such a portrait is the task of the present chapter.

Physically, Newman's university consisted of a fine Georgian mansion on the south side of St. Stephen's Green, at No. 86. Dr. Cullen had purchased it in the summer of 1852, and in 1854, on November 3, Newman opened its doors to a group of twenty adventurous boys. The boys lodged on the top floors and ate in the basement. In between, on the ground and first floors, were lecture rooms in which Newman and a handful of assistants taught the rudiments and as far beyond as they could get. Gradually the numbers increased, other buildings were taken, and a church was built, but even to the very end one must think of the Catholic University as a tiny, intimate community, a very pleasant one apparently, whose activities had neither the scope nor the advanced character which one normally associates with university learning.

And yet to think of it solely in this way would be doing it wrong. For there are two elements, Newman was accustomed to say, which go into every educational institution, the element of discipline or law and the element of influence. Influence is Mark Hopkins on one end of a log and a student on the other, and Newman considered this to be the heart of the educational process. It was his own mode of working, and it was what he necessarily depended on almost exclusively in the early days of the university. But law—the element of system and organization—was also important. Law took over where influence failed, supported influence in moments of weakness, steadied her and guided, helped her transcend herself, provided her with a form which she could seldom fill completely but which she would always be striving to fill as completely as she could. Law was petrified influence, the deposit or encrustation of many individual influences, and although normally it was the product of centuries, for a university which had no past, it had to be manufactured *de novo*. Newman realized this, and therefore in his official publications he set about constructing on paper the university which he knew would have to be delayed as a matter of fact. He laid out faculties and systems of government, higher curricula and specimen examinations, forms of oaths and the ritual and regalia of presentations, at a time when there was no one—literally no one—who could make any use of these things and when he knew perfectly well that this was the case. His university consisted of a handful of people sitting on a log, but in Newman's view it was tremendously important that they should not envisage themselves in that circumstance. Rather they should see themselves as in the midst of a great university, spacious in its grounds, splendid in its antiquity, multifarious in its learning and treasures, for such a vision would give a tone to their thoughts which the more homely scene would not give. It would make them a university from the very first, and even if it were in some degree a paper university, that element in the institution would be no less real and significant than any other.

The government of the university, as it was finally established, followed very closely the form which had been recommended by the subcommittee of three in 1851. Its powers were to be divided among the rector, the Rectorial Council, and the University Senate. The rector was "supreme throughout the University" [2] though he was of course limited by his final dependence upon the bishops. The Rectorial Council, which was composed of the vice-rector, the deans of faculties, and three additional members of the faculty of philosophy and letters with one vote among them, had as its object "to give counsel and support to the

Rector. It originates nothing, and executes nothing; but the Rector avails himself of its assistance . . . at least once a month in term time, and cannot do any public act, except the suspension of Professors, . . . against two-thirds of its vote." [3] As for the Senate, that was the legislative body of the university. It was composed of the vice-rector and secretary, the professors, the heads and tutors of collegiate houses, and the fellows of the university, and it had the office of prescribing the course of study and the subjects and forms of examination, of conferring degrees, of expelling, of preparing addresses and petitions, appointing committees and the auditors of accounts, and of exercising jurisdiction over the university press. "The Senate is the representative of the collective university. . . . Its presence is the presence of the University, and its acts are University acts." [4]

Formally, this scheme of government was modeled upon the University of Louvain, but actually the model of Louvain gave Newman just the opportunity which he desired to criticize the system he had known at Oxford. The government of Oxford had been marred by two great evils—first, that the university was simply lost in a congeries of colleges, and secondly, that the working body of tutors and professors was without any effective power. Both of these evils were due largely to the oligarchy of the Hebdomadal Board, for that board was composed of the various heads of houses and it alone had the power to initiate legislation. But they were also due to the fact that the House of Congregation, which represented the teaching body, had decayed into a purely formal institution, and that the more powerful House of Convocation included all Regents in Arts who had kept their names on the books of a college or hall and who could come up on any occasion to swamp the resident body by their votes. These evils were largely removed by the Oxford University Bill of 1854, but Newman was ahead of Oxford in providing against them in his own institution. In the office of rector he had a power which represented the university at large, and the heads of houses he had reduced to a purely domestic function. They were not even members of the Rectorial Council, which was now purely advisory and which departed from the Louvain plan to include three professors from the important faculty of arts.[5] Moreover, in the Senate Newman had a body with the powers of Convocation—indeed, with greater powers—but with a membership more nearly resembling that of Congregation. Here, too, he departed in one respect from the Louvain plan, for he added to the Senate a body of "Fellows of the University," that is "learned persons scattered through the country" who, after the university had been in operation for some years, would normally have the degree of doctor in one of the faculties. They would provide in the Senate what had been wholesome about the Oxford Convocation, namely, that it offered a corrective upon the interests of the resident body; but since they were limited in number to one-fourth of the entire Senate, they could not usurp from the residents the normal ruling power. This arrangement, Newman believed, would make the constitution of the university "as perfect as possible in itself," [6] and it is interesting that he found this perfection in a combination of Louvain, not with Oxford as he had known it, but with Oxford as it was currently being reformed by a liberal administration.

The faculties of the university were to be five, the traditional four with the addition of science, which was raised from a subdivision of arts to an independent school as it was at Louvain. At Oxford all the higher faculties existed largely on paper, but except for the school of theology, which Newman regarded as simply impractical at the time and which he turned over to the bishops to establish or not as they saw fit, he made a definite effort to realize all the others. With law, however, he could do nothing. There was a dispensation of some years of study to those who attended the lectures at Trinity College, Dublin, and this was an advantage too great to be overcome. Science, too, although it was inaugurated with a dean and three professors, never had any students, and no classes were formed. [7] The principal reason for this was that the students could not enter the school until they had passed through two years of arts, but as the university lost most of its students after two years, science was never needed. This difficulty also operated in the engineering school, which was subsidiary to arts and which opened in the autumn of 1855 with the proposal of a five-year course. [8] Once again there was a professor, very well qualified, but it does not appear that he ever had any students.

Only the faculties of medicine and arts, therefore, were really a success. The former seemed especially important to Newman because the various hospitals and medical schools of Dublin were entirely controlled by Protestants. Obviously, in a profession whose duties were so intimately involved with religion, this was an intolerable situation, and yet it was only by good fortune that Newman was able to remedy it. In the summer of 1854 there was brought into the market a fully equipped medical school which had been operated for some years by the Dublin Apothecaries' Hall. Newman purchased this school with all its equipment, and in November it reopened under the auspices of the university with a qualified staff of Catholic practitioners and forty-three students. None of these students had been through the two years' course in arts and they were not regular members of the university, but Newman recognized that this was likely to be the case even after their numbers increased, and in 1858 he tried to give them some of the benefits of collegiate life by opening a medical lodging house where they could find rooms that were inexpensive and yet free from the dangers of an unsupervised lodging. From the very first the school itself was one of the most complete of any in the United Kingdom outside of London, and in the following years Newman was able to add to its facilities a distinguished medical library of five thousand volumes, acquired from Germany, and to fit up a first-rate chemical laboratory which was also to serve the needs of the school of science. As a result, in the autumn of 1856 the school was formally recognized by the official medical bodies of Ireland, and it continued to flourish until it was finally absorbed into the National University in 1908.[9]

Although the medical school was always the most flourishing department of the university, the school of philosophy and letters remained the heart of Newman's conception. Needless to say, it was deeply modified by the actual needs of the Irish youth, for Newman quickly learned that they were neither so well grounded as those who came up to Oxford and Cambridge nor were they able to delay their profession for so many years. Therefore, he was reduced to providing a course of about two years' duration which would be complete in itself and yet, although it was little more than what would be done in the last years of an English school, would lead into a course which might be considered of university caliber. He did this by the following plan: after an entrance examination in the elements of Latin, Greek, ancient history, geography, mathematics, and one Gospel and the Catechism,[10] the student devoted two years, normally those from age sixteen to eighteen, to the further study of these same subjects. At the end of that time he took an examination, which was not unlike Responsions at Oxford, in three of the following four subjects, the second and one item from the third being required: 1. the text and matter of one Greek book; 2. the same of one Latin book; 3. Philosophy, criticism, geography, chronology, mathematics, logic, physical science (i.e. one or two recommended texts on these subjects); and 4. one modern language and literature. "Besides these three subjects of examination," said the university Rules, "every Candidate must be prepared with an exact knowledge of the matters contained in some longer Catechism and in the four Gospels, and with a general knowledge of ancient history, geography, chronology, and the principles of composition." [11]

The candidate who passed this examination was awarded the degree of Scholar, and at this point he might either retire from the university or enter one of the other faculties or continue in philosophy and letters. If the last, he devoted two more years to studies which were selected with some view to his final profession and which normally emphasized "subjects" rather than classical "books." This course resulted in an Academical License, corresponding to the B.A. elsewhere (for the university never had a charter for granting the standard degrees), and this license might be of a grade either Satisfactory or Meritorious (the Oxford Pass and Honors). In either case the candidate had to pass an examination at the end of his third year in 1. a knowledge of the Four Gospels and Acts, Old Testament history, and an extended Catechism; 2. logic, six books of Euclid, and algebra to quadratics; and 3. one Latin historian or orator. In the fourth year the candidate for a Satisfactory License was further examined in one Greek orator or historian and in one out of the six tercentenaries of profane history since the Christian era. The candidate for the Meritorious License, on the other hand, was examined in a minimum of one subject under each of the following four heads:

1. Christian Knowledge - (1) The Church. (2) Holy Scripture, (3) Literature of Religion, (4) Philosophy of Religion.
2. Philosophy - (5) Logic, (6) Metaphysics, (7) Ethics, (8) Schools of philosophy, ancient and modern, (9) Politics and Law of Nations, (10) Political economy, (11) Political geography, (12) Ethnology, (13) Polite criticism and Science of taste, (14) Philology, (15) Geometry.
3. Literature - (16) Latin classics, (17) Greek classics, (18) Celtic language and literature, (19) English language and literature, (20) Two foreign literatures, (21) Hebrew.
4. History - (22) Greek history, (23) Roman, (24) Medieval - Eastern, (25) Medieval - Western, (26) Modern, (27) Ecclesiastical.[12]

From specimen examinations it appears that by "Greek or Latin classics" (items sixteen and seventeen) Newman meant at least four authors in each and that by the other subjects he meant one or two standard texts which treated them. The curriculum was thus somewhat easier than that at Oxford, but it was hardly more theological and certainly was much broader and more varied in scope.

After the licentiate, if any proceeded so far, came the rank of Fellow of the University, corresponding to Master or Doctor elsewhere and carrying with it a seat in the University Senate. This degree, however, was not an automatic honor, as at Oxford, but was to be granted only after three more years of study, presumably in one of the professional faculties and after the passing of an examination or some other test.

In this academic course, although one can see the pressure of circumstance, one can also see the ideas which Newman had come to believe in at Oxford. The establishment of an entrance examination,[13] the provision that all students should begin their year in November ("if they came at any other time, they would lose so much of the year"[14]), the emphasis on "subjects" at the expense of classical "books," the frequent examinations, and the provision for extended study after the Bachelor's degree, are all changes which Newman would gladly have made in the Oxford system had he been able. The great change which he actually attempted to make, that in the role of the tutor, is also preserved here, although in a form strangely modified by the circumstances of a nascent university.

In the Oxford of Newman's day, it will be recalled, there were three classes of instructors: the professors, who did little or nothing; the tutors, who "lectured" to small classes of undergraduates, either their own pupils or another's; and the private coaches, who were hired by the undergraduates to give them individual instruction and so get them through the examinations. The effort of Newman in his quarrel with Hawkins had been to get the official tutor to employ the intimate method of the private coach and also to assume the office of a minister of religion. Now, after twenty years, his ideas had not significantly changed, but because of the modest way in which the university was beginning they were rather queerly distorted.

Initially, Newman's idea of a professor was that he would be pretty much for show.[15] He would be a person eminent in his own field and would attract students by the brilliance of his name to a university which was otherwise unknown. W. G. Ward, Döllinger in Germany, and Brownson in America are examples of persons whose services he attempted to secure.[16] In many cases these professors would be nonresident and would deliver only an occasional series of lectures, but if they were able to attend more regularly, they would serve as university examiners, would have the care of museums and collections within their field of study, and would write and publish books. In Newman's idea, they would be the guardian or custodian of the particular department of learning which they undertook, and so little would they be considered as teachers that they were not "bound by duty," though they might be "advantageously induced by circumstances," to adapt themselves to the understanding of their hearers.[17] Later, when Newman found that he could neither secure such rarities nor afford their upkeep when he got them, he employed the term "professor," and also "lecturer," to describe an office which combined the Oxford university professor with the Oxford college tutor. Thus all his actual professors, although they did deliver the formal inaugural dissertations and the occasional "display" lectures on which attendance was not required, also "lectured" three times a week to the small recitation classes which constituted the real instruction of the university. These classes were called "professors' lectures," but in form and content they were exactly like the tutors' lectures at Oxford.[18]

The name "tutor," then, Newman reserved for what at Oxford was called a "private tutor" or "cram coach." [19] "They should be young men," he wrote in his first annual report, "not above two or three years older than their pupils, and such as have lately passed their own course of study in the University, and gained honours on examination . . . They would be half companions, half advisers of their pupils, that is, of the students; and while their formal office would be that of preparing them for the Professors' Lectures, and the Examinations, or what in this place is technically called 'grinding,' they would be thrown together with them in their amusements and recreations; and, gaining their confidence from their almost parity of age, and their having so lately been what the others are still, they may be expected to exercise a salutary influence over them, and will often know more about them than any one else." [20] However, since young graduates would obviously not be available at once, Newman proposed to start with four older scholars who would also be occupied in planning the course of studies, selecting texts, forming examinations, and so forth, and who in that capacity would be called "prefects" or "moderators of studies." [21] These four were to be "the basis of the whole real system," [22] and for that reason Newman proposed to pay them well. Unfortunately, the four persons whom he had in mind were all Englishmen, two from Oxford and two from Cambridge, and thus, when he suddenly became aware of the jealousy against English appointments, he was constrained to allow two of them to retire and to make the other two into a professor and a lecturer, positions more commensurate with the salaries they were expecting to receive.[23] As a result, the office of tutor dwindled in importance and does not seem to have been satisfactorily performed.[24] From being a distinct position requiring a distinct type of person, it became simply a function which might be assumed by anyone, even by a married professor who simply came in of an evening for the purpose. Thus the three classes of instruction known at Oxford—university professor, college tutor, and private coach—were in Newman's plan reduced to two, and these two were often held by a single person.

But what of the principle for which Newman had contended so fiercely at Oxford, that the tutor's office should be considered a pastoral one? Strangely enough, the principle is not emphasized in the plan of the Catholic University. The duty of the tutor, as defined by the Rules and Regulations, is "certainly the moral, but more directly the intellectual care of his pupils," [25] and if one may say of this phrase that it simply takes for granted what Newman had contended for at Oxford, one may also say that, by taking it for granted, it gives it a subordinate place. For the Catholic University was at once more secular and more religious than the University of Oxford. Not being under the necessity, as Oxford was, of combining a place of general education for youths who wished to enter the world with a training school for the priesthood, it did not need to combine an irreligious spirit with an ecclesiastical faculty. Its faculty could be lay and its spirit religious, and as such, it was to the spirit of the place, rather than to any particular individual, that Newman entrusted the moral and religious needs of the student.

A chief element in Newman's plan for ensuring the religious character of undergraduate life was the system of residence. From the very first he had felt that to settle the university in the midst of a large city, though there were many compelling reasons for doing so, was to expose the undergraduates to unusual temptations, and he believed that

> *the only way* to hinder the disorder incident upon a University in a town is to do what they were forced to do at Oxford and other Universities in the middle ages—to open *Inns* or *Halls*, as they were called (which, when endowed, became Colleges) . . .
>
> I would have these lodging-houses or halls large enough to hold twenty students each. A Dean should preside over them, or some other officer (I do not care about the names) if the Dean was Confessor, one or two Lecturers, and the Tutors of the Community (i.e., 20) should lodge there too. Thus there would be some sort of governing body in each house, or what would ultimately become such. There should also be two or three scholars, *i.e.*, youths holding burses, in each of the Communities, if possible, who would act as a sort of medium between the governing body and the independent students. . . . Each of these [houses] should have its private Chapel (and the Chaplain might be the Confessor).[26]

As in the Middle Ages, Newman thought that these houses might be established by the various religious orders for their own members, or else by the various faculties or dioceses, or even reserved for various "nations." Thus, the first house, St. Patrick's, which occupied the upper floors of the main university building, was considered an endowed house for the Irish; and when Newman set up one of his own at No. 6 Harcourt Street, he thought of it as providing a center for English youths.[27] He had about eight pupils in his house, he himself acting as dean, tutor, chaplain, bursar, and general factotum, carving for the boys at dinner and locking the door at night after they were in bed. It was a new experience for him, the first time he had ever "kept house," but in some ways it was a realization of his wishes. He called the house St. Mary's, the name he had thought of for Littlemore when he wished to make it a hall dependent upon Oriel, and the whole plan of these houses is clearly the outcome of the discussions held with Froude and Pusey some twenty years before.

All the establishments planned by the Tractarians, however, had a distinctly strained and monastic flavor, whereas in the Dublin houses there was a wonderful lightness and informality. The discipline, of course, was perfectly regular and religious—mass at seven or eight, then breakfast, lectures from nine until one or two, dinner at five, and indoors by a fixed hour in the evening which varied according to the season.[28] But although the discipline was regular, it was marked by none of the fierceness which had characterized Newman when he was a "new broom" at St. Alban's and Oriel. In his first report to the bishops he put forth a theory of discipline which was not only humane and moderate but even very novel considering the date at which it was written. Its guiding principle was that "the young for the most part cannot be driven, but, on the other hand, are open to persuasion, and to the influence of kindness and personal attachment; and that, in consequence, they are to be kept straight by indirect contrivances rather than by authoritative enactments and naked prohibitions." [29] Moreover, among the "indirect contrivances" which he planned were many amusements which he had long ceased to allow himself and had formerly frowned on as used by others. The theater, for instance, he had not frequented since the early twenties, but now he went out of his way to secure its pleasures for his own pupils, and for a time he contemplated licensing a theater so as to bring it under the control of the university.[30] This plan was never realized, but he did borrow £160 from the university to convert one of the stables at the rear of St. Patrick's into a billiard room. This was partly done to keep the undergraduates from the tables in Dawson's Lane, where they might form undesirable acquaintance and hear the betting news, but some such room had been in his plans from the very beginning.[31] So, too, had a cricket ground and facilities for fencing, boating, games, and parties. In the collegiate dining hall he planned to "range the tables in small messes, like a coffee room, that students may invite their friends, to breakfast or dinner," and whereas at Oxford he was said to have summoned the porter when the undergraduates had parties, here he planned "one or two rooms, like common rooms, for private parties, for breakfast or wine extra." [32] Again, at Oxford it was young Mr. Newman who protested to Copleston about the conduct of the gentlemen-commoners, but here it was Dr. Cullen who protested to him—and with no better avail. Some of the collegians, it appeared, had been going to plays and hunting in pink, and on one occasion the Archbishop held forth to Newman for an hour and a half about it. "But then what can I do," he complained afterward, "when Dr. Newman just listens to me without speaking, and then says, 'I will think about it,' and then everything goes on just as it was before?" [33]

Perhaps the most interesting of Newman's projects for undergraduate recreation is that of the debating society, for it clearly illustrates how his views narrowed during the Tractarian phase and then relaxed again after he became a Catholic. It will be remembered that when he was an undergraduate at Trinity, he and his friend Bowden had projected a fortnightly debating society which was to range in its discussions over the whole field of history, poetry, and the fine arts. But then in 1834, in the midst of the controversy over the admission of Dissenters, when such a debating society actually existed, Newman pointed to it as an example of the dangers of "unbridled speculations and sophistical reasonings." [34] Twenty years later, however, he was back where he had started, for one of his first acts as rector of the Catholic University was to found a debating society in the basement of University House. [35] He felt he could do this, of course, simply *because* the university was Catholic. Where religion was secure of its place, the mind could run freely without danger of error, and this was the explanation for the whole spirit of freedom which Newman was attempting to foster.

Indeed, in Newman's view everything in a university, the education as well as the conduct, depended upon what he called the spirit of the place, the *genius loci*; and much of his thinking was expended upon the problem of how this intangible but all-important power was to be shaped. Normally, of course, it was not shaped. It came into being slowly, unconsciously, not the work of any individual, but simply growing up as an invisible presence which none could define and yet which all acknowledged to be the soul of the life about them. It combined in itself the power of discipline with the power of influence, for though its ways were secret and indirect and personal, it had all the authority of law and all the consistency of a living idea. It was almost synonymous with tradition, and Newman's main problem, as he conceived it, was that of creating in his nascent university something which would supply the absence of tradition. [36] One way in which he hoped to do this was through the intimacy of the tutorial system and especially through the harmony of those who were to form, along with himself, the "real working team" of the university. Because they understood one another so thoroughly and came from a common academic tradition, they might almost engraft that tradition upon the new stock which they were planting, and make what Oxford possessed the possession of Dublin as well. [37]

Even more than upon the tutors, however, Newman depended upon the students themselves, for he was firmly persuaded that at least half of the education that really matters in a university is that which the undergraduates give to themselves. In the Dublin *Discourses* he had stated that "when a multitude of young men, keen, open-hearted, sympathetic, and observant, as young men are, come together and freely mix with each other, they are sure to learn one from another, even if there be no one to teach them; the conversation of all is a series of lectures to each, and they gain for themselves new ideas and views, fresh matters of thought, and distinct principles for judging and acting, day by day." [38] The principles, needless to say, must be of the right sort, a stimulus to learning, not to idleness, and for this purpose a spirit of emulation ought to be fostered among the youths. To a degree this would be done by their division into houses, but it might also be done by establishing exhibitions to be given away on *concursus*, for this would bring forward the more studious to become a center of influence among the rest. Then, if these exhibitioners were given some slight privileges and functions to perform, but "without having a shadow of jurisdiction over the rest," they would constitute a "middle party" between the teacher and students and act as a spontaneous channel of communication between them. [39]

The final and supreme source of a genius loci, however, was the presence in a university of the spirit of religion. This was the thing which brought together the professor of logic and the professor of chemistry, the student in arts and the student in medicine, the rector from England and the freshman from Ireland, and united them in a common act of worship and learning. So strongly did Newman feel this that he declared a university could not have a genius loci while it had professors of different religions; [40] and so clearly did he remember how the pulpit at St. Mary's had been an instrument, such as Oxford had hardly known before, for fostering and molding a genius loci, that almost his first thought as rector was to build a university church which would be the center of such an influence again. It "will give a unity," he wrote, "to the various academical foundations" of which the university is composed, "and it will maintain and symbolize that great principle in which we glory as our characteristic, the union of Science with Religion." [41]

The spirit which was proper to a university, and which was thus symbolized by the presence of religion in its midst, was the spirit of universality. This idea was the very heart and soul of Newman's conception, and yet this was the part of his conception which, by the action of his superiors, seemed most deeply imperiled. The Holy See had decided upon a university, and the bishops had ratified that decision, and yet from the very beginning there seemed to be a disposition to be content with something less. In the Papal Brief of March 20, 1854, the words "Lyceum" and "Gymnasium" were sometimes substituted for "Universitas," and Newman, whose use of language was ever precise, could hardly suppose that this was done without a meaning.[42] Moreover, the delays in commencing, the remark of Dr. Cullen that "three or four" professors would do to open with, and of Dr. Forde that of course there would be no professor of law [43]—these and other indications led Newman to fear that the committee would "shirk off into a college instead of a university from ignorance and from fear." "If so," he added, "I have nothing to do with it." [44] His own conception of a university was that of a "*Studium Generale*, or 'School of Universal Learning,'" [45] and although he recognized that historically such schools normally grew up out of colleges or other smaller bodies, he felt that in this day and place, when partiality was not regarded as a defect but was often adopted as a deliberate philosophy, there were compelling reasons for starting with the idea of a university, even if its reality was only achieved by the gradual process of time.[46]

The idea of a *Studium Generale* implied, according to Newman, not only a universality of studies but also a universality of students, and this was another aspect of the question which was continually at issue between Newman and his Irish superiors. Was the university to be, as the Rescripts from Propaganda implied, a place of resort for all Catholics who spoke the English tongue, or was it to be a purely Irish institution? Once again, the former conception had emanated from the Holy See, had been distinctly recognized by the Irish bishops, and had been acclaimed not only in words but also in contributions by England, Scotland, France, India, and both North and South America.[47] Clearly, the conception of an "Imperial University" was the only basis on which an Englishman could be invited to be rector, and it was the basis on which Newman had accepted. He put it forward distinctly in his opening remarks to the first students who entered the university, and in his report to the bishops he again spoke of the need for a Catholic university in "that wide world in which the English tongue is spoken." [48] Properly considered, the university was not the Catholic University *of* Ireland but the Catholic University *in* Ireland—although Ireland, Newman believed, was the proper soil to produce it and Dublin was its natural seat.

To many persons the choice of Ireland as the seat of an international university was preposterous, but Newman with his characteristic energy of vision had already devised a theory to explain it. The world, he wrote, had grown away from the south and west of Europe into five continents, and Ireland stood in "the centre of the Catholicism of the English tongue, with Great Britain, Malta (perhaps Turkey or Egypt), and

India, on one side of it, and North America, and Australia, on the other." [49] Students from all these countries would come flocking to Ireland as to their center. Turbans would mingle with top hats and fezzes with coonskin caps, and the cosmopolitanism of the Middle Ages would be realized again. In other words, Newman's division of his university into "nations" was not a piece of idle medievalism but was a practical preparation for the foreign students who he really believed were coming. "We expect soon, not at once," he wrote, "from 60 to 100 Yankees," though at the moment he was not sure of a dozen Irish, and in the spring of 1854 he seriously considered going to America and lecturing about the university in all the principal cities. [50]

Needless to say, the Yankees never arrived, nor did the Australians or Turks or even many Englishmen. "Who in his senses," said the convert Phillips de Lisle, "would send his children to a province at a distance for the completion of education? . . . It is a joke. An Imperial University in Ireland is an absurdity." [51] There is no question that he was right, but like many absurdities it was generously conceived, and it gave rise to one of Newman's most beautiful essays, on the "Site of a University." After considering what it was in clear air of Athens and the south bank of the Seine and the meadows about Oxford which made them in their turn the schools of civilization, the author seeks on behalf of the age to come for a city less inland than Oxford was and a country closer upon the highway of the seas. "I am turning my eyes towards a hundred years to come," he says—and they have just come—

> and I dimly see the island I am gazing on, become the road of passage and union between two hemispheres, and the centre of the world. . . . The capital of that prosperous and hopeful land is situate in a beautiful bay and near a romantic region; and in it I see a flourishing University, which for a while had to struggle with fortune, but which, when its first founders and servants were dead and gone, had successes far exceeding their anxieties. Thither, as to a sacred soil, the home of their fathers, and the fountain-head of their Christianity, students are flocking from East, West, and South, from America and Australia and India, from Egypt and Asia Minor, with the ease and rapidity of a locomotion not yet discovered, and last, though not least, from England,—all speaking one tongue, all owning one faith, all eager for one large true wisdom; and thence, when their stay is over, going back again to carry over all the earth "peace to men of good will." [52]

Had Newman's prophecy come true, this passage might have been read at the hundredth anniversary of the founding of his university, and people might have remarked upon his acumen in predicting the Shannon airport. But it did not come true—no great university did arise—and the causes are not far to seek. The lack of a charter for granting degrees, the division and hostility among the bishops, the dearth of pupils, and the simple poverty of the land—these are the reasons for the relative failure of Newman's university. But although the university languished and the nations of the world never came flocking to Dublin for their education, there did go forth from Dublin a conception of education which has deeply influenced the universities of the English-speaking world. And in this sense one might say that the institution at Dublin did become an "Imperial University."

The Idea of a
Liberal Education

CHAPTER 9

The Circle of the Sciences

> And it is a matter of common discourse of the chain of sciences
> how they are linked together, insomuch as the Grecians, who had
> terms at will, have fitted it of a name of *Circle Learning*.
> —Francis Bacon

NEWMAN'S labors in behalf of the Catholic University
of Ireland resulted in three volumes on university education which complement each other in a peculiarly systematic way. In the final arrangement of his works, two of these volumes were brought together under the title *The Idea of a University*, and Newman indicated what he conceived to be their relation in the words which follow: *Defined and Illustrated I. In Nine Discourses Delivered to the Catholics of Dublin; II. In Occasional Lectures and Essays. . . .* It would not be stretching a point to consider that "Defined" goes especially with the *Nine Discourses* and "Illustrated" with the *Occasional Lectures and Essays*, for this is exactly the character which the two volumes have. The former presents a philosophic definition of the "idea," the inner form or principle, of university education, and the latter, which is subtitled *University Subjects* and which consists largely of lectures delivered upon the occasion of opening the various schools of the university, illustrates that idea in respect to the subjects which a university teaches. The third volume, the *Rise and Progress of Universities*, was placed in the final arrangement among the *Historical Sketches*, and though one might say that it illustrates historically the same idea which was illustrated philosophically in the *University Subjects*, it is quite properly set apart from the other two volumes as being less directly concerned with the "idea" of a university and more specifically with its actual manifestations in time and place.

The fact that Newman called his work *The Idea of a University* is interesting because characteristically he named his books from their literary form rather than their subject matter. With only a few exceptions his works are all *Sermons, Lectures, Discourses, Tracts, Verses, Historical Sketches, Essays in Aid of a Grammar of Assent,* an *Apologia,* and the like. Even the *Idea of a University,* in the first edition of its two parts, was entitled *Discourses* and *Lectures and Essays*, and these formal designations were retained in the secondary title of the third edition. But they were preceded there by the phrase "the idea of a university" because it was that idea which gave unity to the two parts and indeed to all of Newman's educational writings.

The idea of a university or, more properly, of the education which a university gives, is that of the integrity of all knowledge and the need of the human mind to reflect that integrity. Alluding to Lord Macaulay's defense of the London University in 1826, Newman declared, "Such writers do not rise to the very idea of a University. They consider it a sort of bazaar, or pantechnicon, in which wares of all kinds are heaped together for sale in stalls independent of each other . . . whereas, if we would rightly deem of it, a University is the home, it is the mansion-house, of the goodly family of the Sciences, sisters all, and sisterly in their mutual dispositions. . . . The majestic vision of the Middle Age, which grew steadily to perfection in the course of centuries, the University of Paris, or Bologna, or Oxford, has almost gone out in night. A philosophical comprehensiveness, an orderly expansiveness, an elastic constructiveness, men have lost them, and cannot make out why. This is why: because they have lost the idea of unity." [1]

That the idea of unity had been lost in the modern world was apparent to Newman wherever he looked—in church, in state, in the field of education—but perhaps the most striking example was to be found in an institution which was much to his purpose because it was almost the exact counterpart of the one with which he was dealing. This was the encyclopaedia. An encyclopaedia, properly considered, is simply a scriptural university, just as a university is an institutional encyclopaedia, and it was no accident in Newman's eyes that what had happened to the one should also have happened to the other. "It is curious," he wrote, "how negligent English writers seem to be just now of the necessity of comprehensiveness and harmony of view, in their pursuit of truth in detail. The very word Encyclopaedia ought to suggest it to them; but the alphabetical order has assimilated the great undertaking so designated to a sort of Dictionary of portions and departments of knowledge." [2] Originally, the word "encyclopaedia," which Bacon translated as "circle learning" and Sir Thomas Elyot as "the circle of doctrine," probably referred simply to the common knowledge in general circulation, but gradually it came to designate the whole body of the arts and sciences, especially those deemed essential to a liberal education. It became "encyclical," that is, not in respect to its dissemination but to its scope, and in this meaning it was applied in the sixteenth century to the sort of compendium of universal knowledge which in the Middle Ages

THE CIRCLE OF THE SCIENCES

had been called a *summa* or *speculum*. These works, both medieval and Renaissance, were all systematic in character. The great encyclopaedia of Johann Heinrich Alsted (1630), for example, begins with the statement, "An encyclopaedia is an ordered assemblage [*methodica comprehensio*] of all the things which ought to be learned by man in this life," and the author notes that whereas the term "encyclopaedia" has often been abused, being applied to various circles within the great circle of universal knowledge, his work is not an encyclopaedia of this or that, "sed *absolutè Encyclopaediam, id est, systema omnium systematum* ενκυκλιων." [3]

It was the last such system. In 1704 John Harris, secretary of the Royal Society, published his *Lexicon technicum: or, An Universal English Dictionary of Arts and Sciences*, which was the first English encyclopaedia arranged according to that "most anti-philosophical" principle, the order of the letters in the alphabet. The principle may have been anti-philosophical, but it had the practical advantage of providing a place for any item of knowledge that could be given a name, and by its means Harris was able to include the growing body of mathematical and physical learning for which Alsted's synthesis did not provide. Moreover, it made this learning easily accessible and so began the transformation of the encyclopaedia from a course of instruction into a work of reference. The problem, of course, was how to secure the advantages of both methods—of unified exposition on the one hand and of ready reference and inclusiveness on the other—and it is highly instructive to see the eighteenth- and early nineteenth-century encyclopaedists struggling with this problem. Chambers' *Cyclopaedia* (1728), for example, adopted the alphabetical arrangement of Harris but proposed to modify it by considering "the several Matters not only absolutely and independently, as to what they are in themselves; but also relatively, or as they respect each other. They are both treated as so many Wholes, and as so many Parts of some greater whole." It proposed to do this by a system of cross references from one article to another, and even prefixed an elaborate analysis of human knowledge with the subdivisions keyed so that a philosophical reader might peruse the articles "in their natural Order of Science, out of which the Technical or Alphabetical one had remov'd them." [4] The resulting labyrinth, however, was beyond ordinary human patience, and certainly the great success of the work was due to the quality of its materials rather than to any imaginary Greek temple which might have been constructed out of them.

When a Society of Gentlemen in Scotland published the first *Encyclopaedia Britannica* in 1773, they too wrestled with this problem and adopted a solution which, although anticipated by the obscure dictionary

[175]

of Dennis de Coetlogon (1745), they have always considered as their "distinctive feature" and a most important element in their success. This was to explain all the detached fragments of knowledge under their own names and at the same time to give a separate and comprehensive treatment of each science as a whole. In the second edition, however, they introduced a change so momentous that the original editor resigned rather than be a party to it. This was the inclusion of historical and biographical material, which, though it had insinuated itself very slightly into the French *Encyclopédie*, had not hitherto formed a part of the traditional dictionary of arts and sciences. It was not included at all in Harris or Chambers; Alsted had relegated it to a section entitled "Farragines disciplinarum"; and his predecessor, Ringelbergh (1541), had placed it in a division at the very end of the book which he called "Chaos." This, indeed, is what resulted from the inclusion of a field of knowledge which was necessarily empirical and miscellaneous in a compendium which at least strove to be rational and systematic. But even in the arts and sciences knowledge was being acquired more rapidly than it could be assimilated, and by the time of the famous ninth edition of *Britannica* (1873), the editors had pretty well ceased to worry about being philosophical and contented themselves with being useful and up to date. As a result, when T. S. Eliot wished to show how the soul of modern man had lost the original simplicity with which it was endowed by God, he had it "Curl up . . . in the window seat / Behind the *Encyclopaedia Britannica*." [5]

The meaning of this development was borne in upon Newman while he was working on the university discourses. He tells us that he took down "an Encyclopædia of name" (it was Brewster's *Edinburgh Encyclopaedia* [1830], which he found in his rooms at Dublin), hoping it would give him some light on the subject he was then considering. He looked up the word "Philosophy," but found no article, simply a reference, "see Natural," "see Moral." He then turned to "Science," a term which he was accustomed to use in the older sense of systematic knowledge, but again found only a notice to the effect that, "whereas *each* science will be found discussed under its own name, there is here a vacant place for enumerating some entertaining problems or curiosities, etc., in science . . . such as 'the Invisible girl,' ventriloquism, sugar from old rags, etc., etc." And this, so far as he had observed, was the case with every modern encyclopaedia except one, the exception being the *Encyclopaedia Metropolitana* (1818-45), which had been planned by the poet Coleridge according to a "truer idea." [6]

Coleridge's dream of mapping all the sciences dates back at least to 1803, when he wrote to Southey about a scheme for a "Bibliotheca

Britannica." At that time he noted "what a strange abuse has been made of the word encyclopaedia. It signifies properly, grammar, logic, rhetoric, and ethics, and metaphysics, which last, explaining the ultimate principle of grammar - log. - rhet., and eth.—formed a circle of knowledge. . . . To call a huge unconnected miscellany of the *omne scibile*, in an arrangement determined by the accident of initial letters, an encyclopaedia is the impudent ignorance of your Presbyterian bookmakers." [7] In the ensuing years Coleridge discovered a "manifest tendency" on the part of all the arts and sciences "to lose their former insulated character, and organize themselves into one harmonious body of knowledge," [8] and by 1817 he had planned the *Encyclopaedia Metropolitana* as a repository for the knowledge so organized. The work would be arranged, said the prospectus, "not according to the letters of the alphabet which happen to form the initials of the English *names* of the Treatises, but in agreement with a PHILOSOPHICAL SYSTEM, based on the *nature* of the Subjects,—a method which causes the entire work to become a rational exposition of the state of human knowledge, and the mutual dependence and relative importance of its different branches." [9] Coleridge recognized that a "strictly *scientific* method" [10] was impractical in a modern encyclopaedia, and so he too provided an eight-volume "Chaos" at the end for miscellaneous material alphabetically arranged. But history and biography were handled chronologically rather than alphabetically, and the various pure, mixed, and applied Sciences were treated comprehensively and were ordered in a scale intended to show their derivation from a single master-thought. "The first preconception, or master-thought, on which *our* plan rests," wrote Coleridge, "is the *moral origin and tendency* of all true Science; in other words, our great objects are to exhibit the Arts and Sciences in their Philosophical harmony; to teach Philosophy in union with Morals; and to sustain Morality by Revealed Religion." [11]

Coleridge himself did no more than conceive the plan of the *Encyclopaedia* and write the general introduction or "Preliminary Treatise on Method." The boldness of his conception, however, "captivated and dazzled" [12] the minds of the younger dons at Oxford and Cambridge, and when the editorship passed in 1822 to the Rev. Edward Smedley, Fellow of Sidney Sussex College, Cambridge, the work rapidly became the organ of the two southern universities in opposition to the Whiggish *Britannica* of the North. Among others, Whately of Oriel was deeply involved, and as this was just the moment when he was taking Newman in hand, he naturally involved his young disciple as well. Whately was to furnish the treatises on logic and rhetoric, and it will be remembered that in the summer of 1822 he got Newman to help in the composition of the former. Two years later, when the editor was disappointed in an article on Cicero, Whately arranged for Newman to supply the deficiency in the brief time of two months,[13] and again in February, 1825 he persuaded him to write on Apollonius of Tyana and the related subject of miracles. A year later Smedley himself wrote to Newman proposing that he do an account of "the Fathers of the second century," but Newman found this too large a subject to be completed in the allotted time of one year, and his alternative proposal, that he be given two years to do "the Fathers of the 2nd and 3rd centuries in one paper," [14] was not acceptable to Smedley. In 1828 he was approached again, but this time, while suggesting the names of Pusey and Hampden as possible contributors, he declared that "for myself, my College engagements do not allow me to keep pace with the Encyclopaedia." [15]

He did not altogether lose sight of it, however. In 1836 the editorship was transferred to the Rev. Hugh James Rose, Newman's close associate in the Tractarian movement, and to his brother, John Henry Rose; and in the 1850's, when Newman was writing his university books, he included as part of his preparatory reading Coleridge's "Preliminary Treatise on Method." [16] Without doubt he regarded his own work as a kind of "Preliminary Treatise on the Method of Education." Coleridge had written on the *Idea of Church and State* and the "idea" of an encyclopaedia—now he, Newman, would write on the "idea" of a university. He would do for the university what Coleridge had done for the encyclopaedia, for the two institutions were not only parallel in themselves but were also confronted by parallel dangers. What the *Britannica* was to the *Metropolitana*, the University of London was to Oxford and Cambridge. And the Queen's Colleges stood in the same relation to the proposed Catholic University of Ireland.

There was, however, one important difference between them. Where the tendency in the encyclopaedia was simply to break up the circle of knowledge into unrelated fragments, in the university there was not only this evil but also that of excluding from the circle one entire area of knowledge, namely, theology. This, of course, was the evil to which Newman addressed himself in the first five discourses, and his argument was that by excluding theology a university did violence to its very name. "A University, I should lay down, by its very name professes to teach universal knowledge: Theology is surely a branch of knowledge: how then is it possible to profess all branches of knowledge, and yet to exclude not the meanest nor the narrowest of the number?" [17]

Newman's argument is often criticized because it seems to be based on a false derivation of the word "university." Rashdall, for example, in his history of the medieval universities, points out that whether it be true or not that a university should teach universal knowledge, no comfort for that opinion can be found in the original meaning of the name.[18] In the Middle Ages the word *universitas* meant merely a group or body of persons taken collectively. Trade guilds, fraternal organizations, municipalities, all sorts of legal corporations and informal societies were "universities," and when a group of scholars or masters associated themselves for mutual aid, they were naturally called by the same name without any suggestion about the range of their studies. The term, in other words, was social and juristic rather than intellectual, and it asserted that the scholars were banded together as one, not that their studies were many. The term which referred more particularly to the studies, or to the institution where they were pursued, was *studium generale*, but once again this did not mean a place in which all subjects were studied, but a place where students from all parts were received. Its universality was geographic rather than intellectual, and it was so called to distinguish it from the ecclesiastical and monastic schools which drew only from the surrounding district. In time it came to have another kind of universality as well, but this too was geographic. The prestige of Paris, Bologna, and Salerno had caused its masters to be received everywhere without fresh examination, and as this valuable prerogative was later extended to other studia by papal or imperial decree, it came to be considered the essence of the studium generale. Thus, when President Hadley of Yale remarked that an institution should base its right to be called a university "not upon the universal range of knowledge that it teaches but upon the universal recognition of the value of its degrees," [19] he was being more historical than he knew, for the *ius ubique docendi*, the right to teach everywhere, was an attribute of the studium generale long before this phrase was mistranslated as "general education." [20]

Such is the criticism made of Newman's argument, and it would be perfectly valid were it not for two facts: first, that Newman was entirely familiar with the primitive meaning of both these terms, and second, that he did not base his argument upon them. It must be remembered that the argument which Newman employs was not original with him but was a commonplace in the debate which raged between the old universities and the new in the decade after 1826.[21] It was given as a reason for not granting a charter to the nonsectarian London University and also as a reason for not admitting Dissenters to Oxford and Cambridge. It was voiced in pamphlet, in Privy Council, and in the monthly reviews, and the errors which it contained were exposed in all the same quarters. Specifically, Sir William Hamilton wrote a learned and authoritative article in the *Edinburgh Review* which presents all the information that is to be found in Rashdall.[22] Newman read this article on its first appearance, and when he came to write the university discourses he went into the subject for himself. His friend Hope, an amateur historian of the medieval university, warned him that the popular etymology was probably wrong, and therefore in presenting his argument Newman distinctly stated that he was not taking his stand "upon the *derivation* of the word, but upon its recognised meaning, however it came to mean it." [23] The case was the same as with "encyclopaedia." Referring originally to the knowledge which was in general circulation, it came to suggest that the knowledge itself was general, that it formed a circle of all that could be known. So too with *universitas*. Originally the word had always been followed by some defining phrase such as *magistrorum et scholarium*, "a university of masters and scholars"; but by the fourteenth century it came to be used absolutely, and in time the phrase which was mentally supplied was *scientiarum*, "a university of sciences." In 1477, when the University of Tübingen was founded, it was described as "a *studium* devoted to all the sciences human and divine," and D'Irsay says that this phrase marks the emergence of the new conception of a university as a place of universal knowledge.[24] In a sense the conception was "incorrect," but as the word itself is ambiguous and as history is never slow to profit by so fruitful an ambiguity as that, who shall condemn her for it? If the conception had no basis in the word, it must have had the greater basis in men's hearts, for the important thing is not whether the word "university" originally contained the idea of universal knowledge, but that men so felt the need of that idea that they imported it into the word and ultimately into the institution itself.

But what is the real meaning of the idea of universal knowledge? Originally it was not a quantitative conception at all. Whereas today the word "universal" means all-inclusive, composed of many parts, originally it meant simply that the parts had been "turned into one"—*uni-versum*. Originally, the concern with universal knowledge was simply the obverse of a much deeper concern with the oneness or integrity of knowledge. It was the desire to see things whole that forced men to look at the whole body of things, and therefore the true character of a university is not that it teaches all the sciences but that whatever sciences it does teach, it teaches in a spirit of universality. It does this, moreover, not to be true to its name, whether in the original or the current meaning, but simply to be true to its function. It teaches universal knowledge because only so can it teach the truth.

This, it should be noted, is Newman's real argument for requiring that a university should teach theology. For rhetorical purposes, in order to establish his entire position briefly, he does employ the syllogistic argument which has been quoted above, but although he devotes one discourse to elaborating the minor premise, that theology is a branch of knowledge, the major premise, that a university by its very name professes to teach all branches of knowledge, he never does elaborate. Instead, he spends two discourses illustrating the thesis that every science has such an intimate bearing upon every other that it is impossible to teach any one, or any group of sciences, except in the context of all the others; and this argument, a philosophical rather than a historical or verbal one, is the real basis of his position.

Not being a trained philosopher or writing for an audience of philosophers, Newman does not attempt to be at all technical in his discussion of the structure of the sciences, but one may say that his general position was Aristotelian. There are many ways, of course, in which the unity of knowledge may be conceived, and Newman was not unaware of these alternatives. In the appendix to the first edition of the *Discourses* he cites a number of authorities in support of his thesis that "the Branches of Knowledge form one whole," and these include Coleridge, St. Bonaventura, and Lord Bacon.[25] Bacon held that the unity of the sciences lay in their method, Coleridge that it lay in the unity of the mind itself, and St. Bonaventura that it lay in their derivation from the single science of theology. But Newman held that "all knowledge forms one whole, because its subject-matter is one."[26] That its subject is one doubtless depended for Newman on the fact that God together with his works comprises all of reality, but this is a question that goes beyond the problem of knowledge. Granted that reality is one and that knowledge is of reality, then knowledge is also one, and if we find that it is actually divided into distinct and separate sciences, this is simply for the convenience of study and because of the limits of the human mind. The mind cannot take in all of reality at a single glance, and therefore it draws off, or abstracts, various aspects of reality for momentary consideration—and these abstractions we call sciences. In their own idea they are perfectly complete, but they are incomplete in relation to their subject. If, for example, we were to take man himself as the object of our contemplation, then at once we should find that we could view him in a variety of relations.

We may view him in relation to the material elements of his body, or to his mental constitution, or to his household and family, or to the community in which he lives, or to the Being who made him; and in consequence we treat of him respectively as physiologists, or as moral philosophers, or as writers of economics, or of politics, or as theologians. When we think of him in all these relations together, or as the subject at once of all the sciences I have named, then we may be said to reach unto and rest in the idea of man as an object of external fact, similar to that which the eye takes of his outward form. On the other hand, according as we are only physiologists, or only politicians, or only moralists, so is our idea of man more or less unreal; we do not take in the whole of him, and the defect is greater or less, in proportion as the relation is, or is not, important, which is omitted, whether his relation to God, or to his king, or to his children, or to his own component parts.[27]

What is true of man in general would also be true of any portion of reality however minute. If we wished to know a single material object—for example, Westminster Abbey—to know it thoroughly, we should have to make it the focus of universal science. For the science of architecture would speak only of its artistic form, engineering of its stresses and strains, geology of the nature of its stones, chemistry and physics of the ultimate constitution of its matter, history of its past, and literature of the meaning which it had in the culture of a people. What each one of these sciences would say would be perfectly true in its own idea, but it would not give us a true picture of Westminster Abbey. For that, all the sciences would have to be recombined, and it was this recombination which Newman declared was the object of university education.

The recombination is not the same as all the sciences taken together but is a science distinct from them and yet in some sense embodying the materials of them all. Newman calls it by various names, sometimes Philosophy or Liberal Knowledge, sometimes *Philosophia Prima*, the Architectonic Science, or the Science of Sciences, and he apparently uses so many names because he feels that no one of them is really adequate. Indeed, it is undeniable that this discipline has a rather mysterious character. In the first place, although it is the formal object of a university, it is not actually taught there. A university "teaches *all* knowledge by teaching all *branches* of knowledge, and in no other way." [28] Philosophy, therefore, merely emerges out of the particular sciences as a kind of *tertium quid* of the intellectual world—and much beyond this Newman is unable to go. Indeed, it is evident that the conception of this science came to him in a rather tentative way and never was fully or explicitly developed. The first time that he mentions it is in a passage summarizing part of the argument of the third discourse, but in that argument itself there is no mention of anything resembling this science, almost as if it were an afterthought, or at least as if he would willingly have been spared the necessity of a formal explanation. And on another occasion it is referred to as "that Architectonic Science or Philosophy, *whatever it be*," [29] as if Newman himself were uncertain whether such a science existed and what it would be like if it did exist.

At least part of the difficulty lies in the fact that Newman is really including two slightly different conceptions under the group of terms which he employs. He is, of course, discussing two different questions. The first, which occupies the first four discourses and the last two, is the question of whether or not a university should teach theology, and Newman's reply is that it should, because such is the integrity of knowledge that it cannot otherwise teach the truth. The second question, which occupies the intervening discourses, asks whether a university should make utility the direct object of its teaching, and Newman's reply is that it should not, because such is the integrity of the human mind that it will be destroyed by those specialized disciplines which alone are useful. These two questions, apparently so unrelated, are brought together by the one principle which supplies the answer to both, the principle of the integrity of knowledge and the need of the human mind to reflect that integrity. In the former discussion that principle is applied to the studies, in the latter to the students, of a university; and the two taken together are but the objective and the subjective sides of a single conception, that of knowledge as universal in extent and unified in form.

And yet there is a further distinction which Newman does not clearly express. What the student requires is simply a recombination of all the sciences into a unified vision of reality, but what is required among the sciences themselves is some discipline which will discriminate among their provinces by studying, not merely the nature of reality, but also the methods, purposes, and interrelationships of the sciences themselves. If, following what is perhaps a tendency in Newman's own usage, we gave to the former the name of Philosophy or Liberal Knowledge and reserved for the latter the names of Architectonic Science and Science of Sciences, we might say that the latter is quite literally a science *of* sciences. It is Philosophy becoming conscious of itself and engaging in a process of self-examination. Instead of operating as a science, it takes up a position external to the sciences and studies them in the same way that they have previously studied reality. Not much is required, of course, to transform the one into the other; the synthesis is easily made the object of self-analysis; but at least in our own analysis we ought to distinguish between that generalized knowledge of all things which is Newman's answer to the problem of a liberal education, and that discrimination among the sciences themselves which is his answer to the even greater problem of the warfare between science and theology.

Where did Newman get the idea of these sciences? The question is important not merely for its historical interest but also because it will help us to clarify the meaning of the *Discourses* themselves. It is obvious, for example, that when Newman makes "Philosophy" into the object of a university education, he is not condemning his undergraduates to a course in Spinoza, Hegel, and the English empiricists. "Philosophy" he is using purely in the sense that it had before Descartes of a general or summary knowledge of all things. "Each of the arts," says Philo, "has detached and annexed some small items from the world of nature which engage its efforts and attention: geometry has its lines, and music its notes, but philosophy takes the whole nature of existing things; for its subject-matter is this world and every form of existence visible and invisible." [30] It is well to remind ourselves that this conception of philosophy, as simply the undifferentiated pursuit of wisdom, had an almost continuous tradition from the time of Pythagoras to the very end of the Renaissance. Even in the period after the death of Boethius, when of actual philosophizing there was almost none, the idea of philosophy as universal science was kept alive by a series of definitions which were repeated again and again in the early Middle Ages. One of these, given wide currency by Cicero, was that philosophy was "the knowledge of things human and divine," the phrase "and of their causes" or "in their causes" being sometimes added. Another was that it was "the art of arts and the science of sciences," [31] and a third identified the wisdom which philosophy pursued with that mentioned in Proverbs—"Wisdom hath builded her house, she hath hewn out her seven pillars." The pillars, of course, were the seven liberal arts, and since seven is a perfect number, this was another reason why philosophy, which the arts supported and by which they were virtually contained, should be regarded as universal. In the twelfth-century *Didascalion* of Hugh of St. Victor, which Newman quotes for its wisdom in such matters, philosophy is "the knowledge of things as they are" and has as many parts as there are "different kinds of things." Its four divisions, theoretical, practical, mechanical, and logical, contain all knowledge (*omnem continent scientiam*), and "all the arts tend to the one end of Philosophy." Indeed, the *trivium* and *quadrivium* are so called because they are the roads (*viae*) by which the living mind enters into philosophy, and "they so hang together . . . that if even one were absent, the others would not be able to make a philosopher." [32]

Newman had in mind a more specific model, however, than simply the ancient and medieval conception of philosophy, and this was the discipline known to Aristotle's followers, though not to himself, as metaphysics. The names which Aristotle employed were the same as several of those used by Newman—Philosophy, First Philosophy, and the Architectonic Science [33]—and it will be remembered that Aristotle does not speak of this discipline as something established but rather as "the science which we are seeking." If it exists at all, it exists as the crown of a hierarchy of knowledge which ascends through the degrees of sensation, memory, experience, and art to that knowledge which is supremely difficult and absolutely universal and which alone is worthy of the name Wisdom. Traces of this same hierarchy may be found in Newman's work, and Aristotle's First Philosophy also resembles Newman's in being sharply distinguished from the "so-called special sciences," which "cut off a part of being and investigate the attribute of this part." [34] First Philosophy studies being *qua* being, the first causes and ultimate principles of things, and although it would be rash to say that Newman had anything quite so rigorous as this in mind for his undergraduates, something of this sort he evidently did have in the background of his thought.

There is one feature, however, in Aristotle's account of First Philosophy which has also contributed to Newman's other conception, that of the Science of Sciences. This is that science which, in Newman's words, "disposes of the claims and arranges the places of all the departments of knowledge which man is able to master." It has as its function "the comprehension of the bearings of one science on another, and the use of each to each, and the location and limitation and adjustment and due appreciation of them all, one with another." [35] To a slight degree this is also the function of First Philosophy, which, as the architectonic or "master" science, knows the ends for which other sciences are pursued. For the most part, however, the idea of a science which has as its subject the very sciences themselves is less closely associated with metaphysics than with certain traditional conceptions of logic, and Newman, who had studied the history of logic with Whately, was probably harkening back to these conceptions in developing his idea of the Science of Sciences. Doubtless he knew, for example, that Plato had given to dialectic the task of seeing the interrelationship of the sciences, and certainly he knew that Aristotle did not consider logic to be a substantive discipline but rather a preliminary study which teaches what sort of proof is to be expected for propositions of various sorts. Hence it was called by Alexander of Aphrodisias (200 A.D.) an *organon*, or instrument, and by Augustine and others a "science of sciences." [36] That Newman's discipline had something of this character is suggested in the lecture on "Christianity and Scientific Investigation," where it is given the office not only of setting boundaries to the various sciences but also of determining "how much can be known in each province of thought; when we must be contented not to know; in what direction inquiry is hopeless, or on the other hand full of promise; where it gathers into coils insoluble by reason, where it is absorbed in mysteries, or runs into the abyss." It will be "familiar with the signs of real and apparent difficulties, with the methods proper to particular subject-matters," [37] and in general will perform the functions which Aristotle assigns to logic. Indeed, in the *Office and Work of Universities*, in a passage in which Newman repeats his fundamental doctrine that "all truths of whatever kind form into one large body of Truth, by virtue of the consistency between one truth and another, which is a connecting link running through them all," he adds that "the science which discovers this connection, is logic." [38] Obviously, this science is not identical with the Science of Sciences, for the one discovers the unity of knowledge by demonstrating its formal coherency, whereas the other discriminates among its parts and does so not formally but in relation to reality. Nevertheless, the Science of Sciences was apparently influenced by traditional conceptions of logic, and might therefore be called a kind of logic of the sciences.

It was also influenced, however, by a discipline which Bacon has described in the *Advancement of Learning*. We know this because, in a passage where Newman is insisting that the rank or value of any particular science cannot be determined by the science itself but only by the Science of Sciences, he quotes Bacon to the effect that "no perfect discovery can be made upon a flat or a level: neither is it possible to discover the more remote and deeper parts of any science, if you stand but upon the level of the science, and ascend not to a higher science." [39] In the *Advancement of Learning* this sentence appears immediately following one in which Bacon complains that "after the distribution of particular arts and sciences, men have abandoned universality, or *philosophia prima*; which cannot but cease, and stop all progression." This neglect of universality is the fifth "peccant humour" of learning, and it would at first appear that Bacon's philosophia prima, which is described as "a parent or common ancestor to all knowledge," [40] was not unlike Newman's. Employing the metaphor of a tree, Bacon likens the individual sciences to the branches and philosophia prima to the trunk, for the latter has as its subject all those axioms which cut across several sciences instead of being peculiar to one, as (to use his own fantastic example) the axiom that it is sweet to follow a discord by a concord is true in music as in human affections. Bacon's hope is that by studying philosophia prima men will be able to apply to their own subject those laws and principles which have already been discovered in respect to another, and thus all the sciences, the backward as well as the precocious, will move forward together in the common advancement of learning.

THE CIRCLE OF THE SCIENCES

The fact that there is a historical connection, and yet so little actual resemblance, between Bacon's discipline and Newman's enables us to see much more clearly than we otherwise could the special significance of what Newman was trying to do. Whereas Bacon devised a "lateral" discipline which would enable scientists to translate more and more of concrete reality into the terms of their own abstraction, Newman devised a "vertical" discipline which would enable the nonspecialist to reduce these abstractions into a true and balanced picture of reality. In Bacon's view the sciences all had a common set of principles and differed only in the subject to which these principles were applied, but in Newman's view it was their subject which they had in common and their principles on which they differed. Both physics and theology treat of the real world about us, but physics abstracts from that world the element of matter, and theology the element of spirit. What is needed, then, in a unifying discipline is not some central exchange for the trading of implements (for what would physics do with the deductive method of theology or theology with the inductive method of physics?) but some means of determining how much of the world is spirit and how much matter and what the relations are between them. In other words, whereas for Bacon the problem of truth was a problem in discovery, for Newman it was a problem in discrimination. It was posed by confusion rather than by ignorance and was to be solved, not by the augmentation of the sciences, but by their pacification. Bacon's desire was for more knowledge, Newman's for a synthesis of the knowledge already existing.

And yet Bacon was himself one of the great synthetic intelligences. In the celebrated essay by Lord Macaulay, which Newman had before him as he wrote, it was said that "the art which Bacon taught was the art of inventing arts. The knowledge in which Bacon excelled all men, was a knowledge of the mutual relations of all departments of knowledge." [41] Curiously enough, the former phrase is a precise description of philosophia prima as Bacon defined it, and the latter of the same science as defined by Newman. For if, in the Novum organum, Bacon taught the art of inventing arts, surely in the Advancement of Learning he excelled all men in a knowledge of the mutual relations of all departments of knowledge. And it may be, therefore, that Newman's inspiration for this science came not so much from any particular discipline which Bacon or another had devised as from the very role which men of that type had played in the intellectual life of their times. Aristotle, for example, was to Newman "the most comprehensive intellect of Antiquity." He it was who "conceived the sublime idea of mapping the whole field of knowledge, and subjecting all things to one profound analysis"; [42] and if this was Newman's opinion, then it was not simply

THE IMPERIAL INTELLECT

for Aristotle's metaphysics that he admired him, but for the whole body of his philosophic work, which established the division and classification of the sciences in essentially their modern form. And as for the medieval schools, it was not simply their conception of philosophy that Newman valued but the whole idea of the unity or integrity of knowledge which, he said, "was realized and acted on in the middle age with a distinctness unknown before; all subjects of knowledge were viewed as parts of one vast system, each with its own place in it, and from knowing one, another was inferred." [43]

CHAPTER 10

The Man of
Philosophic Habit

His knowledge differed from that of other men, as a Terrestrial
Globe differs from an Atlas which contains a different country on
every leaf. The towns and roads of England, France, and Germany,
are better laid down in the atlas than in the globe. But while we
are looking at England we see nothing of France; and while we are
looking at France we see nothing of Germany. . . . "I have
taken," said Bacon, in a letter written when he was only thirty-one,
to his uncle Lord Burleigh—"I have taken all knowledge to be my
province."

—Macaulay, "Lord Bacon"

IF the task of the educator does not extend to deciding what
kind of people he ought to produce, but merely to devising means of
producing them, then the *Idea of a University* is not an educational work
at all, for it deliberately omits any consideration of means and con-
centrates exclusively upon ends. It is concerned with constructing an
intellectual and cultural ideal, and therefore it belongs less with the
great educational classics properly so called than with the classics of
idealized portraiture. The ideal ruler of Plato, the ideal orator of Aristotle
and Cicero, the medieval saint, the perfect prince and poet of the
Renaissance—these are the figures from which Newman's ideal of the
perfect student is descended, and if we find, therefore, that he is
like something we have never seen, we must remember that he is like
something never seen by Newman either. He is an aspiration, an object
of desire, an idealized type, and his value is the inspirational value of any
unattainable ideal.

Newman was rather at a loss what to call him. The term "gentleman"
could hardly be avoided altogether since it was almost a commonplace
that the education of a gentleman was what the two older universities
provided, but Newman did not like it. It reminded him of the gentlemen-commoners who had been such a trial at Oxford, and he felt that
it would remind the Irish of their English oppressors. Therefore he
strongly repudiated the notion that his university would "result in

nothing better or higher than in the production of that antiquated variety of human nature and remnant of feudalism . . . called 'a gentleman.' " [1] But if not, what then was it to result in? The English language did not supply any other term by which to express, simply and generally, the idea of intellectual perfection or well-being, as the word "health" expresses the well-being of the body and "virtue" that of our moral nature. Therefore, in default of any recognized term, Newman called the perfection of the intellect by the name of "philosophy, philosophical knowledge, enlargement of mind, or illumination," [2] and the one who possessed these qualities he called the man of "philosophic habit."

Who is the man of philosophic habit? "That only is true enlargement of mind," wrote Newman in one of the most famous passages of his extended portrait,

> which is the power of viewing many things at once as one whole, of referring them severally to their true place in the universal system, of understanding their respective values, and determining their mutual dependence. . . . Possessed of this real illumination, the mind never views any part of the extended subject-matter of Knowledge without recollecting that it is but a part, or without the associations which spring from this recollection. It makes everything in some sort lead to everything else; it would communicate the image of the whole to every separate portion, till that whole becomes in imagination like a spirit, every where pervading and penetrating its component parts, and giving them one definite meaning. . . .
>
> To have even a portion of this illuminative reason and true philosophy is the highest state to which nature can aspire, in the way of intellect. . . . The intellect, which has been disciplined to the perfection of its powers, which knows, and thinks while it knows, which has learned to leaven the dense mass of facts and events with the elastic force of reason, such an intellect cannot be partial, cannot be exclusive, cannot be impetuous, cannot be at a loss, cannot but be patient, collected, and majestically calm, because it discerns the end in every beginning, the origin in every end, the law in every interruption, the limit in each delay; because it ever knows where it stands, and how its path lies from one point to another. [3]

It is apparent from this portrait that the man of philosophic habit is simply a living embodiment of Newman's conception of knowledge. As this knowledge was at once universal in scope and unified in character, so the man who possesses it is a kind of walking encyclopaedia or miniature university, in the older senses of those terms. But to note this is to notice a problem. It is one thing to say that a university or an encyclo-paedia ought to take all knowledge for its province, but it is quite an-other to say that an individual ought to do so. Admittedly, Newman does qualify his statement by what is humanly possible. When he says that the "perfection of the Intellect . . . is the clear, calm, accurate vision and comprehension of all things," he adds, "as far as the finite mind can embrace them." [4] But on the other hand, it is very obvious, by the mere force of the terms employed, that the finite mind cannot embrace all things in any clear and accurate vision. Milton's scheme of education was not a bow for every man to shoot in, but Newman's is not a bow for any man to shoot in, and to say that it is an ideal is not to justify it, for there is no point in a *quantitative* ideal—in an adjuration merely to do more abundantly that which we already know we ought to do as abundantly as we can.

If the ordinary reader does not feel this exasperation at Newman's ideal, it is because the very general terms in which it is presented are undeniably winning, and because whenever Newman descends to specific directions the directions are always couched in a negative form. They tell us to avoid certain errors, and as these are errors which can and should be avoided, it is only when we bring them all together and see that they fall into a series of contrasting pairs—not to be narrow, on the one hand, or superficial, on the other; to avoid the dead fact but also the glittering generality—that we realize they once again add up to doing the impossible. Indeed, it may well be that the man of philosophic habit is not so much a creature of impossible virtues as a creature from whom an impossible number of vices have been subtracted. Certainly the best way to approach him is to thread the narrow passage between the Scylla and Charybdis of these opposing errors.

In the first place, we are told that the man of philosophic habit is neither narrow in the range of his studies nor superficial in his mastery of them. What he knows he knows thoroughly, and he knows every-thing. He is not narrow in the range of his studies for the same reason that the university is not—because the omission of any part of knowl-edge does injury to all the rest and to the truth itself. In the case of the university the practical danger was that it would exclude some one area of knowledge and allow the others to encroach upon a territory not their own. In the case of the individual the danger was rather that he would exclude all areas except one and would pronounce upon matters appro-priate to those areas in the light of his own specialty.

Lord Bacon has set down the abuse, of which I am speaking, among the impediments to the Advancement of the Sciences, when he observes that "men have used to infect their meditations, opinions, and doctrines, with some conceits which they have most admired, or *some Sciences which they have most applied*; and give all things else a *tincture* according to them *utterly untrue and improper*. . . . So have the alchemists made a philosophy out of a few experiments of the furnace; and Gilbertus, our countryman, hath made a philosophy out of the observations of a lodestone. So Cicero, when, reciting the several opinions of the nature of the soul, he found a musician that held the soul was but a harmony, saith pleasantly, 'hic ab arte sua non recessit,' 'he was true to his art.' But of these conceits Aristotle speaketh seriously and wisely when he saith, 'Qui respiciunt ad pauca, de facili pronunciant,' 'they who contemplate a few things have no difficulty in deciding.' " [5]

Newman should not be misunderstood as condemning all specialization. He is not concerned, for example, with the extraordinary man— the genius, the saint, the hero—but only with the person whose mind is formed by a deliberate process of training. Neither does he doubt that most people will have to specialize for the sake of their livelihood; he simply adds that for the sake of their intellectual health they ought to correct this specialization by a broad general culture. Obviously, in the conception of this culture he is giving voice to an ideal which has been part of the humanistic tradition since the days of the Sophists, but he doubtless felt that it had a peculiar urgency in his own day because of the strength of the forces which were aligned against it. In the first place, never before had there been so much to know. Not that there ever was a time when the individual could master all the knowledge, even the formal, academic knowledge, which was generally available, but it was only by the mid-nineteenth century that the very idea of such an attempt had become laughable. The great scientists of the century before—Franklin, Watt, Cavendish, and Priestley—were notable for nothing so much as their versatility, but by Newman's day, with the breakup of "natural philosophy" into its specialized areas and with the rise of the whole company of the social sciences, the figure of the geological divine and the scholar tobacconist was rapidly becoming a thing of the past.[6] Newman himself was still accustomed, in selecting professors for his new university, to pick his man first and only later to discuss with him the question of whether he would teach Greek literature or ecclesiastical history or the science of anatomy—but this was a last-ditch stand. By the sixties and seventies, in the words of G. M. Young, England had marched "through the gateway of the Competitive Examination . . . out into the Waste Land of Experts, each knowing so much about so little that he can neither be contradicted nor is worth contradicting." [7]

The trend toward specialization, however, was due not merely to the increase in knowledge but also to a new attitude which was abroad concerning the purpose of knowledge, namely, that it was power. This utilitarian view, which emphasized the fruits of knowledge rather than knowledge itself, was naturally coupled with the most efficient method of realizing those fruits, which, according to Adam Smith, was that of the division of labor. But Newman perceived that the division of labor was the fragmentation of the human being, and therefore, in order to preserve wholeness, he made his man of philosophic habit into the most inefficient of all human types, the jack-of-all-trades.

This is one side of the picture. The other is that, if Newman deplored specialization and urged universality, he was equally concerned to distinguish his type of universality from that which formed a popular evil of the day. This evil had been noticed by Lamb in his essay on "The Old and the New Schoolmaster." "The modern schoolmaster," wrote Lamb, "is expected to know a little of everything, because his pupil is required not to be entirely ignorant of anything. He must be superficially, if I may so say, omniscient. He is to know something of pneumatics; of chemistry; of whatever is curious or proper to excite the attention of the youthful mind; an insight into mechanics is desirable, with a touch of statistics; the quality of soils, etc., botany, the constitution of his country, *cum multis aliis*." What Lamb is describing here is the effect of that vast movement in popular education, conducted for the most part on utilitarian principles, which manifested itself in the Mechanics' Institutes, in Popular Reading Rooms, in Scientific Museums, and in the publications of the Society for the Diffusion of Useful Knowledge. In the range of its interests this movement did convey a kind of universality, but it was not the universality that Newman meant. For if Newman was sure that the exclusive pursuit of one science was bad, he was equally sure that "the practical error of the last twenty years . . . [has been] to force upon [the student] so much that he has rejected all. It has been the error of distracting and enfeebling the mind by an unmeaning profusion of subjects; of implying that a smattering in a dozen branches of study is not shallowness, which it really is, but enlargement, which it is not; of considering an acquaintance with the learned names of things and persons, and the possession of clever duodecimos, and attendance on eloquent lectures, and membership with scientific institutions, and the sight of the experiments of a platform and the specimens of a museum, that all this was not dissipation of mind, but progress. All things now are to be learned at once, not first one thing, then another, not one well, but many badly." [8] So strongly does Newman feel upon this subject that he is inspired to a famous passage in which he draws a picture of two imaginary universities, the one dispensing with residence and tutorial superintendence and giving its degrees to any person who passed an examination in a wide range of subjects, and the other having no professors or examinations at all but merely bringing its young men together for a period of years and then sending them away again—and he declares that apart from the *moral* problem which is raised by idleness, he would prefer the latter. The two universities, of course, are not imaginary. The second is Oxford and the first is the bustling new University of London, which, with its enlarged curriculum and its professorial system, was regarded by its critics as no better than a kind of bazaar or raree show of the learned world. The diversion which it provided was innocent but it was no more than diversion, and it must not be confused with education, which was a high and solemn word.

The second pair of extremes which Newman would have his ideal student avoid concerns not the scope of his knowledge but its form. Knowledge involves learning, Newman tells us, but "mere learning" is not enough.

> There are men who embrace in their minds a vast multitude of ideas, but with little sensibility about their real relations towards each other. These may be antiquarians, annalists, naturalists; they may be learned in the law; they may be versed in statistics; they are most useful in their own place; I should shrink from speaking disrespectfully of them; still, there is nothing in such attainments to guarantee the absence of narrowness of mind. If they are nothing more than well-read men, or men of information, they have not what specially deserves the name of culture of mind, or fulfils the type of Liberal Education.[9]

Schoolboys are such persons, and with them it is well enough, for the business of a schoolboy is simply to store the memory against a future day. But with some persons that day never comes, they remain boys all their lives, and whether they are simple persons like the sailors on the vessel which carried Newman to the Mediterranean or persons of a deep and multifarious learning, nothing that they see or know "carries them forward or backward, to any idea beyond itself." They are at the mercy of an overstimulated memory, and "they measure knowledge by bulk, as it lies in the rude block, without symmetry, without design."[10] Such a rude block is Mosheim's *Ecclesiastical History*, and anyone who has looked into this work will immediately understand what Newman had in mind. The arrangement of the material is by centuries, and each century is divided into two parts, the External and the Internal History of the church. The External History is then subdivided into Prosperous and Calamitous Events and the Internal into 1. Learning, 2. Ministers and Form of Government, 3. Doctrine, 4. Rites, and 5, Heresies; and this pattern is repeated, without any variation, for each of fifteen centuries! Only at the beginning of the Reformation does the learned author concede that "the order and method, that have been followed in the former part of this work, cannot be continued, without the greatest inconvenience," [11] and one may assume that the reader as well as the author is included in this commiseration.

Newman's conception of how history ought to be written, on the other hand, perfectly exemplifies the positive side of his ideal. In 1854, in inviting T. W. Allies to become professor of the philosophy of history at the Catholic University of Ireland, he explained (to a rather bewildered candidate) his notion of what that subject involved. "My notion of the Philosophy of History, is, the science of which historical facts are the basis, or the laws on which it pleases the Almighty Providence to conduct the political and social world. The fault of Schlegel's work, as far as I recollect it, is, that it has no *view* - only a number of detached remarks. Gibbon's is a philosophical history, i.e. a history written, not as Fleury writes, viz. as a collection of facts, but with reference and subservience to a certain philosophy, and a bad one!" [12] History, of course, is just an example. Any subject, as treated by the man of philosophic habit, would turn into a kind of philosophy of that subject, for the essential character of this type of mind is that it generalizes its materials. It orders them, it delineates relationships, and perceives the inner idea which animates them and gives them form. The image which Newman always uses is that of a traveler lost in some deep, rich country or in a strange city, where he has no map of the streets, and who mounts to some high hill or church tower by way of reconnoitering the neighborhood and so getting a "view." For a "view," more than anything else, is what characterizes the man of philosophical habit.

The word is worth investigating, for it was part of the jargon of Newman's group at Oxford, Froude having apparently given it currency in the early thirties.[13] It expressed what seemed to Newman the greatest need of the day, for whereas the liberals had a coherent, positive philosophy, the church did not, and "those who have a *view*, have indefinite power over those who have none." Hence his alarm, on going to Rome in 1846, to discover from a Jesuit father that even the Catholic church had no view. Aquinas was not in favor there, and when he asked what philosophy they did adopt, he was told, none. "Odds and ends - whatever seems to them best - like St. Clement's Stromata. They have no philosophy. *Facts* are the great things, and nothing else." This was confirmed a few years later in the confusion surrounding the re-establishment of the hierarchy in England, for Newman complained bitterly that "we want Seminaries far more than Sees. We want education, *view*, combination, organisation." [14] And Hope, writing about the new university, agreed that "there is no one . . . who has any *view* (an Oriel Term I think,). . . . All seems insulated and partial, and so the strength of all is comparatively useless." [15]

It is in *Loss and Gain*, however, that the fullest explanation of this term is given. Of the two friends Charles Reding and William Sheffield we are told that neither

> had what are called *views* in religion; by which expression we do not here signify that neither had taken up a certain line of opinion . . . but that neither of them . . . had placed his religion on an intellectual basis. It may be as well to state more distinctly what a 'view' is, what it is to be 'viewy,' and what is the state of those who have no 'views.' When, then, men for the first time look upon the world of politics or religion, all that they find there meets their mind's eye as a landscape addresses itself for the first time to a person who has just gained his bodily sight. One thing is as far off as another; there is no perspective. The connexion of fact with fact, truth with truth, the bearing of fact upon truth, and truth upon fact, what leads to what, what are points primary and what secondary,—all this they have yet to learn. It is all a new science to them, and they do not even know their ignorance of it. Moreover, the world of to-day has no connexion in their minds with the world of yesterday; time is not a stream, but stands before them round and full, like the moon. . . . They hear of men, and things, and projects, and struggles, and principles; but everything comes and goes like the wind, nothing makes an impression, nothing penetrates, nothing has its place in their minds. They locate nothing; they have no system. They hear and they forget; or they just recollect what they have once heard, they can't tell where. Thus they have no consistency in their arguments; that is, they argue one way to-day, and not exactly the other way to-morrow, but indirectly the other way, at random. Their lines of argument diverge; nothing comes to a point; there is no one centre in which their mind sits, on which their judgment of men and things proceeds.[16]

A few pages later, however, we are told that Sheffield, "without possessing any real view of things more than Charles, was, at this time, fonder of hunting for views, and more in danger of taking up false ones. That is, he was 'viewy,' in a bad sense of the word. He was not satisfied intellectually with things as they are; he was critical, impatient to reduce things to system, pushed principles too far, was fond of argument, partly from pleasure in the exercise, partly because he was perplexed." [17] Thus there is a bad sense of the word "view" as well as a good one, and it is the second dilemma of Newman's ideal student that he must realize the one without becoming guilty of the other. On one page of the *Idea of a University* he will read that "Science and Philosophy, in their elementary idea, are nothing else but this habit of *viewing*, as it may be called, the objects which sense conveys to the mind, of throwing them into system, and uniting and stamping them with one form." But on another page he will find a denunciation of "that spurious philosophism, which shows itself in what, for want of a word, I may call 'viewiness' "; [18] and he may be at a loss to state the difference between viewing and viewiness, between having a view and being viewy. One difference would seem to be that in the former instance you have only one and in the latter you have a great many and at a moment's notice and not necessarily in harmony with one another. Hence they may also be described as unreal, another word which was a favorite with Newman and which means partly that a set of opinions has no consistency within itself and partly that it has no relation to reality. [19] This, certainly, is the chief difference between views and viewiness—that the former are grounded in reality and the latter are reared in the insubstantial air. Viewiness, therefore, is the opposite extreme from "mere learning." As mere learning was fact without system, so viewiness is system without fact. The one is reason run mad as the other was memory forgetful of its place. And between these two, with a judicious admixture of reason *and* memory, of fact *and* system, the man of philosophic habit is asked to construct a broad but accurate *view*.

Casting up the accounts, one may say that to become a man of philosophic habit we need to do three things, and that these three things are arranged in a hierarchy of ascending intellectual attainment. First, we must achieve accuracy of mind; we must really know what we know. Secondly, we must achieve universality; we must know everything. And thirdly, we must integrate our knowledge into a single, unified vision. Neither can we avoid the dilemma—or the trilemma—with which we are thus confronted by saying that Newman's real interest is in only one of these points and that the other two are more or less secondary or incidental. He is interested in all of them, and he insists upon all of them with very nearly an equal force. "I hold very strongly," he says in relation to the first point, "that the first step in intellectual training is to impress upon a boy's mind the idea of science, method, order, principle, and system; of rule and exception, of richness and harmony. This is commonly and excellently done by making him begin with Grammar; nor can too great accuracy, or minuteness and subtlety of teaching be used towards him, as his faculties expand, with this simple purpose." [20] And similarly with the other two points, which have already been illustrated sufficiently.

Once again, then, we are confronted with the query—what did Newman mean? How seriously did he intend this impossible ideal to be taken? And did he have in mind any specific technique by which it could be realized? Let it be said at once that if he did, he published no blueprints on the subject, and also that whatever he may have said, the ideal remains in any ordinary sense impossible. But he did intend it to be taken seriously, and he did have a notion, although not one that he very specifically developed, of how his ideal might be realized at least in some sense and to a certain degree.

When Imlac was describing to Rasselas the training and knowledge necessary for a poet, the latter perceived the "enthusiastic fit" coming on and cried out, "Enough! thou hast convinced me, that no human being can ever be a poet." [21] The episode reminds us that Newman's man of philosophic habit is not the only person of whom universal knowledge has been required. From ancient times it has also been a requisite of the poet, especially the epic poet,[22] and the eulogists of other professions have been fain to claim it for their specialty as well. Cicero, Quintilian, and Aristotle, in passages with which Newman was perfectly familiar, made it an attribute of the ideal orator,[23] and Isidore of Seville spoke in the same way of the physician. In the practice of his profession he needed to know all of the seven liberal arts, and indeed, his own art was not included among them only because "they embrace separate subjects, but medicine embraces all." [24] Vitruvius, too, in planning the education of an architect, declared that "he should be a man of letters, a skilful draughtsman, a mathematician, familiar with scientific inquiries, a diligent student of philosophy, acquainted with music; not ignorant of medicine, learned in the responses of jurisconsults, familiar with astronomy and astronomical calculations." [25] It is difficult to remember, after all this, that he is just an architect, but so he is, and like the poet, the orator, and the physician, he provides an example of a role which is sufficiently limited to be within the compass of a single man and yet which includes, at least in some sense, the entire range of knowledge.

It is evident that the universality of the architect and the physician (presumably of the poet and orator as well) is due to the fact that their disciplines are not really sciences, with a definite subject matter of their own, but practical activities which involve a variety of different subject matters. As the sciences are formed by abstracting from reality one particular aspect for isolated consideration, they do not give us, as Newman insisted, a true picture of concrete reality; and conversely, any portion of reality, however minute, can be known in its concreteness only by a knowledge which is universal in extent. The problems of building a theater or treating a disease radiate out infinitely into all creation, and theoretically there is no point at which they can be cut short. They are all "flowers in the crannied wall," and it is perfectly true that if we could understand them "root and all, and all in all," then we would understand the entire universe, even to the nature of God and man.

Tennyson underlines the *if*, and indeed the view which he expresses is not a solution to Newman's problem but simply a restatement of it. It is *because* the unity of knowledge requires universality for the solution of a concrete problem that Newman would give to his student this attribute—but the fact does not explain *how* the student gets it. It does not explain it, that is, unless there is some sense in which the knowledge of a flower or of medicine or archiecture, taken as these things are normally understood, implicitly contains a knowledge of all other facts and relations as well. Something of this view is of course embodied in any mystical or symbolistic approach to reality, and it is an important element in English Romantic thought. As applied to the question of a cultural ideal, it holds that one comes closest to general humanity, not by being complete man, but by being intensive man, by carrying one's particular humanity to its furthest reach. "Any road," wrote Carlyle, "this simple Entepfuhl road, will lead you to the end of the World." And echoing Wilhelm Meister, he added, "Not this man and that man, but all men make up mankind, and their united tasks the task of mankind." [26] It would be wrong to say that Newman is not haunted and even infected by this view, but formally he is against it. Formally, his position is the classical one that man is human because he is totally human. He is a little world, not because he is an atom in a homogeneous universe, but because he is a microcosm, mirroring in his own person every aspect of a fully diversified universe.

Newman's formal solution to his problem, then, is not that there is a knowledge of particulars which implicitly contains a knowledge of all other things, but rather that there is a mode of knowing which is perfectly satisfactory to one whose purposes are not technical and that this mode of knowing is less exacting in its mastery than technical knowledge is. Actually, this is the kind of knowledge that Vitruvius demanded of the architect. "For an architect ought to be and can be no critic like Aristarchus, yet not without culture; no musician like Aristoxenus, yet not without knowledge of music; no painter like Apelles, yet not unskilled with his pencil; no sculptor like Myron or Polyclitus, yet not ignorant of the plastic art; nor in fine a physician like Hippocrates, yet not unskilled in medicine; nor in other sciences excelling in a singular manner, yet in these not unskilled." [27] The problem is, how can a knowledge which is simply not-ignorance and a skill which is simply not-awkwardness be prevented from becoming the viewiness or "smattering" which Newman stigmatized? What is this mode of knowing which magically enables us to know without involving us in the labor that ordinary knowledge requires?

Once again Newman is not very precise, and the most we can say is that there are certain recognizable elements which seem to have been present to his mind. One of these was a classical tradition which was developed more in connection with the practical arts than with the theoretic sciences, and which therefore took the form of a distinction between knowledge which enables one to do and knowledge which merely enables one to understand or evaluate what has been done by others. When the epic poet, for example, employed a simile from bee-keeping or the making of an axletree, this demonstrated to the ancients that his work had an encyclopaedic character. But at the same time it was obvious that the knowledge he possessed did not extend to the actual keeping of bees or the making of an axletree—it extended merely to the meaning of these activities in human life. So too with the orator. He must be able to speak about things which he could not do, and therefore Aristotle in the *Rhetoric* treats the various subjects which the orator must understand in merely a loose and popular way, and he refers the reader for a more technical handling to the various specialized treatises.[28] That something of this rhetorical tradition was present in Newman's mind is evident from the emphasis which he places upon the polite accomplishment of conversation. Conversation is simply the oratory of the drawing room, and just as Cicero might be called upon to speak on naval affairs' one day and agrarian the next, so the man of philosophic habit, without being either an admiral or a farmer, might be expected to converse on an equally wide range of subjects. Such an ability is the mark of a "gentleman," and it is a delightful refinement of this idea by Ruskin, that if the education of a gentleman befits him to converse about things he cannot do, then the education of a lady must befit her, not to converse about things she cannot do, but simply to follow the conversation of a gentleman![29]

The tradition of a nontechnical knowledge was not purely rhetorical, however, for it also included the ability to pass judgment on the excellence or appropriateness of things which we cannot ourselves produce. "It might be objected," wrote Aristotle, "that he who can judge of the healing of a sick man would be one who could himself heal his

disease, and make him whole—that is, in other words, a physician. . . .
But physicians are of three kinds:—there is the ordinary practitioner,
and there is the physician of the higher class, and thirdly the intelligent
man who has studied the art: in all arts there is such a class; and we
attribute the power of judging to them quite as much as to the professors of the art." [30] In music Aristotle thinks it may be "difficult, if not
impossible, for those who do not perform to be good judges of the
performance of others," [31] but there are many arts in which this is not
the case. "For example . . . the master of the house will even be a
better judge than the builder, just as the pilot will judge better of a rud-
der than the carpenter, and the guest will judge better of a feast than
the cook." [32] And if these are trivial examples, their purpose is to show
that the people in a democracy may safely be assigned deliberative and
judicial offices for which they are not expertly qualified. The franchise,
the jury system, the desire for an amateur in policy-making positions are
all based upon the assumption that one can correctly judge of things
which he cannot rightly do.

It is not difficult to perceive, however, that in many of these examples
knowledge has been transmuted into desire. The guest does not really
judge of the feast, but of what he likes, and so too with the householder,
the voter, and the maker of policy. They are not showing knowledge *of*
a situation but are expressing their will *in* a situation, and insofar as they
are doing anything more than this one may doubt whether their competence really does extend beyond their technical knowledge. They are
examples of what Aristotle calls "practical wisdom," of which the good
state is "truth in agreement with right desire"; and to some extent it is
this practical wisdom that the man of philosophic habit possesses. But
he also possesses a knowledge more purely theoretic in character, such as
is to be found in Aristotle's conception of "philosophic wisdom," for like
the man of philosophic habit, the Aristotelian wise man is "wise in
general, not in some particular field or in any other limited respect." [33]
He "knows all things, as far as possible, although he has not the knowledge of each of them in detail," and Aristotle explains that the characteristic of "knowing all things must belong to him who has in the highest
degree universal knowledge [i.e. knowledge of universals]; for he knows
in a sense all the instances that fall under the universal." [34] Philosophic
wisdom, therefore, is a combination of intuitive reason, which apprehends the universals, and scientific knowledge, which is the capacity to
demonstrate what may follow from them.[35]

Newman certainly does not limit his conception of philosophy to the
eternal and invariable, which alone is the object of philosophic wisdom,
but in the conception of a knowledge which, in apprehending the first

principles of things, apprehends all that follows from those principles, he does have a specific and respectable mode of achieving universality. Moreover, he had seen this mode applied to the problems of education in Richard Whately's famous distinction between the two kinds of "smattering,"/ that which gives a superficial, and that which gives an elementary, knowledge of a subject. The former, said Whately, consists in cdd bits of information, the latter in underlying principles, and it is the latter which provides the solution for the problem of general education.

It is evident that a man cannot learn all things perfectly. Some may say it befits a gentleman to have a slight and general knowledge, as much however as he can gain, of every dignified and curious pursuit; others say, "Let him make one study . . . his main object, lest the mind be distracted by the multiplicity of pursuits. . . ."

I should say it is best for a man to make *some* pursuit his main object, according to his, 1st, calling; 2nd, *natural* bent, or, 3rd, opportunities . . . then let him get a slight knowledge of what else is worth it, regulated in his choice by the same three circumstances, which should also determine in great measure, where an elementary, and where a superficial, knowledge is desirable.

Generally speaking, however, the elementary is the more philosophical, the superficial the more showy, and also the more practically useful. . . . (vid. 'Aris. Eth.' 6).[36]

Whately then goes on, in a passage already quoted, to admit that his own learning is "of a very singular kind, being more purely elementary than anyone's I know. I am acquainted with the elements of most things, and that more accurately than many who are much versed in them, but I know nothing thoroughly, except such studies as are intrinsically of an elementary character." [37]

A knowledge of the elements or first principles of things, however, is not the only means by which the man of philosophic habit can achieve a species of universality. He can also achieve it by a knowledge of the methodology of the sciences. This knowledge is not one which judges but is unable to do; rather it is able to do but has not yet done. It puts the student in the *way* (as the Greek *methodos* implies) of acquiring knowledge which in point of fact he has not acquired. When men say that next to knowing a thing, the best is knowing where to find it, or that next to being an authority, the best is being able to discern who is an authority and who is not, they are simply recognizing the possibilities of a knowledge of method.

It was Aristotle, however, who made this knowledge into the hallmark of general culture. In famous passages in the *Ethics*, the *Metaphysics*, and the *Parts of Animals*, he declared that the ability to judge what degree of precision may fairly be expected in any inquiry is the mark of an educated man: such a person would not accept probable reasoning from a mathematician or require demonstration from an orator.[38] Whately apparently included this ability, as well as a grasp of first principles, in the knowledge which he called "elementary," for in the account of his own learning he uses the Aristotelian illustration. "I can explain the nature of mathematical reasoning," he declares, "better than some practised mathematicians, and describe the peculiar nature of theology, and give advice as to the study of it, better than many learned divines. I know pretty accurately the peculiar character of each branch of study, the misconceptions of it which men are liable to form, and the errors in pursuing it, the faculties which it calls for, and the habits it tends to cultivate, and there I stop. . . . Practically, and with a view to general utility, I resemble one whose trade is to make instruments for others to work with, being occupied in training others to do more than I can do myself. . . ." [39]

Such training was not limited to a knowledge of what method is appropriate to each science; it also included (at least for Whately) the method which is common to all, namely, logic. For although "the Statesman is engaged with political affairs; the Soldier, with military; the Mathematician, with the properties of numbers and magnitudes; the Merchant, with commercial concerns, &c.," the one thing in which "*all* and each of these*" are engaged is reasoning. "They are all occupied in deducing, well or ill, Conclusions from Premises; each, concerning the Subject of his own particular business." If, therefore, the process "going on daily, in each of so many different minds, is, in any respect, the *same,*" [40] then a knowledge of that process should not, indeed, at once make a person a statesman, a soldier, a mathematician, or a merchant, but it should put him *in the way* of mastering any one of these subjects with ease and readiness. Indeed, not merely formal logic but, more generally, the ability to think is independent of particular subject matters and so is the instrument of all. "The man who has learned to think," wrote Newman, "and to reason and to compare and to discriminate and to analyze . . . will not indeed at once be a lawyer, or a pleader, or an orator, or a statesman, or a physician, or a good landlord, or a man of business, or a soldier, or an engineer, or a chemist, or a geologist, or an antiquarian, but he will be placed in that state of intellect in which he can take up any one of the sciences or callings I have referred to, or any other for which he has a tasto or special talent, with an ease, a grace, a versatility, and a success, to which another is a stranger." [41] Actually his knowledge will be limited, but potentially it is unlimited. It is unlimited in the sense that there is no direction in which it cannot be extended whenever the occasion requires.

Some element of all these traditions, then, is present in Newman's conception of the man of philosophic habit, but perhaps more interesting than the source or the exact nature of this ideal is the question of this basic antinomy, and that they arise out of Newman's conception of what it meant to Newman himself. Why was he drawn to this ideal rather than to some other? It is not, as some have said, that in the man of philosophic habit Newman was depicting himself, for surely nothing could be farther from the truth. Newman was a seminal rather than an architectonic intelligence, and therefore it is more likely that the man of philosophic habit represents all that he wanted to be rather than all that he was. The ideal was the image in his mind's eye rather than the image in his glass, for it provided the solution to the central intellectual problem of his formative years.

This was the problem of the One and the Many. It will be noted that all the antinomies involved in the man of philosophic habit are forms of this basic antinomy, and that they arise out of Newman's conception of the very nature of philosophic knowledge. With the problem of knowledge as such Newman was not deeply concerned—when he thought about it at all, he inclined to the commonsense view—but with the problem of how the mind can reconcile the unity which is the deepest need of its own nature with the multiplicity which is the most obvious character of the external world, he was deeply and even passionately concerned. In the first place, he could not doubt either of these two premises. He believed, on the one hand, that there is an invincible tendency in the human mind to be "ever seeking to systematise its knowledge." [42] "When we give reasons for alleged facts and reduce them into dependence on each other, we feel a satisfaction, which is wanting when we receive them as isolated and unaccountable," [43] and so strong is this feeling in us that we prefer even "the completeness and precision of bigotry to a fluctuating and homeless scepticism." [44] On the other hand, Newman also believed that, whatever may be the ultimate character of the world about us, the appearance which it initially presents is that of a welter of undifferentiated sensations.

It has often been observed [he writes] that, when the eyes of the infant first open upon the world, the reflected rays of light which strike them from the myriad of surrounding objects present to him no image, but a medley of colours and shadows. They do not form into a whole; they do not rise into foregrounds and melt into distances; they do not divide into groups; they do not coalesce into unities; they do not combine into persons; but each particular hue and tint stands by itself, wedged in amid a thousand others upon the vast and flat mosaic, having no intelligence, and conveying no story, any more than the wrong side of some rich tapestry. The little babe stretches out his arms and fingers, as if to grasp or to fathom the many-coloured vision; and thus he gradually learns the connexion of part with part, separates what moves from what is stationary, watches the coming and going of figures, masters the idea of shape and of perspective, calls in the information conveyed through the other senses to assist him in his mental process, and thus gradually converts a calidoscope into a picture.[45]

What happens, with man and beast alike, in the process of perception, continues in the case of man in the process of intellection. "The intellect of man . . . energizes as well as his eye or ear. . . . It seizes and unites what the senses present to it; it grasps and forms what need not have been seen or heard except in its constituent parts. . . . It distinguishes between rule and exception, between accident and design. It assigns phenomena to a general law, qualities to a subject, acts to a principle, and effects to a cause. In a word, it philosophizes." [46]

That is to say, it philosophizes if it can; for as the mind takes in larger and larger bodies of material, the burden upon it becomes almost intolerable, and it was this burden which produced in Newman the five shattering illnesses which form the basic pattern of his undergraduate and liberal years. Gifted with a ranging and curious intellect, he was led again and again into novel sciences and extracurricular studies, until at last, breaking under the strain or thrown into a panic by some approaching examination, he found that he had not mastered his materials at all, that his mind was "a labyrinth more than anything else." In almost every case the disordered state of his knowledge was symbolized by the very form which his illness took—he felt "a twisting of the brain, of the eyes," and it seemed that his "head inside was made up of parts"—as if the divine vengeance were chastising his arrogance by confirming him in the very state in which he had sinned.[47]

And yet one need not draw solely upon these abnormal experiences to illustrate Newman's problem. In 1825, when he was simultaneously vice-principal of Alban Hall, curate of St. Clement's, and contributor to the Encyclopaedia Metropolitana, he wrote that he was pleased at his ability to make such various tasks "go on together in perfect harmony." "I can pursue two separate objects better than at first," he told his mother. "It is a great thing to have pulled out my mind." [48] But a year later, when he had dropped these various tasks for the single one of tutor, he wrote again, "My work is *all of a kind* - not various, multiform, a convenience which I have long been denied." And to his sister a few days later, "I have felt much the delight of having *one* business. No one can tell the unpleasantness of having matters of different kinds to get through at once. We talk of it *distracting* the mind; and its effect upon me is indeed a tearing or *ripping open* of the coats of the brain and the vessels of the heart." [49]

The point of interest here is Newman's imagery. In the first passage the mind is a sort of elastic container which can be "pulled out" to advantage, but in the second it is a vital organ and is simply destroyed by such treatment. "It is astonishing," wrote George Eliot, "what a different result one gets by changing the metaphor! Once call the brain an intellectual stomach, and one's ingenious conception of the classics and geometry as plows and harrows seems to settle nothing. But then it is open to someone else to . . . call the mind a sheet of white paper or a mirror, in which case one's knowledge of the digestive process becomes quite irrelevant." [50] So in the *Idea of a University* Newman has two sets of images which run through the entire book and which reveal the underlying conflict in his intellectual ideal. According to one set, the mind is a storehouse or container, and as the virtue of a storehouse is to be "capacious" and its vice to be "narrow" or "confined," so the object of education is mental enlargement, and the phrase "enlargement of mind" becomes one of the key phrases in the *Idea of a University*. But according to the other set, the mind is a living organism, either a stomach which "digests" the crude and raw materials of knowledge or else a plant which has to be "cultivated"—in either case, something which is alive, not mechanical; active, not passive; something which does not merely accumulate foreign bodies but assimilates these bodies into its own organic form.

Newman seems to have been quite unconscious of the discrepancy between these two sets of images. Indeed, there is one delightful passage in which, having made "enlargement of mind" into the end of education, he is apparently disturbed by the quantitative implications of the phrase and so goes on to say that "true" enlargement is "a digestion of what we receive, into the substance of our previous state of thought; and without this no enlargement is said to follow!" [51] And yet he should have been conscious of the discrepancy, because the two sets of images reveal the presence in his ideal of two different intellectual traditions. The organic imagery and the emphasis upon unity of mind derive from the school of Coleridge, whereas the mechanical imagery (the "storehouse" is simply

THE MAN OF PHILOSOPHIC HABIT

a *tabula rasa* with raised edges) derives from the liberal tradition of the Enlightenment. The view that "enlargement of mind" is the most important thing in the world Newman found asserted in a dozen places in the literature of the two centuries before his own, and by dint of continuous repetition by Bacon and Locke and Ephraim Chambers, by Isaac Watts, Gibbon, Macaulay, and the two Mills, by Copleston, Whately, and indeed by the entire liberal tradition,[52] the mind of man was so far "enlarged" that by the nineteenth century it went beyond its limits and became fully "open." In our own day the open mind is the ideal, but of this achievement Newman was skeptical. Or at least, whereas the liberals believed that the object of opening the mind was simply opening the mind, Newman believed (as Chesterton once said) that the object of opening the mind, as of opening the mouth, was to shut it again on something solid. "For without digestion no enlargement is said to follow."

Perhaps the best way to illustrate Newman's relation to the liberal ideal, however, is through his use of a work which perfectly represents that ideal, *The Improvement of the Mind: Or, a Supplement to the Art of Logick* (1741) by Isaac Watts. In one of his Oxford university sermons, delivered in 1841, Newman attempted to define what is meant by "enlargement or expansion of mind," and he gave twelve examples of what it does consist in and five of what it does not. At least half of the first group of twelve have some parallel in Watts's chapter "Of enlarging the Capacity of the Mind," and it is probable that they were actually taken from that work, with which Newman had long been acquainted. The borrowed examples include the experience of seeing wild and awful scenery for the first time, "the view of the heavens, which the telescope opens upon us," the sight of strange beasts of prey and other foreign animals, an acquaintance with the physical sciences and with history, and "what is called seeing the world . . . travelling," etc.[53] If these positive examples are a measure of Newman's agreement with Watts, however, the five negative examples are a measure of his disagreement, for they show that true enlargement does not consist in the mere addition to our knowledge, though that is a necessary preliminary, but in the integration of the new knowledge with the old.

Even with this correction, however, Newman was not yet done. Eleven years later he incorporated a considerable part of this sermon into the sixth discourse of the *Idea of a University*. According to his own note, he took it over "almost *verbatim*," [54] but actually there are revisions in phrase which bring out very strikingly his fundamental disagreement with his source. In the sermon, enlargement of mind was an experience which carried along with it a feeling of exhilaration and wonder, a sort

[207]

of "wild surmise," which might produce some momentary tumult in the breast but was certainly nothing to give concern. By 1852, however, the experience had become heady, intoxicating, and even dangerous. It is compared to Eve's giddiness on eating the apple and to the mad vision of the drunken king in the *Bacchanals* of Euripides. The view of the heavens, for example, no longer "fills and possesses the mind," but is regarded as a temptation which, "*if allowed* to fill and possess the mind, may almost whirl it round and make it dizzy." The wild scenery now makes us lose our "bearings," and the sight of strange beasts "throw[s] us out of ourselves into another creation," if one may so express the "temptation" which comes upon the mind. Physical science "almost takes away [one's] breath," whereas the enlargement afforded by religion, we are told, is "an enlargement, not of tumult, but of peace." [55]

Perhaps the most interesting example, however, is that of travel. Watts had urged that we survey the various customs and beliefs of mankind because we should thereby discover that in every party there were "Persons of good Sense and Virtue, persons of Piety and Worth, Persons of much Candour and Goodness," and this would teach us tolerance. In 1841 Newman recommended the same broadening experience but declined to comment on what we would find. By 1852, however, he says that we will learn "how various yet how alike men are, how low-minded, how bad, how opposed, yet how confident in their opinions," [56] which is approximately the attitude that Watts was trying to correct!

In Newman's own travels, it will be recalled, he did not experience any of "that largeness and expansion of mind" which one of his friends told him privately he would get,[57] and on the whole it was probably just as well that he did not. In a sermon preached a few years before his departure, he had warned his hearers that "any thing new or unexpected is dangerous to you," and this included new books, new people, new sights. "See that you are not *unsettled* by them," he urged; "this is the danger; fear becoming *unsettled*. Consider that stability of mind is the chief of virtues, for it is Faith." [58] Believing this, he must have been genuinely alarmed to discover that the idea of a winter in the Mediterranean was so "very tempting" that it "quite unsettled" him and showed how "little real stability of mind I have yet attained." A more cowardly man would have stayed at home, but Newman was a minister of religion and so needed to understand the temptations that he would have to preach against. "I wish to experience the feeling and the trial of expansiveness of views if it were but to be able to *say* I had, and to know how to meet it in the case of others." [59]

Travel, of course, is only an example, but it sufficiently indicates the strange ambivalence of Newman's attitude toward novel information.

THE MAN OF PHILOSOPHIC HABIT

In the abstract, he had no fear of it at all. If it were true, it could not hurt the truth he already knew, and his reason would have no difficulty in seeing that this was so. But this was in the abstract. Actually and concretely, it is not the reason of man that is troubled by these things but his imagination. It is the imagination which is caught up and swept away by the great and engrossing interest of the new sciences and which becomes so totally absorbed in them that, without denying the older truths of revelation or morality, it simply puts them to one side as a dull and troublesome business. Newman felt this danger and felt it keenly. Indeed, it was precisely because he was so interested in the new sciences, and in all novel information, that he alternately decided to reject them so that they would not be tempting and to master them so that they would not be novel. The former, one is happy to say, was only an occasional impulse, whereas the latter was his deliberate and seasoned resolve.

This reveals the practical reason for Newman's concern with universal knowledge. No novel information means *nil admirari*, nothing but a serene philosophic calm. The mind is put

> above the influences of chance and necessity, above anxiety, suspense, unsettlement, and superstition, which is the lot of the many. Men, whose minds are possessed with some one object, take exaggerated views of its importance, are feverish in the pursuit of it, make it the measure of things which are utterly foreign to it, and are startled and despond if it happens to fail them. They are ever in alarm or in transport. . . . But the intellect, which has been disciplined to the perfection of its powers, which knows, and thinks while it knows, which has learned to leaven the dense mass of facts and events with the elastic force of reason, such an intellect cannot be partial, cannot be exclusive, cannot be impetuous, cannot be at a loss, cannot but be patient, collected, and majestically calm, because it discerns the end in every beginning, the origin in every end, the law in every interruption, the limit in each delay; because it ever knows where it stands, and how its path lies from one point to another. It is the τετράγωνος of the Peripatetic, and has the "nil admirari" of the Stoic.[60]

Like the Greek and Roman philosophers, who are Newman's model in the description of this calm, the man of philosophic habit stands aloof and secure amid the tumults which rage about him or in the dust of the valley below. But whereas for the ancient philosopher these tumults were political or social or personal, for the man of philosophic habit they are purely intellectual, the conflict of the old sciences with the new.

THE IMPERIAL INTELLECT

And whereas the ancient philosopher withdrew from the fray as from a battle whose issue did not concern him, the man of philosophic habit is deeply concerned, and refrains from the conflict only that there may be someone, when once the armies are exhausted, who can heal the breach and apportion the territories where they rightfully belong.

CHAPTER 11

The Uses of Knowledge

Alcibiades the Athenian in his boyhood was being trained in the
liberal arts and sciences at the home of his uncle, Pericles; and
Pericles had ordered Antigenides, a player on the pipes, to be sent
for, to teach the boy to play on that instrument, which was then
considered a great accomplishment. But when the pipes were
handed to him and he had put them to his lips and blown, dis-
gusted at the ugly distortion of his face, he threw them away and
broke them in two. When this matter was noised abroad, by the
universal consent of the Athenians of that time the art of playing
the pipes was given up.

—Aulus Gellius, XV.xvii (tr. Rolfe)

AT approximately the moment that Newman was de-
scribing the man of philosophic habit in terms of the nil admirari of
the Stoics, the rest of England was flocking by the thousands to wonder
at the marvels of the Great Exhibition in Hyde Park. Indeed, a writer in
the *Times* ironically contrasted the thanks given to Sir Joseph Paxton
for the invention of the glass house and to Mr. Stephenson for the
tubular bridge, "objects truly Catholic," with those given to Dr. Newman for his lectures on the *Present Position of Catholics*.[1] If Newman
was fined a hundred pounds for those lectures, however, he should have
been fined a thousand for the *Idea of a University*, for the wrong which
he did to Achilli was as nothing compared with the wrong which he did
to the average Englishman in supposing that he would ever allow his
son to be made into anything so useless as a man of philosophic habit.
At one time this might have been possible, but over the past hundred
years the Englishman had taken to himself a new hero, the "active self-
helping character" which John Stuart Mill declared was "the foundation
of the best hopes for the general improvement of mankind."[2] James
Brindley, the almost illiterate son of a Midlands collier, who created the
canals that made Manchester and Liverpool prosperous; John Rennie,
who drained the Lincolnshire fens and built the Waterloo Bridge and
the Plymouth breakwater; "blind Jack of Knaresborough," road-builder
and engineer; Hargreaves, Crompton, Watt, and Arkwright—these men
of no general culture but of a shrewd, practical energy marked the

emergence of a new ideal which was commanding a wider and wider attention.[3] Hence it was that, after developing his conception of philosophy and the philosophic habit, Newman anticipated that "cautious and practical thinkers" would ask him, "What is the *use* of it?" [4]

If he had been perfectly honest, he would have replied that it was of no use whatever, for this was not only true but it was the entire point of the classical and Renaissance tradition to which Newman's thinking belonged. The aristocratic Greek or Roman who could judge of things that he could not do was admired not merely for his ability to judge but also for his inability to do. Inquiring whether music should be part of the education of a freeman, Aristotle asks, "Why should we learn ourselves instead of enjoying the performances of others? . . . In the poets Zeus does not himself sing or play on the lyre. Nay, we call professional performers vulgar; no freeman would play or sing unless he were intoxicated or in jest." Or if he did play, at least he would be careful not to do so too well, for this would suggest that he had devoted more time to the art than was becoming or had submitted himself to a discipline that was somehow degrading. And therefore, although music and drawing were arts "quite proper for a freeman to acquire," they were proper "only in certain degree, and if he attend to them too closely, in order to attain perfection in them, the same evil [i.e. degrading] effects will follow." [5] In the Renaissance this feeling was embodied in the idea of *sprezzatura*, the sort of easy negligence with which the courtier performed all his varied accomplishments, and once again the emphasis was not merely upon the ease but also upon the negligence. The courtier did not wish to fence so well that he might be taken for a fencing master, or to draw so that his pictures would delight anyone besides himself and a circle of intimate friends. The precise degree of excellence which he might be allowed to achieve was perhaps difficult to determine, but in the seventeenth century Locke suggested that he might have just "so much insight into perspective, and skill in drawing, as will enable him to represent tolerably on paper any thing he sees, except faces." [6]

What was true of the varied accomplishments of the courtier was also true of the varied knowledge of the philosopher—it was useless and it was prized because it was useless. This, indeed, was the entire theme of an ancient form of literature, the "protreptic," which endeavored to win the assent of a young man to the philosophic or theoretic life and which openly acknowledged that that life could not be justified by ordinary practical considerations. Plato's *Euthydemus*, Aristotle's *Protrepticus*, and Cicero's *Hortensius*, the last two unhappily lost, are examples of this form. Typically it made use of a traditional body of anecdote about the earliest Greek philosophers which represented them as the type of the unworldly and withdrawn student—Thales falling in a well and being mocked by a servant girl, Democritus and Anaxagoras neglecting or giving away their inheritance, and Pythagoras replying to a question about the purpose of human life, that it was "to contemplate the heavens." It was Pythagoras, too, according to Heraclides of Pontus, who explained the words "philosophy" and "philosopher" by reference to the festival of Olympia, where some persons came to do business and enjoy themselves, some to win the wreath, and some merely as spectators. The third sort, he said, are the philosophers.[7]

These anecdotes arose, as Professor Jaeger has shown, at a time when the theoretic life was being made by Plato and Aristotle into a conscious philosophic ideal, but in later times they became part of the regular apologetic for the life of literary and philosophical ease. The feeling which they embody is found in Cicero's *De officiis*, which Newman quotes, and in a "multitude" of other authors whom he does not quote, although he says that he could.[8] Perhaps the most directly pertinent passage, however, is that in the first book of the *Metaphysics* (itself a reworking of material from the lost *Protrepticus*), which presents "the science which we are seeking" as distinctly without practical utility and to be deemed worthy of the name of "wisdom" for this very reason. "That it is not a science of production," says Aristotle, "is clear even from the history of the earliest philosophers. For it is owing to their wonder that men both now begin and at first began to philosophize. . . . And a man who . . . wonders thinks himself ignorant . . . therefore since they philosophized in order to escape from ignorance, evidently they were pursuing science in order to know, and not for any utilitarian end. And this is confirmed by the facts; for it was when almost all the necessities of life and the things that make for comfort and recreation had been secured, that such knowledge began to be sought. Evidently then we do not seek it for the sake of any other advantage; but as the man is free, we say, who exists for his own sake and not for another's, so we pursue this as the only free science, for it alone exists for its own sake."[9]

It was all very well for Plato or Aristotle to say this, but for Newman, living as he did after the rise of the Baconian philosophy, it would sound "strange." And yet this is exactly what he did say. The knowledge which he would make the object of his university does not serve any practical end, but is "its own end." It is not "a means to something beyond it, or the preliminary of certain arts into which it naturally resolves, but an end sufficient to rest in and to pursue for its own sake."[10] It is "liberal" knowledge, and whether this be conceived as the knowledge appropriate to a freeman (*liberalis*) or as a knowledge which itself is "free," in either case it is without practical issue, and Newman, in his analysis of the word, makes this negative characteristic into its defining principle. When we inquire, he says, what is meant by the epithet "liberal," we are at first led to oppose it to "servile," as belonging to the mind and not the body. But then we recall that there are mental exercises, such as medicine in ancient times and commerce now, which afford scope for the highest powers of mind but which are not technically called "liberal," and, on the other hand, that there are bodily exercises, such as the palaestra and the Olympic games, which are so called. "Why this distinction? because that alone is liberal knowledge, which stands on its own pretensions, which is independent of sequel, expects no complement, refuses to be *informed* (as it is called) by any end, or absorbed into any art, in order duly to present itself to our contemplation. The most ordinary pursuits have this specific character, if they are self-sufficient and complete; the highest lose it, when they minister to something beyond them." [11]

Aristotle had made this distinction in regard to possessions. "Of possessions," he says in a passage quoted by Newman, "those rather are useful, which bear fruit; those liberal, which tend to enjoyment. By fruitful, I mean, which yield revenue; by enjoyable, where nothing accrues of consequence beyond the using." [12] A shuttle, for example, is useful since something else is made by it, whereas a garment has its use in itself and so may be called "liberal." [13] In the opening section of the *Ethics* Aristotle extended this distinction from possessions to activities—indeed, it applies to possessions largely as they represent activities. "Every art and every inquiry, and similarly every action and pursuit, is thought to aim at some good. . . . But a certain difference is found among ends; some are activities, others are products apart from the activities that produce them. Where there are ends apart from the actions, it is the nature of the products to be better than the activities." [14] The end of weaving, for example, is the garment produced, and the garment is better than the activity of weaving; but from wearing a garment nothing issues except the benefit and enjoyment of the activity itself. One might say that warmth and adornment are the "products" which issue from wearing a garment, but the point is that warmth and adornment, unlike the garment, are not separable from the activity which produced them. Indeed, the distinction becomes most fruitful and most precise if we abandon the conception of a product, which is suited only to an art or industry, and describe liberal activities as those whose value is intrinsic or substantial *with* the activity, and useful activities as those whose value is extrinsic or consequent *upon* the activity.

[214]

Newman does not attempt to say which kinds of knowledge are liberal and which are useful, and indeed, a complete economy of knowledge would be so elaborate that we may restrict ourselves to three statements. First, it is clear that many kinds of knowledge have both intrinsic and extrinsic value. To Kepler, for example, the value of astronomy lay in the utter loveliness of the truths which it contemplates, and this value is inseparable from the contemplation; but astronomy is also valuable to people who never heard of these truths, for it ensures the safety of navigation and aids in the production of crops. Secondly, it seems likely that no form of knowledge is utterly without intrinsic value, although the value may be so slight that we can neglect it in practice. The chief value of the knowledge involved in plumbing, for instance, is not to the plumber himself but to the person whom he serves; yet one could hardly say that there is no satisfaction at all in the art and practice of plumbing. It is merely that the satisfaction is so rudimentary that a human being does not willingly rest in it, and hence, although "liberal" to a degree, it could hardly be made the basis of a liberal education. And thirdly, it does seem likely that some forms of knowledge are completely without extrinsic value. What is the value to other people of one's knowing a poem? There must be some, we feel, because the scholar is paid to know poems, and wages are a sign of value received. But the value received *is* the knowledge. He teaches the poem or writes books about it, which is another form of teaching, and there seems to be nothing else that he can do with it. The value which he finds in a poem may be such as will transform his entire life, but he cannot distil this value into a serum and inoculate his students while they sleep. For good or ill, the value which he finds is inseparable from the process by which he found it. He may explain it to others, but he will convey only an explanation and not the value itself. He may write it up in books or monographs, but in so doing he will only produce another knowledge with a slightly different value—and again with no value except as it, too, is known. He has no way of conveying the value except by conveying the knowledge in which it inheres, for the value of knowing a poem is inseparable from the knowledge itself.

Newman would not restrict his university to this third type of knowledge, but he would ask that whatever knowledge it made the subject of its contemplation it should contemplate only under this aspect. It would prize astronomy because, in the loveliness and precision of its truths, it has the power of recreating and refining the mind. That it also has the power to guide the sailor and assist the farmer is a reason for gratitude, but it is not this power which a university considers. The power of knowledge to relieve pain, to ensure safety, to construct open and wholesome cities, to order society, to accelerate movement, and to release great energy —all these powers are wonders with which we could not dispense but with which, as a university, we are not concerned. We are concerned only with the power which knowledge has to perfect the human intellect. To open it, refine it, correct it, to discipline its powers and give it mastery over itself—this is the end which is served by liberal knowledge, and since this is also the end of man, we may properly say that such knowledge is "its own end" or may be pursued "for its own sake."

There is a difficulty in this view, however, which Newman does not specifically face. If we pursue liberal knowledge as a kind of mental gymnastic, a mere exercise of the mind, are we not in danger of sacrificing the power which knowledge has of placing us in communion with reality? Logic will perfect our faculties as well as history, and alchemy as well as chemistry; what need, then, if this is their only function, for supplementing formal knowledge by real or even preferring true knowledge to false? For it must be obvious that the distinction between liberal and useful knowledge is simply a translation into value terms of the distinction between subjective and objective truth. Useful knowledge is power, and it is validated by its ability to manipulate the external world. Liberal knowledge, however, is understanding, and it is validated by our willingness to rest in the understanding which it conveys. Overtness is the sign of the one and inwardness of the other, and the real usefulness of this distinction is to inform us what kinds of values we should expect from the various disciplines which we pursue.

When a witch doctor makes an image of his enemy and sticks it full of pins, is he trying to kill him or simply to express his feelings about him? If the former, then his skill is useful (though mistaken); if the latter, then it is liberal (and correct). If his rain dance is to bring rain, it is useful and should be called work; if it is to express his feelings about the rain, it is liberal and is a ritual. If a discipline proposes merely to be interesting but turns out to be true as well—as Riemannian geometry did when Einstein employed it in the theory of relativity—then it passes from the class of the liberal to that of the useful, or rather to both at once. But if it proposes to be useful—as did astrology, alchemy, and magic—and fails, then it passes into the category of the useless, which includes everything that is neither objectively true nor subjectively true but simply false—and this means exploded science on the one hand and bad art on the other, for however different these may be in the motive that produced them, in themselves they are absolutely the same.

Where does religion fall in this discussion? In the primitive and the Catholic view, religion is a useful discipline. It speaks of a reality which is external to the individual, and the information that it gives is of ex-

[216]

trinsic value. Prayers are not merely good for the soul—they are also answered; and belief is not merely inspiriting to the believer—it effects his salvation. But does it? Atheism would assert that religion is really exploded science, and that just as alchemy has been superseded by chemistry so religion will be superseded by psychiatry, and if so, then the only difference between them is that religion has intrinsic value as well. Prayers *are* good for the soul even if they are not answered, and this, of course, is the idea behind liberal Protestantism. Indeed, the ultimate effect of the Protestant Reformation was simply that it transformed religion from a useful into a liberal discipline. When T. H. Huxley said that the Ten Commandments were certainly not divine but that he could give ten good human reasons for obeying them, he was typifying the process that was occurring everywhere in nineteenth-century thought. Everywhere, values which had once been objective were being internalized, subjectivized, given a psychological status. The good was not absolute, it was what you liked; God was not a Person, He was the sum total of your best moments; Hell was not a place where people went after they were dead, it was the actual degradation which evil-doing brings upon the living; and so on and on. In the words of Matthew Arnold, religion had "materialised itself in the fact, in the supposed fact," and the fact had failed it. Therefore, said Arnold, lest its values be discarded entirely, let us recognize what the true nature of religion is. The Bible is not dogma but literature; religion is not exploded science but poetry; and one may prophesy that the future of poetry is immense, because in poetry there are no facts to be exploded. In poetry "the idea *is* the fact." [15]

Poetry for Arnold was subjectively true but objectively false; science was objectively true but subjectively false; religion had pretended to be science and was actually poetry. In the face of this dilemma Arnold delivered a lecture, "Literature and Science," in which he tried to deal with the same problem that Newman had dealt with under the terms of useful and liberal knowledge, and it will be remembered that his answer is strangely perplexing. We need science, he says, to tell us about the world in which we live, but we also need literature to enable us to live in this grim world of science. Science tells us that "our ancestor was a hairy quadruped furnished with a tail and pointed ears, probably arboreal in his habits," and in one sense this is true. But it is not a livable truth. For that we must go to Genesis or to *Paradise Lost*, where we will learn that really our ancestors were "two of far nobler shape erect and tall." This is a livable truth, it is validated in our personal experience; but unfortunately it is not validated in the fossils and the rocks. How do we bridge the gap? It is no criticism of Arnold, but rather a tribute to his intellectual honesty, to say that he found no means except that afforded by personal stoicism.

Did Newman find any means? Newman does not have the religious problem because he considered religion to be a useful discipline, but in those disciplines which he did consider to be liberal the identical problem arises. How can he be sure that the knowledge which will best refine and discipline the mind will also inform us truly about the external world? Or, to put it another way, how can he be sure that the world has such a character that knowledge of it will constitute the perfection of the mind?

Let it be said, in the first place, that Newman did not believe with Coleridge, to whom he otherwise owed so much, that the mind in its creative power can be the source of its own perfection. On the contrary, he believed that "the soul would not think without some external stimulus; that if it were cut off from all external communication from the external world, it would pass this life in a sort of torpor." [16] This being so, it was evident that "our nature, unlike that of the inferior creation, does not at once reach its perfection, but depends, in order to it, on a number of external aids and appliances," of which knowledge is one of the chief.[17] But this knowledge was not ready-made as an instrument of human perfection. Where Bacon had distributed the parts of knowledge according to the faculties of the human mind—memory, imagination, and reason—and had thereby ensured that the pursuit of universality would be the pursuit of our own perfection, Newman did no such thing. He distributed the parts of knowledge according to their subject matter. And where the ancients had distributed the parts of the mind according to the four elements, declaring with Empedocles that "it is with earth that we see Earth, and Water with water; by air we see bright Air, by fire destroying Fire. By love do we see Love, and Hate by grievous hate," [18] Newman again did no such thing. He agreed that man was in some sense a microcosm and that his knowledge did depend ultimately upon an identity between the mind and the object known, but he did not agree that this one-to-one relation corresponded to our experience of the actual process of knowledge.

For knowledge was a process. In Newman's conception it might be likened to a pyramid based broadly in sense perception but rising into the unity of understanding, and although in this pyramid there was no solution of continuity—the apex rested upon the base—nevertheless the difference between the apex and the base was a symbol which did not exaggerate the apparent unlikeness between the mind and its object. The one was to the other as active to passive or as form to matter. The mind invaded the anarchy of sense perception like the

Creator putting forth his virtue over chaos. It energized what was inert, purged off what was accidental and arbitrary, and drew the multiplicity of fact up into the unity of a significant order. And yet the order was *in* the fact. Writing to T. W. Allies to explain what he meant by the "Philosophy of History," Newman declared that the "laws" of history "are a sort of facts *in* the subject matter," [19] and in the *Idea of a University* he observed that the relations which the philosopher contemplates are "relations which our minds have no power of creating, but which we are obliged to ascertain." [20] These laws and relations comprise philosophical knowledge, and hence Newman could declare of this knowledge that it was good "*both* because it secured to the intellect the sight of things as they are, or of truth, in opposition to fancy, opinion, and theory; *and again*, because it presupposed and involved the perfection of its various powers." [21]

It did these two things because it was informed with reason. It is reason, says Newman in his most exact and deliberate statement of the matter, which is "the principle of that intrinsic fecundity of Knowledge, which, to those who possess it, is its especial value, and which dispenses with the necessity of their looking abroad for any end to rest upon external to itself. . . . The principle of real dignity in Knowledge, its worth, its desirableness, considered irrespectively of its results, is this germ within it of a scientific or a philosophical process. This is how it comes to be an end in itself; this is why it admits of being called Liberal." [22] And this is also why it admits of being called knowledge. It is the rational character of reality together with the rational nature of man which enables philosophy to be at once the record of the one and the fulfillment and perfection of the other.

Such is Newman's reply to those "cautious and practical thinkers" who had questioned the value of philosophical knowledge, and one feels that this portion of his argument is rigorous and winning and genuinely fruitful. Would that he had stopped with this portion! Would that he had not gone on, in the seventh discourse, to reinforce a good argument with a bad by telling us that the knowledge which he had just recommended as "not useful" was actually, if we considered the matter closely, more useful than "useful knowledge" itself. What he says is doubtless true, but it is rather like the preacher who tells his congregation to be virtuous even if it doesn't pay and then adds that they may be sure it will pay in the long run anyhow. Perhaps it will, but the added incentive leaves one in doubt on the basic principle, and this is precisely the effect which Newman's seventh discourse has.

In a sense it was not his fault. This is the lecture in which Newman simply steps aside as the defender of liberal education and allows the argument to be conducted by two of his former associates at Oriel, Edward Copleston and John Davison. In the early years of the century they had been engaged in a controversy over the utility of the Oxford curriculum, and although it was perfectly natural for Newman to make use of their argument, it may be doubted whether he would have done so, at least to so large a degree, if it had not come to him with such very personal associations.

The controversy had arisen with the publication of three articles in the *Edinburgh Review* in the years 1808–09. The first of these, a review by John Playfair, professor of natural philosophy at Edinburgh, of Laplace's *Traité de mécanique céleste*, was not otherwise concerned with Oxford than by a single sentence, at the very end of the review, which blamed the two southern universities, and especially Oxford, for the low condition of mathematics in England. The second article, written by Richard Payne Knight (not Lord Jeffrey, as Newman supposed), was an attack upon a splendid new edition of Strabo which had been printed at the university press; and the third, a review by Sydney Smith of R. L. Edgeworth's *Essays on Professional Education*, was made the occasion of a forceful and witty attack upon the Oxford classical curriculum. As the insults mounted in number and force, "the whole university," we are told, "was kept in hot water" over them.[23] Troubled alumni wrote up from the country to inquire what was wrong, and their delighted sons replied in verse:

> Since the cold cutting gibes of that Northern Review
> Have tormented and teased Uncle Toby and you,
> I'm exceedingly happy in sending you down
> A defence, which is making much noise in the town,
> Of all our old learning and fame immemorial,
> Which is said to be writ by a Fellow of Oriel.[24]

The "defence" was Edward Copleston's *Reply to the Calumnies of the Edinburgh Review* (1810), a pamphlet of some two hundred pages, which he later supplemented by a *Second Reply* and a *Third*. It was answered by Playfair, Knight, and Smith in a joint review and was supported by two articles in the *Quarterly* by John Davison. In addition to these, there was an entire flood of Observations, Remarks, Letters to the Editor, and Poetical Accounts, which did not subside until the very end of the year 1811.[25]

Most of the controversy was the merest quibbling and vituperation, but occasionally it did rise to a statement of principle, and when it did, the position of the Oxonians was that liberal knowledge, although distinct in its nature from useful, did have an ultimate utility both in the conduct of one's profession and in the larger life which we are all called upon to lead simply as members of human society. It had a professional utility for two reasons. The first was, that since there are no divisions in reality corresponding to the division between the professions, the specialist really needs to know more than his own specialty, and indeed, not knowing more, will not know even that. Hence the broad training demanded by Vitruvius for the architect and by Isidore of Seville for the physician. A more important consideration, however, was that a liberal education trains the good mind, and the good mind is useful in one's profession. Of this second argument one can only say that, however true it may be, it could hardly have arisen except in a period when the professions were so untechnical that they required little more than the good mind for their successful practice. Certainly when this was no longer the case the argument itself came under fire, for it was then seen to depend on what educational psychologists call "transfer of training," that is, the possibility that training acquired in one subject, such as Latin grammar, will be of use in learning another subject, such as chemistry; and the early investigations of Thorndike and others seemed to show that this transfer does not occur. Today, however, there is a disposition to admit that it does occur under somewhat broader conditions than was at first supposed, and in point of fact these conditions correspond very closely to the kind of training which Oxford provided.[26] What is required is a degree of similarity between the two fields in question, and as this is usually achieved by a process of generalization, it is in the abstract or formal disciplines that transfer is most complete. The abstract nature of mathematics, for example, provides for an absolute transfer of mathematical training—having learned to count apples, one can count chickens or stars or any countable thing—and so too with logic. Logic teaches the framing of arguments which are correct independently of the subject to which they are applied, and since these formal disciplines were the very essence of the Oxford curriculum, one may say that Oxford was not really ignoring the problem of transfer of training but, on the contrary, was attempting to make it into a science. They were not teaching particular subjects with the naive hope that their benefits would carry over into other situations, but were teaching the very method of carrying benefits from one situation to another, and this is especially true of the science which Newman called philosophy.

The second kind of utility claimed for liberal studies by Newman and the Oxford defenders is their utility to society at large. Here the distinction between useful and liberal knowledge is resolved into a distinction between specialized and general knowledge. Useful knowledge is necessarily specialized because the useful arts are merely the tangible issue of particular sciences; but philosophy, the knowledge which integrates other knowledge, has no corresponding art, and hence liberal knowledge is necessarily general.[27] Or, to put the matter in the language of Adam Smith, useful knowledge is specialized because only by the division of labor can one achieve the excellence which makes that labor useful. There are, of course, exceptions. Any work of coordination is both useful and general, but in a highly organized society it is for the most part true that useful knowledge will be specialized and that knowledge which is general will be too elementary to be useful. Copleston and Davison accepted this view as correct, but they observed that the specialization which improves the individual as a worker impoverishes him as a human being. True, there are emergencies in which the good to be achieved by specialization is worth the sacrifice that it requires. Military training destroys the soldier in order to save the republic, and the scientist who narrows his life to discover a cure for poliomyelitis is justified by the lives of the children he saves. But the problem is not merely to balance the individual's loss against society's gain, for society reflects both the loss and the gain. What it gains in the skilled worker it loses in the judicious citizen, and this is a necessary result of the two principles on which society is organized. Productively, society is a whole because it integrates many parts, but culturally and politically it is a whole because it is an aggregate of wholes. As workers we are responsible for only a tiny segment of life, but as citizens and human beings our duties are as various as life itself. The wide sphere of these duties must be anticipated by a wide sphere of knowledge, and such knowledge is necessarily liberal. Thus, says Newman, "if . . . a practical end must be assigned to a University course, I say it is that of training good members of society." [28]

Such is the conclusion, the rather grudging conclusion, of Newman's seventh discourse. "If one *must* have a utilitarian end to education, this is it." But why "must" one have such an end? The whole burden of the fifth discourse was that one must not, that liberal knowledge is its own end, and now, under the guise of carrying this argument a step further, Newman has actually reversed it. Where before he had rejected utility as a criterion for evaluating knowledge, he now accepts that criterion and merely claims that liberal knowledge is useful too. In other words, he has done precisely what Bentham said that every opponent of the utilitarian philosophy must do, he has combated the principle of utility with reasons drawn "from that very principle itself." [29]

And yet it was in no way necessary that he do this. In all the classical texts with which Newman was most familiar, in Cicero and Aristotle and in the long debate between Stoic and Epicurean over the *utile* and the *honestum*, he found the relation between these concepts of the "good" and the "useful" thoroughly worked out. The useful is that which we desire not for its own sake but for what it leads to, whereas the good leads to nothing and is desired simply for its own sake. Actually, however, of things that we desire there are three classes: that which is simply useful, that which is both useful and good, and that which is simply good. It is in the second of these classes that Newman places liberal knowledge: it would be desired for its own sake even if it led to nothing; but it does in fact lead to something, and therefore it is desired for that as well. Useful knowledge, on the other hand, may fall either in the first class (for "the useful is not always good" [30]) or in the second; and if it falls in the second, then there is no means of distinguishing it from liberal knowledge. The one forms the good mind in the process of being useful, and the other enables the mind to be useful by virtue of giving it form.

We find our way out of this maze only by the principle, which is the very heart of Aristotle's teleology but which Newman has momentarily ignored, that ends and means (or the good and the useful) are arranged not merely in series but in a hierarchical series. Moreover, this series has an end. We desire one thing for the sake of another and that for the sake of a third, but "if we do not choose everything for the sake of something else (for at that rate the process would go on to infinity, so that our desire would be empty and vain)," we must come to "some end . . . which we desire for its own sake (everything else being desired for the sake of this)," and "clearly this [end] must be the good and the chief good." [31] It could not be called useful because, although it redounds with all possible goods, which indeed it contains, these goods are all less worthy than itself. Nothing that it produces is so desirable as that which it is.

The real issue, therefore, between Newman and the utilitarians is the question, what is the chief good, the final end, of man? Bentham said that it was happiness, but Newman (the religious answer apart) said that it was the full development of man's own nature. Newman would place before the student the vision of an ideal human type, of one who is the summation of all the intellectual virtues, and ask him to use this type as a standard whereby to correct and discipline his own nature. Bentham, on the other hand, would place before him nothing—or rather he would show him his reflection in the glass and tell him to model himself upon what he already was. What he liked was what he ought to pursue, and since he could like nothing that was not a function of his own nature, he would pursue nothing but himself. He would be Narcissus gazing in the pool, and he could not turn away his eyes to anything higher or better because nothing higher or better existed. Happiness was simply the satisfaction of desires, and as desires did not differ in quality but only in strength and duration, the satisfaction of one was as good as the satisfaction of another. In the phrase of the master, "push-pin is as good as poetry," and to be a pig satisfied (an errant disciple notwithstanding) is as good as being Socrates satisfied, is much better than being Socrates dissatisfied.[32]

The only problem which life presents to the utilitarian, therefore, is that of simultaneously satisfying all the desires of all the people, or at least of achieving the greatest happiness of the greatest number. The way to do this, according to the Benthamite philosophy, was to see that the interest of the individual was identified with that of the community at large, either by persuading him to desire only those things which would least conflict with the desires of others or by devising social, political, or even material mechanisms which would channel his existing desires into socially acceptable forms. Both of these ways involved a kind of education, but it was not education in Newman's sense of the term. True, there were in the Benthamite society a few philosopher-statesmen at the top who saw the problems and devised the solutions and wrote the directives, and these were essentially "men of philosophic habit" with an economic cast. But they were only the few. The rest of society was an ant-hill, and although happiness was the end proposed, this end was not to be achieved directly, in what people were or did, but indirectly, in the benefits which flowed back upon them from the civilization which they created. They were to be happy as consumers rather than as workers, for in the latter role their whole being was sacrificed to the achievement of some specialized task. They were simply cogs in a great political and technological machine, and if they assumed a certain shape in the performance of their duties, even one that was not recognizably human, that was quite to be expected and was even in the interests of efficiency. Moreover, even as citizens they did not receive a general education which would fit them to cope with the complex problems of society, for it was not desirable that they should think before they voted, but merely that they should vote correctly. And under the associationist psychology, which the utilitarians accepted, this could be achieved most easily by setting up in the mind of the citizen those "trains of ideas" which would lead inevitably to the desired behavior. For as the citizen not only ought to, but necessarily did, pursue his own pleasure, one had only to establish favorable associations with social conduct and unfavorable associations with unsocial conduct in order to achieve the perfect society without involving anyone in the unpleasantness of self-denial.

Indeed, the wonderful thing about the Benthamite utopia was that it was so easy. Where old-fashioned philosophers had tried for centuries to secure the good society by the troublesome expedient of securing good human beings to compose it, Bentham side-stepped that difficulty, which he regarded as perfectly insuperable, and achieved the good society without the slightest annoyance to anyone. He devised assembly lines which would produce complicated mechanisms without the necessity of the workers' understanding the mechanisms that they produced. He devised a model prison which, by a simple architectural principle, automatically reformed the criminals within it, whether they would or no. His ancestor, Lord Bacon, devised a scientific method which had this advantage, that it dispensed with the necessity of genius on the part of those persons who used it. It "levels men's wits . . . ," boasted its inventor, "and leaves but little to their excellence; because it performs everything by the surest rules and demonstrations." [33] And as though to prepare for this method, Bell and Lancaster in the nineteenth century devised a system of elementary education whereby children could be instructed in subjects they did not understand by slightly older children who did not understand them either. To some persons this lack of understanding might seem a drawback, but Lord Brougham pronounced it "a capital discovery, in every point of view." To think, he declared, that all sciences which "admit of a symbolical notation . . . are . . . capable of being communicated by a person ignorant of them, but able to read, to as many others as can hear the sound of his voice at once." [34] Had he survived into the *Brave New World* of Aldous Huxley, he would have been even more enraptured, for there the living voice is replaced by hypnopaedia, by the radio under the pillow, which inculcates in the children their social attitudes while they sleep. For this purpose the system worked very well, but when an attempt was made to teach the children geography it failed—and quite rightly, says Huxley, for "you can't learn a science unless you know what it's all about." [35]

"O brave new world—that has such people in it." The conclusion of the phrase is the point that Huxley would make. Happiness the end of life? Even the moronic elevator boy in the Central Conditioning Center was happy. Rising to the roof, he would blink stupidly at the sunlight and cry out, "O roof, o roof," which was his god. And when he descended to the basement, there was soma to make him happy there. But happiness of such a kind! Deliberately to create a moron because only a moron will be happy in running an elevator, to make a human being into an instrument and elevation into an end, this was what Newman, like Huxley, could never endure. Not that he totally ignored the workaday world in his conception of education. In the actual institution which he established at Dublin he came far closer to the modern conception of a university, with its professional schools, its specialized research, and its program of service to the community at large, than did either of the English universities which he took as his model. Indeed, it is in this respect that a study of the Catholic University of Ireland provides the most significant corrective to the Dublin *Discourses*, for whereas in the latter Newman had insisted upon a curriculum exclusively liberal, in his actual university only the first two years were so; [36] and whereas in the *Discourses* he had repudiated the notion that research was a function of the university, in Dublin he made it a very prominent function.[37] Apparently, seeing the needs of Ireland at firsthand and thinking more largely and practically about the problems of society than he had before, he did actually attain to a broader and more realistic conception of a university than that which he had expressed in his lectures. But after all, those lectures do not pretend to say everything about a university that can be said. Despite their title, they do not speak of a university in toto but only of the arts portion and of that portion only in its inner idea. On that idea, however, Newman stood firm. He held, then and forever, that the end of education is the human being himself, the simple perfection of his own nature. It is not the means of transforming the world but rather of transforming ourselves. It is a conversion, an exaltation of the individual from what he is into what he would like to be, and if this conversion is attended with pain (as all learning is, according to Aristotle), it is a pain that we willingly suffer for the sake of the quality which in our suffering we achieve. We would rather be Socrates dissatisfied than a pig satisfied, and indeed, if we are really wise, we would rather be Socrates dissatisfied than Socrates satisfied, for only so can we make it perfectly plain that our true end is not satisfaction but Socrates.

CHAPTER 12

The Religion of Philosophy

The fullest and freest development of the intellect, joined to the
most cheerful and implicit submission of the whole man to God's
will, this is surely the highest triumph which a system of Education can achieve.

—An Oxford pamphlet (1839)

ONE of the strangest experiences to be had in reading
the *Idea of a University* comes in the eighth discourse, on "Knowledge
Viewed in Relation to Religion." From its title that discourse would
seem to be the continuation of a pattern established by the two preceding discourses, "Knowledge Viewed in Relation to Learning" and
"Knowledge Viewed in Relation to Professional Skill." Actually it is not
a continuation of a pattern but its direct reversal. It tells us that the
ideal which has been presented for our admiration through three discourses is not admirable at all, and that if we pursue knowledge for its
own sake, if we erect it into a self-sufficient and independent principle,
we are making a religion out of our own minds. Such a person, whom
Newman had once glorified by the name of philosopher, he now stig-
matizes as a "mere Philosopher," and the words "reason," "philosophy,"
and "civilization," which previously had characterized his cultural ideal,
are now transmuted by the very veneration we had been asked to give
them into the "Religion of Reason," the "Religion of Philosophy," and
the "Religion of Civilization." What Newman means by these terms is
simply humanism, and therefore one may say that, whereas Newman
had presented in the three previous discourses a cultural ideal which was
distinctively and purely humanistic, he now looks back upon this ideal
from the religious point of view and notes wherein it is deficient. He does
not repudiate humanism, but he goes beyond it, and the problem of this
chapter is to determine why he goes beyond and what is left of his humanism once he has gone.

One's first thought is that the conflict between the religious and humanistic elements in Newman's ideal reproduces a conflict which was
central to his own educational experience. Newman has said that the
Idea of a University is based upon two great controversies, that over the

admission of Dissenters and that between Oxford and the *Edinburgh Review*, but really it is also based upon a third, the controversy in Newman's own nature between his intellectual aspirations, his yearning for "the sweet food of sweetly uttered knowledge," and his sense that this knowledge was somehow forbidden. During the years 1816 to 1833 this conflict erupted in a series of illnesses which were so humbling in their power that there was simply no relation, by Newman's own account, between the vainglorious person who went into the illness and the docile and submissive creature who emerged. By a kind of exaggeration one might say that these two persons were respectively the author of the humanistic and the religious discourses in the *Idea of a University*. In the former, with their fine panegyric of the philosophic habit of mind, we hear the voice of the young man who read Paine and Hume at the age of fifteen and made himself giddy by their novel and un-Christian speculations; who dabbled in the works of Gibbon and found that the elegance of the style palliated the fact that he was not a better man; who in 1822 aspired to a seat beside the Noetics of Oriel and was soon deep in the nominalism of Whately's all-corroding logic; who drifted in 1827 "in the direction of the liberalism of the day," and who later, to prevent narrowness of mind, deliberately tempted himself with a passionate exploration of the pagan beauties of the Mediterranean world. On the other hand, in the discourses which go beyond humanism, we hear the voice of the young evangelical who was converted by Mr. Mayers, of the youth made docible by his failure in the Schools, of the examinee who took comfort in the motto *Pie repone te*, and of the voyager who turned his back on the beauties of Sicily and prayed to the Kindly Light, "Lead Thou me on."

With such riving forces beneath the surface of the book it is no wonder that the humanistic ideal is presented with some ambivalence. The wonder rather is that Newman was able to present it with the generosity and fairness that he does. But in truth, by 1852 the conflict was no longer severe. It had arisen partly out of the problems of adolescence and partly out of Newman's evangelical background, with its deep distrust of all intellectual achievement. Hence, as adolescence passed and as Newman moved into a religious position which was not distrustful of intellect, the conflict gradually resolved itself into the precarious balance which is achieved in the *Idea of a University*.

The balance of that work is due, however, not solely to the development of Newman's own attitude but also to the change in the audience for which he was writing. When he was in Oxford, he was in a school which had lapsed, since the Middle Ages, to "that level of mere human loveliness, which in its highest perfection we admire in Athens." [1] It was

THE RELIGION OF PHILOSOPHY

the very type of humanism without religion. Indeed, if there were an official seat or center, a kind of Holy See of the Religion of Philosophy, surely that See was to be found at Oxford, and for twenty years Newman had preached against this religion in the very temple of its worshipers. In the end they had turned against him and driven him out, and with his expulsion that particular sermon had come to an end. There was no need to preach in Dublin against the vices of Oxford. There was rather a need to import into Dublin the virtues of Oxford. Dublin could do with some of that "mere human loveliness" which was the special virtue, almost the sole virtue, of the English Protestant gentleman; and there-fore, by supplying the deficiencies of one group from the excesses of an-other, Newman achieved in his writings a kind of reconciliation of oppo-sites which he had already achieved in his own person and which gives to his cultural ideal a rich and interesting ambivalence.

The ambivalence of Newman's attitude toward intellectual culture may be seen very clearly in the examples by which he has chosen to illustrate the Religion of Philosophy. In almost every case these are iden-tical with the examples by which he had previously illustrated his ideal of the philosophic habit. It is not surprising, of course, that Newman should sometimes admire in point of intellect a person whom he could not admire in point of character, but it is a little surprising to discover that almost the only intellects which he found admirable were those coupled with characters that were not admirable. The magnanimous man of Aristotle, whose incidental and unstudied greatness of mind contrib-uted very largely to Newman's ideal of the philosopher, was neverthe-less "deformed by an arrogant contempt of others, a disregard of their feelings, and a harshness and repulsiveness of external manner." [2] Cicero, who was praised in one place for understanding that knowledge may be pursued for its own sake, was censured in another for the trifling and sophisticated nature of that pursuit.[3] In the appendix of the *Dis-courses* the story is told of the Athenian philosophers who were expelled from Rome by Cato "lest their arts of disputation should corrupt the Roman youth." But in the text of the *Discourses*, where the story is told again, these arts represent liberal knowledge, and Cato, transformed from the type of the moralist into the type of the utilitarian, is taunted for despising "that refinement or enlargement of mind of which he had no experience." [4] Gibbon's "Essay on the Study of Literature" is quoted extensively by Newman to illustrate the true nature of liberal knowledge, and at the same time the sentiments of a "godless intellectualism" are illustrated from the account, in the *Decline and Fall*, of the dying mo-ments of Julian the Apostate.[5] Goethe is cited as one of the "truly great intellects" of all time, and yet the tenor of this intellect, as Newman shows by copious extracts from a contemporary biography, was toward an aloofness and self-sufficiency which is cold and repellent and ultimately un-Christian.[6]

It was largely from classical antiquity and the eighteenth century that Newman had drawn his conception of the philosophic habit, and it was largely from these same periods that he drew his examples of that spurious philosophism which was simply the same habit unrectified by religion. Moreover, the habit which he both admired and contemned he seemed to admire and contemn for the same reason, for as he was attracted to the classical ideal by its gift of a serene philosophic calm, so, on reconsideration, he was repelled by it for its possession of this same complacent feature. There were moments when man had no right to be calm, relations in which he had no business to be philosophic, seasons in which he could do no better than grovel in terror before a Maker of whom his solipsism had told him nothing. The view of the world which was presented by the humanistic tradition was all very well for a sunny day, and in the Stoic version it would even give support in periods of moderate gloom. But it told nothing of the awful dark and the blinding bright which lay below and above the tiny, pastoral world of man considered solely as man. It did not whisper to him of his ruined state or of his utter inability to gain heaven by any efforts of his own, it did not speak of the moral certainty of losing his soul if left to himself, of gloom and terror, of martyrdom and wrath. It said nothing of the inconceivable evil of sensuality and the imperative and obligatory force of the voice of conscience, of the simple absence of all rights and claims on the part of the creature in the presence of the Creator, and of the illimitable claims of the Creator on the service of all his creatures. It spoke much of Nature but nothing of Grace, much of the mean but nothing of extremes. It told man of no perfection beyond the type of his own species, and it gave him such hopes of achieving that perfection that it led insensibly into a kind of conscious pride which, although it was the highest conception of pagan ethics, was also the root of all the Christian sins.[7]

When Newman first went up to Oxford, he was warned by Mr. Mayers never to be of that school which holds that "Ridicule is the test of truth," [8] and now, in his analysis of the difference between the humanistic and the religious position, he heeded that warning by depending chiefly upon the *Characteristics* of Lord Shaftesbury to illustrate the moral implications of this Religion of Philosophy.[9] To say that ridicule is the test of truth is to say that satire occupies the same place in the classical tradition as is held in the Christian tradition by the sermon. It is no accident that the one form is dominant in the eighteenth century

and Augustan Rome and the other in the seventeenth and nineteenth
centuries and the Middle Ages, for within its own period each performs
the same function, that of censuring deviations in conduct from a norm.
How, then, do they differ? Most obviously in the fact that the one employs laughter whereas the other does not, and if we ask whence this
difference arises, we must reply that it arises from the nature of the norm
to which each makes its appeal. Satire appeals to a human norm, to the
ideal of rational conduct, and as everyone makes a kind of pretense to
such conduct simply by virtue of his human nature, so the failure to
achieve it involves an incongruity which excites laughter. But the norm
of religion is supernatural, superhuman, transcendent, and therefore
there can be no pretensions of achieving it, no expectation of its achievement by others, and no laughter when they fail. Failure to achieve this
norm is normal—and also it is dire. Hence, whenever it occurs, it excites
not laughter but religious horror and commiseration.

Laughter and commiseration, which are respectively the humanistic
and the religious attitude toward the errors of others, are replaced in the
case of our own errors by self-reproach and fear. If the philosopher does
wrong he is angry and calls himself a fool, whereas if the Christian does
wrong he calls himself a sinner and is afraid. Sin is the transgression of
a law, and as a law implies a lawgiver and a judge, so the injury done is
to another than oneself, and it requires confession to make the matter
open, and contrition to make it right. Folly, on the other hand, is simply
a deviation from our own nature as a rational being. If there is injury
at all, it is an injury to ourselves, and although we may feel remorse or a
sense of degradation, the most that this requires is that we make to
ourselves the apology which is due to our own nature. We have acted in
a way which is unbecoming, which is not seemly, and this failure in
decorum, which the Christian in his exaggerated terminology describes
as vice, is really just a kind of deformity. It is a failure to realize the perfection of our own nature, and conversely, when we do realize this, we
achieve a propriety in our own kind, a harmony and beauty of our own
type, which the Christian absurdly denominates virtue. The faculty by
which we discriminate the beautiful from the deformed is good taste,
and therefore taste rather than conscience (so reasons the philosopher)
is the faculty by which we guide ourselves in the conduct of our life.
Admittedly, there might be some difficulty as to how our nature can be
guided by something which is no more than the appetitive part of our
nature. It would seem as though we were lifting ourselves by our own
bootstraps or modeling our features upon their reflection in the glass,
but since the matter is all between ourselves, since there is no third party
to spy into what we are doing, since, indeed, the whole problem is simply

to see that our own features *are* modeled upon their reflection in the glass, there will be no difficulty on this score. How can we avoid being moral when morality consists in simply being what we already are?

The difference, therefore, between religious and philosophical morality is that the former takes us out of ourselves, whereas the latter confines us within the round of our own being. The former places us in relation to a Being with whom we are simply incommensurate, and by so doing it gives us the means, which we do not possess within ourselves, of exalting our nature and rectifying our will. The latter places us in no relation with any being except ourself and the types of ourself, and by thus intruding into every situation the problem of the self, it radically alters the meaning, when it does not actually alter the outward form, of every moral act. Indeed, as between Christianity and Civilization, for all that they have in common, for all that the fastidiousness and refinement of the one, its shrinking from the grosser forms of evil, may contribute to what is also desired by the other, the real tenor of their ethical codes is simply distinct. What the one accounts as a virtue the other considers to be a vice, and the vice of the one is the virtue of the other. The nobility of mind and independence of spirit which was the ideal at once of the Roman philosopher and the American savage, of the chivalric warrior and the eighteenth-century gentleman, is known to the Christian by the opprobrious name of pride. Humility, on the other hand, which the Christian accounts a virtue, is held by the philosophical moralist to involve a cringing and self-abasement, a meanness and abjectness of spirit which is unworthy a rational being. "As has been often observed," wrote Newman, "ancient civilization had not the idea [of humility], and had no word to express it: or rather, it had the idea, and considered it a defect of mind, not a virtue, so that the word which denoted it conveyed a reproach." [10]

Modern civilization was in even a greater predicament. Having the word and knowing that it was supposed to denote a virtue, it was yet unable (literally unable) to achieve the quality which the word represented. When Benjamin Franklin decided to perfect himself in all the virtues and kept a weekly chart of his progress, he found that he did very well in everything except humility, but there all his efforts were unavailing, for if he were successful, his very success had the effect of making him proud. Obviously, he had gone about the matter in the wrong way. If he had forgotten about his own humility and given thought to the greatness and majesty of God, he would have been humbled in a trice and without any effort on his own part. But this his philosophy did not permit: he was determined to develop in himself a virtue which consists in the annihilation of the self, and it goes without saying that he failed. What he should have attempted (and did actually achieve) was modesty, for modesty is the form which humility takes in the Religion of Civilization. Modesty is humility made decorous, just as pride is made decorous by calling it self-respect. These two, indeed, are the twin virtues of the civilized world. They teach us what is due to ourselves and what is due to others, and in a world where nothing is due to God this is the whole rule of deportment. Newman considers that they differ from their religious opposites as a counterfeit differs from the true—they are content with setting right the surface of things, whereas religion regenerates the very heart [11]—but this is not fair to the sincerity of the humanistic virtues. Modesty does not simulate humility but is simply that degree of humility which is appropriate in our relation to our fellow men. Neither does self-respect try to conceal its real inward pride. It *is* pride, but it is simply that degree of pride to which we are entitled when we compare ourselves with others. In comparison with God we are entitled to none: our humility is absolute and our pride is simply egregious.

Newman achieved an understanding of the relation between religious and humanistic morality at a very early age. Prior to his Oriel examination he had written to his mother that when he reflected upon his own weakness he "shuddered at himself," and yet, he declared, he did not disvalue himself "relatively to others." This paradox he developed in his examination paper by showing that self-confidence(i.e. self-respect) differs from arrogance (or pride) in that "the arrogant man thinks himself positively excellent," whereas the self-confident man "is aware his excellence . . . is relative only." Moreover, by considering that his excellence is relative not merely to "his own race" but also to "beings of such comprehensive powers, that the difference which exists in mental ability or cultivation between himself and his fellow creatures dwindles into nothing," [12] this attitude of self-confidence, which is simply the Aristotelian mean between self-conceit and diffidence, is transformed into true Christian humility.

So Newman wrote in 1822, but by 1826, when he was "drifting in the direction of the liberalism of the day," he preached a sermon in which the difference between the religious and the humanistic position was rather obscured. It was entitled "The Philosophical Temper, First Enjoined by the Gospel," and it declared that "some of those habits of mind which are throughout the Bible represented as alone pleasing in the sight of God, are the very habits which are necessary for success in scientific investigation." These habits are earnestness in pursuit of truth; modesty, patience, and caution; distrust of system; and cooperative spirit; and although Newman admitted that some scientists are not good Christians, a fact which he explained by saying that Christianity requires a far deeper humility than is necessary for science, nevertheless he found himself in the position (which must have astonished him later) of praising the Scriptures for being "the first to describe and inculcate that single-minded, modest, cautious, and generous spirit, which was, after a long time, found so necessary for success in the prosecution of philosophical researches." [13]

The sermon is thoroughly out of character, and yet it has brought forward a fact which Newman nowhere recognized in the *Idea of a University*, namely, that the philosopher, like the Christian, is also confronted by a great external fact which has the power of taking him out of himself, and that this is the fact of knowledge. The vast reaches of external reality, both known and yet to be known, though not a philosophical absolute nor a supreme good, are yet an object of which the contemplation will chasten natural pride. The historian Ranke once expressed the wish to extinguish his own personality in order to become the pure mirror of things,[14] and although one may doubt whether "things" are worthy of this sacrifice, certainly the sacrifice is possible. Newman had said that the philosopher was the "victim of an intense self-contemplation," [15] but any true philosopher contemplates his object, and it is quite as possible to lose the self in the object of knowledge as it is in the object of religious adoration.

Is not this the truth upon which the humanism of Matthew Arnold is based? When Arnold prophesied that the future of poetry was immense, that more and more poetry would take the place of religion, he was founding his prediction not merely upon the subjectivity of poetic truth but also upon the greater degree of objectivity which poetry, as a real formal structure, had over a religion which was rapidly crumbling into myth; and one may say that the whole effort of Arnold's critical essays was to give to the body of world literature the character of an objective standard of excellence. The diseases of his countrymen were all diseases of the self—on the one hand, the eccentricity of Romantic individualism, and on the other, the partisan zeal of political and religious conflict—and the cure for these diseases was a system of value which was larger than the self and perfectly distinct from it. Such a system Arnold found in culture, "the best that is known and thought in the world," and his interest in the culture of France and of ancient Greece was due not solely to the catholicity of those cultures within themselves but also to their distinctness from the culture of nineteenth-century England. They provided the chronological and geographical corrective of modern Britain which modern Britain might equally have provided for them. They formed a "power not ourselves which makes for righteousness," a Literature which becomes Dogma by materializing itself in the fact of its own extrinsic form.

To ensure for literature the quality of apartness, of transcendence, Arnold adopted many expedients. He urged the poet to choose a subject remote from his own time, to delineate an action rather than give vent to an emotion, and to subordinate the felicities of his own expressive power to the rule of a traditional literary structure. The critic he urged to abandon a "personal" judgment for one which was "real," and in his celebrated "touchstones" he devised a kind of poetic litmus paper for rendering such judgments after the manner of an exact science. Actually, of course, his touchstones are as purely personal as any that can be imagined, and one may say that at every turn his search for objectivity failed. When he played with the idea of an English Academy which should provide for the Religion of Philosophy the center of authority which the Vatican provided for Rome, he came right up to the point and then shied away again by deciding that each individual should have his own academy within him. And when he sought, in the idea of the state, a central organ of political authority, he finally placed that authority in the collective body of our "better selves." Indeed, wherever he attempted to expel the self he ended by reintroducing it under another guise. But one may say that the "guise" was the very point of all his endeavors. It is the very means by which values, which have their origin within us, assume their apartness from us. Their transformation *is* their extradition, and as the success with which they are extradited is the measure of the sanction with which they come, so the corrective power of the humanistic values lies in the great, distinct, and objective image of human nature which has been erected in the culture of the past.

Why did Newman fail to recognize, except in that one youthful sermon, the real existence of this power? In his essay on "Christianity and Letters" he had set forth in more satisfactory terms than Arnold would ever do the image of Civilization as a great, distinct, and objective fact, an *orbis terrarum* which was co-extensive with Christianity and more than coeval in point of time. Why did he not acknowledge the power of that fact, so obviously bigger than any individual or any nation or any single epoch, to take men out of themselves, to provide a standard by which they could correct and discipline their own nature?

On one level the answer lies in the attitude which Newman had toward all secular knowledge, an attitude which was conditioned by the highly competitive nature of the English educational system. The awarding of scholarships and fellowships on the basis of grueling examinations; the great importance attached to the Class List, so that a man might be marked for life by his failure to secure Honors in the Schools; the public nature of the Final Examination, which made success into a general triumph and failure into a personal humiliation—all these features, which led the youth to measure himself against his fellow students rather than against the fact of what there was to be learned, created a moral situation which was distinctly unhealthy and which led naturally into the vanity and pride which Newman continually discovered in himself and which he supposed was a necessary part of all intellectual pursuits when uncorrected by religion.

But this was not all. A second factor in Newman's attitude was the Oriel apologetic for liberal knowledge. Strange as it may seem, this apologetic ended by dissolving the real defenses of humanism, for it turned the attention of the student away from the object of knowledge, with the veneration which it ought to excite, toward the contemplation of the self which was being cultivated by that knowledge. In other words, it ran against the same paradox that had baffled Franklin in his pursuit of humility, the paradox that it is psychologically impossible to realize an inner condition which we consciously pursue. John Stuart Mill had discovered this in respect to happiness. Happiness is the end of life, but if you make it your object in life, it mysteriously eludes you. Why? Because it depends on the satisfaction of desires, and thus there must be objects which really are desired if the happiness of achieving them is to be a real happiness. Better forget about happiness, said Mill, and set your heart on something else; then, when you achieve that, you will achieve happiness by the way, and you will not achieve it otherwise.

What is true of humility and happiness is likewise true of every other intrinsic value and hence of every activity which we call liberal—they have an end which is different from their object and one must pursue the object in order to gain the end. This may be illustrated from the case of games, which are the very type of a purely liberal activity. The object of golf is to get the ball in the cup, but no one would say that this was the reason for playing it. The reason for playing it, its end, is the health and recreation which it affords, and it is well to keep this in mind, because one could become so intent upon getting the ball in the cup that he would destroy his health and forfeit his recreation. On the other hand, if one went about the game with *no* persuasion that its object was important, it would not be the means of those advantages which he really hopes to secure. He must both know, and not know, that the object of the game is not the reason for playing it. He may know it as an analyst, but as a player he must not know it. As a player he must really believe that it is of crucial importance to get the ball in the cup.

Something like this is also the case with knowledge. Presumably it is true that the end of liberal knowledge is the perfection of the intellect, but the problem is, will an intellect be perfected by pursuing knowledge in this spirit? One would suppose that it must forget about its own perfection and propose truth as its sole object. Then, if it pursues this object in honesty and sincerity and self-forgetfulness, the perfection will come as a matter of course, and it will not come otherwise. True, we must, in the remote regions of our consciousness, remain aware that knowledge is made for man and not man for knowledge, for in the pedant we see one who has forgotten this, who has become so intent upon the object of the game that he has forgotten the reason for playing it, but this awareness must stay remote and is merely a safeguard. The object before us must always be the truth, the means of our perfection and not the perfection itself. Santayana has said that the only value of possessing great works of literature lies in what they can help us to become, and this is true. But if we go to literature in that spirit, we will simply reduce it to an approximation of our own mind and will not become anything. We must go to literature to discover the truth about what it is, and only by submitting ourselves to the discipline of that discovery shall we emerge with the perfection which is our end.

What is the solution to this problem? Mill's solution was to adopt an "as if" attitude toward life, to act *as if* the objects he did not desire were really desirable, and *as if* the happiness he really wanted was not in his thoughts at all. He called this attitude, which involves a kind of intellectual prestidigitation, a not-letting-your-right-hand-know-what-your-left-hand-is-doing, by the name of Carlyle's "anti-self-consciousness theory." [16] But the trouble is that by being "anti-self-conscious" one does not become unconscious—he simply adds a further degree of sophistication to the self-consciousness he already has. Indeed, once it happens that man has made himself an object of study, once he has written the natural history of his own religious, moral and intellectual behavior, that behavior can never again be the same. By a kind of psychological indeterminacy principle the act of observation affects the thing observed, and it is for this reason that the Noetic defense of a liberal education acted as a solvent upon the education it was trying to defend.

The third and perhaps the chief reason why Newman could not give to literary culture the value which Arnold accorded it was that his conception of this culture was stubbornly naturalistic. In his essay on "Literature" he distinguished the writing which merits that name (and under which he included the whole range of the humanities) from science on the one hand and theology on the other by its intensely personal character. It is not something that could be produced by a group of persons working in concert or by a machine or a natural process, but it bears upon it the mark of an individual human mind. Indeed, it is no more than the extension of that mind into the realm of language, and so far is it from achieving autonomy by virtue of its symbolic form that that form is simply the radiance cast by the light of the mind, the motion imparted by the life of the mind, the shadow thrown by the form of the mind, upon the ground of public communication. Divide the light from its radiance, the shadow from its form, the motion from its life, and then you may divide the twofold *logos* of human speech and human reason. But until then, to employ literature, which is simply "the Life and Remains of the *natural* man," [17] as a means of improving man is like trying to save the soul of a highwayman by reading him the history of his adventures on the road.

The Religion of Philosophy, therefore, is really a naturalistic religion. It might call itself humanism, but in a philosophy which knows no excellence beyond the standard of human nature, to do this is simply to dwell upon the adjective and forget the noun. Generically it is a naturalism, and even if it be a "human" naturalism it still provides no means for transcending the limits of the natural man. Like Archimedes, it lacks a point outside its own universe from which its universe can be moved, and therefore all its jostling serves only to shift its weight and never to alter its center of gravity. It is in the position of a moral tautology: what it strives to be, it already is, and if it strives to be anything else, it becomes a contradiction in terms. It occupies, in relation to man, the position which Natural Theology occupies in relation to God, for Natural Theology is also a Theological Naturalism. It argues from the world of nature to the existence of God, but just as it cannot deduce a God who is greater than his handiwork, so it would not suggest that He be edified by the contemplation of his handiwork. Why, then, should one suggest that man be so edified? Is he to be regenerated by the productions of his unregenerate nature or to receive the Life Everlasting from that which received its portion of life from him? Obviously not. Obviously, the best that one can do with any humanistic discipline is to raise individuals to the level of their fellows, make them conform to their own nature as embodied in the society about them—make them, in short, into gentlemen.

As Newman's celebrated portrait of the "gentleman" contains his finest comment upon the Religion of Philosophy, it is ironic that this portrait should often be taken as a serious expression of Newman's positive ideal. Presumably the mistake could never have happened if the passage had not been so often detached from its context and reprinted separately as an anthology piece, but even so there is no better evidence of the truth of Newman's view that the Religion of Philosophy is the religion of the world than the fact that some part of the world should be willing to model itself upon the gentleman as Newman describes him. "It is almost a definition of a gentleman," the description begins, "to say he is one who never inflicts pain," and in this one sentence are presented both the ethical standard and the literary method which characterize the entire portrait. The standard, as befits the devotee of a naturalistic philosophy, is pleasure, but no positive act is ever attempted in behalf of this standard. Perhaps one-third of the sentences which describe the gentleman are couched in the negative form, and another third imply a negative by the nature of their verb. The gentleman is "mainly occupied in merely *removing* the obstacles which hinder the . . . action of those about him"; "he *concurs* with their movements rather than takes the initiative himself"; he "carefully *avoids* whatever may cause a jar or a jolt in the minds of those with whom he is cast." He is analogous to an easy chair, which gives way wherever pressure is applied, and indeed his habitual act is an act of deference. If he is standing, he steps aside; if he is sitting, he rises; and he does this not out of any pusillanimous spirit but because "his great concern [is] to make every one at their ease and at home." "He has his eyes on all his company; he is tender towards the bashful, gentle towards the distant, and merciful towards the absurd; he can recollect to whom he is speaking; he guards against unseasonable allusions, or topics which may irritate; he is seldom prominent in conversation, and never wearisome." [18] He does nothing remarkable because it is his desire to avoid remark. If he has vices, he conceals them out of a sense of propriety, and if he has virtues, he would not embarrass others by their display. He is all things to all men because he is really nothing in himself. He has no inner nature or essential form; he simply assumes, in rapid succession, the forms and natures of the various persons with whom he comes in contact. If he believed in some principle, he might be positive in its defense, but he does not and so he is pliable in the extreme. He has no allegiance except to society, and society asks nothing of him except that he conform. It does not tell him what to conform to, for it does not know. The fashions of tomorrow are not the fashions of today—if they were, they would not be fashionable. The only rule is to change with the changing scene, to take your colors from the foliage of the season and your tone from the vibrations in the air. The rule is the rule of decency and decorum, but as the decent and the decorous are simply that which is fitting, without being fitting to anything in particular, there can be no positive rule but only the general admonition not to go counter to the things that are currently being done.

The work which seems to be the chief literary influence upon Newman's portrait of the gentleman is James Forrester's *The Polite Philoso-*

pher: or, An Essay on the Art which makes a Man happy in himself, and agreeable to others (1734). As Newman read this work in an edition of Lord Chesterfield's *Advice to His Son*, where it was published anonymously, he seems to have supposed that it was by Chesterfield himself,[19] and certainly it does belong to that school. It presents the ideal of the Polite Philosopher as one characterized by Reason, Calmness, and Good-Nature (or Sense, Moderation, and Sweetness), and it declares that "his chief aim [is] to be well with all." To this end he eschews the example of Honorius, who "speaks bluntly what he thinks, without regarding the company who are by," and he imitates Garcia, who does not. He never willingly speaks of himself, and he avoids political topics, on which "it is almost impossible to say any thing that will please all." He never speaks contemptuously of religion, "because he knows it will give the person to whom he speaks pain; a thing ever opposite to the character of a polished philosopher." In other words, Forrester offers seriously the advice which Newman offers ironically, and he concludes by observing, "I have shewn you what you are not to be; in a word, I have explained politeness negatively: if you would know it positively, you must seek it from company and observation." The company which he especially recommends is that of the "fair sex," for if we would consider the matter carefully, "politeness can be no other way attained. Books may furnish us with right ideas, experience may improve our judgments: but it is the acquaintance of the ladies only, which can bestow that easiness of address, whereby the *fine gentleman* is distinguished from the *scholar* and the *man of business*." [20]

To trace out the historical affiliations, is to follow up the ultimate implications, of the man who makes a religion out of Civilization. He belongs, says Newman, with Lord Chesterfield and the ladies. Holding as he does that virtue is a kind of beauty, he will end by finding it in a beauty that is not even virtuous, and thus "that very refinement of Intellectualism, which began by repelling sensuality, ends by excusing it." [21] The most striking example of this that Newman can give, all the more striking because it comes from one so grave and wise as Edmund Burke, is the extravagance into which that statesman was betrayed in his famous lament over Marie Antoinette and his valediction to the spirit of chivalry. "It is gone," cried Burke, "that sensibility of principle, that chastity of honour, which felt a stain like a wound; which inspired courage, while it mitigated ferocity; which ennobled whatever it touched, and under which *vice lost half its evil by losing all its grossness*." [22]

In the judgment of Newman this was not merely a memorable, but also a precise, statement of what the Religion of Philosophy could do and of what it often presumed to do but could not. It *could* make one lose all his grossness; it *could not* make him lose even half his evil. It could prepare him to enter into polite society; it could not prepare him to enter into the presence of God. The paradox that one who was fit to see God might be unfit to be seen by anyone else was one which dwelt upon Newman's imagination with great insistence. He expressed it by drawing a contrast between a typical English gentleman of the Oxford stamp and some wretched Sicilian beggar-woman who had thrown herself upon him in the course of his travels. Scabrous and diseased, almost bestial in the filth with which her garments and even her hair were matted, dissolute, drunken, improvident, she ran beside him whining her importunate professional whine. Out of simple humanity he could not refuse her the money and even the silk handkerchief which he knew that she or another would one day steal, and if he then turned to the beauties of the landscape, it was with a real sorrow that she, who gazed upon them daily, should see them with so blank an eye. Her world began and ended with her allotted "beat." Of yesterday and tomorrow, of the world of Europe and the world of thought, she knew nothing. He gazed into the hills and saw the site of a Roman villa, built on the ruins of a Greek temple and providing the foundations of a Christian shrine, and if he did not enter the shrine, as the woman had done before sunrise, it was because the understanding he had of the rise and fall of successive civilizations had taught him to be tolerant of all human opinions and no more than respectful of any. His Greek Testament he had not brought with him this time—the course of travels which he intended would not take him into the regions which it described—but he was no less familiar with it than with the classical poet which he had substituted, and he did not know which volume inspired and refreshed him the more. Neither did he feel any repugnance as he observed the woman turn from counting her money to counting her beads, for he perfectly understood that her superstition was simply the effect of her ignorance. What he did not understand was that she, for all her ignorance and unsavory character, would be saved, and that he, for all his far-ranging views, would be damned.[23]

If Newman had had his choice of being an English gentleman or a Sicilian beggar, *such* an English gentleman and *such* a beggar, he would have chosen without the slightest hesitation to be the scabrous and drunken beggar. Happily these were not the only alternatives—one could be both. Abstractly and in their own idea, there were no two ways of life more distinctly opposed than the humanistic way of making all things tributary to man and the religious way of making man entirely tributary to God. But they were only opposed as the left leg is opposed to the right—taken together, they enabled one to cease halting and to walk. They enabled man to fulfil his own nature and then to place that nature, fully developed, at the service of God. They provided neither for a godless humanism nor a Christian asceticism, but rather for a Christian humanism which fulfilled the idea of perfection by providing an apex for a pyramid which was not without a base. Newman's ideal, in its completed form, has this pyramidal or hierarchical structure, and any inconsistencies which seem in one part or another to mark it may well arise from the fact that Newman builds it up stage by stage and defends each new stage by the way in which it supplements or contrasts with the old. In the first instance, there could be no knowledge without a broad basis of fact, but in the second, this knowledge would be "mere learning" if it were not organized into a philosophic view. This view, in turn, would be a mere spurious "philosophism" if it were not placed in the service of religion; and thus we have a hierarchy of Nature in tribute to Man and Man in tribute to God. We have universal learning, rising by degrees into the integrity of knowledge, and crowned at last by the gift of the Catholic faith.

No less than the saint is the full scope of such an ideal, but not every saint fulfills it. Some take the way of thorns and harsh flints, of matted hair and self-laceration—no less than the way of the Sicilian beggar. It is remarkable, therefore, that Newman's special devotion was reserved, not for a St. Anthony or a St. Francis, but for one who combined the winning charm of a civilized age with the humility and devotion of the rudest times. And if Newman concludes his *Discourses* with a tribute to the father and patron of the Oratory, St. Philip Neri, this is not merely a pious acknowledgment to the one under whose auspices he speaks but also an exemplification of the principles about which he has spoken. For St. Philip, if he had not been a saint, might well have been a courtier or a philosopher instead, or rather he already was these things and then erased them in the superaddition of saint. In his youth, so says his biographer, he studied philosophy and theology until "he was reckoned one of the most distinguished scholars . . . in the schools of Rome," but when he had made "sufficient advancement in learning, not for his own use only, but also for the edification of others," "he laid his studies aside, and applied himself wholly to that science which is found in the crucifix." Gradually, as he gathered about him a band of followers, the first Congregation of the Oratory was formed, and it knew no rule except the rule of its founder's life. "He did not indeed forbid them to study, but he bade them give themselves to studies suitable to the institute, and not to seek to have the name of being scholars, or to make a show of learning in the presence of others; the servant of God ought, he said, to try to acquire knowledge, but not to display it; nor again, to pursue it with excessive application, for in that there might even be sin." [24]

Philip was no medieval saint but a saint of the Renaissance, and not of stern Viterbo or the harsh, unyielding North, but of Florence, the city of art, and of Rome, the city of worldly culture. "He lived," wrote Newman, "at a time when pride mounted high, and the senses held rule . . . when medieval winter was receding, and the summer sun of civilization was bringing into leaf and flower a thousand forms of luxurious enjoyment; when a new world of thought and beauty had opened upon the human mind, in the discovery of the treasures of classic literature and art." He saw the dangers which they presented, but he also saw that whatever might be the methods of others in meeting them, his own method must be that of mildness and moderation, of patience and a sweet, attractive charm. "He preferred to yield to the stream, and direct the current, which he could not stop, of science, literature, art, and fashion, and to sweeten and sanctify what God had made very good and man had spoilt." [25]

It is a little remarkable that the one passage from the *Life of St. Philip* which Newman has chosen to quote in his own description is one which is so consonant with the principles of a gentleman that it could almost find a place in the *Polite Philosopher* or Lord Chesterfield's *Advice to His Son*. "In the words of his biographer," wrote Newman, quoting the *Life* by Bacci, " 'he was all things to all men. He suited himself to noble and ignoble, young and old, subjects and prelates, learned and ignorant. . . . When he was called upon to be merry he was so; if there was a demand upon his sympathy he was equally ready. He gave the same welcome to all. . . . In consequence of his being so accessible and willing to receive all comers, many went to him every day, and some continued for the space of thirty, nay forty years, to visit him very often both morning and evening, so that his room went by the agreeable nickname of the Home of Christian mirth.' " [26] If the mirth were laughter and not merely a smile, then this was one difference between Lord Chesterfield and the Saint. But another was, that whereas both professed to be "all things to all men," it was only Philip who knew to complete the phrase in the manner which Paul intended: "I became all things to all men, that I might save all."

CHAPTER 13

Secular and Religious Knowledge

To me conversions were not the first thing, but the edification of
Catholics. So much have I fixed upon the latter as my object,
that up to this time the world persists in saying that I recommend
Protestants not to become Catholics. And, when I have given as
my true opinion, that I am afraid to make hasty converts of educated men, lest they should not have counted the cost, and should
have difficulties after they have entered the Church, I do but imply
the same thing, that the Church must be prepared for converts, as
well as converts prepared for the Church. How can this be understood at Rome? . . . And Catholics in England, from their very
blindness, cannot see that they are blind. To aim then at improving
the condition, the status, of the Catholic body, by a careful survey
of their argumentative basis, of their position relatively to the
philosophy and the character of the day, by giving them juster
views, by enlarging and refining their minds, in one word, by education, is (in their view) more than a superfluity or a hobby, it is
an insult. It implies that they are deficient in material points. Now
from first to last, education, in this large sense of the word, has been
my line. . . . I should wish to attempt to meet the great infidel
&c. questions of the day, but both Propaganda and the Episcopate,
doing nothing themselves, look with extreme jealousy on anyone
who attempts it.

—Newman's Journal, January, 1863

EVERYTHING is miserable," wrote Newman to his
sister Jemima in February, 1840. "I expect a great attack upon the
Bible - indeed, I have long expected it. At the present moment indications of what is coming gather. Those wretched Socialists on the one
hand, then Carlyle on the other, a man of first-rate ability, I suppose,
and quite fascinating as a writer. His book on the French Revolution is
most taking (to *me*). I had hope he might have come round right, for
it was easy to see he was not a believer, but they say that he has settled
the wrong way. *His* view is that Christianity has good *in* it, or is good
as far as it goes, which, when applied to Scripture, is of course a picking
and choosing of its contents. Then again you have Arnold's school, such

SECULAR AND RELIGIOUS KNOWLEDGE

as it is, (I do hope he will be frightened back) giving up the inspiration of the Old Testament, or of all Scripture, (I do not say Arnold himself does). Then you have Milman clenching his History of the Jews by a History of Christianity, which they say is worse, and just in the same line. Then you have all your Political Economists, who *cannot* accept, (it is impossible) the Scripture rules about almsgiving, renunciation of wealth, self denial &c. And then you have Geologists giving up parts of the Old Testament. All these and many more spirits seem uniting and forming into something shocking." [1]

In such terms did Newman describe the great issue of his day, the conflict between science and religion, but in 1840 this issue was not the full scope or extent of his fears. "I begin to have serious apprehensions," he continued, "lest any religious body is strong enough to withstand the league of evil but the Roman Church," and a dozen years later, when he was a member of that church, he felt, though with very different emotions, that his prophecy had been fulfilled. "He who believes Revelation with that absolute faith which is the prerogative of a Catholic," he wrote, "is not the nervous creature who startles at every sound, and is fluttered by every strange or novel appearance which meets his eyes. He has no sort of apprehension, he laughs at the idea, that any thing can be discovered by any other scientific method, which can contradict any one of the dogmas of his religion." He knows that his religion is true, and since "truth cannot contradict truth," he is perfectly sure that "if anything seems to be proved by astronomer, or geologist, or chronologist, or antiquarian, or ethnologist, in contradiction to the dogmas of faith, that point will eventually turn out, first, *not* to be proved, or, secondly, not *contradictory*, or thirdly, not contradictory to anything *really revealed*, but to something which has been confused with revelation." [2]

This was Newman's position as a Catholic on the conflict between science and religion. Given the integrity of knowledge, there was no possibility of dissension among its branches. "Nature and Grace, Reason and Revelation, come from the same Divine Author, whose works cannot contradict each other." [3] And yet, despite the fact that they cannot, their adherents continually do. Throughout the ages there has always been an antagonism between the advocates of religion on the one hand and the physical philosophers on the other, and the problem arises— why do they quarrel if they really have nothing to quarrel about?

They quarrel, says Newman, because each side encroaches upon the territory which belongs to the other. In point of fact these territories are almost perfectly distinct. The one concerns the natural and the other the supernatural world, and as these worlds differ not merely in what they are but also in the means by which we know them, so the study of these worlds will differ not merely in their subject matter but also in their method. The one will be an induction from natural phenomena, the other a deduction from God's revelation of himself, and it would seem that two sciences so perfectly distinct would be "incapable of collision," would need "at most to be connected, never to be reconciled." [4]

So it would seem, but actually it was the very distinctness of these sciences that brought them into collision. The physical scientists, considering that the great triumph of the Baconian school was to have expelled the deductive method from physical investigations, were irritated to find that there was still one subject matter in which it remained. They asserted that by deduction no new truth could be gained; theologians agreed but added that, as regards religious truth, they had not to seek at all, for they had it already. "Christian Truth is purely of revelation; that revelation we can but explain, we cannot increase, except relatively to our own apprehensions; without it we should have known nothing of its contents, with it we know just as much as its contents, and nothing more." [5] In the sciences a vast and omnigenous mass of phenomena lies before the inquirer, all in a confused litter, and needing the arrangement and analysis which induction can give.[6] But in theology such varied phenomena are wanting, or rather, if one were to take the Scriptures as a collection of such phenomena, inviting the Christian to an inductive process by which he might arrive at his own religious conclusions, then one would indeed have an inductive science of God, and it would be such a science as goes by the name of Protestantism. For this is what Protestantism is: it is the application to the Book of God of the same method which the Baconian applies to the Book of Nature, and the fact that in the course of three hundred years it has come to such a variety of conclusions does not indeed at once prove any one of them to be wrong, but it does cast a grave doubt upon the propriety of the entire method.

As to the particular subject matters which are the province of science on the one hand and theology on the other, these are no less distinct than are their appropriate methods. The one is nature and the other the Author of nature; the one is matter and the other is Mind or Spirit; the one is the ordering laws which govern the phenomenal world and the other is the extraordinary Giver of those laws who can dispense with them whenever he sees fit. It is true, of course, that "these two great circles of knowledge . . . intersect; first, as far as supernatural knowledge includes truths and facts of the natural world, and secondly, as far as truths and facts of the natural world are . . . data for inferences about the supernatural"; [7] but even where they intersect they will consider their common subject only under the aspect of their own idea, and they will be impatient at the intrusion of any other. The scientist, asking the cause of volcanoes, will be indignant at being told it is "the divine vengeance"; and the theologian, asking the cause of the overthrow of the guilty cities, considers it preposterous to be referred to the volcanic action still visible in the neighborhood. The one is inquiring into final causes and so for the moment passes over the existence of established laws; the other is inquiring into physical causes and so passes over for the moment the existence of God. Neither intends to deny the causes which he does not study; he simply holds that they are irrelevant to his purpose, and he asks that his investigation not be spoiled by having them obtruded upon him.[8]

It is not merely in their general drift, however, but even in the very nature of their common subject matter that science and theology are found to be distinct. When the former argues from nature to the God of nature, it is doubtless engaged in a divine work and cannot issue in untrue religious conclusions. "But at the same time it must be recollected that Revelation has reference to circumstances which did not arise till after the heavens and the earth were made. They were made before the introduction of moral evil into the world: whereas the Catholic Church is the instrument of a remedial dispensation to meet that introduction. No wonder then that her teaching is simply distinct, though not divergent, from the theology which Physical Science suggests to its followers." [9]

Science and theology, then, are perfectly distinct in their method, their general drift, and their subject matter, and no occasion for conflict should arise between them were it not that individuals occasionally attempt to extend the method or drift or subject matter of their own discipline into the province of the other. Normally, Newman felt, this was not done as a deliberate act of aggression but simply as a result of narrow-mindedness. It would happen that a particular scientist or theologian would be preoccupied with his own discipline to the exclusion of everything else, and although this was perfectly justified from the point of view of advancing his studies, it gave to his writings the outward appearance of one who not merely ignored, but also denied, the things which he was temporarily excluding from view. On others this might have a startling effect, and in the end it would have a similar effect upon himself, for what had once been a deliberate and even arduous act of abstraction would gradually become the habit of his mind, and by long familiarity with one subject he would eventually be indisposed for any other. The subject itself, however, would remain, and by virtue of forming a part of the world, and a world which touched upon his own, he could not always avoid handling it, and he would necessarily handle it in his own way. The vacuum which he had created in his own mind he would fill up with the pressure of his own thoughts, and necessarily he would fill it up wrong. Hence the appearance of conflict between his discipline and that upon which he was encroaching.

Either the scientist or the theologian might be guilty of such an encroachment, but there was a special temptation to which the former was liable and the latter was not. The world treated by the scientist was so obvious, so various, so strangely compelling and deeply absorbing that it was very liable to carry one away into a neglect of that other world spoken of by theology—a world not obvious, but invisible; not various, but thin and meager; not novel and dazzling, but, to minds of a certain cast, barren, of a rude simplicity, stern, and even repelling. Moreover, to be taken up on the mountain top of the modern world and to be shown by the astronomer reaches of almost infinite distance and by the geologist reaches of ageless time, to look with the chemist into the infinitesimal organization of matter, to learn of cities and societies and living forms which have had their place and have passed away, to view nature in "its infinite complexity, its awful comprehensiveness, and its diversified yet harmonious colouring," is to gain a view of the world so different from that presented by the simple record of faith that the imagination is bewildered and swims with a sense of the distance between the two. Not that there is anything in the view of science, or anything that can be deduced from that view, which is contrary to the faith, but then it is not the reason of man that is perplexed but his imagination. Merely by the "terrible influence" of that faculty, which Butler called "the author of all error," [10] is he borne away from one truth, not by its contrariety but by its strangeness, to another.

To exemplify how this may happen Newman instanced a number of cases from the intellectual history of recent times. The first was that of a professional man, eminent in London in the early years of the century, who "so treated the subject of Comparative Anatomy as to seem to deny the immateriality of the soul." [11] Without doubt this was William Lawrence, professor of anatomy in the College of Surgeons, whose course of lectures in 1816 was attacked by John Abernethy, the celebrated physician, and then by a host of others in books and pamphlets which continued to appear for over a decade.[12] The charge was that Lawrence had denied that life was anything more than the result of organization, "the assemblage of all the functions," [13] and this was found so contrary to Scripture that Lord Eldon refused an injunction to protect the rights of the author in his own works, the chief effect of this action being, as usual, to send those works through a number of editions which they never would have achieved of their own merit.

A second example, one which came within Newman's personal observation, was provided by Henry Hart Milman's *History of the Jews*, published in 1829. Milman has been called "a kind of Christian Gibbon, without the indecency and without the fun," [14] but he was not a rationalist historian of the stamp of Grote or Macaulay but simply an Anglican clergyman of the school of Arnold who was trying to apply the critical method of Barthold Niebuhr to the history of the chosen people. His leading principle was that of accommodation, the view that the Divine Spirit in manifesting itself through the Jewish people necessarily accommodated itself to their particular stage of development. It showed itself as barbarous when they were barbarous, as ignorant when they were ignorant, and had to wait upon their refinement to become the civilized religion of later times. It was not this principle, however, which caused the greatest scandal, but rather the minimizing of the supernatural element in the Old Testament miracles. In telling how the bitter waters of Marah were made sweet by the branch of a tree, Milman would add the comment, "whether from the natural virtue of the plant seems uncertain"; [15] and in general he emphasized the natural means by which a miracle was accomplished rather than the Supernatural Agent by whom these means were employed.

The outcry against the work was immediate and sensational. Dr. Faussett, Margaret Professor of Divinity at Oxford, preached a sermon against it in St. Mary's, and Bishop Mant addressed two letters to the author imploring him to withdraw the work from publication, a step which was eventually taken.[16] Newman himself wrote to Pusey that he thought it "a very dangerous work," [17] but on the whole his judgment was less severe and based upon rather different grounds than that of many of his contemporaries. To a young friend who was still writing *his* protest more than a year later, Newman advised that it was unnecessary and, moreover, that he himself did not always agree. "Sometimes I am on M[ilman]'s side against you," he declared. "It seems to me that the great evil of M's work lies not in the *matter* of the history, but in the profane *spirit* in which it is written. In most of his positions I agree with him - but abhor the irreverent scoffing Gibbon-like tone of the composition." [18]

A decade later, when Milman's *History of Christianity* appeared ("worse, and just in the same line"), Newman wrote a lengthy review in the *British Critic* [19] in which he set forth fully and precisely his objections to treating sacred history in the same manner as profane. It was not that the two subjects did not have an element in common or that this element could not be isolated and treated in a strictly historical manner, but simply that in sacred history this element was completely trivial. If Christ really were the Son of God, then that was the most momentous fact about him, and to leave it out of account in a history of his work was to ignore the very reason for our being interested in that work at all. Furthermore, it was to lose the meaning of everything that he did. And as for miracles, they were assuredly natural events—every event was—and since their real character as miracles lay not in their violation of natural law but in their coherence with God's larger purpose, one could make them as naturalistic as he pleased without destroying their supernatural character. The difficulty with Milman was that he pressed the matter too hard; he limited God's power by the extent of his own credulity, and when he traced elements in the Christian religion to their source in some oriental culture, he felt that he had somehow disposed of them. Newman had "so little antecedent difficulty" about the fact of their heathen origin that he readily granted it. He only denied that *because* they were heathen they could not also be Christian, that *because* they were human and natural they could not also be divine. The natural in God's dealings with his people was simply the vehicle, the sacrament, the visible type, of the supernatural, and to speak of the former without mentioning the latter was like omitting the spring from the year or playing Hamlet without the prince.

A third instance, which did not give rise to any controversy, was provided by Nassau Senior's inaugural lecture as first professor of political economy at the University of Oxford in 1826. To understand this instance one must remember that in the early years of its history political economy was regarded not merely as a "dismal science" but also as a peculiarly intrusive one. It was engaged in constructing an abstract "economic man" who was motivated solely by the desire for wealth, and since such a figure was distinctly un-Christian, it was popularly supposed that there was some scheme afoot to replace the Gospels by the doctrines of Malthus and Ricardo.[20] So general, indeed, was this concern that in 1810 Copleston was reluctant to admit into the curriculum a science "so prone to usurp over the rest," and in 1825, when the Drummond professorship was endowed, the founder made it perfectly clear that he relied on the university to keep the new study "in its proper place." [21]

Nassau Senior, a friend and pupil of Whately, was the person appointed to this task, and Newman concedes that most people would find his lecture to be temperate and modest in its tone. Nevertheless, it was part of the tradition of an inaugural lecture that it should state not merely the objects and principles of the science in question but also its scope and importance, and Whately urged his young friend to enlarge upon the latter as the thing that most needed to be said.[22] Enlarge upon it he did, as Newman shows. Concerned lest his audience should think that a science which dealt only with the pursuit of wealth was a low or inferior occupation, he ventured to predict that in the course of a very few years "it will rank in public estimation among the first of *moral* sciences in interest and in utility." Warming to his subject, he declared that "the pursuit of wealth . . . is, to the mass of mankind, the great source of *moral* improvement," [23] and he implied that any institution which discouraged this pursuit, as Christianity presumably does, was really a mischievous institution.

Given that wealth is to be sought, says Newman, the political economist can tell us that this or that is the method of seeking it. But that is as far as he has a right to go. The question of whether it ought to be sought or whether it is the way to virtue or the price of happiness is an ethical question; and the question of the rank of political economy is obviously not one to be decided by the science itself but belongs to that special science "which disposes of the claims and arranges the places of all the departments of knowledge," [24] the Science of Sciences.

Indeed, the answer to all these problems lies with the Science of Sciences. If the conflict between science and religion is simply a matter of one discipline encroaching upon the province of another, then the whole issue can be solved by the accurate delimitation of their provinces. And that, of course, is why philosophy was regarded by Newman as the study appropriate to a citizen in the nineteenth century. Just as today one might educate for peace or for democracy, so in Newman's day one educated for intellectual peace, for a discrimination among the rival claims of conflicting disciplines. And if the individual, for all of his catholicity, could do this only imperfectly, at least he had in the university an organ which could do it for him with fine dispassion. The university was, or ought to be, the intellectual tribunal of the age. It was the mother of sciences and the arbiter of truth, and to say this is simply to say—what Newman was conscious of at all times—that it was a medieval institution.

It is in the *Rise and Progress of Universities* that Newman shows himself most conscious of his medieval heritage, and although one may say that it was only natural, in one who was founding a Catholic university in Ireland, to recur in thought to the founding of the first universities of Europe, it is clear that Newman did not do so from the mere appropriateness of the occasion but because he regarded his own work as repeating in some sense the work of the Middle Ages. He saw a deep and pervasive analogy between the intellectual problem of the twelfth century and that of his own day, for both periods were confronted with the task of bringing a vast body of new knowledge, suddenly acquired, into harmony with the more traditional wisdom of a rather different character; and he hoped that in the great synthesis of the thirteenth century, and especially in the role played by the university in achieving that synthesis, he might find a means of adjusting the claims of science and religion in the modern world. It is worthwhile, then, to remind the reader briefly of this analogy, because it shows that Newman's reiterated statement, "truth cannot contradict truth," is not a mere rationalistic commonplace but is a belief grounded deep in the actual experience of the church.

An encyclopaedist of the eleventh century might well have claimed that the entire formal knowledge of his day was contained in the seven liberal arts and the Scriptures with the comment of the Fathers, but by the early thirteenth century all this was changed. It was not merely that the arts themselves had undergone a remarkable elaboration, although that was so, but that entire new sciences had sprung up outside the framework which the arts provided. Roman law, for example, of which only a meager information had survived in the practice of Italian notaries, was revived at Bologna in the early twelfth century, and canon law was first formulated by Gratian in about 1140. Somewhat earlier the study of medicine, of which there had been a continuing but minor tradition in southern Italy, became more intensely conscious of the writings of Hippocrates, Galen, and certain Arabian physicians, and flowered forth into the University of Salerno. Farther north, the application of logic and philosophy to the problems of faith converted the exegesis of Scripture into the new science of theology, but even more remarkable than this was the rise of logic itself. Originally a minor part of the Trivium, it soon burst quite out of the framework of the arts and became an independent science to which all the others were merely preliminary, and here the great impetus was the new translations of Aristotle. "Of his works," says Professor Haskins, "the early Middle Ages had access only to the six logical treatises of the *Organon* as translated by Boethius, and as a matter of fact all of these except the *Categories* and the *De interpretatione* dropped out of sight until the twelfth century. These two surviving treatises came to be known as the *Old Logic*, in contradistinction to the *New Logic*—the *Prior* and *Posterior Analytics*, *Topics*, and *Elenchi*—which reappeared in various forms soon after 1128. By 1159 the most advanced of these, the *Posterior Analytics*, was in course of assimilation, and the whole of the Aristotelian logic was absorbed into European thought by the close of the century." [25] The *Physics* and lesser works on natural science were translated not long before 1200, the *Metaphysics* about the same time, and in the course of the next sixty years the rest of the Aristotelian *corpus* was added: the various books *On Animals*, the *Ethics* and *Politics*, and, in an imperfect form, the *Rhetoric* and *Poetics*.[26]

The immediate effect of this new learning was, as Newman says, intoxicating. It dazzled the imaginations of men and "carried them away." [27] It broke up the old structure of knowledge without bringing any new structure in its stead, and so the world of learning became, for the moment, anarchic, sciences jarring angrily together, swerving out of their accustomed course, and striving hotly for place. Law, which had traditionally been taught at Bologna as a subdivision of rhetoric, the branch called "judicial oratory," came rapidly to overshadow the entire arts course, and the same was true of logic at Paris. Thus the circle of the sciences became a ring of contention, and the metaphor of a battle of the books, which Swift was to apply to a similar clash of thought in his own day, was actually used by a thirteenth-century *trouvère*, Henri d'Andeli, in his poem *The Battle of the Seven Arts*. Grammar, the champion of Orleans, goes out against Logic of Paris, but is badly worsted, for "Logic has the students." [28] Logic, indeed, was pre-eminent in the age and not only was pursued to the neglect of other disciplines but also infected with its own method those studies which it could not expel. Grammar, for example, it transformed from an empiric to a speculative discipline, replacing Donatus and Priscian by the *Doctrinale* of Alexander de Villedieu (1199),[29] but its greatest struggles were with the study of literature on the one hand and theology on the other.

The revived study of classical authors in the schools of Chartres from about 1090 to 1150 and at Orleans for the hundred years thereafter provides a pleasant humanistic episode in an age where the main movement was all the other way. If Orleans had its champion in Henri d'Andeli, the champion of Chartres was John of Salisbury (c. 1115–80), an Englishman who has left a famous account of the teaching in its schools and who was perhaps the most attractive figure in the entire age. Persons qualified to judge say that he writes the best Latin to be found before the Renaissance and that he is the most learned man of his time, especially in the classics, which he quotes lovingly and profusely. To Newman he is the very type of medieval universalism, exemplifying by his wanderings from school to school and teacher to teacher that cosmopolitanism which is but the geographical expression of a deeper habit of mind, a habit of wide sympathies, of sanity and moderation. John was not anti-logical. His *Metalogicon* is the first work of the Middle Ages which displays a knowledge of the entire *Organon* of Aristotle, and its main purpose is to defend logic against those who would debase it. The first part of the work, however, is a defense of grammar and rhetoric against the logicians. John tells how he studied logic at Paris under Abelard and how, returning there twelve years later, he found his former associates exactly where he had left them, still solving the same syllogisms and propounding the same questions as before, and he wisely observes that logic is bloodless and barren unless it draw its material from other studies. It is an integral part of the Trivium, and the Trivium is an integral part of the whole scheme of knowledge, leading on to the Quadrivium and thence to natural philosophy and moral philosophy, which is the crown of all the sciences.[30] Here, then, is one who in the first onset of the revival of learning had the breadth and stability of mind to master the new sciences without throwing away the old, and Newman sees in his spirit the means of maintaining the humanistic tradition against the encroachments of the Baconian, as formerly against the Aristotelian, logic.[31]

The conflict between logic and literature, however, was much less intense than that between logic and theology, for the latter came to involve the most fundamental problem in medieval thought, that of the relation between faith and reason. As usual, the champions of the new science did not practice restraint. Berengar of Tours declared, "It is the part of courage to have recourse to dialectic in all things," [32] although this was the very question—whether there was a sphere in which dialectic, at least as humanly exercised, ought to submit itself to the authority of revelation or of personal religious feeling or of the historic experience of the church. The doctrine of the Trinity, for example, presented exactly the kind of problem which was tantalizing to a logician but was not to be handled safely by logic alone. Thus Roscelin of Compiègne was condemned by one church council for sacrificing the unity of the Divine Substance and Abelard by another for sacrificing the distinctness of the Persons,[33] and both were led into their false positions by a presumptuous and uncorrected use of logic. The spirit of the time was symbolized for Newman by the narrative of Simon de Tournay, struck dead for crying out after lecture, "Ah! good Jesus, I could disprove Thee, did I please, as easily as I have proved." [34]

An even better symbol was to be found in Abelard. Through the lurid and garbled versions of his autobiography and letters to Heloise, which had poured from the English and French press in the last two centuries, Abelard had become a sort of martyr of rationalism, almost the prototype of the eighteenth-century *philosophe*, anticipating Rousseau in his

amours and Voltaire in his conflict with religion. We know now that
whatever he was to Heloise, to the church he was not a Voltaire. "I would
not be a philosopher," he says, "if that meant a denial of Paul, nor an
Aristotle if that involved separation from Christ." [35] But if his error was
not religious, it was intellectual, and this is precisely Newman's point.
Abelard studied logic much and early and theology only very little and
late, and he was personally so self-assured and pugnacious that he was
called by a contemporary "that rhinoceros." Thus, both by nature and
training he was the very type of an intellectual partisan. He approached
theology with no tool except dialectic, and he treated it as a series of
isolated propositions which the mind could sometimes grasp and sometimes could not. When it could not, or when it was deceived in thinking
it could, he had no idea of appealing to the rich religious experience of
all kinds, both institutional and personal, out of which theology had
really grown, for all that experience lay outside both his studies and his
own character.[36]

By a natural reaction, Abelard begot St. Bernard of Clairvaux, who
faced him across the Council of Sens in 1140 and secured his condemnation. Gilbert Porrée, whose work on logic was placed by the age beside
that of Aristotle, was present at the trial, and Abelard whispered to him
that he would be next, for the excesses of reason had in fact produced
an excess, if one may so speak, of faith. But the wonderful thing was that
when the synod met in 1147 and 1148, Gilbert was acquitted by the
Pope. The claims of faith and reason, or rather the excessive claims of
rationalism and obscurantism, had found their proper level, and Gilbert's
was the last trial of this sort in the Middle Ages.[37]

What was true of the new logic was also true of the new philosophy.
When Aristotle's works on natural science and metaphysics were introduced to the Western world about 1200, men seized upon them with an
avidity which alarmed the faithful. The alarm had some justification,
for there are doctrines in Aristotle, such as the eternity of matter and
the unity of the active intellect, which run counter to Christian ortho-
doxy. They are not particularly emphasized by Aristotle himself, but in
the "great comment" of Averroës, by which Aristotle was attended,
they are brought into the foreground and elaborated. Thus, says Haskins, the writings of Averroës produced on the Christian world "a shock
which extended to those of Aristotle himself. In 1210 the newly arrived
natural philosophy of Aristotle and the commentaries thereon were forbidden by a provincial council at Paris; in 1215 the prohibition was repeated and specifically applied to the *Metaphysics*; in 1231 the Pope
prohibited the study of these works at Paris until they should have been
purged of all error by a special commission. No actual expurgation, how-

ever, seems to have taken place; the difficulties were simply smoothed out and explained away, and the Arabic interpretations were swept aside, until, by 1255, the whole of the new Aristotle is prescribed at the University of Paris for the degree of Master of Arts." [38] The "smoothing out" and "explaining away" was done largely by Albertus Magnus and Thomas Aquinas, and the result was not merely that Aristotle was made respectable again, but that the whole structure of his thought was pressed into the service of existing Christian doctrine. Thus, within little more than two centuries Western Europe had passed from one synthesis to another, from the seven liberal arts of Isidore and Alcuin to the elaborate structure of Thomistic thought, and although the transition had certainly been troubled, nevertheless it had been made. The new learning had been incorporated successfully into the old.

What most impressed Newman about this process was the role played by the university.[39] The actual work of adjusting the Aristotelian philosophy to the needs of the church might well belong to individual minds such as Albertus and St. Thomas, and the authority which sanctioned this work, once it was done, could of course only be that of the pope; but between initiation and acceptance there was a third task which required some organ free from the peculiar weakness of both the individual mind and the administering authority. Authority is always conservative, and the papacy, with its heavy cares for the welfare of the faithful, was rightly reluctant to risk so much that was so precious for the sake of so doubtful a gain. The individual intellect, on the other hand, was shortsighted and eccentric; it struck out brilliant things but was rash in its inquiries and crotchety in its judgments; it could not be trusted. What was needed was a collective mind, some organ which could be judicious because it was not a mere individual and yet receptive to new truth because it did not have the responsibility of finally accepting it. Such an organ was the university, and in the conflicts of 1255 and 1270–77, by which the Thomistic synthesis was finally established, Newman saw the university acting in its true function. Through its triumphant handling of these conflicts it became, according to its latest historian, "the supreme and clearly acknowledged intellectual tribunal of the Middle Ages." Poets hailed it as "mère de toute science et marâtre d'hérésie," and as

> l'université qui garde
> La clef de la crestienté.[40]

What was to prevent it from reassuming this position in the modern world? There were the Baconian sciences which were now causing scandal in the world as the Aristotelian had before, but which might yet be brought to useful and reverent issue. There were the Oriel Noetics who glorified logic much as Abelard had done, and on the other side there was Archbishop Cullen standing in the place of St. Bernard. It was perhaps the twelfth century now rather than the thirteenth—not yet the time for a great new synthesis, if indeed a complete synthesis would ever again be possible, but surely time for some spirit of moderation and many-sidedness, a John of Salisbury or Hugh of St. Victor, to come and prepare the way. Surely it was time for a university in which a body of informed opinion could canvass these new sciences, and with a sense of duty, but of duty only to truth, could present their final judgment to the pope for him to act upon as he saw fit. Necessarily he would consider *all* the three needs of the church, the needs of devotion and rule as well as the needs of truth,[41] but at least he would act in the light of the best secular knowledge of the time. Looking back six hundred years, Newman saw that it was no accident that the universities of Europe should have come into being just at the moment when Europe needed them for ordering its mind. Europe needed them again, and so a new university was being founded and again was dedicated specifically to this task.

How seriously Newman took the task may be seen from his efforts to make the Science of Sciences, which he had treated in the Dublin *Discourses* as hardly more than an idea, into a practical and existing discipline. Obviously, if the Science of Sciences was to be a reality, it must have a professor, but who should this professor be? Not the advocate of any particular science, for to allow this would be to make one of the parties in the quarrel into the judge of his own case. It must be someone who represented no particular discipline but who in some sense was the representative of them all, and this could only be the rector of the university himself. As rector, then, the chair of the Science of Sciences was filled by Newman, and we may see him practicing this science in the lectures which form the second part of the *Idea of a University*. Seven of the ten lectures included there, most of which were delivered on the occasion of opening or reconvening one of the various schools of the university, are concerned with defining the relation of the studies of that school to the other major departments of knowledge. Thus the relation between Christianity and literature, between literature and science, between science and Christianity, and between Christianity and medicine are successively passed in review, and Newman indicates in several passages that his choice of these subjects was not accidental but was a deliberate attempt to map out the provinces of the intellectual world.

THE IMPERIAL INTELLECT

What these provinces were is not so important here as the larger question of Newman's fitness for the attempt. Was he capable of giving the sciences a fair deal? This is the question by which many readers, at least non-Catholic readers, of the *Idea of a University* are deeply troubled, for as they go through the discourses they seem to detect a certain shifting of ground, a discrepancy between the enunciation of principles, which are fair enough, and the application which they fear will be made of these principles in practice. They find that they are easy and happy about the discourses which treat of liberal knowledge but that they are uneasy and unhappy about those that treat of the role of theology. They find that they do not really understand what that role is, and they wonder if Newman did or if he is hedging. They find, to be specific, that he employs two different images to describe the structure of knowledge, that of the circle of the sciences and that of the hierarchy of the sciences, and that he makes no attempt to reconcile the two. The former, which is of classical origin, implies that theology occupies one segment of a circle which is presided over by the Science of Sciences, but the latter, which is of medieval origin, implies that she is the queen of the sciences and herself has the ruling of all the rest. They notice, moreover, that in the third discourse, "The Bearing of Theology on other Branches of Knowledge," Newman explains how the omission of theology will allow other sciences to encroach upon its province, and that in the next discourse, "The Bearing of Other Branches of Knowledge on Theology," where they might expect to hear the other side of the case, they only hear more of the same. Indeed, they find that throughout the book the examples of theology doing injury to another discipline are brief and vague and supposititious, whereas the examples of injuries suffered by theology are lengthy and specific and all too real. And they wonder if this will not always be the case, if the tears will not always be for the theologian whose Deluge is spoiled by the rocks and never for the geologist whose rocks must anyhow tell the story of the Deluge.

There is no one answer to this problem, for what will seem like impartiality to one person will be arrant bias to the next. Nevertheless, it is possible to show that Newman's position was not so illiberal as would appear simply from the Dublin *Discourses*. For one thing, his position developed, and it was more advanced even at the time of writing the *Discourses* than the *Discourses* themselves would suggest. The portions of that work which are most hostile to science are the third and fourth discourses, but the entire matter of these discourses dates from a period twenty to thirty years before. Their argument derives from the attack on the new London University in the late 1820's and from the controversy over the admission of Dissenters in 1834–35. Moreover, all the examples which Newman uses derive from the same period. Lawrence's lectures were in 1816, Senior's in 1826, and Milman's *History* in 1829. Why, one asks, did Newman recur to these almost forgotten instances? Were there no more recent examples of books which had gone out of their way to attack religion? Of course there were, and one can only suppose that he did not use them because they no longer troubled him as they had in the period twenty and thirty years before. In 1840 he had expressed his fears that only the Roman church could withstand the league of evil which was forming against the Bible, and now that he was a member of that church and his religion was less dependent upon the Bible, he found that he too could withstand it more easily than he had before.

The one thing that he forgot was that his hearers were also members of that church, and as the bearing of any statement is partly determined by the needs of the person to whom it is addressed, so Newman soon discovered that words which had one meaning in Protestant Oxford had quite another in Catholic Dublin, and that he, who had been counted a conservative in the former place, was likely to end up a liberal in the latter. A striking example of this change is furnished by one of the leading positions of the discourses, namely, that the end of a university is intellectual, rather than moral or religious. This position was developed by Newman while yet an Anglican in opposition to the school of Lord Brougham, which would have assigned to education the work that properly belongs to religion. Ultimately the basis of this school was the Benthamite view that the morality of an act lay in its consequences, and therefore that the problem of morality was simply one of foreseeing consequences and also of understanding that one's own true interest was identical with the interest of the greatest number. So conceived, virtue was not a matter of rectifying the will but of enlightening the intellect, and the whole effort of Brougham's popular education movement was to instruct the lower classes in farming and political economy, animal husbandry and navigation, so as to make their lives not merely more agreeable, "but better." [42]

The place in which Newman has most fully expressed his opinion of this school is in a series of letters, later called "The Tamworth Reading Room," which was published in the *Times* in February, 1841. They were written at the invitation of one of the proprietors and were an attack upon an address delivered by Sir Robert Peel to his constituents at Tamworth upon the occasion of opening a public reading room in that city. In this address, which was later published, Peel had embraced the philosophy of Brougham so openly that in a caricature which was

THE IMPERIAL INTELLECT

circulated at Oxford he was depicted as Nicholas Nickleby approaching
Mr. Squeers (Lord Brougham) and asking, "Do you want an assistant?"
Newman had little difficulty in making him appear ridiculous, but he
did not confine his attentions to Peel alone. He also drew examples from
two other works of this school, Lord Brougham's *Discourse of the Objects, Advantages, and Pleasures of Science* (1827) and G. L. Craik's
The Pursuit of Knowledge Under Difficulties.[43] Both of these books
receive further mention in the *Idea of a University*,[44] but what most
definitely connects that work with the "march-of-mind" school is the
fact that, in the passage where Newman explicitly repudiates the notion
that the end of liberal knowledge is virtue, he is evidently replying to
Macaulay's essay on Bacon. In that essay Macaulay had drawn a contrast between the low aim of the Baconian philosophy (to supply man's
material needs) and the exalted aim of the older philosophy (to make
him virtuous), and he declared that for himself he preferred the former
on the ground that an acre in Middlesex is better than a principality in
Utopia. But at this point Newman interposes. It is *not* the aim of philosophy, he says, to make man virtuous. "It is as real a mistake to burden
it with virtue or religion as with the mechanical arts," for "its object is
nothing more or less than intellectual excellence." [45]

This, then, was the original bearing of Newman's thesis that the end
of a university is intellectual and not moral or religious. But as he composed the sixth discourse, in which the thesis is expressed, he suddenly
realized that a view which was objectionable to Lord Brougham for one
reason might be equally objectionable to Archbishop Cullen for another. The Archbishop might consider that the end of a Catholic university *was* the inculcation of faith and morals. Not that he would agree
with Brougham that it was *sufficient* to that end or could *supersede* the
church in its performance, but that, considering the church was interested in a university only insofar as it ministered to religion, he would
be in practical agreement with Brougham on the question of what the
end of a university ought to be.

Alarmed by this possibility, Newman wrote the brief Introduction to
Discourse VI which has already been described [46] and sent it with copies
of his lecture to various Catholic friends. From one, Father Joseph
Gordon of the Oratory, he received the objections which he had appre-
hended. Father Gordon denied that the end of a Catholic university was
the cultivation of the intellect; it was "making men Catholics or making
Catholics *good* Catholics," and he declared that in Newman's view religion was put "so absolutely apart from the object of a Catholic University that if it only turned out highly accomplished and clever Devils
it *would not be a failure*." [47] This, of course, was true. Newman con-

ceded that a Julian or a Gibbon, as well as a Basil or a Pole, could be the product of a university. That fact defined the limits of what a university could do. It could teach knowledge, and since faith and morals were matters of knowledge, it could teach them too—but simply *as subjects*. It could not teach one to *believe* the dogmas of faith or to *practice* the precepts of morals, for this was a matter of the will, not the intellect. Obviously the faith and morals of the students were not to be neglected while they were resident in a university. The church would be present there to care for these things just as a doctor might be present to care for the students' health. But the point was, the university would not *be* a church, just as it would not be a hospital, and this was all that Newman was arguing.

The point is made in the various drafts of his Introduction and the letters in which he discussed it, and one may wonder whether, if Newman was simply making a distinction in logic which could never be made in fact, it was really worth all the attention he gave it. In the end it proved to be, for although Newman was willing to concede that the university might be used by the church for its higher purposes, he soon found that some of the Irish clergy wished to use it *before* it was a university. It was Edward Butler, Newman's professor of mathematics, who observed that "the Irish bishops, not having themselves had a University education, did not properly understand what it was, and, with one or two exceptions, did not really want such a university as Newman had in mind; their idea was a glorified seminary for the laity." [48] In view of the fact that Newman had been accused by Pattison of wishing to make Oxford into such a seminary, this is a striking measure of the distance which he had traveled since the 1830's. Indeed, if Pattison, judging from what he knew of Newman at Oxford, had attempted to predict the kind of university he would create at Dublin, he would hardly have hit it right in any detail which concerned the place of religion in the institution. He would have assumed that the tutor's office would be a pastoral one, when in point of fact it was not. He would have assumed that there would be religious tests and that non-Catholics would be excluded, but actually they were not excluded and there were no tests. [49] Theology he would have expected to be a flourishing discipline and secular subjects to be practically neglected, whereas the truth of the matter was that Newman refused to form a theological school [50] and poured all his energies into the medical school, the school of science and engineering, and the school of arts. Realizing that Oxford was the private preserve of the Anglican church and that nearly all its officers were clergy, Pattison would have expected that this would be the case in Dublin as well. "Priest-ridden" is the word that he would have used.

But actually it was a great point with Newman that all the professors, except in the subjects of theology and mental science, be laymen.[51] Moreover, his first act on being installed as rector was "to invite a number of Laymen in both countries to place their names on the University books," [52] and one of the principal reasons for his eventual resignation was that he could not secure from the bishops a measure of lay control. Writing to an officer of the university in 1873, he declared,

> One of the chief evils which I deplored in the management of the affairs of the University twenty years ago, was the resolute refusal with which my urgent representations ever met that the Catholic laity should be allowed to co-operate with the Archbishops in the work. As far as I can see, there are ecclesiastics all over Europe, whose policy is to keep the laity at arm's length, and hence the laity have been disgusted and become infidel, and only two parties exist, both ultras in opposite directions. I came away from Ireland with the distressing fear that in that Catholic country, in like manner, there was to be an antagonism, as time went on, between the hierarchy and the educated classes.
>
> You will be doing the greatest possible benefit to the Catholic cause all over the world, if you succeed in making the University a middle station at which clergy and laity can meet, so as to learn to understand, and to yield to each other—and from which, as from a common ground they may act in union upon an age which is running headlong into infidelity.[53]

To secure an educated Catholic laity it was absolutely necessary, in Newman's view, that their education should not be confined to works which were morally or doctrinally "safe." If they were to meet the arguments of Protestants and of infidels they must understand the attractiveness of these positions, as well as the rightness of their own, and if they were to be thrown upon the blandishments of the world they must have some knowledge of the world in advance.[54] Thus, on a slip of paper dated October 19, 1852 which seems to be an outline for a course in "English Literature," Newman lists the names of Bacon, Hobbes, Bentham, Dryden, and Pope (with a note that the last two "have translated some of the most licentious classics"), Swift, Gibbon, and Hume (with a note that "I hardly put in Hume, except because his style makes him a classic").[55] Some years later, when Thomas Arnold, the brother of the poet, who was Newman's professor of English literature, submitted a syllabus of the course he proposed, Newman suggested the addition of Gibbon, though he admitted that he had "a great difficulty" about him.[56] In the end Archbishop Cullen would not allow it, but if Newman's recommendation seems to us like a little thing, one should remember that even Arnold *père* "dared not" use Gibbon at Rugby.[57]

About the same time Newman faced the problem of prohibited books. He felt that it was absolutely necessary both in the course in English literature and in those preparing for government examinations that students be acquainted with some works on the Index, and since there was a question whether the Index was binding in Ireland he felt that it would be best to go quietly ahead without raising the issue. However, when he consulted E. J. O'Reilly, professor of dogmatic theology, and also Dr. Cullen, he found that they were more cautious. They did not object to the fact so much as to the look of the thing, and it was nearly nine months before Newman secured the Archbishop's sanction "for quietly availing ourselves in our lecture rooms of books which, though prohibited, are not like Gibbon, decidedly dangerous, and are necessary for the intended professions of our students." [58] Later he raised the same question, and with the same results, about the use of Protestant works for examination in the philosophy of religion.

The general problem with which Newman was dealing was of course of long standing, but it had recently been made into an issue, and feelings on the subject had been exacerbated by the so-called Gaume controversy in France. In 1851 the Abbé Jean-Joseph Gaume published a book, *Le ver rongeur des sociétés modernes*, in which he attributed the moral and religious deterioration of the age to its use of the pagan classics as an instrument of education. In his view the remote cause of all evil was to be found in the Renaissance, which had resurrected the paganism of antiquity and prepared the way for the French Revolution, and the only means of combating its influence was to exclude the classics from all but the three highest grades in school and replace them by catechetical instruction and the reading of Christian authors. As his work was espoused by several influential prelates and supported by the articles of Louis Veuillot in *L'univers*, it provoked a lively controversy in which the chief antagonist was Msgr. Dupanloup, bishop of Orleans. The latter boldly instructed the superiors and professors of his little seminaries to go on, as they had been doing, giving to the ancient authors their honored place and not to be troubled lest they were slighting the Holy Scripture and the Fathers. For this he was attacked by Veuillot, and the quarrel raged sharply for several years until it finally terminated, pretty much in a compromise, on instructions from Rome.

The point is that it occurred just at the moment when Newman was entering upon his university lectures. On September 16, 1851, writing to Dr. Cullen to inquire the subjects on which he should speak, he added, as though to intimate his own feelings in advance, "Have you got the good Abbé Gaume's book? It is a startling one, to judge from a very partial inspection of it. He seems to give up Classics altogether. Is Aristotle to be given up with the rest?" [59] The subject was not a new one to Newman, for even at Oxford many religious persons had been troubled at giving so large a portion of their time to heathen authors and especially to heathen ethics, and several of Newman's friends had written pamphlets resolving the difficulty. Usually they took the line that heathen ethics analyzed the nature of a moral action, which revelation then provided us with the motive for doing, or that heathen ethics showed us how far mere reason would take us toward the truth and so, by its very deficiencies, helped us properly to value the gift of revelation.[60] But no one suggested giving up the classics, and thus when Newman found himself entering the field of Catholic education at the very moment that it was agitated by this suggestion, he was deeply concerned to reject it. In several places he refuted the historical part of Gaume's work, that the classics had not been widely employed in the Christian schools of the first centuries and the Middle Ages, and his entire essay on "Literature" may be regarded as a protest against it.[61] "I well remember," wrote Aubrey de Vere, "the look of stern disapproval with which he [Newman] spoke to me of the Abbé Gaume's theory of education, one that must have excluded the Greek and Latin classics from the schools of Christian youth, or left them but a small place therein." [62]

Against this background one may turn to the most precise general statement which Newman has given us concerning the relation of secular and religious knowledge. In the original fifth discourse, speaking of the organic unity of philosophic knowledge as the Catholic conceives it, Newman observes that he is "claiming for Theology nothing singular or special, or which is not partaken by other sciences in their measure. . . . Far indeed am I from having intended to convey the notion . . . that Theology stands to other knowledge as the soul to the body; or that other sciences are but its instruments and appendages. . . . This would be, I conceive, to commit the very error, in the instance of Theology, which I am charging other sciences, at the present day, of committing against it. On the contrary, Theology is one branch of knowledge, and Secular Sciences are other branches. Theology is the highest indeed, and widest, but it does not interfere with the real freedom of any secular science in its own particular department." [63] Years later, in writing the memorandum of his connection with the Catholic University, Newman made a reference to this passage. He noted that in the Brief of March 20, 1854, which established the University, "the Pope exhorts the Bishops to make 'divina nostra religio *tamquam anima totius litterariae institutionis*' in the University, that is, *the form.* 'Omnes disciplinae' are to go forward in the most *strict league* with religion, that is, with the assumption of Catholic doctrine in their *intrinsic* treatment: and the Professors are directly to mould '*totis viribus*' the youth to piety and virtue, and to ground them in literature and science in conformity with the Church's teaching. I wrote on a different idea my 'Discourses on University Education' in 1852, vid. especially the original 5th discourse." [64] As Father McGrath has pointed out, when the intent of the two documents is taken into consideration, they do not really disagree.[65] The Brief is concerned simply with repudiating secular education, whereas Newman is concerned with defining the precise way in which education should be religious. Nevertheless, the fact that Newman chose to comment on the passage gives to his words a deliberateness which they would not otherwise have. It shows that he distinguished sharply between the science of theology and the divine matters which are the subject of that science. The latter occupy a place in human life which is simply supreme, and therefore, if one were to speak of their relation to other matters, one would naturally employ the image of a hierarchy or the metaphor of a queen. But this relation between the subjects of the sciences does not affect the speculative relation between the sciences themselves. As sciences, they are completely isolated from one another. They are isolated by the very act of abstraction which brought them into being and made them one science rather than another, and theology shares this isolation as absolutely as any other. It is not the soul or form of all knowledge, for Philosophy is that. It is simply one science out of many, and like all the others it has its province allotted to it by the Science of Sciences.[66]

The real test of this view comes in those areas which are treated both by theology and the secular sciences. According to Newman, there are two such areas, for on the one hand, supernatural knowledge may include truths and facts of the natural world, thereby giving rise to the historical and cosmological statements of Scripture, and on the other, truths and facts of the natural world may be data for inferences about the supernatural, thereby giving rise to the science of natural or physical theology.[67] Actually these were the two areas in which the conflict between science and religion was most intense, religion being pretty much on the defensive in the former but in the latter being still confident and ebullient. Hence the usual position of the religious-minded person was to make as much as he could of natural theology, emphasizing the way in which the findings of science, as interpreted by the argument from design, gave comfort to the religious position, and to cling to the biblical statements as long as he could, retreating from one interpretation to another only as this became absolutely necessary. It is very striking that Newman's position was exactly the reverse of this.

In reference to the Bible, Newman held that the number of statements which it contains of a physical or natural character are extremely few, "so few that they may be counted." "It speaks of a process of formation out of chaos which occupied six days; it speaks of the firmament; of the sun and moon being created for the sake of the earth; of the earth being immovable; of a great deluge; and of several other similar facts and events." But the meaning of these statements "has not yet engaged the formal attention of the Church, or received any interpretation which, as Catholics, we are bound to accept. . . . And this being the case, it is not at all probable that any discoveries ever should be made by physical inquiries incompatible at the same time with one and all of those senses which the letter admits, and which are still open." [68] True, there always have been in Christendom a number of "floating opinions" about the meaning of these statements, not the unanimous consent of the Fathers but "more or less appended to the divine tradition; opinions which have a certain probability of being more than human, or of having a basis or admixture of truth." Such were the opinions about the millennium and about the Antichrist, about the existence of the antipodes and the Ptolemaic conception of the universe. But these opinions "admit of no test, whence they came, or how far they are true, besides the course of events," [69] and in many cases events have disproved them. Indeed, it is almost an argument for the divinity of the church that she never did, during all the centuries when these opinions were generally received, formally adopt them as her own. Considering that it was her business to make comments on the sacred text and that these opinions were the natural comment to make, it was almost inevitable that she should have acknowledged them to be true. But she never did acknowledge them, and therefore Catholics are not burdened with their defense.[70] They can quit the fort which others are holding because they know that it never was their own.

Hence it was that Newman was less excited by the theory of evolution than were most of his contemporaries. In his review of Milman in 1840 he had mentioned speculations about "man's being originally of some brute nature, some vast mis-shapen lizard of the primeval period, which at length by the force of nature, from whatever secret causes, was exalted into a rational being, and gradually shaped its proportions and refined its properties by the influence of the rational principle which got possession of it. Such a theory," he had observed, "is of course irreconcilable with the letter of the sacred text, to say no more," [71] but the fact that he presented the theory as a precise analogy to Milman's treatment of Christianity, which he regarded not as false but simply as one-sided, suggests that he did not regard the theory of evolution as necessarily untrue.

This, of course, was long before Darwin, but a year after the publication of the *Origin of Species* a friend who questioned Newman on the subject found him unperturbed.[72] Keble was still holding out for Genesis and declared that if there were fossils in the rocks, then God must have placed them there so as to give things the appearance of having evolved, but Newman simply laughed at this and even used its absurdity to highlight the equal difficulty of special creationism. "There is as much want of simplicity," he wrote in a notebook in 1863, "in the idea of the creation of distinct species as in that of the creation of trees in full growth, or of rocks with fossils in them. I mean that it is as strange that monkeys should be so like men, with no *historical* connection between them, as that there should be no course of facts by which fossil bones got into rocks. The one idea stands to the other idea as fluxions to differentials. Differentials are fluxions with the condition of time eliminated. I will either go whole hog with Darwin, or, dispensing with time and history altogether, hold, not only the theory of distinct species but that also of the creation of fossil-bearing rocks." [73] During the next two decades Newman was in frequent correspondence with St. George Mivart, the great Catholic zoologist, receiving and reading his works on evolution and teaching him in turn, according to a proposed dedication to Mivart's *Contemporary Evolution,* "to unite in one the Theistic and Naturalistic conceptions of the world about us." [74] Doubtless Newman was sympathetic with Mivart's attempt to demonstrate the insufficiency of natural selection as the mechanism of evolution, but he declared that "you must not suppose I have personally any great dislike or dread of his theory." [75] And to another friend he wrote on Easter Eve, 1874, "I see nothing in the theory of evolution inconsistent with an Almighty God and Protector." [76]

As a matter of fact, Newman cared less for Paley, whose *Natural Theology* was pretty well crushed by Darwin, than he did for Darwin himself. Natural theology he had "ever viewed . . . with the greatest suspicion," for it was "a most jejune study, considered as a science," and really was "no science at all," but merely "a series of pious or polemical remarks upon the physical world viewed religiously." [77] It served, as Bacon had noted, "to confute atheism, but not to inform religion," for whereas "it is written, that 'the Heavens declare the glory of God' . . . we nowhere find it that the Heavens declare the will of God; which is pronounced a law and a testimony that men should do according to it." [78]

More precisely, natural theology teaches only three of the Divine Attributes—Power, Wisdom, and Goodness—and of these, most of Power
and least of Goodness. Of mercy, long-suffering, and the economy of
human redemption, of religion as something relative to us, it can say
nothing. Indeed, it "cannot, from the nature of the case, tell us one word
about Christianity proper," because it is "derived from informations
which existed just as they are now, before man was created, and Adam
fell." [79] More than this, it has a tendency, if contemplated exclusively,
to dispose the mind against Christianity, because it speaks only of laws
and cannot tell of their suspension, that is, of miracles. In effect, it
reduces God to a mere collection of his laws and makes him "just as
high and deep and broad and long as the universe, and no more." He
is not something separate from nature but is "Nature with a divine glow
upon it." [80] And if He is really no more than that, if He is merely a
function or correlative of the natural world, coincident with it in every
way, then the science of natural theology is really neither theology nor
is it natural. It tells us nothing of God that is distinctive of Him and
nothing of nature that is distinctive of it; rather it mingles the two to
the utter confusion of both.

In the great lecture on "Christianity and Scientific Investigation,"
never delivered because it was considered by theological censors to be
"inexpedient," [81] Newman emphasizes from the point of view of the
scientist what he had already emphasized for the theologian, namely,
the need for absolute freedom in investigation. He does not mean, of
course, that the scientist is free to come into collision with actual points
of dogma, or that he may venture out of his own province into matters
of religion, or that his teaching, as distinct from his research, should be
entirely free, or that he may scandalize the weak and the immature by
discussing openly matters that ought to be handled in the journals and
conclaves of his own profession—but within the limits of these reserva-
tions, in the investigation of his own science he must be "free, independent, unshackled in his movements." He must not be forced to
digress into Final Causes or square his theories with the first ten chapters
of Genesis; neither must he be made apprehensive by a continually
watchful and intrusive church. If he seems to go astray he must be allowed to continue, so that his investigations will bring him home in the
end. "Great minds need elbow-room. . . . And so indeed do lesser
minds, and all minds." If we wish, says Newman, we can "refuse to
allow of investigation or research altogether; but, if we invite reason to
take its place in our schools, we must let reason have fair and full play.
If we reason, we must submit to the conditions of reason. We cannot
use it by halves." [82]

Such was Newman's public pronouncement, and one final illustration, a private letter, may be allowed to supplement it. When T. W. Allies was writing to Newman to ask what he meant by the "Philosophy of History," whether it was not "the results of history viewed by the light of final causes," Newman replied that " 'Providence' comes into the definition accidentally. In physical nature, an atheist talks of efficient causes, and the theist of final, but the *laws* are the same." Augustine, whom Allies had suggested as a model, Newman thought too theological, and when Allies questioned this severance of theology from the philosophy of history, Newman replied, "For myself, I cannot help thinking that laws are a sort of facts *in* the subject matter which is in question. In chemistry latent heat involves certain laws. These the religious mind rightly considers to have been determined by the Creator for a good end; but the end is not part of the law, as in the corresponding case of morals, 'finis praecepti non cadit sub praeceptum.' Bacon seems to me to state correctly, that the doctrine of final causes (when actively introduced) *spoils* physics. First let us ascertain the fact—then theologize upon it. Depend upon it, when once the laws of human affairs are drawn out, and the philosophy into which they combine, it will be a movement worthy of the Lawgiver, but if we begin speaking of Him first of all, we shall never get at His laws. I can quite understand a Professor drawing religious conclusions from historical laws or ordinances, as from physical, but he must first find his laws." [83]

For the sake of truth, for the welfare of the university, and also for the health of the individual, Newman wished science to be conjoined with religion. He stipulated that "they should be found in one and the same place, and exemplified in the same persons," so that "the same spots and the same individuals [should] be at once oracles of philosophy and shrines of devotion." [84] But the disciplines themselves he wished to be kept distinct. He would not have them united in one person by being assimilated to each other. Their virtue was in themselves, and their peace lay in going their own way. Taken together, they formed a unified body of truth which Newman called "Philosophy," and in his younger days and at the beginning of his work in Ireland he had been entranced by the beauty and perfection of this ideal. There is no reason to suppose that he ever ceased to be entranced by it, but he did become less confident, as the years went by, that it could be realized easily or at once. He seemed to feel more keenly than he had before the dangers of too easy a synthesis as well as the vacancy and absence of none at all. He saw that for a long time to come one might not be able to say just how one science lay in respect to another. He saw that one might have to live with perplexities for many years and make the best of them, that hitches and doubts would be with us, and that the Science of Sciences was not to be exercised "by rules reducible to writing, but by sagacity, wisdom, and forebearance."

I observe, then . . . that the philosophy of an imperial intellect, for such I am considering a University to be, is based, not so much on simplification as on discrimination. Its true representative defines, rather than analyzes. He aims at no complete catalogue, or interpretation of the subjects of knowledge, but a following out, as far as man can, what in its fulness is mysterious and unfathomable. Taking into his charge all sciences, methods, collections of facts, principles, doctrines, truths, which are the reflections of the universe upon the human intellect, he admits them all, he disregards none, and, as disregarding none, he allows none to exceed or encroach. His watchword is, Live and let live. He takes things as they are; he submits to them all, as far as they go. . . . If he has one cardinal maxim in his philosophy, it is, that truth cannot be contrary to truth; if he has a second, it is, that truth often *seems* contrary to truth; and, if a third, it is the practical conclusion, that we must be patient with such appearances, and not be hasty to pronounce them to be really of a more formidable character.[85]

Appendices
and Notes

Bibliographical Appendix

1. MANUSCRIPT SOURCES

Manuscripts from sources other than the great collection at the Oratory, Edgbaston, Birmingham, are identified simply by the place where they are preserved, e.g. (Oriel Library). The Oratory collection is divided into two parts: the Letters, which are housed in the Archivum, and the Miscellaneous Papers, which are housed in Newman's own room.

A. THE LETTERS

These are divided into seven major collections, which are referred to in this study by the following abbreviations:

CL	Copied Letters (22 volumes)
FL	Family Letters (4 volumes)
ML	Miscellaneous Letters (68 volumes)
OL	Oratory Letters (60 volumes)
PC	Personal Collection (171 volumes)
PubL	Publishers' Letters (9 volumes)
VC	Various Collections (76 volumes)

There are also many letters included among the Miscellaneous Papers.

B. MISCELLANEOUS PAPERS

These papers have never been very scientifically catalogued, and it is customary for scholars simply to quote them without any system of identification. I have felt, however, that they ought to be more widely known and used than they are at present, and therefore I have referred to them in the notes by the following descriptive titles, which in many cases were supplied by Newman himself. To enable the reader to identify the manuscripts more precisely, however, I also give below the letter and number which they bear and by which they are listed in the *Catalogue of the Contents of the Cupboards* prepared by Edward Bellasis in 1920. The occasional quotations are from notes made by Newman on the manuscripts.

Admission of Dissenters to Oxford (A27.9)
Analysis of Aristotle's *Rhetoric* (A6.4)
Analysis of Herodotus (A6.1)
Analysis of Livy (M27)
Analysis of Thucydides (A6.2)
Autographic Remains, 1804–21 (B1.1)
Autographic Remains, 1816–32 (B1.5)

THE IMPERIAL INTELLECT

Catholic University, Formal and Documental (A34.2)
Chronological Notes (A4.3) An abstract made by Newman himself
    from his Private Diary.
Circular and Correspondence (Archivium)
Correspondence, Public, 1828–36 (B11.8)
Correspondence with Friends, Personal, 1822–36 (B12.1–2)
Dublin University Correspondence, 1851–53 (C6.37)
Early Private Account Books (A22.5)
Examination School (A6.19)
Journal of JHN, 1859–76 (A1.2) "I am dissatisfied with the whole of
    this book. It is more or less a complaint from one end to the other.
    But it represents what has been the real state of my mind, and what
    my Cross has been."
Literary, Classical, and Mathematical (A6.22)
Memoranda, Personal and Most Private, I (A10.1) "The following
    reminiscences of my life up to August 1816, were written first in
    1820, 1821. Then faithfully transcribed with additions in 1823.
    Then faithfully transcribed with omissions in the Lent of 1840. Now
    to be partially and finally re-transcribed, with great omissions and
    put aside for good. The copies which were superseded were all burned
    carefully." (Dated Dec. 31, 1872)
Memoranda, Personal and Most Private, II (A10.2) "Book, or Part 2
    re-copied. Edgbaston. July 22, 1855. Extracts from my Private Jour-
    nal of 1821–1828. I have altered nothing, only omitted."
Memoranda, Personal and Most Private, III (A10.3)
Memoranda, Personal and Most Private, IV (A10.4) On the inside
    cover of this notebook is a solemn adjuration for anyone into whose
    hands the book may fall to "burn it without reading." This is dated
    July 13, 1834, but below is added, "I revoke this. December 1, 1851.
    JHN," and again in pencil, "I revoke all this. It is lawful to read it."
Memorandum Book about College Pupils (A6.15)
Memorandum Relating to the Catholic University (A3.8)
Miscellaneous Papers (A11.8)
My Connection with the Catholic University (A34.1)
My Connection with the Catholic University (rough draft) (B4.1)
My Illness in Sicily (A10.8)
Notes, Classical and Mathematical (A6.8–9)
On the Study of Modern History (A6.20)
On the Study of Modern History (another copy) (B7.2)
Oriel Tutorship (VC,61)
Papers on Theological Subjects, 1816–34 (A9.1) "Papers on Theological
    Subjects (including Hebrew) from 1816 to 1834. None of them
    are worth any thing but burning. I leave them as illustrations of the
    historical fact, what I have been doing with myself all my life?
    May 12, 1874. JHN."
Papers relating to the *Undergraduate* (A18.8)
Preparatory Work for "Office and Work" (D5.15)
Private Diary (A1.1) A series of bound copybooks each with the printed
    title: *The Private Diary: arranged, printed, and ruled, for receiving
    an account of every day's employment, for the Space of one Year*
    (London, n.d.). Volumes exist for the years 1824–46, 1850–51,
    and 1853.

Records of Studies, 1817–19 (A6.7)

Records of Undergraduate Work (A6.6)

Sermon on "Mediatorial Kingdom of Christ," 1827 (A8.1)

Sundries, Unconnected (A46.3) "NB. Sept. 24, 1888 - Table of Book *Discursive Exercises* on *metaphysical* subjects. Sept. 22. What I write I do not state dogmatically, but categorically, that is, in investigation, nor have I confidence enough in what I have advanced to warrant publication."

Suppressed Chapters of Autobiographical Memoir (A15.1) "These passages, cut out from Ch. IV [of Autobiographical Memoir] as being severe upon Hawkins, will give elbow-room *private* information to a Memoir Writer. For this reason I add them."

Theological Commonplace Book (D18.1)

University Journal (A34.2) "My University Journal, private, (contemporaneous) day by day 1854 &c."

Whately's Dialogues on Logic (A6.21) "These are curious, as Dr. Whately's compositions, never published, and the original shape and the basis of his Treatise on Logic.

"The probability is that no one else has a copy of them, except (I suppose) Miss Whately. July 30, 1874. JHN."

Whately's Fallacies (A6.24) "Whately's Logic in its original form, transcribed by FWN [Francis Newman] from Whately's copy."

Whately's Logic, Miscellaneous (A6.23)

2. NEWMAN'S SCHOOL AND COLLEGE TEXTS

The following selected list of books owned by Newman and now preserved at the Oratory is presented as a supplement to the account of Newman's education in Chap. 1. The dates in brackets (or, lacking a date, the place) are those written in Newman's autograph on the flyleaf or cover and presumably indicate the date when the book was acquired. The quoted comments are also Newman's.

A. ELOCUTION

Enfield, William. *Exercises in Elocution; selected from various authors, and arranged under proper heads.* New ed. London, 1804. [August 24, 1810]

Walker, John. *The Academic Speaker; or, a Selection of Parliamentary Debates, Orations, Odes, Scenes, and Speeches, from the best writers, proper to be read and recited by Youth at school . . .* 7th ed. London, 1812. [May 25, 1812]

B. FRENCH

Chambaud, Lewis. *A Grammar of the French Tongue.* London, 1812. [Feb. 12, 1814]

————. *The Treasure of the French and English Languages.* 13th ed. London, 1810.

Genlis, Mme. la Comtesse de. *Théâtre à l'usage des jeunes personnes.* 3 vols. London, 1813. [Sept. 6, 1814]

Perrin, John. *The Elements of French Conversation.* 17th ed. London, 1813. [August 16, 1814]

Wanostrocht, N. *A Grammar of the French Language.* London, 1815.

C. GENERAL LITERATURE

Bacon, Francis. *Works.* 12 vols. London, 1815. [1818]

Cowper, William. *Poems.* 2 vols. Chiswick, 1819.

Denon, Vivant. *Travels in Upper and Lower Egypt, in company with several divisions of the French Army under the command of General Bonaparte,* trans. F. Blagdon. London, 1802. [See Chap. 1, n. 10]

Lamb, Charles. *Tales from Shakespear.* 2 vols. London, 1810. "J. H. Newman / Prize for Speaking / 1811." "We were allowed to *choose* our prizes for speaking. I chose this. My second choice was Denon's Travels, and it was long before an English abridgment of the book could be found, such as was reasonable in price. Afterwards I chose Milton. Afterwards Cooper's Homer. JHN."

Milton, John. *Paradise Lost.* London, 1806. [Dec. 10, 1811]

————. *Paradise Regained,* ed. T. Newton. London, 1806.

Peacock, Lucy. *The Visit for a Week; or Hints on the Improvement of Time. Containing Original Tales, Anecdotes from Natural and Moral History, &c. designed for the instruction and amusement of youth.* 6th ed. London, 1806. [Feb. 21, 1809] "I was in the little school in Ealing, when this book was [given?] round to me to read in class, I believe in Feb. '09 as I have put it in the beginning of the book. Instead of keeping it for school time as a lesson, I put myself in the large open window, my legs hanging out or along it and read it right through, or at least as far as time would allow, one half holy day. I have often thought of this book and thought it was lost for ever. It has just come to me from T. Mozley. April 17, 1854."

Shakespeare, William. *Works.* 8 vols. London, 1811. "I bought this copy of Bowden for £2 when an undergraduate, either in 1818 or 1819."

Tasso, Torquato. *Jerusalem Delivered,* trans. Hoole. London, 1809. A gift of Charles Newman on June 26, 1814.

Turner, R., jr. *An Easy Introduction to the Arts and Sciences.* 11th ed. London, 1806. "This book I had at Ham, i.e. before September 1807. I have just received it from T. Mozley, and on opening it at pp. 186–190, I recollect perfectly rhodomontading out of it to my nursery maid in the shrubbery there, near the pond, at the end of the diagonal of the paddock or path from the house, and telling her that, when I was at Brighton I had seen four different fish, describing from pp. 186–190, the whale, the shark, &c. and, when she could not make out what the fish were, and guessed wrong, I said, 'it was a whale' 'it was a tortoise' &c. 'which I saw.' Edgbaston April 17, 1854 Easter Monday."

Watts [Isaac]. *Directions for the improvement of the mind. Chiefly from Dr. Watts.* Stourport [etc.], 1810. "I think, given to me by my Mother about the year 1815–17. JHN."

D. GREEK CLASSICS

Aeschylus. *Tragœdiæ,* ed. C. G. Schütz. 2 vols. Oxford, 1810. [August, 1820]

Aesop. *Fabulae Graeco-Latinae*. Eton, 1807. "My first Greek book Autumn 1811."

Aristotle. *De poetica liber*, ed. T. Tyrwhitt. 4th ed. Oxford, 1817. [July, 1820] "These notes are written by me in two hands, my hand of 1820, and then the matter is, I suppose, from Tyrrwhit - and my hand of 1827–8, when I suppose the matter is my own. Jan. 19, 1871.

"I was preparing for the office of Examiner in the Schools in the Long Vacation of 1827."

——. *De rhetorica libri tres*. 2d ed. Oxford, 1809. [Nov., 1818]

——. *Ethicorum Nichomacheorum libri decem*, ed. G. Wilkinson. 4th ed. Oxford, 1815.

——. *A New Translation of the Nichomachean Ethics*. Oxford, 1819. [1820]

——. *The Rhetoric, Poetic, and Nichomachean Ethics*, trans. T. Taylor. 2 vols. in 1. London, 1818. [1818]

Euripides. *Tragoediae viginti*, ed. Joshua Barnes. 6 vols. in 3. Oxford, 1811. [1818]

——. *Tragoediae viginti*, ed. Joshua Barnes. 2 vols. in 1. Oxford, 1811. "I bought this copy in May 1818, to stand with at the Trinity College examination, as we were told to bring a Euripides with us. JHN."

——. *Tragoediae*, ed. R. Porson. Lipsiae, 1807.

Herodotus. *Musae sive historiarum libri ix*, ed. J. Schweighaeuser. 5 vols. Strasbourg and Paris, 1816. [1817]

Homer. *Ilias*. 2 vols. Oxford, 1811. [May 25, 1812]

——. *Clavis Homerica: sive lexicon vocabulorum omnium, quae continentur in Homeri Iliade et potissima parte Odysseae*, ed. S. Patrick. New ed. Edinburgh, 1811. [May 25, 1812]

Sophocles. *Tragoediae septem*, ed. R. F. P. Brunck. 2 vols. Oxford, 1812. [June 18, 1816]

Thucydides. *De bello Peloponnesiaco libri octo*, ed. E. L. Baverus. 3 vols. Oxford, 1811. [1818]

Xenophon. *Anabasis*, ed. J. G. Schneider. Oxford, 1813. [August 29, 1816]

——. *Cyrus's Expedition into Persia; and the Retreat of the Ten Thousand Greeks*, trans. E. Spelman. Oxford, 1811. [Feb., 1817]

——. *Memorabilia Socratis. Cum apologia Socratis*, ed. J. G. Schneider. Oxford, 1813. [Nov. 14, 1816]

E. LATIN CLASSICS

Adam, Alexander. *Roman Antiquities: or, an account of the manners and customs of the Romans*. 7th ed. London, 1814. [Dec. 13, 1821]

Cicero. *Cato major, and Laelius*, ed. E. H. Barker. London, 1813. [August 17, 1816]

——. *De natura deorum*, ed. J. Davis. Oxford, 1807.

——. *De officiis libri tres*, ed. J. M. and J. F. Heusinger. Oxford, 1810.

Gradus ad Parnassum. London, 1807.

Horace. *Opera*, ed. L. Desprez . . . in usum Delphini. 20th ed. London, 1810. [1817]

THE IMPERIAL INTELLECT

Juvenal and Persius. *Satirae*, ed. L. Prateus in usum Delphini. London, 1810. [May 24, 1815]
Labbé, Philip. *Eruditae pronuntiationis catholici indices*. London, 1812. [August 17, 1816]
Latin Dialogues, collected from the best Latin Writers. 2d ed. Reading, 1803. [June 12, 1817]
Ovid. *Metamorphosis* [title page missing]. [May 25, 1810]
Tacitus. *De moribus Germanorum, et de vita Agricolae*, ed. G. Brotier. Cambridge, 1813. [Trinity]
Terence. *Comoediae sex*, ed. N. Camus . . . in usum Delphini. London, 1811. [Great Ealing School]

F. LOGIC

Artis logicae rudimenta. Oxford, 1817. [August 27, 1817]
Artis logicae rudimenta. With Illustrative Observations on each Section. 2d ed. Oxford, 1821. [Nov. 6, 1821]
La logique ou l'art de penser. 6th ed. Paris, 1724.

G. MATHEMATICS

Bridge, B[ewick]. *An Elementary Treatise on Algebra*. 3d ed. London, 1815.
———. *Six Lectures on the Elements of Plane Trigonometry*. London, 1810.
Dealtry, William. *Principles of Fluxions*. Cambridge, 1816.
Hutton, Charles. *The Compendious Measurer; being a brief, yet comprehensive, treatise on mensuration and practical geometry. With an introduction to decimal and duodecimal arithmetic*. 7th ed. London, 1812. [May 8, 1815]
Robertson, A[braham]. *Elements of Conic Sections . . . designed as an Introduction to the Newtonian philosophy*. Oxford, 1818. [1818]
Schemata geometrica. Ex Euclide et aliis. Oxford, 1806.
Vince, S[amuel]. *The Elements of the Conic Sections*. 5th ed. Cambridge, 1817.
———. *A Treatise on Fluxions*. 5th ed. Cambridge, 1818.

H. NATURAL SCIENCE

Bingley, William. *Useful Knowledge: Or a Familiar Account of the Various Productions of Nature, Mineral, Vegetable, and Animal, which are chiefly employed for the use of man*. 2d ed. 3 vols. London, 1818. "The kind present of the Rev. J. Wilson, M.A. Mar 19th 1821."
Vince, S[amuel]. *The Elements of Astronomy*. 4th ed. Cambridge, 1816.
———. *The Principles of Hydrostatics*. 4th ed. Cambridge, 1812.
Wood, James. *The Elements of Optics*, 4th ed. London, 1818.

I. SCRIPTURE

White, J[oseph], ed. *Diatessaron: sive integra historia Domini Nostri Jesu Christi Graece, ex IV. Evangeliis inter se collatis*. 4th ed. Oxford, 1808. [March 23, 1812]

Notes

Chapter 1. Undergraduate at Trinity

1. W[illiam] Tuckwell, *Reminiscences of Oxford* (London, Cassell, 1900), p. 3.
2. JHN to his father, Dec. 8, 1817 (FL,I); see *Letters and Correspondence of John Henry Newman*, ed. Anne Mozley (London, 1891), I, 38.
3. *Letters and Correspondence*, I, 26.
4. *Ibid.*, p. 18.
5. [Harriett (Mrs. Thomas) Mozley], *Family Adventures* (London, 1852), pp. 17, 46, 13, 164.
6. Extracts are preserved in MS Autographic Remains, 1804–21, from which most of the following information is taken. See *Letters and Correspondence*, I, 18n. For a complete account of Newman's schooldays see Henry Tristram, "The School-days of Cardinal Newman," *Cornhill Magazine*, N.S. LVIII (June, 1925), 666–77. The description of "Old Mr. Black's" education in Newman's *The Idea of a University* (4th ed. London, 1875, pp. 366–71) is thinly veiled autobiography.
7. See Bibliog. App., Pt. 2, for a list of Newman's school and university texts as preserved at the Birmingham Oratory.
8. Newman's copy of E. H. Barker's edition (1813) is dated August 17, 1816. He apparently returned to the work the following year, for his papers include two pages headed, "October 28th 1817. The following are extracts from the Notes of E. H. Barker Trin. Coll. Cant's Edition of Cicero's *Cato Major*, and Laelius." MS Records of Undergraduate Work; see also MS Record of Studies, 1817–19, Oct. 27 and 28, 1817.
9. *Idea of a University*, p. 278; cf. De Quincey's account of the same incident in *Collected Writings*, ed. David Masson (Edinburgh, 1889–90), V, 112f.
10. Newman's copy of Vivant Denon's *Travels in Upper and Lower Egypt* (2 vols. London, 1802), contains the following note on the inside cover of Vol. I: "When I was a boy, I chose Denon's Travels for a prize which was to be given me at School, not knowing it was a large work. I was obliged to put up with this." On the flyleaf facing, the note continues: "The first prize I chose (in a former year) was Lamb's Tales of Shakespeare. Another prize I chose was Milton. Another Cooper's Homer." See Bibliog. App., Pt. 2, under Lamb.
11. Edward Bellasis, *Cardinal Newman as a Musician* (London, 1892), p. 21. Bellasis, who had his information from Newman himself, includes only the last three roles, but it is evident from the appearance of Newman's text that Hegio is also to be included. According to Henry Tristram, it was the first role Newman played, in 1813, the others following over the next three years in the order given.
12. Autographic Remains, 1804–21.
13. Robert Ornsby, *Memoirs of James Robert Hope-Scott* (2d ed. London, 1884), II, 253.
14. *Apologia Pro Vita Sua. The Two Versions of 1864 and 1865*, ed. Wilfred Ward (London, Oxford University Press, 1913), p. 107. Preserved among Newman's papers is a packet of "infidel pamphlets" which includes Thomas Paine, *The Age of Reason*.

Part the Third (London, 1811) and John Hollis, *Free Thoughts. Consisting of remarks occasioned by Paley's reply to Hume* (London, 1812).

15. *Letters and Correspondence*, I, 22.

16. The fullest account of this episode is in Sean O'Faolain, *Newman's Way. The Odyssey of John Henry Newman* (New York, Devin-Adair, 1952), pp. 49–52.

17. MS Journal of JHN, 1859–76, June 25, 1869.

18. Writing to the Rev. R. Greaves (Feb. 27, 1828, Oriel Library) about the death of Mr. Mayers, Newman declared, "Whatever religious feeling I have within me, to his kind instructions when I was at school I am especially indebted for it - and it may (I think) be safely said, that had it not been for my intimacy with him, I should not have possessed the comfort of that knowledge of God which (poor as it is) enabled me to go through the dangerous season of my Undergraduate residence here without wounding my conscience by any gross or scandalous sin."

19. O'Faolain, *Newman's Way*, p. 46.

20. *Letters and Correspondence*, I, 22.

21. Record of Studies, 1817–19, from which all the information in this paragraph is taken.

22. JHN to his father, June 16 and 27, 1817 (FL,I); see *Letters and Correspondence*, I, 30.

23. *Letters and Correspondence*, I, 27.

24. *Loss and Gain* (6th ed. London, 1874), pp. 354–5; see *Letters and Correspondence*, I, 48.

25. June 16, 1817 (FL,I); see *Letters and Correspondence*, I, 30.

26. June 16, 1817 (FL,I).

27. JHN to his father, June 19, 1817 (FL,I).

28. *Idem*, June 27, 1817 (FL,I); see *Letters and Correspondence*, I, 31.

29. Record of Studies, 1817–19.

30. MS Memoranda, Personal and Most Private, I, Nov. 10, 1817.

31. JHN to his father, June 11, 1817 (FL,I); see *Letters and Correspondence*, I, 29.

32. C. E. H. Edwards, *An Oxford Tutor. The Life of the Rev. Thomas Short, B.D. of Trinity College, Oxford* (London, Stock, 1909), p. 39.

33. JHN to his mother, Nov. 28, 1817 (FL,I); see *Letters and Correspondence*, I, 34.

34. JHN to his mother, Oct. 22, 1817 (FL,I).

35. *Idem*, Oct. 28, 1817 (FL,I); see *Letters and Correspondence*, I, 31–2.

36. JHN to his mother, Nov. 13, 1817 (B1.5); see *Letters and Correspondence*, I, 32.

37. *Ibid.*

38. MS Notes, Classical and Mathematical.

39. JHN to his mother, Nov. 21, 1817 (FL,I); see *Letters and Correspondence*, I, 33. These terms appear in Edmund Scarburgh, *The English Euclide* (Oxford, 1705), pp. 180–2.

40. JHN to his mother, Nov. 28, 1817 (FL,I); see *Letters and Correspondence*, I, 34.

41. Record of Studies, 1817–19.

42. JHN to his mother, Nov. 13, 1817 (B1.5).

43. *Ibid.* Newman's Latin diary also records the event: "Id. Nov. Me decanus laudat per declamationem meam, mihi decus afferentem. Me Tutor meus laudat propter Euclidi propositionem ad unguem demonstratam." Memoranda, Personal and Most Private, I.

44. JHN to his mother, Nov. 28, 1817 (FL,I).

45. Nov. 13, 1817 (B1.5).

46. JHN to his father, Dec. 8, 1817 (FL,I); Record of Studies, 1817–19.

47. JHN to his mother, Feb. 13, 1818 (FL,I).

48. Record of Studies, 1817–19.

49. *Letters and Correspondence*, I, 34n.

50. JHN to his mother, April 7, 1818 (FL,I).

51. JHN to his father, April 14, 1818 (FL,I).

52. "On Wednesday, the 29th of April I determined to stand for the Scholarship in consequence of the advice of my Tutor, who thought I might be likely to attain it. And my heart beat within me, and I was sanguine that I should gain it, and I was fearful that I should be too much set upon it." Memoranda, Personal and Most Private, I, May 19, 1818.

53. Letters and Correspondence, I, 36.

54. Memoranda, Personal and Most Private, I, May 19, 1818.

55. JHN to his mother, May 14, 1818 (FL,I).

56. Idem, May 25, 1818 (FL,I); see Letters and Correspondence, I, 35.

57. Letters and Correspondence, I, 35n.

58. JHN to his mother, May 26, 1818 (FL,I).

59. Record of Studies, 1817–19, May 13–19.

60. Memoranda, Personal and Most Private, I. A note written in later adds, "It was on the 18th, Trinity Monday, the Gaudy, that I was obliged to leave the Scholar's wine party, to avoid being made drunk. I never went to it in the years which followed."

61. Autographic Remains, 1804–21; Record of Studies, 1817–19; JHN to his mother, April 7, 1818 (FL,I).

62. JHN to his mother, June 28, 1820 (FL,I); see Letters and Correspondence, I, 42.

63. "May 13, 1874. I have noted in various letters, that the time in which I relaxed in my reading for the Schools, and amused myself with general literature, was the Long Vacation of 1818 and the two terms following." Written above this is the query, "? up to March 1819." MS Analysis of Thucydides; cf. Letters and Correspondence, I, 39, 53; JHN to H.H.H. [Hans H. Hamilton], [May ?], 1821 (FL,II).

64. JHN to his mother, Oct. 19 and Dec. 2, 1818 (FL,I).

65. Analysis of Thucydides. On the flyleaf of this copybook Newman noted on May 13, 1874 that "this analysis, which implies reading up the whole of Thucydides, was one of the works of that time [the Long Vacation of 1818]." The Analysis itself, however, is dated "Dec. 1818," and a letter from Newman to his mother on Oct. 19, 1818 implies that he and Bowden were just then beginning their Thucydides (FL,I); see Idea of a University, p. 322.

66. Notes, Classical and Mathematical.

67. MS Analysis of Aristotle's Rhetoric; see Record of Studies, 1817–19. Newman's copy of the Rhetoric is dated Nov., 1818.

68. JHN to his mother, Feb. 13, 1818 (FL,I).

69. Idem, Nov. 12, 1818 (FL,I).

70. JHN to his father, Feb. 2, 1819 (FL,I).

71. March 23, 1819 (FL,I). Newman's brackets.

72. JHN to his mother, Feb. 24, 1819 (FL,I).

73. Newman's annotations on a copy of the Undergraduate preserved at the Oratory attribute No. 1 to himself and Nos. 2 and 3 to Bowden; of the author of Nos. 4–6 he is uncertain.

74. The Undergraduate, No. 1 (Feb. 8, 1819), p. 4.

75. Ibid., No. 3 (Feb. 22, 1819), pp. 22–3.

76. MS note on the half title of Newman's copy of the anonymous Letter to the Oxford Spy, from the Bigwig's Friend (Oxford, 1818). Newman's library also contains two copies of [J. S. Boone], The Oxford Spy (Oxford, 1818). See Newman, An Essay in Aid of a Grammar of Assent (4th ed. London, 1874), p. 47n.

77. MS Papers relating to the Undergraduate.

78. Historical Sketches (London, 1872–73), III, 24.

79. Lilian M. Quiller-Couch, Reminiscences of Oxford by Oxford Men, 1559–1850 (Oxford, 1892), p. 241.

80. The tone of Kinsey's relation with Newman is indicated by the following letter which he wrote to Newman on April 5, 1828 (B12.1). The explanations in brackets are Newman's own.

Yes, my dear Newman, not only what you mention - but I recollect also your cachinnation at a Livy Lecture [when I was an Undergraduate] in Hall to the great discomfort of the Lecturer [himself - the Revd W.M.K.] in moral philosophy and Rhetoric - the same risibility through all the turnpikes from London to Oxford - the geological walks to the Selenite and rag district of Shotover - the mineralogical notes, and the entry of the Responsions names by your own pen in the Junior Proctor's Book [viz. Revd W.M.K.], and that for the first time! You know you were always welcome to my sincerest friendship and regard.

Kinsey was junior proctor in 1821.

81. *Letters and Correspondence*, I, 41.

82. *Ibid.*

83. Mrs. [Anna J.] Gordon, *The Life and Correspondence of William Buckland* (New York, 1894), pp. 31, 53; Tuckwell, *Reminiscences of Oxford*, p. 38.

84. JHN to his mother, June 4, 1819 (FL,I).

85. *Letters and Correspondence*, I, 41, 42.

86. Memoranda, Personal and Most Private, I; JHN to his mother, Oct. 25, 1819 (FL,I); see *Letters and Correspondence*, I, 47.

87. Memoranda, Personal and Most Private, I.

88. [First week in] Oct., 1820 (FL,II).

89. JHN to Harriett Newman, Jan. 19, 1822 (FL,I); cf. also JHN to H[amilton]. [May ?], 1821 (FL,II).

90. JHN to H[amilton], [May ?], 1821 (FL,II).

91. Analysis of Aristotle's *Rhetoric*. Pasted on the cover of this copybook is a list in Newman's autograph of the books "I took up for my degree Examination in November 1820." It includes, in addition to those given above, Homer's *Iliad* (12 books). Juvenal, and Cicero, but each with a query which indicates that the fact was uncertain in Newman's own mind. As none of these works appears in the very detailed record of Newman's studies for the six months before the examination (Analysis of Aristotle's *Rhetoric*), it seems unlikely that he actually did present them. Xenophon's *Hellenica*, on the other hand, does not appear on the list, but as Newman was reading it only a month before the examination and reviewing its history only four days before, it should probably be added.

92. JHN to his mother, June 19, 1819 (FL,I).

93. MS Analysis of Herodotus.

94. JHN to his mother, Oct. 25, 1819 (FL,I); *Letters and Correspondence*, I, 41.

95. JHN to Jemima Newman, Dec. 10, 1819, in Eleanor Mozley, "Some Unpublished Letters of Cardinal Newman to his Mother and Sisters," *Catholic Woman's Outlook* (1926), p. 61.

96. JHN to his mother, Dec. 18, 1819 (FL,I).

97. *Letters and Correspondence*, I, 52.

98. JHN to [his mother?], Jan. 21, 1820 (FL,I).

99. MS Autographic Remains, 1816–32.

100. *Letters and Correspondence*, I, 52; *Idea of a University*, p. 150.

101. JHN to his father, May 18, 1820 (FL,I).

102. Record of Studies, 1817–19; JHN to H[amilton], [May ?], 1821 (FL,II).

103. Analysis of Aristotle's *Rhetoric*; JHN to H[amilton], [May ?], 1821 (FL,II); MS account in PC [171], published by Henry Tristram in *A Tribute to Newman, Essays on Aspects of his Life and Thought*, ed. Michael Tierney (Dublin, Browne and Nolan. [1945]), pp. 257–9.

104. Analysis of Aristotle's *Rhetoric*.

105. Mark Pattison, *Memoirs* (London, 1885), p. 137; *Report of Her Majesty's Commissioners Appointed to Inquire into the State, Discipline, Studies, and Revenues of the University of Oxford* (London, 1852), p. 63. Hereafter cited as the *Oxford University Commission Report* (1852).

106. MS account in PC [171]; see Tristram in Tierney, ed., *Tribute to Newman*. p. 259.

NOTES [pp. 18–24]

107. JHN to his father, July 12 and Sept. 28, 1820; JHN to his mother, July 25, 1820 (FL,I).

108. JHN to Francis Newman, August 17, 1820, and to his sisters, August and Sept. 1820 (FL,II).

109. JHN to F. Newman, August 17, 1820 (FL,II).

110. *Letters and Correspondence*, I, 44.

111. JHN to Mayers [about Sept. 20, 1820] (FL,II).

112. Memoranda, Personal and Most Private, I, Sept. 17, 1820.

113. [First week in] Oct. 1820 (FL,II).

114. *Ibid.*

115. JHN to his mother, Oct. 18, 1820 (FL,I).

116. *Idem*, Nov. 8; to his father, Nov. 12, 1820 (FL,I).

117. JHN to Mayers, Jan. 1821 (FL,II).

118. Dec. 1, 1820 (B1.5).

119. Mrs. Newman to JHN, Dec. 4, 1820 (FL,I).

120. JHN to Mayers, Jan. 1821 (FL,II).

121. JHN to his mother, Dec. 3, 1820 (FL,I); see *Letters and Correspondence*, I, 47.

122. *Oxford Apostles. A Character Study of the Oxford Movement* (London, Faber, 1933), p. 59. Most readers find Faber overly Freudian.

123. Thomas Vowler Short, *A Letter addressed to the very Reverend the Dean of Christ Church on the State of the Public Examinations in the University of Oxford* (Oxford, 1822), p. 21. Short (not to be confused with Newman's tutor) was one of the examiners at the time that Newman came up. Newman possessed a copy of his *Letter* (2d ed. 1829), which is preserved at the Oratory.

124. "This analysis is a specimen of the labour, but the unremunerative labour as regards the Schools, which I gave to my books. I began it August 9, and finished it September 9. In consequence, (strange to say), 'Sept. 9' has been a date in my memory ever since. It is written in that pseudo-Gibbonian style, which at that time was my amusement. JHN. May 13, 1874." Note in Newman's hand on flyleaf of Analysis of Herodotus.

125. JHN to Mayers [first week in] Oct., 1820 (FL,II).

126. MS account in PC [171]; see Tristram in Tierney, ed., *Tribute to Newman*, p. 258; *Idea of a University*, p. 366.

127. *Letters and Correspondence*, I, 39. A letter from Dr. Nicholas, Newman's master at Great Ealing, also explains his failure as due to youth. Autographic Remains, 1816–32.

128. MS account in PC [171].

Chapter 2. Fellow of Oriel

1. MS On the Study of Modern History.

2. I (1855), 294–6, reprinted in the *Idea of a University*, pp. 366–71.

3. [Edward Copleston], review of T. D. Whitaker, *De motu per Britanniam civico*, in *Quarterly Review*, V (February, 1811), 84–100.

4. JHN to Harriett Newman, August 2, 1822 (FL,I). Newman's extracts from Copleston run to 4 pages and are included in Records of Undergraduate Work.

5. *Idea of a University*, p. 368.

6. *Ibid.*, pp. 368–9.

7. JHN to his mother, March 28, 1821 (FL,I); see *Letters and Correspondence*, I, 61. On March 21 Harriett had written, "Your chemical affairs make but slow progress. Only the Nitro-sulphate of Copper ceases to turn the Litmus paper; and I have today begun to evaporate it, which process is now going on." (FL,II)

8. JHN to his mother, March 28, 1821 (FL,I); JHN to Jemima Newman, March 31, 1821, in E. Mozley, "Unpublished Letters of Cardinal Newman," p. 68.

9. *Letters and Correspondence*, I, 62; MS Early Private Account Books, March 13, 1822 and March 9, 1823; JHN to Harriett Newman, June 13, 1822 (FL,I).

10. JHN to his father, March 20, 1821 (FL,I). A note in Memoranda, Personal and Most Private, II, says that in 1821 "Mineralogy was my principal pursuit, (as chemistry had been in the Christmas vacation) - and musical composition."

11. The course was given in Lent Term, 1821. Newman's notes, which run to 28 pages, are preserved in MS Substance of Lectures on Mineralogy. Early Private Account Books, Feb. 12, 1821; JHN to Jemima Newman, March 31, 1821, in E. Mozley, "Unpublished Letters of Cardinal Newman," p. 68.

12. June 8, 1821 (FL,I); see *Letters and Correspondence*, I, 61; Early Private Account Books, May 22, 1821. The course was given in Act Term, 1821. On June 5 Newman noted in his private journal, "Buckland has just noticed in his geological lecture the extraordinary fact, that, among all the hosts of animals which are found and are proved to have existed prior to 6000 years ago, *not one* is there which would be at all serviceable to man; *but* that directly you get within that period, horses, bulls, goats, deer, asses &c. are at once discovered. How strong a presumptive proof from the face of nature of what the Bible asserts to be the case." Memoranda, Personal and Most Private, I. In the same diary, under date Oct. 15, 1821, Newman gives six "Reasons in behalf of the Mosaic length of the earth [6000 years]," which are probably also from Buckland.

13. Memoranda, Personal and Most Private, II. A note dated July 1, 1822, says, "The greater part of 1821 I gave myself to Chemistry, to Mineralogy, to Geology, to the composition of Music, so as to acquire a smattering in each, and, lastly, with most attention to the study of the Scriptures." Analysis of Aristotle's *Rhetoric*; see also *Letters and Correspondence*, I, 61-2.

14. MS Papers on Theological Subjects, 1816-34.

15. *Ibid.* The essay is entitled, "On the analogous nature of the difficulties in the Mathematics and those in Religion," March, 1821. It was published in the *Christian Observer* (1821) and was privately reprinted by Newman in *Two Letters Addressed to the "Christian Observer"* (1871).

16. *Letters and Correspondence*, I, 54-5.

17. Papers on Theological Subjects, 1816-34.

18. JHN to J. W. Bowden, April 15, 1822 (PC); see *Letters and Correspondence*, I, 48.

19. *Loss and Gain*, pp. 354-5; *Letters and Correspondence*, I, 48, II, 223. The High Street was first lighted with gas in 1819. G. V. Cox, *Recollections of Oxford* (2d ed. London, 1870), p. 98.

20. Memoranda, Personal and Most Private, II.

21. F. R. Thresher to JHN, April 12, 1822, in *Letters and Correspondence*, I, 74.

22. Pattison, *Memoirs*, p. 8.

23. D. W. Rannie, *Oriel College* (London, Robinson, 1900), pp. 54-6, 73, 163-4, 185. The *Oxford University Commission Report* (1852) found that of 542 fellowships at Oxford only 22 were really open (p. 149).

24. Henry P. Liddon, *Life of Edward Bouverie Pusey* (4th ed. London, 1894-98), I, 67.

25. *Memoirs*, p. 158.

26. W. J. Copleston, *Memoir of Edward Copleston* (London, 1851), p. 188.

27. Sandford's review was of Andrew Dalzel's *Substance of Lectures on the Ancient Greeks*, in *Edinburgh Review*, XXXV (July, 1821), 302-14. Subsequent pamphlets were: [A. W. Hare], *A Letter to Daniel K. Sandford . . . in Answer to the Strictures of the Edinburgh Review on the Open Colleges of Oxford* (Oxford, 1822); D. K. Sandford, *A Letter to the Reverend Peter Elmsley, A.M. in Answer to the Appeal Made to Professor Sandford, as Umpire between the University of Oxford & the Edinburgh Review* (Oxford, 1822). Newman possessed copies of all these, and on the inside front cover of the *Edinburgh Review* noted, "The first number of this

volume [the July number] is of exceptional value, because there were alterations in a second edition, viz. the pp. 311, 312."

28. JHN to his father, April 12, 1822 (FL,I); JHN to Charles Newman, April 13, 1822 (FL,I).

29. JHN to his mother, March 6, 1822 (FL,I); see *Letters and Correspondence*, I, 68.

30. Memoranda, Personal and Most Private, II, Nov. 15, 1821; see *Letters and Correspondence*, I, 67.

31. Memoranda, Personal and Most Private, II.

32. March 6, 1822 (FL,I); see *Letters and Correspondence*, I, 58.

33. March 12, 1822 (FL,I).

34. *Ibid.*; see *Letters and Correspondence*, I, 59.

35. JHN to his father, March 15, 1822 (FL,I); see *Letters and Correspondence*, I, 69.

36. JHN to his father, Feb. 15, 1822 (FL,I).

37. Memoranda, Personal and Most Private, II, Feb. 5, 1822. Autographic Remains, 1816–32, contains a slip of paper with "the information which the Provost of Oriel gave me in Febr. 1822, when I called on him to ask his leave to stand for a fellowship. JHN. Sept. 18, 1850."

38. Memoranda, Personal and Most Private, II, March 7, 1821; cf. the different version in *Letters and Correspondence*, I, 69.

39. Memoranda, Personal and Most Private, II, March 18, 1821; see *Letters and Correspondence*, I, 70.

40. He learned this from Kinsey's cousin on Nov. 15 and apparently confirmed it in his interview with Copleston on Feb. 5. Later, however, he told Bowden that the information was based on "an *induction* of particular instances." JHN to Bowden, April 15, 1822 (PC).

41. Memoranda, Personal and Most Private, II, March 18, 1821; see *Letters and Correspondence*, I, 69.

42. JHN to his father, March 15, 1822 (FL,I); see *Letters and Correspondence*, I, 69.

43. MS Literary, Classical, and Mathematical. On November 6, 1821 Newman bought a copy of the *Artis logicae rudimenta* (2nd ed. Oxford, 1821), which is now preserved at the Oratory.

44. Tom Mozley, *Reminiscences, Chiefly of Oriel College and the Oxford Movement* (London, 1882), I, 29–30. Newman's copy of Edward Copleston's *Praelectiones academicae* (Oxford, 1813) is preserved at the Oratory.

45. *Idea of a University*, p. 369.

46. *Reminiscences*, I, 29.

47. Some of these materials are preserved in MS Analysis of Aristotle's *Rhetoric* and MS Literary, Classical, and Mathematical.

48. The opening paragraphs of this paper will illustrate Newman's concern with the whole as opposed to the part:

The art of composition is only to be learned by a careful study of the most approved authors—treatises on the subject can but *set you in the way*.

For (1) you must not suppose that good writing consists merely in the use of certain words and phrases, or even in composing sentences; but especially in *framing paragraphs*. Attention to this last particular will alone give an air of ease, vigour, freedom, originality. It alone will make a foreign language, as it were, *sit well* upon you. Without it, you will appear drest up in borrowed garments, however choice your words and elegant your phrases. It often happens in faces that every feature is good and yet the general effect unpleasant;—as on the other hand harsh or irregular features not unfrequently combine into an agreeable or gentlemanlike expression of countenance.

Nor (2) are rules sufficient even for the minuter excellencies of words and phrases. They cannot of themselves inspire taste or impart delicacy of expression. A critic may analyze the beauties of Cicero, but can lay down no sufficient rule for recomposing the sentence of its separate parts; just as the chemist decomposes the diamond without being able to restore it.

Literary, Classical, and Mathematical.

49. *Ibid.*

50. Two copies of this essay, both the one submitted for the prize and another, are preserved in Literary, Classical, and Mathematical. On the latter copy appears the following note: "I succeeded at Oriel mainly by my Latin writing. Accordingly, when Dr. Copleston, the Provost, heard that I had written for the Latin Essay . . . he asked to see my attempt. When he saw it, he was much disappointed, and saw at once it would not succeed. In truth I had *learned* to write Latin, *while* I composed the Essay, and therefore what I produced at the examination was far superior to any thing I wrote during the term or months before it, (for when I once caught the *idea* of Latin composition, I rapidly made progress.) The Provost, then, in his kindness went through it with me, thoroughly correcting it. JHN. July 30, 1874." On the next page the note continues, "These corrections in pencil and ink (not in my hand) are Dr. Copleston's, who was kind enough to look it over, just after I was elected at Oriel. JHN."

51. Memoranda, Personal and Most Private, II.

52. Literary, Classical, and Mathematical. The theme occupies a single sheet and took Newman "between 4 and 5 hours." A note in his later hand explains, "When I was preparing to stand for Oriel, I practised myself in Latin, and *timed* myself."

53. Memoranda, Personal and Most Private, II, March 30, 1822.

54. JHN to Charles Newman, April 13, 1822 (FL,I); JHN to Bowden, April 15, 1822 (PC); Pattison, *Memoirs*, p. 162.

55. Literary, Classical, and Mathematical contains part of a copybook (13 pages) headed "This is my Oriel Examination April 1822." Autographic Remains, 1816–32, contains "Rough copies of Papers of my Oriel Examinations for Fellowship, written in Oriel Hall, 1822," and also a fair copy, made for Charles Newman in 1822, of the passage of Latin translation.

56. Candidates brought their own volume, for among Newman's papers is a small slip of paper with the words, "Spectator Vol 4 at 10 o'clock." Newman explains that this is the "Notice for Oriel Examination for fellowship, sent down to me at Trinity, advertising me of its beginning on Saturday, April 6, 1822 at 10." "This Hawkins' writing," he adds. Autographic Remains, 1816–32.

57. *Ibid.*

58. JHN to Bowden, April 15, 1822 (PC); Memoranda, Personal and Most Private, II.

59. Newman's letter to Bowden, cited above, says 4, but his examination paper shows that he answered 5. Literary, Classical, and Mathematical.

60. Memoranda, Personal and Most Private, II.

61. JHN to his mother, May 3, 1822 (FL,I); the same list is given toward the end of Newman's examination paper, but with Lysias replacing Aeschines. Literary, Classical, and Mathematical.

62. JHN to his mother, May 3, 1822 (FL,I); Francis Newman to his father, April 12, 1822 (FL,I); *Letters and Correspondence*, I, 70–1.

63. Memoranda, Personal and Most Private, II.

64. Journal of JHN, 1859–76, Jan. 21, 1863.

65. W. J. Copleston, *Memoir of Edward Copleston*, p. 188.

66. March 11, 1822 (FL,I); see *Letters and Correspondence*, I, 58.

67. "Illud γνῶθι σεαυτόν noli putare ad arrogantiam minuendam solum esse dictum, verum etiam ut bona nostra norimus." *Ep. ad Quint. frat.* III, v–vi. 7.

68. Literary, Classical, and Mathematical.

69. Newman's interleaved copy of Aristotle's *Ethics*, ed. G. Wilkinson (4th ed. Oxford, 1815) contains the following note opposite p. 150 (*Eth.* 1123a): "Many

men are moral cowards; they have powers, but not having a just estimate of them, they shrink from claimants of inferior merit. Others rate themselves too highly. Μεγαλόψυχια, i.e. selfconfidence, arising from a knowledge of one's own excellence, is the mean, and evidently the summit and perfection of virtue (vid. p. 152.) For it presupposes all virtues; since they must *exist* to be *known*." He then cites the remark of Cicero quoted above.

70. Literary, Classical, and Mathematical.

71. JHN to Pusey, Jan. 24, 1836 (PC); see Jer. 45:5: "And seekest thou great things for thyself? seek them not: for, behold, I will bring evil upon all flesh, saith the Lord, but thy life will I give unto thee for a prey in all places whither thou goest." One recalls that as an undergraduate Newman hoped "great things" for himself. See above, p. 15.

72. JHN to his mother, May 3, 1822 (FL,I); see *Letters and Correspondence*, I, 72.

73. JHN to his father, April 16, 1822 (FL,I).

74. *Edinburgh Review*, XXXVI (October, 1821), 254n.; JHN to his father, April 16, 1822 (FL,I).

75. JHN to C. Newman, April 13, 1822 (FL,I).

76. John W. Burgon, *Lives of Twelve Good Men* (London, 1888), I, 386–7.

77. R. W. Church, *Occasional Papers* (London, 1897), II, 345.

78. *Letters and Correspondence*, I, 114.

79. *Narrative of Events Connected with "Tracts for the Times"* (London, 1883), pp. 19–20.

80. Liddon, *Life of Pusey*, I, 58; George A. Denison, *Notes of My Life, 1805–1878* (Oxford and London, 1878), p. 50.

81. Pattison, *Memoirs*, p. 79; T. Mozley, *Reminiscences*, I, 20.

82. Pattison, *Memoirs*, p. 79.

83. Literary, Classical, and Mathematical.

84. Cox, *Recollections*, p. 182.

85. *Reminiscences*, I, 80.

86. Pattison, *Memoirs*, p. 8.

87. [Hare], *Letter to D. K. Sandford*, p. 52.

88. *Idea of a University*, p. 157.

89. W[illiam] Tuckwell, *Pre-Tractarian Oxford. A Reminiscence of the Oriel "Noetics"* (London, Smith, Elder, 1909), p. 54.

90. W. J. Copleston, *Memoir of Edward Copleston*, p. 38; see also pp. 30, 31.

91. *Letters and Correspondence*, I, 104–5; see JHN to William Monsell, later Baron Emly, Oct. 10, 1852 (PC): "When I was elected fellow of Oriel thirty years ago, I was so shy and bashful no one could make me say a word or knew what to make of me - so, I was committed to Dr. Whately's care, then married and in lodgings, to bring me out. He most kindly undertook the task."

92. Burgon, *Twelve Good Men*, I, 385.

93. Blanco White to JHN, July 16, 1828 (PC).

94. E. J. Whately, *Life and Correspondence of Richard Whately* (London, 1866), I, 38–9; Tuckwell, *Pre-Tractarian Oxford*, p. 18.

95. JHN to William Monsell, Oct. 10, 1852 (PC).

96. E. J. Whately, *Life and Correspondence of R. Whately*, I, 62.

97. T. Mozley, *Reminiscences*, I, 25.

98. E. J. Whately, *Life and Correspondence of R. Whately*, I, 10.

99. Richard Whately, *Miscellaneous Remains from the Commonplace Book of Richard Whately*, ed. E. J. Whately (London, 1864), pp. 55–6.

100. E. J. Whately, *Life and Correspondence of R. Whately*, I, 10, 19.

101. Richard Whately, *Elements of Logic. Comprising the Substance of the Article in the Encyclopaedia Metropolitana. With Additions, &c.* (3d ed. London, 1829), p. xviii.

102. Tuckwell, *Pre-Tractarian Oxford*, pp. 23, 67.

103. R. Whately, *Logic*, p. xi.

104. *Letters and Correspondence*, I, 106.
105. Both manuscripts are preserved at the Oratory: MS Whately's Dialogues on Logic and MS Whately's Fallacies. In addition, there is a third packet of 32 miscellaneous sheets of Whately's own manuscript: MS Whately's Logic, Miscellaneous.
106. Memoranda, Personal and Most Private, II.
107. *Letters and Correspondence*, I, 106.
108. *Ibid.*
109. Newman's table of studies for the Long Vacation of 1822 records, for the week of July 1–6: "by myself—began a sketch of logic for the Encyclopaedia Metropolitana from Whateley's dialogues"; July 8–20: "continued the sketch of logic"; July 29–August 3: "revised and completed my sketch of logic." Analysis of Aristotle's *Rhetoric*.

His progress with the work is further illustrated by a letter to Whately dated July 25, 1822 (B12.1):

I have looked into the selection from Aristotle's Organon you mentioned, and find neither Preface nor Notes; in short, no remark whatever to throw light upon the History of Logic. I therefore conjecture you alluded to an Edition now out of print. However, I have been hunting in the Library, and I have discovered several books which have given me some information. Two questions I want answered - 1. did the Stoics take their dialectics from Antisthenes? I *believe* they did - 2 Did the Peripatetics pay attention to Aristotle's logical system before the Christian era? I find Aristotle's works were *lost* for the 200 years immediately following his death, and, when discovered, were for some time hardly studied even by his own sect; yet does not Cicero argue according to the Aristotelian method?

I am at a loss how to introduce my notice of singular and common terms. From ambiguous terms I proceed to Definition; and from singular and common terms I go to Abstraction and Division; but I am at a loss how to connect Definition with common and singular terms.

For the treatment of these matters in the published work, see R. Whately, *Logic*, pp. 47–9, 60–1, 68–71, 71–5.

110. *Ibid.*, p. ix.
111. Nov. 14, 1826 (B12.1); see *Letters and Correspondence*, I, 107. The version of this letter given in the text is from a transcription made by Newman in 1860, presumably from a fair copy which he had retained but later destroyed. The rough draft of the letter, preserved in MS Miscellaneous Papers, presents the following variants: *contributed . . . materials*: had any share in forming its materials; *an Undergraduate exercise*: a schoolboy's exercise; *regards . . . doing it*: it gave me an opportunity of submitting a composition of mine to your correction.
112. Nov. 20 [1826] (B1.5).
113. *Ibid.* He wrote the comment directly *on* the letter, i.e. at bottom of the page.
114. Literary, Classical, and Mathematical.
115. Whately to JHN, Jan. 17 and Feb. 5 [1834?]; JHN to Whately [Feb., 1834?] (PC).
116. T. Mozley, *Reminiscences*, I, 29.
117. Miscellaneous Papers.
118. *Letters and Correspondence*, I, 119.
119. *Ibid.*, p. 118.
120. Burgon, *Twelve Good Men*, I, 439.
121. *Ibid.*, p. 441.
122. *Ibid.*, p. 459.
123. *Apologia*, ed. Ward, pp. 111–12.
124. Denison, *Notes of My Life*, p. 50; Tuckwell, *Pre-Tractarian Oxford*, p. 59.
125. E. J. Whately, *Life and Correspondence of R. Whately*, I, 27.

Chapter 3. Tutor of Oriel

1. Newman wrote twice for the Latin essay prize, in 1822 on the subject "An, re vera, praevaluerit apud eruditiores antiquorum polytheismus" (see above, p. 30), and in 1823 on "Conditio servorum apud antiquos." Two copies of the latter are contained in MS Literary, Classical, and Mathematical. The same MS contains two loose sheets headed, "Preparations for an Essay never written." This was evidently for the English essay of 1823, "On Public Spirit amongst the Ancients."

2. Memoranda, Personal and Most Private, II; *Letters and Correspondence*, I, 136–7, 197.

3. JHN to Bowden, August 10, 1834 (PC).

4. Bowden to JHN, July 14, 1834 (B12.2). In 1845 Newman could not make out the German address of his brother Charles, saying, "I can't read him and don't know German." JHN to Jemima Newman, Feb. 24, 1845 (MS Letters to Jemima, 1832–61).

5. JHN to his father, June 25, Oct. 19. and Nov. 14, 1821 (FL,I); see also JHN to his mother, June 11, 1821 (FL,I).

6. JHN to his father, Jan. 25 and Sept. 6, 1822 (FL,I); MS Chronological Notes, Jan. 22, 23, 24, and 29, 1822.

7. JHN to Harriett Newman, Oct. 4, 1822 (FL,I); cf. *Letters and Correspondence*, I, 76, where the text is joined to that of another letter.

8. Memoranda, Personal and Most Private, II; see *Letters and Correspondence*, I, 78.

9. JHN to his mother, Feb. 14, 1823 (FL,I); see *Letters and Correspondence*, I, 78.

10. Chronological Notes, Dec., 1825.

11. Chronological Notes, May 25, 1823.

12. MS Private Diary.

13. March 29, 1825 (FL,I).

14. Private Diary, under dates April 15, 1825 to March 15, 1826; Chronological Notes, under date April 16, 1825; Miscellaneous Papers.

15. *Oxford University Commission Report* (1852), p. 27; see also Cox, *Recollections*, 2d ed., p. 188; C. E. Mallett, *A History of the University of Oxford* (New York, Methuen, 1928), III, 223.

16. Memoranda, Personal and Most Private, II. The matter within brackets is Newman's.

17. *Letters and Correspondence*, I, 62, 117, 189. John Sargent's *Memoir of the Rev. Henry Martyn, B.D.* was published in 1819.

18. *Letters and Correspondence*, I, 117–18.

19. Sir J. T. Coleridge, *A Memoir of the Rev. John Keble* (3d ed. London, 1870), p. 73. Keble also considered the provostship to be a "pastoral employment." Burgon, *Twelve Good Men*, p. 400.

20. Memoranda, Personal and Most Private, II; see *Letters and Correspondence*, I, 148–9.

21. Memoranda, Personal and Most Private, II; see *Letters and Correspondence*, I, 149.

22. *Letters and Correspondence*, I, 84.

23. Chronological Notes.

24. *Apologia*, ed. Ward, p. 111; see also *Loss and Gain*, pp. 191–2, and R.F.C., "The Early Life of Cardinal Newman," *The Month*, LXXI (March, 1891), 311n.

25. *Letters and Correspondence*, I, 91.

26. Memoranda, Personal and Most Private, II.

27. *Letters and Correspondence*, I, 149–50. Actually, the pastoral conception of the tutorship seems implicit in the following note, written July 1, 1822: "The present long vacation I purpose to spend in Oxford, and I have someone with me whose studies I am to direct—Prosper Thou the works of my hands upon me, Good Lord, oh prosper Thou my handywork." Analysis of Aristotle's *Rhetoric*.

28. Memoranda, Personal and Most Private, II, Feb. 21, 1826. Newman accepted the tutorship on Jan. 20, arranged to give up St. Clement's on Feb. 16, and noted on Feb. 21 that he was to be succeeded at Alban Hall by Samuel Hinds. *Ibid.*; Private Diary.

29. Memoranda, Personal and Most Private, II.

30. March 21, 1826 (FL,I).

31. Sunday, May 7 [1826].

32. Thomas Hughes, *James Fraser. . . . A Memoir* (London, 1887), pp. 24–5.

33. *Letters and Correspondence*, I, 132.

34. Pusey to JHN, Jan. 9, 1827 (B12.1).

35. Memoranda, Personal and Most Private, II, April 13 [1823] and Feb. 21, 1824.

36. *Letters and Correspondence*, I, 79–80, 127.

37. Newman, letter to the *Daily News*, Oct. 28, 1884.

38. JHN to Harriett Newman, Nov. 1, 1826 (FL,I). The matter within brackets is Newman's.

39. *Letters and Correspondence*, I, 164.

40. *Ibid.*, p. 165.

41. Sir Herbert Maxwell, *The Honourable Sir Charles Murray, K.C.B. A Memoir* (Edinburgh and London, 1898), pp. 56–8. Tom Mozley says that Tyler "was on very good terms with most of the undergraduates. His special fondness, however, was reserved for the Gentlemen Commoners, above all for one 'dear boy,' who in after life became the pet of the world, and who was probably indebted to Tyler for no small part of his spoiling. This was Charles A. Murray." *Reminiscences*, I, 82.

42. Earl of Malmesbury, *Memoirs of an Ex-Minister. An Autobiography* (London, 1884), I, 18.

43. *Daily News*, Oct. 13, 1884.

44. Lord Malmesbury's apology was published in the *Globe* on Oct. 30, 1884, and reprinted in the *Daily News* on Oct. 31. Newman's acceptance appeared in the *Globe* on Nov. 4. All the papers relating to the controversy are preserved at the Oratory (VC,2).

45. C. J. Plumer, who was a Fellow of Oriel from 1821 to 1830, testified that James was the victim. On the other hand, Lord Cranbrook (formerly Gathorne Hardy) knew a "legend (existing in 1833–4) . . . of various repetitions of the offence, ending (not in passive sufferance on your part - but) in some rustications." Newman doubted this on the ground that "rustication &c. had been impossible in Copleston's time" (but see above, p. 54); moreover, *his* table was "large and heavy, not on castors but on a carpet, and a dozen youths sitting round it." (VC,2)

46. *Daily News*, Oct. 28, 1884.

47. *Prelude*, III, 412–16.

48. [John C. Colquhoun], *An Appeal to the Heads of the University of Oxford* (London, 1822); [Edward Hawkins], *A Letter to the Author of "An Appeal to the Heads of the University of Oxford" upon Compulsory Attendance at the Communion* (Oxford, 1822). Newman possessed copies of these pamphlets, which are preserved at the Oratory. He discusses them briefly in a letter to Lord Blachford, Oct. 22, 1884 (VC,2).

49. JHN to Lord Blachford, Oct. 22, 1884 (VC,2); see *Letters and Correspondence*, I, 151–2, and for Newman's later views, I, 265 and *Fifteen Sermons Preached before the University of Oxford* (London, Longmans, Green, 1906), pp. 152–3 and n.

50. June 26, 1827 (FL,II); see *Letters and Correspondence*, I, 165.

51. Journal of JHN, 1859–76, June 25, 1869.

52. *Letters and Correspondence*, I, 164.

53. T. V. Short, *Letter on the State of the Public Examinations* (2d ed. Oxford, 1829), app., p. 30. In 1830–31 Newman urged the heads of houses to reduce the number of examining masters from 6 to 3, because the larger number "involves a difficulty of finding men sufficiently qualified. Indeed there are few examiners . . . who have time to qualify themselves. Books are not uncommonly present[ed] by

candidates, of which they know little or nothing, and which they are accordingly obliged to cram for the occasion; e.g. Aristotle's Politics, and Categories, Plato's Dialogues, some of Cicero's Treatises, Xenophon's vii Hellenica, the Greek Orators." MS Examination School.

54. The volumes are listed in Examination School.
55. Memoranda, Personal and Most Private, II.
56. Ibid.
57. Letters and Correspondence, I, 177.
58. Ibid., p. 178.
59. Memoranda, Personal and Most Private, II.
60. Letters and Correspondence, I, 181, 184, 186.
61. Ibid., p. 45.
62. Memoranda, Personal and Most Private, II, Feb. 21, 1823.
63. Apologia, ed. Ward, pp. 116–17.
64. Ibid., p. 118.
65. Ibid., p. 119.
66. JHN to Lord Blachford, Nov. 4, 1884 (VC,2).
67. Rannie, Oriel College, p. 191.
68. Letters and Correspondence, I, 219.
69. MS Sermon on "Mediatorial Kingdom of Christ," 1827.
70. Chronological Notes, August 14, 1828. A fortnightly dinner club which Newman founded on April 29, 1828 included Froude and Wilberforce among its members. Ibid., April 29, 1828; Letters and Correspondence, I, 184.
71. Short, Letter on the Public Examinations, app., p. 31n.
72. Sept. 3, 1828 (B12.1). This letter is erroneously attributed to Wilberforce in Letters and Correspondence, I, 191–2.
73. Feb. 6, 1829; see Letters and Correspondence, I, 198–9.
74. Hawkins to JHN, May 15, 1830 (VC,61). MS Suppressed Chapters of Autobiographical Memoir. The Oriel system seems to have been in general use, at least in the smaller Oxford colleges, at this period; both Corpus and Balliol had it. Coleridge, Memoir of Keble, pp. 11–12; R. T. Davidson and W. Benham, Life of Archibald Campbell Tait (3d ed. London, 1891), I, 71, 108.
75. Rannie, Oriel College, pp. 201–2.
76. Reprinted in Historical Sketches, III, 75.
77. Letters and Correspondence, I, 152.
78. Reminiscences, I, 136.
79. Letters and Correspondence, I, 182.
80. Ibid., p. 152.
81. JHN to Hawkins, April 25, 1830 (VC,61). The public lectures scheduled for 1830 were 10 in number: Senior Greek Play, Junior Greek Play, Greek Lecture "for idle men," Latin Lecture for idle men, Rhetoric, Senior Latin prose, Junior Latin Prose, Analytical Mathematics, Second Analytical Mathematics, and one term each for Euclid, Articles, and Logic. A letter from Froude to Newman on Jan. 20, 1831 (PC,46) shows the private lectures of that year as including: Art[icles ?], Thucydides, Politics, Ethics, Livy (Decade II), Mathematics, Hellenica, Pindar, and "G.P" [Greek Poets ?]. The number of pupils in the private lectures varied from 1 to 6.
82. MS Oriel Tutorship, July 9, 1830.
83. J. Dornford to JHN, Dec. 26, 1828 (VC,61).
84. JHN to Keble, Dec. 19, 1827 (PC).
85. Suppressed Chapters of Autobiographical Memoir.
86. Ibid.
87. Note dated Sept. 15, 1850, in Oriel Tutorship.
88. Newman recounts the episode in Suppressed Chapters of Autobiographical Memoir; Letters and Correspondence, I, 200–7; and Historical Sketches, III, 231–2.
89. Suppressed Chapters of Autobiographical Memoir.
90. Chronological Notes, Feb. 13 and 14, 1829.

91. JHN to his mother, March 13, 1829 (FL,III); see *Letters and Correspondence*, I, 204-6.

92. JHN to his mother, March 1, 1829 (FL,III); see *Letters and Correspondence*, I, 202-3.

93. *Letters and Correspondence*, I, 199-201.

94. Burgon, *Twelve Good Men*, I, 415; T. Mozley, *Reminiscences*, I, 229-31.

95. T. Mozley, *Reminiscences*, I, 229.

96. Newman wrote to Hawkins on June 8, 1830 (VC,61): "My chief private objection to the system you propose, is, that, in my own case as I know from experience (whatever others may be able to effect) the mere lecturing required of me would be incompatible with due attention to that more useful private instruction, which has imparted to the office of Tutor the importance of a clerical occupation." Froude wrote in the same sense on June 10 (VC,61); see *Letters and Correspondence*, I, 157-8.

97. *Addresses to Cardinal Newman, with his Replies, 1879-81*, ed. W. P. Neville (London, 1905), p. 184. Pattison gives the same interpretation of the quarrel in *Memoirs*, p. 87.

98. Hawkins to JHN, June 9, 1830 (VC,61); Burgon, *Twelve Good Men*, I, 410-12.

99. JHN to Hawkins, May 5, 1830 (VC,61).

100. Rannie, *Oriel College*, pp. 201-2.

101. Chronological Notes, under date June 11, 1831. Actually, although Newman finished his lectures at this date, he still had 4 (possibly 6) pupils whom he wished to prepare for their examination, so that he was not altogether out of the tutorship until the summer of 1832. JHN to Hawkins, April 13, 1831 (VC,61); see *Letters and Correspondence*, I, 159.

102. Pattison, *Memoirs*, p. 88.

103. Rannie, *Oriel College*, p. 203.

104. Suppressed Chapters of Autobiographical Memoir. Newman's own note explains, "only 'partially restored;' as has been said, because the innovation had made its mark on the College, and Mr Newman, though not Tutor, was Dean and Vicar of St. Mary's."

105. *Ibid*. Newman wrote to Froude on June 15, 1834 (PC): "I have in writing my prediction given in to the Provost 4 years since, that, if our system of Tuition were stopped, the Classes would fail - and I referred him to the fact that when Tyler, Keble, and Whately ceased to take private pupils, the series of honors stopped in 1823. Now observe Eden came up the term before, Bliss the term after I was Tutor - they are the two first new honors of *our* series—Rogers took his honors two years since, he was the last of my pupils - and the last of our (classical, i.e. in-college) honors. Nothing is doing now. Men like young [James] Mozley who might have been any thing, are doing nothing. Well - Den[ison] [the Tutor] now wishes to *found Scholarships* . . . in order to *encourage* reading. . . . [N.B. Oct. 17, 1860. I believe that from that time till now, and in spite of the Scholarship scheme being carried out, Oriel has never regained its place in the Class list.]" The matter within brackets was supplied by Newman in a transcription of the letter in MS Correspondence with Friends, Personal, 1822-36.

A second letter to Froude, Nov. 17, 1835 (PC), continues: "Denison is going to give up the Tuition at Christmas. He has been 5 years Tutor! He professes one especial reason has been his disgust at finding men *will* take private pupils. You recollect this was the very reason for our system which I put on paper for the Provost, before our controversy. The remarkable thing is, our view should have been *proved* to be correct in so short a time. Is it not remarkable that Denison, clever and popular man as he is, *has not got for the College one first class?* They say Utterton is soon to have one - but he is a private pupil of Rogers' - *the old succession*."

106. George Moberly, *A Few Remarks on the Proposed Admission of Dissenters into the University of Oxford* (Oxford, 1834), p. 14; [C. P. Eden], *Self-Protection*.

The Case of the Articles (Oxford, 1835), pp. 17–18. Even A. C. Tait, tutor of Balliol, who was no friend of the Tractarians, has this note in his diary (Nov. 16, 1839): "What can be done for the College servants? what to make more of a pastoral connection between the tutors and their pupils? What can be done for making the tutor more fully superintend his individual pupils' reading without mere reference to the Schools?" Davidson and Benham, *Life of Tait*, I, 72; see also I, 87. Balliol had the same system as Oriel under Copleston.

107. *Memoirs*, p. 64; see T. Mozley, *Reminiscences*, I, 177, 181.

108. *Memoirs*, pp. 65–6.

109. *Reminiscences*, I, 237.

110. JHN to Hawkins, Jan. 18 and 24, 1828 (Oriel Library).

111. *Loss and Gain*, p. 183.

112. *Aristotelis ethicorum Nichomacheorum libri decem*, ed. G. Wilkinson (4th ed. Oxford, 1815), opp. p. 7.

113. *Ibid.*, opp. p. 59.

114. E. J. Whately, *Life and Correspondence of R. Whately*, I, 394.

115. JHN to the Rev. Dr. Nares, July 18, 1825 (A11.8).

116. JHN to Arthur Tarbutt, Dec. 4, 1827 (CL).

117. JHN to his mother, Feb. 14, 1823 (FL,I).

118. *Letters and Correspondence*, I, 76.

119. *Reminiscences*, I, 232.

120. Examination School. The paper is headed, "Proposals about the rules of examination proposed to my fellow examiners 1827," with the date 1828 queried and then confirmed on another page. The latter date is also indicated by a letter from H. A. Woodgate, one of the examiners, to Newman on July 23, 1828, about the Proposals (B12.1).

121. The revised examination had three full days of written papers, including logic, translation of English into Latin, and a moral essay. Mallett, *History of Oxford*, III, 228–9; Lord Blachford, *Letters*, ed. G. E. Marindin (London, 1896), pp. 8–9.

122. Private Diary, June 9, 1828. Under the same date in Chronological Notes Newman writes, "we introduced paper examinations into Collections," and on June 24, 1829, "first day of *hall* collections," "N.B. called last year 'paper examinations' . . . it was one of the innovations we made, by right of Tutors, in the terminal examinations." The innovation was dropped after Newman ceased to be tutor. See Private Diary, March 19, 1833.

123. Examination School. It was usual for examiners to serve three terms, which in Newman's case would have been Michaelmas, 1827, Easter Term, 1828, and Michaelmas, 1828. Newman broke down in his first term, however, and was replaced by Dornford in his second. The third he attempted, but again fainted and had to be replaced for at least a few days by Miller and Woodgate. Private Diary, April 19, Oct. 25, Dec. 2, 3, 5, 1828; Chronological Notes, April 19 and Nov. 10, 1828.

124. Examination School.

125. *Idea of a University*, pp. 109–10.

126. *Reminiscences*, II, 412.

127. Various student themes, with Newman's comments on them, are preserved in MS Memorandum Book about College Pupils.

128. *Reminiscences*, I, 181–2.

129. *Ibid.*, II, 413.

130. JHN to his mother, Oct. 24, 1831 (ML); see also JHN to J. Bliss, same date (ML).

131. Memorandum Book about College Pupils.

132. *Reminiscences*, I, 181; see *Letters and Correspondence*, I, 131–2, 166.

Chapter 4. Sicily and Adam de Brome

1. Cox, *Recollections*, 2d ed., p. 261.
2. Chronological Notes, June 28, 1830; Froude to JHN, July 1, 1830 (B12.1).
3. JHN to Froude, July 28, 1830 (B12.1); see *Letters and Correspondence*, I, 232.
4. R. I. Wilberforce to JHN, Dec. 13, 1830 (B12.1).
5. JHN to Froude, July 28, 1830 (PC and B12.1); see *Letters and Correspondence*, I, 232; also Chronological Notes, June 30–July 17, 1830 and Jan. 10, 1831.
6. JHN to J. F. Wood, Sept. 4, 1832 (PC).
7. *Letters and Correspondence*, I, 273–4.
8. *Ibid.*, p. 286.
9. *Idea of a University*, p. 136.
10. *Letters and Correspondence*, I, 370–2.
11. *Ibid.*, p. 297.
12. *Ibid.*, p. 367.
13. *Ibid.*, p. 331.
14. *Ibid.*, p. 344.
15. *Ibid.*, pp. 377–8.
16. *Ibid.*, p. 403.
17. MS My Illness in Sicily.
18. *Ibid.* This version differs in many particulars from that in *Letters and Correspondence*, I, 413–30.
19. *Letters and Correspondence*, I, 412.
20. Private Diary, Oct. 17, 1833; Chronological Notes, same date.
21. JHN to Jemima Newman, August 27, 1832 (Letters to Jemima, 1832–61); Froude to JHN, Sept. 9, 1832 and JHN to Froude, Sept. 24, 1832 (PC); *Letters and Correspondence*, I, 262–3.
22. JHN to Froude, Sept. 24, 1832 (PC).
23. Oriel Tutorship; William Lockhart, *Paternoster Review*, I (Oct.–Nov., 1890), 24.
24. *Memoirs*, p. 169.
25. MS Analysis of Livy.
26. T. Mozley, *Reminiscences*, I, 142; Pattison, *Memoirs*, p. 98.
27. *The Statutes of Oriel College*, Oxford (London, 1855), pp. 9, 18.
28. Coleridge, *Memoir of Keble*, p. 248.
29. Memoranda, Personal and Most Private, IV. From 1835 to 1845 Newman prepared long thin slips of paper containing notes for prayers and lists of people and institutions to be prayed for, many of them extremely long lists. This is one of them.
30. T. Mozley, *Reminiscences*, I, 143.
31. *Memoirs*, p. 99.
32. *Reminiscences*, I, 144. Mozley admits that this is a matter of opinion, but of the 17 elections made between 1829 and 1840, by which date Newman's interest was waning, 5 of the 6 who can be identified as his candidates are noticed in the *Dictionary of National Biography*, and only 2 of the other 11. The 5 are Mozley, Eden, Marriott, Rogers, and Church.
33. J. B. Mozley, *Letters* [ed. Anne Mozley] (London, 1885), pp. 57, 60; Liddon, *Life of Pusey*, I, 338–9.
34. J. B. Mozley, *Letters*, pp. 75–6.
35. *Ibid.*, p. 78; Pattison, *Memoirs*, pp. 180–1.
36. J. B. Mozley, *Letters*, pp. 78, 107; Pattison, *Memoirs*, pp. 182–3; *Letters and Correspondence*, II, 297; R. D. Middleton, *Newman at Oxford* (London, Oxford University Press, 1950), p. 169.
37. Liddon, *Life of Pusey*, II, 139.
38. Jan. 29, 1840 (PC).

39. JHN to Hope, March 7, 1840 (PC).
40. *British Critic*, 4th ser. XXVIII (April, 1840), 369.
41. *Ibid.*, p. 376.
42. *Ibid.*, pp. 379–80.
43. *Ibid.*, pp. 385, 395.
44. JHN to James Hope, March 18, 1840 (PC); cf. Ornsby, *Memoirs of Hope-Scott*, I, 196.
45. Liddon, *Life of Pusey*, II, 135. It was on March 7 and 18 that he wrote to Hope praising his review and on March 17 that he wrote to Pusey about the Littlemore plan. On March 21 he sought through Frederic Rogers the advice of Hope as to whether the plan was compatible with his obligations as a Fellow of Oriel. *Letters and Correspondence*, II, 302.
46. Liddon, *Life of Pusey*, II, 37–8.
47. *Ibid.*, pp. 136–8.

Chapter 5. Tractarian Education

1. JHN to Bowden, Feb. 15, 1832 (PC). In 1827 the university received from the estate of Joseph Boden, lieutenant-colonel in the East India Company's service, property for "the erection and endowment of a professorship in the Sanskrit language . . . , [the donor] being of opinion that a more general and critical knowledge of the language will be the means of enabling my countrymen to proceed in the conversion of the natives of India in the Christian religion, by disseminating a knowledge of the Sacred scriptures among them, more effectually than by all other means whatever." *DNB*.
2. JHN to Bowden, Feb. 15, 1832 (PC); see also JHN to Froude, Feb. 18, 1832 (PC).
3. R. I. Wilberforce to JHN, Feb. 13, 1832 (B12.1).
4. S. Rickards to JHN, Feb. 25, 1832 (B12.1).
5. Bowden to JHN, March 5, 1832 (B12.1).
6. Private Diary, March 15, 1832.
7. Sept. 2, 1833 (B12.2).
8. JHN to Bowden, Feb. 9, 1834 (PC).
9. *Idem*, Nov. 17, 1833 (PC). This letter is incorrectly dated in *Letters and Correspondence*, II, 16.
10. JHN to Bowden, Feb. 9, 1834 (PC).
11. J. B. Mozley, *Letters*, pp. 39–40.
12. Rivingtons to JHN, March 5, 1834 (D2.7). At the head of this letter Newman wrote, "NB I was so sure of being elected Moral Philosophy Professor, that I wished the title inserted in my titlepage to my Sermons. I thought, however, it had been volume 2 - but the date of this letter shows it was volume 1. JHN Dec 27/51." Newman's first volume of *Parochial Sermons* appeared March 11. *Letters and Correspondence*, II, 16.

Two years later Newman was urged by President Routh of Magdalen, one of the electors who had voted for him on the first occasion, to become a candidate again, but Newman declined as being too busy and as favoring William Sewell, who had already announced his candidacy. M. J. Routh to JHN, March 11, 1836 (B12.2); JHN to Froude, June 15, 1834 (B12.2).
13. Ornsby, *Memoirs of Hope-Scott*, I, 183; J. B. Mozley, *Letters*, pp. 37–8.
14. *Society for the Diffusion of Useful Knowledge* [n.p., n.d.]. A copy of this statement of the aims of the society is preserved among Newman's books at the Oratory.
15. *Penny Magazine*, I (1832), preface.
16. Francis Trench, *A Few Notes from Past Life. 1818–1832* (Oxford, 1862), pp. 106, 108, 76.
17. Cf. *Idea of a University*, p. 145.

18. *Statement by the Council of the University of London, explanatory of the nature and objects of the institution* (London, 1827), p. 12. Newman possessed a copy of this work, now preserved at the Oratory, and quotes from it in the *Idea of a University*, pp. 33–4.

19. "Christianus" [pseud. of George D'Oyly], *A Letter to the Right Hon. Robert Peel, on the Subject of the London University* (London, 1828).

20. F. J. C. Hearnshaw, *The Centenary History of King's College, London, 1828–1928* (London, Harrap, 1929), p. 41.

21. V. A. Huber, *The English Universities. An Abridged Translation*, ed. Francis W. Newman (London, 1843), II, Pt. 1, 346n.; see Francis W. Newman, *The Relations of Professional to Liberal Knowledge* (London, 1859), pp. 24–5.

22. The best account of the Cambridge side of the controversy is in D. A. Winstanley, *Early Victorian Cambridge* (Cambridge, The University Press, 1940), pp. 83–96. See also *Annual Register*, LXXVI (1834), 163–221.

23. 4 Will. IV.—Sess. 1834. A Bill To remove certain Disabilities. . . . 21 April 1834.

24. H. J. Rose to JHN, March 10, 1834 (PC); JHN to Rose, March 17, 1834 (PC); *British Magazine*, V (April 1, 1834), 445–8. The rough draft of Newman's article is preserved in MS Admission of Dissenters to Oxford.

25. *British Magazine*, V (April 1, 1834), 446.

26. Newman's brief letter to the *Standard* (published August 7, 1834) simply corrects a statement of some speakers in Parliament to the effect that Pusey himself had acknowledged that all the religious instruction given at Oxford might be compressed within a fortnight. Pusey had already corrected the error in the *British Magazine* in June, 1834. See MS Correspondence, Public, 1828–36.

27. JHN to Bowden, April 21, 1834 (PC); Private Diary, April 22, 1834.

28. Private Diary, May 2, 1834; My Illness in Sicily.

29. *Declaration of Professors, Deans, and Tutors*, April 24, 1834.

30. JHN to Froude, June 15, 1834 (PC); JHN to Bowden, Saturday [? May 3, 1834] (PC).

31. John Griffiths of Wadham College, who made a collection (now in the Yale Library) of the pamphlets in this controversy, notes that about 2,670 persons were entitled to sign the 3 declarations of heads of houses, professors and tutors, and members of Convocation. Of these, 2,015 signed, about 170 could not be found, and about 485 were opposed, so that the ratio was more than 4 to 1 against the bill.

32. These figures are derived in the first 3 instances from copies of the printed petitions, in the third and the remaining instances from Newman's correspondence. How closely in touch with the work he was is shown by the almost daily bulletins he is able to issue on the progress of the petitions. See his letters to J. W. Bowden on April 27, May 2, 3, and 7, 1834 (PC), and to Jemima Newman on May 18 and June 2, 1834 (Letters to Jemima, 1832–61). Many letters to Newman from W. Palmer, Keble, Rose, A. P. Perceval, and Bowden on this subject are preserved in Correspondence, Public, 1828–36.

33. *Declaration of Professors*, April 24, 1834.

34. The phrasing is characteristic. Moreover, Sewell says that the idea was not his but was suggested by "a friend" who apparently had the actual phrasing of the declaration already in mind. As Sewell was writing on April 21, the day of the meeting of the Committee of Defense, the friend may well have been a member of that committee, and Newman is certainly a better candidate than Burton or Faussett. However, it might have been Pusey. See William Sewell, *Letter of April 21, 1334* [sic].

35. Bowden to JHN, April 3 and 18, 1834 (B12.2).

36. Keble to JHN, April, 1834 (B11.8).

37. JHN to Froude, June 14 and 15, 1834 (PC). The matter in brackets is Newman's.

38. Rose to JHN, August, 1834 (B11.8); see *Letters and Correspondence*, II, 55–63, 131.

39. The Oxford University Bill of 1854 abolished tests for matriculation and for

the B.A. degree, but retained those for the master's degree, for a vote in Convocation, and for admission to fellowships. In 1871 the University Tests Act removed all tests except those for theological degrees and professorships. Mallett, *History of Oxford*, III, 325, 332.

40. Moberly, *A Few Remarks on the Proposed Admission of Dissenters*, pp. 9–11.

41. In the debate over the London University, Mr. Wilberforce had suggested the propriety of making the students read Paley's *Evidences of Christianity*. He received the reply, "You do not consider our Jews." Mr. Wilberforce then proposed Paley's *Natural Theology*, and the answer was, "You do not consider our infidel." *Annual Register*, LXXVI (1834), 190n.

42. Sewell, *Letter of April 21, 1334* [sic], p. 1.

43. August 20, 1834 (PC). The "Declaration" is the Declaration of Heads of Houses and Proctors on May 2, 1834; see R. D. Hampden, *Observations on Religious Dissent* (Oxford, 1834), p. 40n.

44. Hampden, *Observations on Religious Dissent*, pp. 5, 8, 14–15, 16, 17, 20.

45. Nov. 28, 1834 (B11.8). The brackets are in Newman's transcription. Newman also transcribed the letter on the verso of the title page of the second edition of Hampden's pamphlet; this, together with his copy of the first edition, is preserved at the Oratory.

46. JHN to Keble, Nov. 10, 1834 (PC); Pusey to JHN, same date (PC).

47. [E. B. Pusey], *The expediency of substituting a Declaration for the signature of the Articles at Matriculation having been widely canvassed . . . : it is hoped . . . that it will not be deemed premature to submit the following Questions. . . .* [Nov. 11, 1834]. John Griffiths of Wadham College noted on his copy that the questions were "circulated in the Common Rooms in Michaelmas Term 1834."

48. The first draft of this protest is given in Newman's letter to Pusey, Nov. 14, 1834 (PC). Three copies of a slightly revised version, all in Newman's autograph, are preserved in ML, 1829–36. As revised it reads:

> We, the undersigned, being informed of an intention on the part of some members of the University to attempt the removal of the Subscription to the 39 Articles at present required at matriculation, lose no time in expressing our deep grief that any such design should be in contemplation. We deprecate any change in so important a matter at the present moment, and we seriously lament, that, for the chance of making the position of the University more intelligible to the adversaries of its highest interests, any persons should consider it their duty to incur the certain evil of introducing differences and divisions into a body which has for a long season enjoyed the blessing of internal peace and unanimity.

49. Pusey to JHN, Nov. 17, 1834 (PC).

50. Vice-Chancellor's Notice of New Statute to be Submitted, April 1, 1834.

51. This is Archdeacon Powell's explanation (1757) as quoted in [George Horne], *A Letter to the Right Hon. the Lord North . . . concerning subscription to the XXXIX Articles. . . .* [1773] [ed. Thomas Vaughan] (Oxford, 1834), p. xviii. Henry Phillpotts, bishop of Exeter, explained in Parliament that subscription at matriculation "is simply tantamount to a declaration that the subscribers belong to the Church of which these are the Articles, and accept them as true on that authority." The second subscription then means that "he now knows and approves for himself." *Speech on occasion of a petition from certain members of the Senate of Cambridge, presented to the House of Lords, On Monday, April 21, 1834* (London, 1834), pp. 5–6, 7.

52. [F. D. Maurice], *Subscription No Bondage* (Oxford, 1835), p. 13.

53. Sir J. F. Maurice, *The Life of Frederick Denison Maurice* (London, 1884), I, 182. Newman's copy of Maurice's pamphlet is preserved in the Oratory.

54. [J. W. Bowden], *A Religious Reason, against Substituting a Declaration of Conformity to the Church, for the Subscription to the Articles* (Oxford, 1835); [Benjamin Harrison], *Latitudinarianism in Oxford in 1690, a Page from the Life of Bishop Bull*

(Oxford, 1835) and 1835 *and* 1772. *The Present Attack on Subscription Compared with the Last* (Oxford, 1835); [C. P. Eden], *Self-Protection. The Case of the Articles* (Oxford, 1835); [Charles Marriott], *Meaning of Subscription* (Oxford, 1835); [H. W. Wilberforce], *The Foundation of the Faith Assailed in Oxford* (London, 1835); [J. F. Christie], *The Views of our Reformers as Bearing on Religious Dissent* (Oxford, 1835); Frederick Oakeley, *A Letter to His Grace the Duke of Wellington . . . upon the Principle and Tendency of a Bill now before Parliament* (Oxford, 1835).

55. [Edward Hawkins], *Oxford Matriculation Statutes* (Oxford, 1835), p. 6.

56. Pusey, *The Expediency of Substituting a Declaration.*

57. A note by Newman to a letter from R. I. Wilberforce, May 6, 1834 (B11.8), gives this as the "accredited" view of "the party of Pusey &c."

58. JHN to the Rev. W. H. Hale, June 3, 1835 (Oriel Library).

59. JHN to Keble, Nov. 10, 1834 (PC). This explanation, however, is not so sharply distinguished either from the Bishop of Exeter's view or from the Declaration of Conformity as was their later position.

60. [Eden], *Self-Protection*, p. 4. Newman found this pamphlet "splendid." *Letters and Correspondence*, II, 106.

61. Many of the replies he received are preserved in Correspondence, Public, 1828–36.

62. Lord Blachford, *Letters*, pp. 23–4. See also Pusey to JHN, Nov. 17, 1834 (B11.8). Chronological Notes, May 20, 1835, gives the vote as 459 to 5, doubtless an error in copying.

63. *Short Studies on Great Subjects*, 4th ser. (N.Y., 1883), p. 168.

64. *Memoirs*, p. 237.

65. *Memorials of Dean Lake*, ed. by his widow (London, Edward Arnold, 1901), p. 54.

66. Dec. 28, 1856 and June 21, 1870 (PC).

67. Froude, *Short Studies*, pp. 183–6.

68. *Ibid.*, p. 185.

69. *Letters and Correspondence*, II, 224.

70. *The Life of Mary Russell Mitford, Related in a Selection from her Letters*, ed. A. G. L'Estrange (London, 1870), III, 273–4, quoted in *Letters and Correspondence*, II, 224–5n.

71. *Essays*, ed. H. Nettleship (Oxford, 1889), II, 269–70.

72. Examination School. This paper is headed, "1830–31. Questions proposed to the Tutors of Oxford by a Committee appointed by Heads of Houses; (with my answers.)." The date is uncertain, however, for on Oct. 5, 1829 Newman "wrote paper on Examinations," which might well be the one in question. Chronological Notes.

73. *Recollections*, pp. 132–3. How liberal his motive was in so voting is uncertain. On Jan. 9, 1830 he wrote to Froude, "If I possibly can, I shall vote for the New Examination Statute—I cannot but fear, if it be rejected, men will be appointed [i.e. as examiners] who are likely to make great innovations, losing sight completely of those old principles which in drawing up this the Provost has kept in view. Cardwell, Mills, Burton, Short, Hampden &c. would they not exclude Aristotle, and bring in modern subjects? I should like to make modern history, or Hebrew, &c. &c. necessary for the M.A. degree." (PC).

74. *Letters and Correspondence*, I, 220; JHN to Froude, June 9, 1830 (B12.1).

75. JHN to Rickards, Feb. 7, 1840 (Oriel Library).

76. Charles A. Bristed, *Five Years in an English University* (3d ed. N.Y., 1873), p. 182.

77. John C. Shairp, *Studies in Poetry and Philosophy* (Edinburgh, 1868), pp. 269–70, 272.

78. *Memorials of Dean Lake*, pp. 29, 41.

79. Froude, *Short Studies*, pp. 185–6.

80. *Unpublished Letters of Matthew Arnold*, ed. A. Whitridge (New Haven, Yale University Press, 1923), pp. 65-6.

81. Henry Tristram, "Newman and Matthew Arnold," *Cornhill Magazine*, N.S. LX (1926), 316.

82. *Memoirs*, pp. 236ff.

83. Quoted in Henry Tristram, "Cardinal Newman at Oxford," *The Tablet* (August, 1939), p. 242.

84. JHN to Jemima Newman, August 13, 1844 (Letters to Jemima, 1832-61).

85. *Apologia*, ed. Ward, p. 327.

86. JHN to Jemima Newman, June 15, 1845 (Letters to Jemima, 1832-61).

87. Both Newman's letter and the rough draft of Hawkins' are in the Oriel College Library.

Chapter 6. The Irish University Question

1. Wilfred Ward, *Life of John Henry Cardinal Newman* (London, Longmans, 1913), I, 312. In the present chapter the author is heavily indebted to two sources— first, an unpublished history of the Catholic University of Ireland by Henry Tristram, and secondly, Fergal McGrath's Oxford dissertation, *Newman's University. Idea and Reality* (London, Longmans, 1951)—but references are necessarily limited to the latter. Readers who wish a more detailed treatment of what is here handled summarily will find it in McGrath, chaps. 1-3.

2. *Lectures on the Present Position of Catholics in England* (2d ed. London, 1851), pp. 170-1.

3. *Chartae et statuta Collegii Sacrosanctae et Individuae Trinitatis* (Dublin, 1822), pp. 55-64, 186-8. A translation of the relevant passages will be found in Robert Bolton, *A Translation of the Charter and Statutes of Trinity-College, Dublin* (Dublin, 1749), pp. 43-51, 158-60.

4. *Report of Her Majesty's Commissioners Appointed to Inquire into the State, Discipline, Studies, and Revenues of the University of Dublin, and of Trinity College* (Dublin, 1853), pp. 4, 53-4, 70.

5. McGrath, *Newman's University*, pp. 7-8.

6. *Ibid.*, pp. 8-10.

7. John W. Adamson, *English Education, 1789-1902* (Cambridge, The University Press, 1930), pp. 6-11.

8. McGrath, *Newman's University*, p. 35.

9. Thomas C. Hansard, ed., *The Parliamentary Debates*, 3d ser. (356 vols. London, 1830-91), LXXX, 360, 353-7.

10. *Ibid.*, LXXX, 378.

11. *Ibid.*, LXXX, 1, 149-50.

12. McGrath, *Newman's University*, pp. 61-2.

13. *Ibid.*, p. 62.

14. *Ibid.*, pp. 62-3.

15. The Latin text is given in J. H. Newman, *My Campaign in Ireland*, ed. W. Neville (privately printed, 1896), pp. lxxiii-lxxiv.

16. Bernard O'Reilly, *John MacHale, Archbishop of Tuam* (N.Y., 1890), II, 122-3, quoted in McGrath, *Newman's University*, p. 66.

17. *My Campaign in Ireland*, p. lxxv.

18. *Ibid.*, p. lxxvi.

19. *The Tablet*, XIII (Jan., 1852), 8, 23.

20. McGrath, *Newman's University*, pp. 74-6.

21. Paul Cullen, *Pastoral Letters and Other Writings*, ed. P. F. Moran (Dublin, 1882), I, 31, quoted in McGrath, *Newman's University*, p. 78.

22. Cullen, *Pastoral Letters*, I, 51-67, quoted in McGrath, *Newman's University*, pp. 100-1.

Chapter 7. The *Discourses*: Composition and Rhetoric

1. MS My Connection with the Catholic University; JHN to Dr. Cullen, July 5 [misdated July 7], 1850 (Diocesan Archives, Dublin).

2. April 15, 1851 (C6.37).

3. Robert Whitty to Fr. Pettit, April 21, 1890; cf. McGrath, *Newman's University*, p. 105, where the date is given as 1895. My text is not from the original but from a copy preserved in the Dublin Diocesan Archives. However, if this is the source used by McGrath, then the date of the letter is not 1895. Whitty's letter to Cullen, which McGrath says is in the Dublin Diocesan Archives, could not be found when I was there in 1951.

4. JHN to Dr. Cullen, April 16, 1851 (Diocesan Archives, Dublin).

5. JHN to Dr. Cullen, April 28, 1851 (Diocesan Archives, Dublin).

6. July 13, 1851 (C6.37). My Connection with the Catholic University gives the date of Dr. Cullen's call as July 6, but Newman's Private Diary and a letter of July 9 to T. W. Allies show that it was the 8th.

7. July 12, 1851 (PC).

8. JHN to Fr. Ambrose St. John, Oct. 3, 1851 (OL).

9. JHN to Dr. Cullen, July 15, 1851 (Diocesan Archives, Dublin); Private Diary, July 18, 1851; My Connection with the Catholic University.

10. Hope to JHN, July 24, 1851 (C6.37). The proposal was made by Dr. Cullen on July 18.

11. My Connection with the Catholic University.

12. *Ibid.*; JHN to Hope, July 23, 1851 (CL); Hope to JHN, July 24, 1851 (C6.37); F. W. Faber to Birmingham Oratory, July 24, 1851 (C6.37); JHN to T. W. Allies, July 25, 1851 (PC).

13. July 23, 1851 (Diocesan Archives, Dublin).

14. Dr. Cullen to JHN, August 12, 1851 (C6.37); JHN to Dr. Cullen, August 19 and 28, 1851 (Diocesan Archives, Dublin); My Connection with the Catholic University; *My Campaign in Ireland*, p. 76.

15. The questions in their original form are given in Dr. Leahy's letter to Newman, August 20, 1851 (C6.37).

16. Dr. Leahy to JHN, Sept. 17 and 23, 1851 (C6.37); JHN to Dr. Cullen, Sept. 29, 1851 (Diocesan Archives, Dublin).

17. The report is given in *My Campaign in Ireland*, pp. 77–87.

18. *Ibid.*, p. 77.

19. *Ibid.*, p. 80.

20. Msgr. F. X. de Ram to Allies, Oct. 2, 1851 (C6.4).

21. JHN to Hope, Oct. 11, 1851 (CL).

22. JHN to Mrs. J. W. Bowden, Oct. 19, 1851 (PC).

23. Dr. Cullen to JHN, Nov. 14, 1851 (C6.37); My Connection with the Catholic University.

24. Dr. Cooper to JHN, Nov. 12, 1851 (C6.37).

25. JHN to Mrs. Bowden, Oct. 19, 1851 (PC).

26. Sept. 15, 1851 (C6.37).

27. Sept. 16, 1851 (Diocesan Archives, Dublin).

28. Sept. 20, 1851 (C6.37).

29. JHN to R. Ornsby, April 18, 1852 (PC).

30. JHN to Dr. Cullen, Sept. 22, 1851 (Diocesan Archives, Dublin).

31. My Connection with the Catholic University (rough draft).

32. JHN to Dr. Cullen, Sept. 22, 1851 (Diocesan Archives, Dublin).

33. My Connection with the Catholic University.

34. Ornsby to JHN, April 16, 1852 (PC); see McGrath, *Newman's University*, pp. 143–8.

35. McGrath, *Newman's University*, p. 144.
36. My Connection with the Catholic University; see Ward, *Life*, I, 335.
37. F. Lucas to JHN, Oct. 9, 1851 (ML).
38. My Connection with the Catholic University; see Ward, *Life*, I, 327.
39. Feb. 4, 1852 (Diocesan Archives, Dublin).
40. Feb. 8, 1852 (C6.37).
41. April 14, 1852 (PC).
42. Private Diary, April 3, 1852.
43. Chronological Notes, April 3, 1852. This phrase is often said, incorrectly, to refer to the next entry below, about the "university discourses." (See McGrath, *Newman's University*, p. 141.) It was the books and papers, however, that Newman was reluctant to leave. Prison would have been a pleasure after the discourses.
44. Jan. 12, 1852 (PC).
45. Henry Tristram, *Newman and His Friends* (London, John Lane, 1933), p. 81.
46. April 14, 1852 (PC).
47. Dr. Leahy to JHN, April 21, 1852 (C6.37).
48. Anonymous to JHN, Dec., 1851 (C6.37).
49. Dr. Cullen to JHN, Feb. 8, 1852 (C6.37); see also Dr. Leahy to JHN, Nov. 5, 1851 (C6.37) and Dr. Cullen to JHN, April 25, 1852 (C6.37).
50. Ornsby to JHN, April 13, 1852 (PC).
51. April 14, 1852 (PC).
52. April 15, 1852 (PC).
53. April 20, 1852 (C6.37).
54. JHN to Ornsby, April 18, 1852 (PC).
55. JHN to Dr. Cullen, Dec. 30, 1851, also Feb. 4 and March 2, 1852 (Diocesan Archives, Dublin).
56. JHN to Dr. Cooper, March 16, 1852 (CL); Dr. Cooper to JHN, April 21, 1852 (C6.37); JHN to Fr. Superior of London Oratory, April 27, 1852 (OL).
57. Private Diary, April 10, 1852. Though Newman had been occupied on the lectures since early Oct., most of the actual writing seems to have been done from Feb. on. On Dec. 30 he wrote that he did not "forget" the lectures, but "how shall I find time?" and on Jan. 14 that after his trial on Feb. 12 he would go to Ireland, "where I am to write my Lectures." In a letter of Feb. 4 he also speaks as if things were not very far along. JHN to Dr. Cullen, Dec. 30, 1851 and Feb. 4, 1852 (Diocesan Archives, Dublin); JHN to Mrs. Bowden, Jan. 14, 1852 (PC); JHN to Fr. Superior of London Oratory, April 27, 1852 (OL); JHN to Ornsby, May 2, 1852 (PC).
58. April 21, 1852 (C6.37). In transcribing this and other letters into My Connection with the Catholic University, Newman replaced the names of the various ecclesiastical authorities with the letters A, B, and C, and then, when he came to make a fair copy of the manuscript some time later, he apparently forgot what he had done and expanded C (standing in this letter for Dean Meyler) into Cullen. McGrath (*Newman's University*, p. 152) quotes the second transcription instead of the original letter and so is obliged to spin a theory as to why Dr. Cullen's mind needed soothing.
This is perhaps the place to correct another error repeated by McGrath from Ward, who got it from Fr. William Neville, Newman's friend and literary executor. Father Neville had said in the advertisement to *My Campaign in Ireland* that Newman's whole course of lectures was nearly relinquished at one time because, after accepting the rectorship, "he had found himself so strangely left alone with regard to his going to Ireland that in the following spring he fixed a day to himself when he would resign, unless, meanwhile, a letter of some sort (this is the way he happened to put it to himself) came to him from Ireland. The day had come without his having received any such letter; his letter of resignation was written, but in the course of the day a letter *did* come from Dr. Cullen, which though not *apropos* to anything calling him to Ireland, nevertheless broke the stipulation he had made with himself." (p. lxiv) Father Neville and Ward give the date as "at the close of April or in the early days of

May, 1852," McGrath as about March 7. (*My Campaign in Ireland*, p. lxv; Ward, *Life*, I, 315–16; McGrath, *Newman's University*, p. 139). It is clear, however, that there was no question of Newman's being called over to Ireland any time in the spring of 1852, and that there was no long period in which he did not receive letters, either from Dr. Cullen or Dr. Cooper. (Letters are preserved from Jan. 26, Feb. 8, 12, 27, March 13, April 21 and 25.) Without doubt, the date of the incident was 1853, and thus it did not jeopardize the delivery of the lectures. (See Ward, *Life*, I, 325; McGrath, *Newman's University*, pp. 205–6.)

59. May 2, 1852 (PC).

60. Ellis, secretary of the Irish Church Missions, to JHN, May 7, 1852 (ML).

61. The Rotunda, or Rotundo, as it was called in the papers of the day, was built in 1764–82 in connection with the Dublin Lying-In Hospital and was the scene of most fashionable gatherings, lectures, and public entertainments in nineteenth-century Dublin. See C. P. Curran, *The Rotunda Hospital. Its Architects and Craftsmen* (Dublin, At the Sign of the Three Candles, 1945).

62. J. H. Newman, *The Scope and Nature of University Education* (2d ed. London, 1859), advertisement.

63. J. H. Newman, *Discourses on University Education* (Dublin, 1852), pp. 25, 27. Referred to hereafter simply as *Discourses* (1852).

64. In 1870 in My Connection with the Catholic University. However, in 1867 he had used this passage under the title "Cathedra Sempiterna" as his contribution to Fr. Cardella's book, *Omaggio Cattolico in varie lingue ai Principi degli Apostoli Pietro e Paolo*, presented to Pius IX on his Jubilee. *My Campaign in Ireland*, pp. lx, 211–14.

65. Newman, *Discourses* (1852), pp. 31, 33.

66. JHN to Fr. St. John, May 11, 1852 (OL).

67. *Freeman's Journal*, LXXXV (May 11, 1852), 3.

68. Lucas to JHN, Wednesday [May 12, 1852?] (C6.37). The chief objector was Fr. John Curtis, S.J., who later, however, so far changed his opinion as to advise Newman, "Don't attempt the University; give up the idea." My Connection with the Catholic University.

69. Newman, *Discourses* (1852), p. 24.

70. The *Freeman's Journal* published reports of each of the five lectures on the day after delivery, and these were reprinted in the *Dublin Evening Post*. It is not certain whether these reports, which are partly a paraphrase and partly a verbatim account, were prepared from Newman's manuscript or from shorthand notes. According to a disappointed Irish editor, Newman forbade note-taking in the hall. JHN to Fr. Gordon, May 13, 1852 (OL).

71. Copy in the National Library of Ireland.

72. *Dublin Evening Post*, XC (May 11, 1852), 3.

73. Fr. Gordon to JHN [May 14, 1852] (OL).

74. JHN to Fr. Nicholas, May 16, 1852 (OL).

75. *Freeman's Journal*, LXXXV (May 11, 1852), 3; see Fr. St. John to JHN, [May 12, 1852] (OL); JHN to Fr. Gordon, May 13, 1852 (OL).

76. JHN to Ornsby, April 18, 1852 (CL); JHN to H. Wilberforce, April 17, 1852 (CL).

77. JHN to Fr. St. John, May 13, 1852 (OL). The first discourse appeared in full in the *Tablet*, XIII (May 15, 1852), 307–9. This apparently preceded the publication of the pamphlet.

78. May 14, 1852 (OL); see Fr. Gordon to JHN [May 14, 1852] (OL).

79. Advertisements in the *Freeman's Journal* for the following dates announce the Discourses as "now ready," "just published," or "this day published": May 19, Discourse I; May 24, Discourse II; May 31, Discourse III; August 18, Discourse VI ("The Seventh and Eighth Discourses are in the Press, and will be published in a few days."); Oct. 13, Discourse VIII; Nov. 9, Discourse IX ("The Tenth and concluding Discourse is in the Press and will be ready in a few days."). Thomas Grant wrote to

Newman on June 7 that he had received the fourth discourse "a day or two ago," (ML) and the *Tablet* advertised it on the 5th.

80. JHN to Fr. Gordon, May 13, 1852 (OL). McGrath (*Newman's University*, pp. 153–4n.) was misled by an error in the *Freeman's Journal* into supposing that Newman used three different rooms for his lectures. Actually, it is clear from the advertisements in both the *Freeman's Journal* and the *Tablet* that he used only two: the Concert Room for the second and the Exhibition Room for the first and all the later ones. (*Freeman's Journal*, May 10, 15, 19, 22, etc.; *Tablet*, May 8, 15, 22, 29, June 2.)

There is some difficulty, however, in identifying the rooms to which these names apply, for the modern building is much altered and the rooms were variously described at different periods. The architect's plan of the building (in A *List of the Proprietors of Licenses of Private Sedan Chairs* [1787], facing p. 6) shows the main Round Room as flanked by a Card Room to the west (66 by about 30 ft.), a slightly smaller Tea Room to the east, and the Grand Ball Room (86 by 40 ft.) to the north. Over the Ball Room was a Great Supper Room of the same size, and there were smaller apartments over the Card Room and the Tea Room. Since the entrance to Newman's Concert Room was from Cavendish Row (advertisement in *Freeman's Journal*, May 15), that must have been either the Ball Room or the Great Supper Room above it, and McGrath is doubtless right in supposing it was the latter. The entrance to the Exhibition Room, however, was from Sackville St. on the south (advertisements of May 10, 19, etc.), and so that must be identified with either the Card or the Tea Room or one of the apartments above them. Newman's reference to the want of light, and the phrase "the spacious *salon* adjoining the round room" (*Freeman's Journal*, June 1) both suggest the Card Room rather than the Tea Room and downstairs rather than up, but it is impossible to be certain.

81. May 17, 1852 (OL). The band was that of the 81st regiment, which was stationed in a side salon and "performed a variety of brilliant music during the day." *Freeman's Journal*, LXXXV (May 18, 1852), 3.

82. Fr. Gordon to JHN, Wed. [May 19, 1852] (OL). Nevertheless, Fr. Gordon was "a little inclined to agree with you in your own criticism." Not so Fr. St. John: "I think your present lectures ought to be what they are, for your credit as Head of the University - and felt it would raise you immensely with France and Germany. Depend upon it, it is very lucky your bright thought did not come out before - Thalaba, Thalaba, trust God and thyself. I distrust everybody's-judgment about your works till they have been in the world some years - Your last 2 sets of lectures have been *too much* for the people you were addressing. I hope you will not come down. There is a meaning in your being directed to take the course you have taken." Fr. St. John to JHN, May 18, 1852 (OL).

83. JHN to Ornsby, April 18, 1852 (PC).

84. JHN to Dr. Cooper, March 16, 1852 (CL).

85. The dates of the lectures were May 10, 17, 24, 31, and June 7. The hour of the first was three o'clock, thereafter at four.

86. JHN to Ornsby, April 18, 1852 (PC).

87. JHN to A. Mills, June 3, 1852 (OL).

88. June 3, 1852 (OL).

89. Thomas Grant admired the fourth "more than its predecessors even, which says a great deal," and Robert Whitty wrote that "All seem pleased with them so far," i.e. through the third. Grant to JHN, June 7 [1852] (ML); Whitty to JHN, May 28 [1852] (C6.37); Faber to JHN, June 4 [1852] (OL); JHN to Fr. Frederic, June 7, 1852 (OL).

90. JHN to H. E. Manning, June 8, 1852 (CL).

91. June, 1852 (OL).

92. The *Tablet* announced Newman's departure on June 12, giving the trial as the reason and implying that the lectures would be resumed in "a few weeks."

93. June 15, 1852 (CL).

94. June 26, 1852, quoted in Ward, *Life*, I, 292.

95. MS Circular and Correspondence. McGrath is incorrect in saying (*Newman's University*, p. 163n.) that Fr. Gordon's objections have not survived. They are in the Archivium at the Oratory.

96. JHN to Fr. B. Dalgairns, July 21, 1852 (OL); Dr. Moriarty to JHN, July 21 and Oct. 24, 1852; JHN to Dr. Moriarty [about July 23, 1852] (Circular and Correspondence).

97. [July 21 or 22, 1852] (Circular and Correspondence).

98. JHN to Fr. Dalgairns, July 22, 1852 (OL).

99. The Introduction was canceled in the first collected edition as being unnecessary once the argument could be seen in full. As a result it is little known and so may be given here:

Introduction

As misconceptions may arise with regard to some of the points treated of in the following pages, in consequence of the impossibility of introducing at once all the safeguards and explanations which they respectively require, the Author would observe,

1. That he is treating here of the Object of a University in the *abstract* and in its *idea*; 2. that, as such, its object is *knowledge*, as such; 3. but that a *Catholic* university will, in all its regulations and appointments, and in its routine, distinctly recognize Catholicism; and 4. that, for its *integrity*, though not for its essence, it ought to be invested with a *coercive* power, enforcing order, discipline, and religious and moral behaviour on its subjects.

Newman, *Discourses on University Education*. . . . *Discourse* VI. *Philosophical Knowledge Its Own End* (Dublin, 1852). See Chap. 13 below for a further discussion of this problem.

100. July 22, 1852 (OL).

101. JHN to Fr. Gordon, May 13, 1852 (OL).

102. JHN to Fr. St. John, August 4, 1852 (OL).

103. Sept. 22, 1852 (OL).

104. JHN to Bowden, Oct., 1852 (OL).

105. Private Diary, Sept. 29, 1852; see JHN to Lord Feilding, Oct. 6, 1852 (CL): "I would gladly take your Sermon, if I could—but I am finishing my University Discourses against time, and am so overworked that I am physically unable. I broke down in a common Lecture this day week."

106. JHN to Sister Mary Imelda Poole, Oct. 22, 1852 (CL). The discourses were probably finished by Nov. 2, on which date Newman wrote to Allies, "My University Lectures have taken out of me, no one can say how much, and I am fit for nothing but to lie on a sofa." (PC) The Preface was apparently completed by Nov. 21, the date of the dedication, and the Appendix a short time after. JHN to Ornsby, Oct. 29, 1852 (PC); JHN to Allies, Dec. 28, 1852 (PC).

107. JHN to H. Wilberforce, Dec. 9, 1852 (CL). Some copies were bound in dark cloth with a stamped design and "Newman's Discourses" in gold on the spine. This was all right with Newman if it was "SMALL gold letters (capitals) - as the Oxford Library of the Fathers." *Ibid*.

108. Feb. 17, 1852 (A46.2).

109. Longman to JHN, Sept. 12, 1856 (PubL).

110. The plan is given on the front flyleaf and in the text of a copy of the first collected edition (1852) preserved at the Oratory.

111. My Connection with the Catholic University.

112. JHN to H. Wilberforce, Dec. 20, 1852 (CL).

113. Ward, *Life*, II, 262.

NOTES [pp. 156–65]

Chapter 8. The Catholic University of Ireland

1. McGrath, *Newman's University.*
2. *My Campaign in Ireland,* p. 106.
3. *Ibid.,* p. 109.
4. *Ibid.,* p. 108.
5. *Ibid.,* pp. 59–60.
6. *Ibid.,* pp. 62–3, 79.
7. *Ibid.,* pp. 182, 206–8.
8. *Ibid.,* pp. 22–3; *Catholic University Gazette,* p. 35.
9. *My Campaign in Ireland,* pp. 20, 53–4, 64–8, 170–9, 295–8, 355–60.
10. *Ibid.,* pp. 126–7, 130–1.
11. *Ibid.,* p. 137.
12. *Ibid.,* pp. 142–3.
13. MS University Journal, Jan. 19, 1854. This document, which both Ward and McGrath were unable to find, is preserved in Newman's room at the Oratory in a packet of papers labeled "Catholic University, Formal and Documental" (A34.2). It was discovered by the author in 1952 and is being published by Henry Tristram in the French edition of Newman's works. See Ward, *Life,* I, 321; McGrath, *Newman's University,* p. xn.
14. MS Memorandum Relating to Catholic University.
15. *My Campaign in Ireland,* p. 276; see Newman's note of Feb. 19, 1853: "Appoint some [Professors] for actual work, some more or less for show (attraction). For show (attraction), Law, Political Economy, Physical Science, Literature, Fine Arts. . . . For hard work - Rhetoric, History, Philosophy of Religion." Memorandum Relating to Catholic University.
16. MS University Journal, Nov. 23, Dec. 15, 1853; My Connection with the Catholic University.
17. *My Campaign in Ireland,* p. 110.
18. *Ibid.,* pp. 84–5, 110.
19. JHN to T. Scratton, May 12, 1852 (CL): "These [i.e. Tutors] would be young men, for the most part unmarried, and would naturally live a good deal with their pupils - not indeed of necessity, but because they would be in the position of private Tutors and Junior Fellows at Oxford." In a letter to Dr. Cullen, July 4, 1852, Newman describes the tutors as "answering to Private Tutors at Oxford" (A34.1), and this is repeated in memoranda of Feb. 19, 1853 and July 17, 1854. Memorandum Relating to Catholic University; University Journal, under latter date.
20. *My Campaign in Ireland,* pp. 41–2; see also pp. 117–20, 277.
21. *Ibid.,* pp. 98–9, 111; University Journal, June 21, 1854. There was also to be another class of tutor, paid only half as much as these four. *Ibid.,* Nov. 5, 10, 12, and 23, 1853.
22. JHN to H. Wilberforce, Nov. 23, 1853 (PC).
23. The four were Henry Wilberforce, Robert Ornsby, E. Healy Thompson, and James Stewart. See University Journal, June 21 and Sept. 24 and 25, 1854.
24. University Journal, March 28, 1856.
25. *My Campaign in Ireland,* p. 117.
26. *Ibid.,* pp. 272–3.
27. *Ibid.,* pp. 47–8; McGrath, *Newman's University,* p. 343.
28. *My Campaign in Ireland,* pp. 33, 120.
29. *Ibid.,* p. 36. Newman admired the management of student discipline at Louvain as "combining freedom in the students with the safeguard of Catholic morality." JHN to Myles O'Reilly, April 2, 1853 (C6.3).
30. *My Campaign in Ireland,* p. xxi.
31. *Ibid.,* p. 44; McGrath, *Newman's University,* p. 346; Memorandum Relating to Catholic University.

[305]

32. Memorandum Relating to Catholic University.
33. Lord Blachford, *Letters*, p. 249.
34. [J. H. Newman], "Universities," *British Magazine*, V (April, 1834), 446.
35. Memorandum Relating to Catholic University; McGrath, *Newman's University*, pp. 254, 337n.
36. *My Campaign in Ireland*, pp. 197–9.
37. JHN to Scratton, May 12, 1852 (CL).
38. *Idea of a University*, p. 146; see also *My Campaign in Ireland*, p. 39, and Memorandum Relating to Catholic University: "The genius loci depends mainly on the intercourse of students *with each other*."
39. *My Campaign in Ireland*, pp. 39–40.
40. *Ibid.*, p. xliv.
41. *Ibid.*, p. 24; see also pp. 290, 305–9; JHN to Ornsby, March 7, 1853 (PC).
42. My Connection with the Catholic University. For the text of the Brief see *My Campaign in Ireland*, pp. lxxix–lxxxii.
43. Dr. Cooper to JHN, Nov. 2, 1852 (A34.1); Fr. St. John to JHN, Sept. 19, 1853 (OL); see McGrath, *Newman's University*, p. 210.
44. JHN to H. Wilberforce, Sept. 30, 1853 (PC). The fact that the university had been mentioned by the synod of Dublin but not by the synod of Thurles in the autumn of 1853 suggested to Newman "the dangerous idea that the University is only to be a *Dublin College*." JHN to Dr. Taylor, Oct. 23, 1853 (A34.1); see also memorandum of Dec. 29, 1853, in My Connection with the Catholic University.
45. Newman, *Historical Sketches*, III, 6.
46. *My Campaign in Ireland*, pp. 6–10.
47. Catholic University of Ireland, *Report of the Committee, and List of Subscriptions* (Dublin, 1852), pp. ix–x; McGrath, *Newman's University*, pp. 148–9.
48. *My Campaign in Ireland*, p. 55, also pp. 19, 321; My Connection with the Catholic University.
49. *My Campaign in Ireland*, p. 94.
50. McGrath, *Newman's University*, pp. 253, 343.
51. W. F. P. Stockley, *Newman, Education and Ireland* (London, Sands [1933]), p. 70. Bishop Ullathorne also told Newman that "the English gentlemen would never send their sons to it" and seemed to acquiesce in their feeling. My Connection with the Catholic University.
52. Newman, *Historical Sketches*, III, 32.

Chapter 9. The Circle of the Sciences

1. *Discourses* (1852), pp. 139–40, 142.
2. *Ibid.*, p. 387.
3. *Encyclopædia* (Herbornae Nassoviorum, 1630), p. 49.
4. E[phraim] Chambers, *Cyclopaedia. Or, an Universal Dictionary of Arts and Sciences* (London, 1728), I, i.
5. "Animula."
6. Newman, *Discourses* (1852), p. 387.
7. Alice D. Snyder, *Coleridge on Logic and Learning* (New Haven, Conn., Yale Univ. Press, 1929), p. 35. This work and Miss Snyder's edition of Coleridge's *Treatise on Method* (London, 1934) contain a full discussion of Coleridge's relation to the *Encyclopaedia Metropolitana*.
8. *Treatise on Method*, ed. Snyder, p. 78.
9. Snyder, *Coleridge on Logic and Learning*, p. 33.
10. *Treatise on Method*, ed. Snyder, p. 72.
11. *Ibid.*, pp. 54–5.
12. The *British Controversialist* (Jan., 1862), p. 7, quoted in Snyder, *Coleridge on Logic and Learning*, p. 39.

13. *Letters and Correspondence*, I, 85 and n.

14. JHN to E. Smedley, Jan. 27, 1826; Smedley to JHN, Feb. 8, 1826 (B12.1).

15. Smedley to JHN, May 17, 1828; JHN to Smedley, May 29, 1828 (B12.1).

16. An analysis of Coleridge's *Treatise* in Newman's autograph is preserved in MS Preparatory Work for "Office and Work." The sheet bearing the analysis is watermarked 1851; the entire packet is dated 1854. It is worth noting that the 1852 edition of Coleridge's *Treatise* bore a subtitle, *The Laws and Regulative Principles of Education*, which emphasized its relevance to Newman's problem.

17. *Scope and Nature of University Education* (1859), pp. 18–19.

18. Hastings Rashdall, *The Universities of Europe in the Middle Ages*, ed. F. M. Powicke and A. B. Emden (Oxford, Clarendon Press, 1936), I, 4–5.

19. Morris Hadley, *Arthur Twining Hadley* (New Haven, Conn., Yale Univ. Press, 1948), p. 153.

20. Rashdall, *Universities of Europe*, I, 6–13.

21. For instances of the argument see: *Quarterly Review*, XXXIII (1825), 271–2; XXXIX (1829), 128, 132–5; [D'Oyly], *Letter to the Right Hon. Robert Peel*, p. 9; W[illiam] Sewell, *A Second Letter to a Dissenter on the Opposition of the University of Oxford to the Charter of the London College* (Oxford, 1834), p. 9; Connop Thirlwall, *A Letter to the Rev. Thomas Turton, D.D. . . . on the Admission of Dissenters to Academical Degrees* (Cambridge, 1834), p. 15; *British Critic*, I (1827), 194–211; *Annual Register*, LXXVI (1834), 191.

22. *Edinburgh Review*, LX (Oct., 1834), 202–30. Newman corresponded with H. J. Rose about the article and helped work up a reply to it for the *British Magazine*. Rose to JHN; Oct. 16 and 22, 1834, JHN to Rose, Oct. 19 and Dec. 8, 1834. (CL)

23. *Discourses* (1852), p. 381.

24. Stephen d'Irsay, *Histoire des universités françaises et étrangères des origines à nos jours* (Paris, Picard, 1933), I, 72, 127, 148, 292.

25. *Discourses* (1852), pp. 387–91.

26. *Idea of a University*, p. 50; see Newman, *Grammar of Assent* (1874), p. 261.

27. *Idea of a University*, p. 48. This view is ultimately Aristotelian (see *Met.* 1003^a, 1025^b), and Newman probably learned it directly from the *Metaphysics*. His own copy of Bekker's edition (1837) shows annotations through I.6 and is opened through X.10. However, he also knew the passage in Whately's *Logic* which says that "when we *draw off*, and *contemplate separately*, any part of an object presented to the mind, disregarding the rest of it, we are said to *abstract* that part." (p. 48) Whately exemplifies the process by the same illustration that Newman used, namely, that an individual "may be considered either in a political point of view, and accordingly referred to the class of Merchant, Farmer, Lawyer, &c. as the case may be; or physiologically, as Negro, or White-man; or theologically, as Pagan or Christian, Papist or Protestant; or geographically, as European, American, &c. &c." (p. 51)

28. *Idea of a University*, p. 166.

29. *Ibid.*, pp. 51, 91.

30. Philo, *De congressu*, tr. F. H. Colson and G. H. Whitaker, XXV, 144.

31. *Ibid.*, XIV, 79; Cicero, *De officiis*, II, ii, 5; Cassiodorus, Isidore of Seville, and Alcuin, in Migne, *Pat. Lat.*, LXX, col. 1167; LXXXII, col. 141; CI, col. 952; Hugh of St. Victor, *Didascalion*, I, iv; II, i.

32. Newman, *Discourses* (1852), pp. 388–9, where most of the references to Hugh's treatise are given. The four divisions are from II, i.

33. *Met.* 983^a 22, 995^a 21, 982^a 1; 1004^a 4, 1026^a 24. In the practical realm Aristotle makes politics the "architectonic" science (*Eth.* 1094^a 10), a passage which Newman echoes in the *Idea of a University*, p. 47.

34. *Met.* 1003^a 25, tr. W. D. Ross. Aristotle instances mathematics as studying the attribute of number, physics that of motion, and grammar that of articulate sounds (*Met.* 1003^a 25, 1003^b 20, 1004^b 13).

35. *Idea of a University*, pp. 91, 51.

36. Plato, *Republic*, VII, 534–7; Aristotle, *De animal. part.* 639ᵃ 4; *Met.* 1005ᵇ 3, 1006ᵃ 6; *Eth.* 1094ᵇ 23; Augustine, *De ordine*, II, xiii, 38.

37. *Idea of a University*, p. 461.

38. *Historical Sketches*, III, 194.

39. Francis Bacon, *Works* (London, 1824), I, 36–7; quoted in *Idea of a University*, p. 90, and paraphrased, p. 139. It is interesting that this same quotation appears as a motto on the title page of F. D. Maurice's *Subscription No Bondage* (1835), which Newman also used in this portion of his argument. Newman, however, knew the *Advancement of Learning* at first hand, and he quotes it three more times in this same connection (*Discourses*, 1852, pp. 391, 392, 403–4). As an undergraduate he had purchased the 1815 edition of Bacon's *Works* in 12 volumes, but here he seems to have used 2 other editions, that of 1824 (see *Discourses*, 1852, p. 404) and an 18th-century paraphrase by Peter Shaw, *The Philosophical Works of Francis Bacon. . . . Methodized, and made English* (London, 1733)—cf. Shaw, I, 86, 262 with *Idea of a University*, pp. 222, 225–6.

40. Bacon, *Works* (1824), I, 100–1; see also pp. 93–5 and *De augmentis scientiarum*, III, iv.

41. *Edinburgh Review*, LXV (July, 1837), 96; see *Idea of a University*, p. 118n.

42. *Historical Sketches*, III, 195.

43. *Ibid.*, p. 194.

Chapter 10. The Man of Philosophic Habit

1. *Idea of a University*, p. x; cf. pp. xi, xvi.

2. *Ibid.*, p. 125.

3. *Ibid.*, pp. 136–8.

4. *Ibid.*, p. 139.

5. *Ibid.*, pp. 77–8; see Bacon, *Works* (1824), I, 37–8.

6. See Charles C. Gillispie, *Genesis and Geology* (Cambridge, Mass., Harvard Univ. Press, 1951), p. 21.

7. *Victorian England: Portrait of an Age* (London, Oxford Univ. Press, 1936), p. 160.

8. *Idea of a University*, p. 142.

9. *Ibid.*, p. 135.

10. *Ibid.*, pp. 127, 332, 136, 140.

11. Johann Lorenz von Mosheim, *An Ecclesiastical History, Ancient and Modern*, trans. A. Maclaine (London, 1826), IV, 3; see *Idea of a University*, p. 140.

12. Sept. 3, 1854 (PC).

13. "I wish I had what Froude calls *a view* on the subject of your Translation - but I only see bits of it, which do not connect together, and which I cannot defend." JHN to Keble, August 30, 1831 (PC).

14. Ward, *Life*, I, 262, 166–7, 260. The italics are Newman's.

15. To JHN, July 12, 1851 (PC).

16. *Loss and Gain* (1874), pp. 16–17.

17. *Ibid.*, pp. 19–20.

18. Pp. 75, xviii.

19. J. H. Newman, *Discussions and Arguments on Various Subjects* (London, 1872), pp. 1–2.

20. *Idea of a University*, p. xix; cf. pp. 334–6.

21. *Rasselas*, chap. xi.

22. "I should not think," wrote Coleridge, "of devoting less than twenty years to an epic poem. Ten years to collect materials and warm my mind with universal science. I would be a tolerable Mathematician. I would thoroughly understand Mechanics; Hydrostatics; Optics, and Astronomy; Botany; Metallurgy; Fossilism; Chemistry; Geology; Anatomy; Medicine; then the mind of man; then the minds of men, in all

Travels, Voyages, and Histories. So I would spend ten years; the next five in the composition of the poem, and the last five in the correction of it." Snyder, *Coleridge on Logic and Learning*, p. 1.

23. Cicero, *De orat.* I.vi; Quint. I.x–xii; II.xxi.14–23; Aristotle, *Rhet.* 1355ᵇ 27; Newman, *Historical Sketches*, I, 280, 282.

24. Migne, *Pat. Lat.*, LXXXII, col. 197–8.

25. *On Architecture*, trans. F. Granger, I.i.3.

26. *Sartor Resartus*, ed. C. F. Harrold (New York, 1937), pp. 95, 7.

27. *On Architecture*, I.i.13.

28. *Rhet.* 1366ᵃ 21, 1366ᵇ 23.

29. "Of Queens' Gardens," in *Sesame and Lilies*, sec. 74.

30. *Pol.* 1281ᵇ–1282ᵃ.

31. *Ibid.* 1340ᵇ; but cf. 1339ᵇ 2.

32. *Ibid.* 1282ᵃ.

33. *Eth.* 1139ᵃ 30; 1141ᵃ 13; see *Idea of a University*, p. 106n.

34. *Met.* 982ᵃ 9, 22.

35. *Eth.* 1141ᵃ 17; 1141ᵇ 3.

36. Whately, *Miscellaneous Remains*, pp. 51–3; see James and J. S. Mill, *On Education*, ed. F. A. Cavanagh (Cambridge, 1931), pp. 141–3.

37. *Miscellaneous Remains*, p. 54. That Newman had something of this sort in mind is suggested by his concern to have T. W. Allies teach, not history, but the "Philosophy of History," at the Catholic University, and also by a memorandum to "teach Undergraduates the *principles* of Law and Physiology." Memorandum Relating to Catholic University of Ireland. The italics are Newman's.

38. *Eth.* 1094ᵇ; *Met.* 995ᵃ; *De animal. part.* 639ᵃ.

39. *Miscellaneous Remains*, p. 55.

40. Whately, *Logic*, pp. xi–xii.

41. *Idea of a University*, pp. 165–6.

42. *Discourses* (1852), p. 140.

43. JHN to Harriett Newman, Oct. 10, 1835 (FL,III).

44. *Discourses* (1852), p. 140; see *Idea of a University*, p. 76.

45. *Idea of a University*, p. 331.

46. *Ibid.*, pp. 74–5; see also pp. 112–13.

47. See above, pp. 19, 59.

48. Nov. 14, 1825 (FL,I).

49. JHN to his mother, Nov. 23, 1826; JHN to Harriett Newman, Nov. 25, 1826 (FL,I). The italics are Newman's.

50. *Mill on the Floss*, Bk. II, chap. i.

51. *Idea of a University*, pp. 133–4.

52. See especially Locke, *Conduct of the Understanding*, secs. 3, 19, 22; Chambers, *Cyclopaedia* (1728), I, xxix–xxx; I[saac] Watts, *The Improvement of the Mind* (London, 1753), I, 203–4, 217–45; Macaulay's essay on Bacon, in *Edinburgh Review*, LXV (July, 1837), 95; James and J. S. Mill, *On Education*, ed. Cavanagh, pp. 21, 46; Richard Whately, *Miscellaneous Lectures and Reviews* (London, 1861), pp. 3–5.

53. J. H. Newman, "Wisdom, as Contrasted with Faith and with Bigotry," in *Sermons, Chiefly on the Theory of Religious Belief, Preached Before the University of Oxford* (London, 1843), pp. 280–1; see Watts, *Improvement of the Mind* (1753), I, 217–45. At the Oratory there is preserved a tiny abridgement of Watts' *Directions for the Improvement of the Mind* (Stourport [etc.], 1810), with the note on the flyleaf, "I think, given to me by my Mother about the year 1815–17. JHN." It was probably not much later that Newman became acquainted with the full work, for he used Watts' *Logick* while working on that subject with Whately (see Whately's *Logic*, pp. 9–10) and also inherited his father's copy (now preserved at the Oratory). Moreover, in Dec. 1827 his sister Mary wrote to him that Samuel Rickards had urged her to read "the Port Royal Art of Thinking (is not that an odd title?) and Watts on the

Mind." (FL,II; see *Letters and Correspondence*, I, 171) Newman himself had just come from a strenuous reading party with Rickards, and so this may reflect what the brother had just finished doing as well as what the sister needed to do.

54. *Idea of a University*, p. 130n.

55. *Sermons, Chiefly on the Theory of Religious Belief* (1843), p. 280; *Idea of a University*, pp. 131–3. The italics are mine.

56. Watts, *Improvement of the Mind* (1753), I, 229; *Idea of a University*, p. 132.

57. *Letters and Correspondence*, I, 372.

58. *Parochial and Plain Sermons* (London, 1870), I, 255.

59. *Letters and Correspondence*, I, 273–4; see above, Chap. 4.

60. *Idea of a University*, pp. 137–8.

Chapter 11. The Uses of Knowledge

1. Quoted in *Dublin Review*, XXXI (Dec., 1851), 547.

2. *Representative Government* (World's Classics), p. 194.

3. Leslie Stephen, *The English Utilitarians* (London, Duckworth, 1900), I, 47–8, 61–2.

4. *Idea of a University*, p. 102.

5. *Pol.* 1339^b 6, 1337^b 15, 25.

6. *Thoughts Concerning Education*, sec. 161. At Oxford music was still considered ungenteel in Newman's day. Mallett, *History of Oxford*, III, 281–2.

7. Werner Jaeger, *Aristotle*, trans. R. Robinson (2d ed. Oxford, Clarendon Press, 1948), pp. 97–8, 426–8, 432.

8. *Idea of a University*, pp. 104–5.

9. *Met.* 982^a 15, 982^b 11–23.

10. *Idea of a University*, p. 103.

11. *Ibid.*, p. 108.

12. *Rhet.* i.5; *Idea of a University*, p. 109.

13. *Pol.* 1254^a.

14. *Eth.* 1094^a.

15. Arnold, *Essays in Criticism*, 2d ser. (London, 1894), pp. 1–2.

16. MS Sundries, Unconnected, Feb. 24, 1859.

17. *Idea of a University*, p. 104.

18. Ernst Cassirer, *An Essay on Man* (New Haven, Conn., Yale Univ. Press, 1944), p. 112.

19. Nov. 16, 1854 (PC).

20. *Idea of a University*, p. 496.

21. *Ibid.*, p. 180. The italics are mine.

22. *Ibid.*, pp. 111, 113.

23. *Blackwood's Magazine*, III (June, 1818), 280.

24. *Ibid.*, p. 281, quoted in Maisie Ward, *Young Mr. Newman* (New York, Sheed and Ward, 1948), pp. 69–70.

25. Newman's account of the controversy is given in *Idea of a University*, pp. 1–2, 153–77.

26. James Deese, *The Psychology of Learning* (New York, McGraw-Hill, 1952), pp. 214–29.

27. *Idea of a University*, p. 102.

28. *Ibid.*, p. 177.

29. Jeremy Bentham, *Works*, ed. J. Bowring (Edinburgh, 1843), I, 2–3.

30. *Idea of a University*, p. 164.

31. *Eth.* 1094^a.

32. J. S. Mill, *Utilitarianism* (London, Dent, 1947), p. 9.

33. Quoted in F. H. Anderson, *The Philosophy of Francis Bacon* (Chicago, Univ. of Chicago Press, 1948), p. 186.

34. *Edinburgh Review*, XVII (Nov., 1810), 74.

35. *Brave New World* (New York, Doubleday, Doran, 1932), p. 29.

36. Memorandum Relating to Catholic University, dated Feb. 19, 1853, notes: "The first 2 years could be classics and elementary mathematics (and English &c. Literature). Then B.A. The next two preparations for Profession, e.g. (1) Ethics, Metaphysics, and History for Theology (2) Physical Science for Medicine 3. Political Economy, History, and Civil Law for Law. Then M.A. It *would* be Arts, tho' each a specific *kind* of Arts. The three last years for Profession, e.g. DD LLD MD." Further, the Rules and Regulations (1856) notes that even the first two years leading to the scholar's degree "can be adapted to the classical student, the ecclesiastic, or those who are intended for engineering, for business, etc." *My Campaign in Ireland*, p. 138; see also pp. 9, 93–4, 147–8, 313–18.

37. *Idea of a University*, pp. ix–xiv. The conception of the university as a research institution arose in Germany in the 18th century but was not generally accepted in England until the 1870's. See Paul Farmer and Charles Gillispie in *The Modern University*, ed. Margaret Clapp (Ithaca, N.Y., Cornell Univ. Press, 1950), pp. 15–16, 47–8; Copleston, *Reply*, 2d ed., p. 151; *Quarterly Review*, XXXIII (Dec., 1825), 266–8.

For Newman's altered conception see Rules and Regulations for the Catholic University (1856), which stipulates that "A Professor is not to be overburdened with lectures, that he may have time for the steady pursuit and thorough mastery of the department of science or learning, which he has undertaken." The marginal summary is more blunt: "Professors to write books." To this end Newman founded a learned periodical, the *Atlantis*, which was not to be "a magazine or review - but simply a place for depositing professorial *work*," and he published at university expense Professor Eugene O'Curry's studies of ancient Irish manuscripts. He also established, or tried to establish, an astronomical observatory, laboratories, research libraries, a school of useful arts, and other "institutions, which will have their value intrinsically, whether students are present or not." *My Campaign in Ireland*, pp. 96–7, 110–11; JHN to Lord Dunraven, March 21, 1857 (PC).

Chapter 12. The Religion of Philosophy

1. *Historical Sketches*, III, 28; cf. 33, 80–1.

2. *Sermons, Chiefly on the Theory of Religious Belief* (1843), p. 30.

3. *Idea of a University*, p. 104; *Discourses* (1852), pp. 410–12.

4. *Discourses* (1852), p. 412; *Idea of a University*, p. 106.

5. *Discourses* (1852), pp. 396, 404–6; *Idea of a University*, pp. 194–6, 211, 309.

6. *Idea of a University*, p. 134; *Discourses* (1852), pp. 423–37.

7. *Idea of a University*, p. 183.

8. See above, p. 6.

9. *Idea of a University*, pp. 196–200; *Discourses* (1852), p. 418.

10. *Idea of a University*, p. 205.

11. *Ibid.*, pp. 204–6.

12. See above, p. 34.

13. *Sermons, Chiefly on the Theory of Religious Belief* (1843), pp. 7, 11.

14. Cassirer, *An Essay on Man*, p. 187.

15. *Idea of a University*, p. 192.

16. J. S. Mill, *Autobiography* (New York, 1924), p. 100.

17. *Idea of a University*, p. 227.

18. *Ibid.*, pp. 208–11. The italics are mine.

19. *Discourses* (1852), p. 437.

20. *Lord Chesterfield's Advice to his Son, on Men and Manners. . . . To which are annexed, The Polite Philosopher: or, An Essay on the Art which makes a Man*

happy in himself and agreeable to others (Philadelphia, 1789), pp. 170, 173, 179, 180, 181, 204, 210.

21. *Idea of a University*, p. 202.

22. *Ibid.*, p. 201. The italics are Newman's. Newman read Burke's *Reflections* in the Christmas vacation of 1829. Chronological Notes. It is interesting that one of the questions in the Final Public Examination at Oxford for Easter Term, 1832, was the following: "Examine the sentiment, that 'Vice loses half its evil by losing all its grossness:' and inquire, generally, how far principles of Taste were admitted by the ancient Moralists as principles of Ethics." Newman was acquainted with the question through the fact that Frederic Rogers, his last pupil, wrote on it. *Examination Papers for Class Candidates* (Oxford, 1832), p. 19; Lord Blachford, *Letters*, p. 8.

23. This paragraph is a free development of Newman's ninth lecture in *Lectures on Certain Difficulties Felt by Anglicans in Submitting to the Catholic Church* (2d ed. London, 1850).

24. P. G. Bacci, *Life of St. Philip Neri* (2d ed. London, 1868), pp. 10, 13, 98–9. Newman used the 2-volume edition (1847).

25. *Idea of a University*, pp. 234–5.

26. *Ibid.*, pp. 236–7. The quotation from Paul (I Cor. 9:22) is also applied to Philip in Bacci, *Life of St. Philip Neri*, p. 154.

Chapter 13. Secular and Religious Knowledge

1. Feb. 25, 1840 (FL,IV); see *Letters and Correspondence*, II, 300.

2. *Idea of a University*, pp. 466–7.

3. *Ibid.*, p. 219.

4. *Ibid.*, p. 431.

5. *Ibid.*, pp. 223–4.

6. *Ibid.*, p. 441.

7. *Ibid.*, p. 430.

8. *Ibid.*, pp. 221–2.

9. *Ibid.*, p. 225.

10. *Ibid.*, p. 402; see Joseph Butler, *Works* (Oxford, 1836), I, 20.

11. *Idea of a University*, pp. 84–5.

12. William Lawrence, *An Introduction to Comparative Anatomy and Physiology, being the two introductory lectures delivered at the Royal College of Surgeons* (London, 1816). Subsequent lectures appeared under various titles, that of the 9th edition, which Newman owned, being *Lectures on Comparative Anatomy, Physiology, Zoology, and the Natural History of Man* (London, 1848). For a partial list of attacks on the book, see *British Museum Catalogue*, s.v. Lawrence.

13. Thomas Rennell, *Remarks on Scepticism* (2d ed. London, 1819), p. 66.

14. Charles Smyth, *Dean Milman* (London, 1949), p. 19, quoted in Duncan Forbes, *The Liberal Anglican Idea of History* (Cambridge, The University Press, 1952), p. 2.

15. [Henry Hart Milman], *The History of the Jews* (London, 1829), I, 90.

16. Godfrey Faussett, *Jewish History Vindicated from the Unscriptural View of it Displayed in the History of the Jews* (Oxford, 1830); [Richard Mant], *A Letter to the Rev. Henry Hart Milman, M.A. . . . Deprecating the Republication of that Work* (Oxford, 1830) and *A Second Letter to the Rev. Henry Hart Milman, M.A.* (Oxford, 1830). Two copies of Faussett's work are preserved at the Oratory.

17. Hawkins wrote to Newman on August 30, 1829: "I am very sorry indeed to hear your account of Milman's book; I have sent for it in consequence." (B12.1) On the following day Newman wrote to Pusey: "My real reason for writing is to withdraw my apparent commendation of the history of the Jews in the Family Library. I am much distressed to find it *is* the work of the person we supposed [the book was published anonymously]. When we spoke of it, I had only opened it, in B. V. White's

room; since I have read it, and if you on reading it do not pronounce it rationalistic, it will be to me a great relief. I think it a very dangerous work - it is a large subject, which I cannot do justice to here. I suppose M. has aimed at 2 things - to exhibit the internal evidence of the truth of the history viewed as a human institution and to give a philosophical view of the second causes etc. which were concerned in the Jewish system; - and to pre-occupy a subject which certain other persons might treat in a worse spirit. To judge by the work itself, I should have said it was written by a Socinian who either thought the whole Mosaic system *merely providential* or almost entirely so - or conceived the record to be the human and traditionary account of a miraculous history, and therefore full of exaggeration." (PC) On Jan. 28, 1830, Jemima wrote, "We are reading of an evening Milman's History of the Jews. I think it not a bit more comfortable to read from knowing he cannot mean what he implies." (FL,II)

18. JHN to S. L. Pope, Oct. 28, 1830 (PC). On Jan. 3, 1831 he added: "I am amused that your original notion was that in Oxford people are afraid of M! - poor fellow, I grieve for him heartily, but think he has got more blows than halfpences by his work. It seems to me he undertook it in a hasty thoughtless irreverent spirit, and not *understanding whither his principles would carry him*. Some persons think he did it to conciliate unbelievers - this may be. Yet, judging from the work, I should say it was the fruit of a supercilious liberalistic spirit, which liked to be (what it thought) philosophical and above the world - and to appear so - to show that a clergyman could take an enlarged view of things, and yet be a firm believer - and he went on, treading on the brink of danger, and now and then letting precious things fall over, without knowing where exactly he was. . . . As far as *scandal* goes and as far as public opinion is concerned, I think he has been protested against quite enough." (PC)

19. "Milman's View of Christianity," *British Critic*, XXIX (Jan., 1841), 71-114, reprinted in Newman, *Essays, Critical and Historical* (1890), II, 186-248.

20. This was the burden of Ruskin's criticism of the science in *Unto This Last*, and it was John Stuart Mill's opinion that the success of his *Principles* was due to the fact that it "treated Political Economy not as a thing by itself, but as a fragment of a greater whole; a branch of Social Philosophy, so interlinked with all the other branches, that its conclusions, even in its own peculiar province, are only true conditionally, subject to interference and counteraction from causes not directly within its scope." *Autobiography* (1924), pp. 165-6.

21. Copleston, *Reply* 2d ed., p. 174; Mallett, *History of Oxford*, III, 215. Writing from Dublin to one of the Oratory fathers on June 1, 1852, the day after delivering the original fourth discourse, Newman asked: "Will you look into my Oxford Calendars (it must be one later than 1825, say 36 or any other - they are on a high shelf in my bookcase between the window and fire) whether 'Henry Drummond Esqr of Albury Park' founded the Political Economy Professorship in Oxford?" (OL); see *Discourses* (1852), p. 124.

22. Whately, *Life and Correspondence*, I, 47.

23. Nassau Senior, *An Introductory Lecture on Political Economy, delivered before the University of Oxford, on the 6th of December, 1826* (London, 1827), pp. 1, 12; *Idea of a University*, pp. 89, 91. Newman's copy of Senior's lecture, with marginal scoring, is preserved at the Oratory.

24. *Idea of a University*, p. 91.

25. Charles H. Haskins, *The Renaissance of the Twelfth Century* (Cambridge, Mass., Harvard Univ. Press, 1939), p. 345.

26. *Ibid.*, pp. 345-6.

27. *Idea of a University*, p. 263.

28. Henri d'Andeli, *The Battle of the Seven Arts*, ed. Louis J. Paetow, in Memoirs of the Univ. of California, IV (Berkeley, Calif., Univ. of California Press, 1914), p. 39.

29. Louis J. Paetow, "The Arts Course at Medieval Universities with Special Reference to Grammar and Rhetoric," *Univ. of Illinois Bulletin. University Studies*, III, No. 7 (January, 1910), 33-66.

30. *Metalogicon*, ii, 9, 10.

31. *Idea of a University*, p. 262.
32. Haskins, *Renaissance of the Twelfth Century*, p. 27.
33. See *Idea of a University*, p. 96.
34. *Ibid.*, p. 384.
35. J. G. Sikes, *Peter Abailard* (Cambridge, The University Press, 1932), pp. 31–2.
36. *Ibid.*, pp. 253–4.
37. Roger Lloyd, *The Golden Middle Age* (London, Longmans, 1939), pp. 159–71.
38. Haskins, *Renaissance of the Twelfth Century*, pp. 347–8.
39. *Idea of a University*, pp. 469–70.
40. D'Irsay, *Histoire des universités*, I, 168n., 170–71.
41. J. H. Newman, *The Via Media of the Anglican Church* (London, 1882), I, xxxixff.
42. Henry P. Brougham, *A Discourse of the Objects, Advantages, and Pleasures of Science* (London, 1827), p. 48.
43. Newman's copy of Brougham's *Discourse*, preserved at the Oratory, is full of scoring and marginalia. Craik's work, which Newman mistakenly ascribed to Brougham in "The Tamworth Reading Room" (*Discussions and Arguments*, p. 256), had come under Newman's censure in the early 1830's. In June, 1834, he was horrified to discover that this work, which is of the "self-help" school, was included in a Catalogue of General Literature put out by a committee of the Christian Knowledge Society, and he and his friend Bowden tried to use their control of the purse strings to force its removal. It does not appear whether or not they were successful, but the episode led to one of Newman's most extreme statements to Froude on Jan. 18, 1835: "The abandonment of state prosecutions for blasphemy &c., and the disordered state of the Christian Knowledge Society, when books are taken cognisant of and condemned, render it *desirable* that there should be some really working court of heresy and false doctrine. . . . The chief advantage of this would be its practical curb upon the exercise of the king's power &c., for if a Maltby were appointed, nay before his appointment, his works would be censured by this Court." (B11.8)
44. *Idea of a University*, pp. 34–5, 103–4.
45. *Ibid.*, pp. 120, 121; cf. 118n.
46. See above, pp. 151–2.
47. Circular and Correspondence.
48. Dom Cuthbert Butler, *The Life and Times of Bishop Ullathorne* (London, Burns, Oates & Washbourne, 1926), II, 312n.
49. *My Campaign in Ireland*, p. lxxi. Newman's Memorandum Relating to the Catholic University (Feb. 19, 1853) contemplates only Catholics: "The beginning of each year . . . each student to go into retreat for one or two days, and then to confession and communion. This too will be the proof that the student is a Catholic." A printed sheet of Directions to Candidates for Entrance, however, shows that there was no kind of oath or test. It does not appear how early non-Catholics were admitted.
50. JHN to Dr. Cullen, July, 1855 and Sept. 13, 1855; JHN to Dr. Leahy, July 25, 1856; JHN to Fr. MacNamara, July 29, 1856; JHN to Dr. Forde, Sept. 10, 1856 (C6.31).
51. Memorandum Relating to the Catholic University; JHN to Ornsby, March 7, 1853 (PC); McGrath, *Newman's University*, pp. 197, 502.
52. JHN to E. L. Badeley, May 11, 1854 (PC,6).
53. JHN to George Fottrell, Dec. 10, 1873 (A22.2).
54. Newman, *Present Position of Catholics*, 2d ed., pp. 372–3; *Idea of a University*, pp. 232ff.; Ward, *Life*, I, 314–15.
55. Preparatory Work for "Office and Work." The list also includes Locke, Shakespeare, Milton, Clarendon, Defoe, Addison, Johnson, and Burke.
56. J. Connop Thirlwall, "Cardinal Newman's Literary Preferences," *MLN*, XLVIII (Jan., 1933), 25.
57. E. J. O'Reilly to JHN, Jan. 17, 1857 (C6.32); Arthur P. Stanley, *The Life and Correspondence of Thomas Arnold* (London, 1844), I, 145; see also p. 206.

58. JHN to E. J. O'Reilly, Jan. 18, 1858. A dozen letters on this subject are preserved in MS Index of Prohibited Books.

59. Diocesan Archives, Dublin. Two newspaper clippings on the controversy are
preserved among Newman's university papers (C6.35), and he was of course familiar
with W. G. Ward's anticipation of Gaume in *The Rambler*, III (Feb. and April,
1849), 446-57, 604-14.

60. Henry A. Woodgate, *The Study of Morals Vindicated and Recommended* (Oxford, 1837); Frederick Oakeley, *Remarks upon Aristotelian and Platonic Ethics, as a
Branch of the Studies Pursued in the University of Oxford* (Oxford, 1837).

61. *Idea of a University*, pp. 9, 260-1, 269, 372. Newman's lists of references and
works to consult on this subject are found in Preparatory Work for "Office and Work"
and MS Theological Commonplace Book, *s.v.* Classics. See also Henry Tristram, "The
Classics," in Tierney, ed., *Tribute to Newman*, pp. 246-7, 271-3.

62. *Recollections* (New York, 1897), p. 281.

63. *Discourses* (1852), pp. 152-3.

64. My Connection with the Catholic University.

65. *Newman's University*, pp. 277-8.

66. At variance with this view is a statement in the report of the subcommittee of
three (Newman, Leahy, and Myles O'Reilly) prepared in Oct., 1851: ". . . the Professors will be bound, not only not to teach anything contrary to Religion, but to take
advantage of the occasion the subjects they treat of may offer, to point out that Religion is the basis of Science." (*My Campaign in Ireland*, p. 80) This report, however,
is not exclusively Newman's work and, like the papal Brief, does not pretend to do
more than assert generally the religious character of the institution. A more difficult
passage is that in the final discourse of the *Idea of a University*, where Newman says
that although a university "had ever so many theological Chairs, that would not suffice
to make it a Catholic University; for theology would be included in its teaching only
as a branch of knowledge, only as one out of many constituent portions, however important a one, of what I have called Philosophy. Hence a direct and active jurisdiction
of the Church over it and in it is necessary." (p. 215) Here, however, Newman is
considering a university, not in its essence, but in its integrity, that is, not in its own
idea, but in its external relations (to the church). He is saying that for a university to
be a Catholic university it must be subservient in its totality to the Catholic church,
but this fact does not alter its internal balance and arrangements as a university.

Nevertheless, this is a delicate point and one on which Newman has been harshly
criticized by Thomas Corcoran in his edition of *Selected Discourses on Liberal Knowledge . . . with an Introduction on Newman's Theory of Liberal Education* (privately
printed, Dublin [1929]). Corcoran's attack, which is directed against Newman's alleged "philosophy of severance" (i.e. the severance of secular from religious knowledge) is too wrongheaded to require refutation at this date. His thesis that Cardinal
Wiseman's sermon, *University Teaching*, preached at Southwark, June 27, 1852, was a
criticism of Newman's original fifth discourse will not stand a candid examination; and
his suggestion that Newman had an insidious motive in suppressing that fifth discourse in the second edition is made without knowledge of the facts. Even William
Neville's account is in error here. Neville states that when Newman was delivering his
lectures in Dublin, he began, so it seemed, "very happily, but it was afterwards brought
home to him that he was on the wrong tack if he hoped to carry the Clergy along
with him. This was a great disappointment; for, had he been left alone, he said, and
heard to the end, they would have found themselves in accord with him. An influence
so great as this could not be let go. This obliged him to alter what he had prepared,
and, indeed, the scheme of the whole course; in doing this, by adjusting, for instance,
part to part, No. V. became, in his opinion, both spoilt and out of keeping with the
rest, and he therefore withdrew it." (*My Campaign in Ireland*, p. lxi) Writing after
the lapse of nearly fifty years, Neville has evidently confused two events, first, Newman's trouble with Discourse VI, which *did* arise from the fact that, in his serial mode
of publication, he felt the clergy would not hear him "to the end" before they began

to criticize, and secondly, the alteration in the *times* of the delivered lectures. It will be recalled that Newman wrote the first three discourses to be delivered as a unit, close together, and that he then intended to go on with what is now Discourse VI. When the lectures were scheduled at weekly intervals, however, he found that it was neither wise to drop the old subject so quickly nor was there time to begin a new one before the trial. Therefore he simply gave further illustrations in IV and recapitulated in V, and if V was later dropped, it was because it never was needed in the first place. But Newman did not drop it as condemning anything in it, for, as Neville notes, "he purposed including it, after corrections, in an intended volume of Pamphlets and Papers." Moreover, at one time he entertained a scheme of revision for the second edition which, while reducing the first five discourses into two, would have retained the greater part of Discourse V (pp. 135-6, 140-53), including the passage quoted above on theology. (MS notes dated Feb. 25, 1857, on flyleaf of a copy of 1852 edition preserved at the Oratory.)

67. *Idea of a University*, pp. 61, 430.

68. *Ibid.*, p. 439.

69. *Ibid.*, pp. 443, 467-9.

70. Newman's final and most precise treatment of this question is found in his essays, "On the Inspiration of Scripture" and "What Is of Obligation for a Catholic to Believe" (1884). There he holds that the inspiration specifically attributed to Scripture by the Tridentine and Vatican Councils is in respect to "faith and morals," and to matters of fact only generally, as manifesting God's providence and grace. Further, the meaning of this inspiration is determined by the church speaking *ex cathedra*, and on points on which it has not spoken, although there is a presumption in favor of interpretations received by the Fathers, nevertheless as the Fathers themselves were not inspired and as there is no canon or list of them, there is no heresy, though there may be impropriety, in advancing an interpretation of one's own which is not in itself contrary to faith. Certainly, no problems of authorship or of composite origin, etc., always saving the inspiration of the final redactor, need create difficulties. J. H. Newman, *Stray Essays on Controversial Points, Variously Illustrated* (privately printed, 1890).

71. *Essays, Critical and Historical*, II, 193-4.

72. Sir Rowland Blennerhassett, "Some of My Recollections of Cardinal Newman," *Cornhill Magazine*, LXXXIV (Nov., 1901), 618-20.

73. Sundries, Unconnected, p. 83 verso.

74. Mivart to JHN, Dec. 5, 1875 (PC). Newman apparently declined the honor of the dedication, for the work is inscribed to Lord Ripon.

75. JHN to Mivart, Dec. 9, 1871 (PC).

76. JHN to Dr. David Brown, principal of the Free Church College, Aberdeen (Oriel Library).

77. *Idea of a University*, pp. 452-3, 61; see also Newman, *Stray Essays*, pp. 104-6.

78. *Idea of a University*, pp. 225-6; Bacon, *Philosophical Works*, ed. Shaw, I, 262.

79. *Idea of a University*, p. 454.

80. *Ibid.*, pp. 38, 39.

81. Ward, *Life*, I, 408-9.

82. *Idea of a University*, pp. 471, 475, 476.

83. Allies to JHN, Nov. 10, 1854; JHN to Allies, Nov. 11 and 16, 1854 (PC); see *Idea of a University*, p. 222.

84. Ward, *Life*, I, 395.

85. *Idea of a University*, pp. 458, 460-1.

Index

INDEX

Harrison, Benjamin, 112
Haskins, Charles H., 252-3, 255
Hawkins, Edward, 26, 27, 35, 37, 38, 50, 57, 77, 120, 141, 286 (n. 56), 298 (n. 73), 312 (n. 17); characterized, 43-4; election as provost of Oriel, 63-5; and college quarrel, 64, 66, 68-73, 85-6, 88, 91, 275, 292 (n. 105); and admission of Dissenters, 112, 115
Hebdomadal Board, at Oxford, 68, 105, 110, 117, 118, 134
Heber, Reginald, 14-15
Hebrew, 298 (n. 73); JHN's study of, 46, 59, 274
Heliose, 254, 255
Heraclides of Pontus, 213
Hermes, The, 82, 194
Herodotus, 2, 7, 10, 11-12, 16, 22, 273, 277
Heron, Denis Caulfield, 124
Hierarchy, of knowledge, 185; of Nature, Man, and God, 240-1; of the sciences, 258, 265-6
Hinds, Samuel, 39, 42
Hippocrates, 252
History, philosophy of, 195, 219, 269, 309 (n. 37); sacred and profane, 249-50
Hobbes, Thomas, 97, 262
Hollis, George P., 6
Hollis' *Free Thoughts*, 280 (n. 14)
Homer, 2, 3, 59, 76, 277, 279 (n. 10), 282 (n. 91)
Hope, James (later Hope-Scott), 92, 94, 98, 132, 180, 196
Horace, 2, 5, 12, 16, 78, 277
Hugh of St. Victor, 184, 257
Humanism, 227-8, 229, 236, 237-8
Hume, David, 4, 36, 228, 262
Humility, as opposed to modesty, 232-3
Hutton's *The Compendious Measurer*, 3, 278
Huxley, Aldous, 225-6
Huxley, T. H., 2, 217

Imagination, dangers of, 113, 248
"Imperial University," 168, 169-70
Implicit faith, 113
Index of prohibited books, 263
"Influence," 157, 166
Inglis, Sir Robert, 126
Ingram, James, 7-8
Integrity, of knowledge, 174, 180-1, 183, 188, 269-70; of mind, 70, 174, 183, 194-7, 204-9; problem of for JHN, 19-20, 70, 205-6

Intellectual pride, JHN's sense of sin through, 4, 11, 16, 19, 28-9, 61, 87, 228
Ireland, 123-70 *passim*; anti-English feeling in, 127, 143, 148, 163; and education, 123-4, 125, 126, 138-9; political unrest in, 124-5; state of society in, 138-9, 142
Irish Church Missions, 144
Irsay, Stephen d', 180
Isidore of Seville, 198, 256
Italian language, 24

Jaeger, Werner, 213
James, William (Oriel tutor), 35, 56, 86
Jeffrey, Lord, 220
Jelf, R. W., 35
Jenkyns, Henry, 35
Jewel, Bishop, 107
John of Salisbury, 253-4, 257
Johnson, Samuel, 13, 198, 314 (n. 55)
Jubber, Miss, 105
Julian the Apostate, 229, 260-1
Juvenal, 2, 5, 32, 278, 282 (n. 91)

Kant, 36
Keble, John, 90, 98, 116, 123, 141, 267; Fellow of Oriel, 26, 27, 35, 292 (n. 105); JHN's first intimacy with, 64; JHN compares self with, 86-7; and admission of Dissenters, 105, 296 (n. 32); and contest for provostship, 63, 64; pastoral conception of tutorship, 50
Kepler, Johannes, 215
King's College, London, 100, 101
Kinsey, Rev. W. Morgan, 7, 9, 12, 24, 26, 28, 32, 47, 281-2 (n. 80), 285 (n. 40); characterized, 14-15
Knight, Richard Payne, 220

Labbé's *Eruditae pronuntiationis catholici indices*, 278
Laity, and CUI, 164, 261-2
Lake, William C., 118-19
Lamb, Charles, 3, 193, 276, 279 (n. 10)
Lancaster, Joseph, 125, 225
Lansdowne, Lord, 47
Laplace's *Traité de mécanique céleste*, 220
Larcher's edition of Thucydides, 16, 22
Latin composition, JHN's study of, 2, 7, 9, 23-4, 29, 30-1, 32, 37, 285-6 (n. 48); JHN's teaching of, 68, 88, 285-6 (n. 48)
Latin Dialogues, 278
Laud, Archbishop, 89

INDEX

Mozley, James, 91, 92, 97, 292 (n. 105)
Mozley, Tom, 30, 36, 37, 43, 53, 67, 71, 72, 75, 77, 79, 80, 91, 294 (n. 32)
Mullins, Rev. John ("a clerical friend of the family"), 1, 26
Multiplicity, 204–5, 218–19
Murray, Sir Charles, 54–5, 67, 75
Murray, Daniel, 126, 127, 139, 147
Music, 3, 13, 17, 24, 310 (n. 6)

Nares, Dr., 15
Narrowness of mind, 82–3, 191–3, 206
Nation, The, 124–5
National Education Act (1831), 125
National University of Ireland, 156, 160
Natural Theology, 15, 265, 267–8
Neate, Charles, 86
Neville, William, 301–2 (n. 58), 315 (n. 66)
New Examination Statute (1800), 8, 37
Newdigate prize, 13
Newman, Francis, 28, 41, 100, 275
Newman, Harriett, 2, 10, 16, 60–1, 152
Newman, Jemima, 10, 60–1, 120, 244
Newman, John (father of JHN), 1, 4, 10, 15, 20, 60
Newman, Mrs. John (mother of JHN), 10, 20, 28, 33, 57, 60
Newman, John Henry: as a boy, 2; attends Great Ealing School, 1–5; conversion, 3–5; matriculation at Trinity, 1, 5; first terms at Trinity, 5–10; wins scholarship, 10–11; "idle" period, 12–16; prepares for Schools, 16–20; failure, 20–2; studies after taking degree, 23–5; stands for Oriel Fellowship, 26–33; self-analysis in examination paper, 33–5, 233; relation with Noetics, 35–45; transitional period in studies, 46–7; takes private pupils, 47; becomes vice-principal of Alban Hall, 47–8; debates whether to be missionary, priest, or tutor, 48–51; ordained deacon, 50; accepts curacy of St. Clement's, Oxford, 51; becomes tutor of Oriel, 52; difficulties of his first year, 52–7; serves as examiner in Schools, 58–60, 61–2, 78; death of his sister Mary, 60–2; helps elect Hawkins provost, 62–3; changing position in Oriel, 63–4; plans college reforms, 64–8, 77–8; college quarrel, 65–74; opposes re-election of Peel, 69–71; as tutor, 74–9; studies advanced mathematics, 80–1; alarmed at liberalism, 81–2; voyage to Mediterranean, 82–7; illness in Sicily, 85–7; elected

dean of Oriel, 87–8; would reconstitute Oriel on medieval lines, 89–95; opens house in St. Aldate's, 91–2; and Littlemore, 94–5; concerned over Sanskrit professorship, 96–7; stands for moral philosophy professorship, 97; active against admission of Dissenters to Oxford, 102–8; and against substituting a Declaration of Conformity for subscription to the Articles, 108–15; his influence on Oxford education summarized, 115–19; resigns Fellowship, 120; asked to deliver University Discourses, 131–2; appointed rector of CUI, 132, 135; appointed to subcommittee of three for CUI, 133–5; sued for libel by Achilli, 135–6; composes Discourses, 136–44, 149–53; delivers them, 144–9, 150; revises for later editions, 153–4; opens and organizes CUI, 156–70

austerity of personal life, 5–6, 25, 53–4, 165; celibacy, ideal of, 51, 94; illnesses and breakdowns, xii, 4, 20, 31–2, 34, 58, 59–60, 61–2, 84, 85–7, 148, 205, 228; integrity of mind, 19–20, 70, 205–6; intellectual pride, self-accusation of, 4, 11, 16, 19, 28–9, 61, 87, 228; liberalism, attitude toward, xii, 58, 62, 81–2, 87, 123, 228, 233–4

works: "An, re vera, praevaluerit apud eruditiores antiquorum polytheismus," 289 (n. 1); *Apologia*, xii, 4, 62; "Apollonius of Tyana," 178; *Arians of the Fourth Century*, 81, 152; "Christianity and Letters," 235; "Christianity and Scientific Investigation," 185–6, 268; "Cicero," 178; "Coliseum, The," 13; "Conditio servorum apud antiquos," 23, 289 (n. 1); *Development of Christian Doctrine*, 155; *Discourses on University Education*, 131–55, 173; "Essay on Miracles," 178; "Essay on the Study of Modern History," 23; *Essays, Critical and Historical*, 249–50, 266–7; *Grammar of Assent*, 78, 155; "Hints on Latin Composition," 30, 285–6 (n. 48); *Historical Sketches*, 173; *Idea of a University*, 78, 131–55, 173–270 *passim*; juvenilia, 3; "Lead, Kindly Light," 86, 87, 228; *Lectures and Essays on University Subjects*, 153, 173, 185–6, 235, 268; *Lectures on Justification*, 155; *Library of the Fathers*, 92; "Literature," 2, 237, 264; *Loss and Gain*, 6, 25–6, 75, 196–7; "Mediatorial Kingdom of Christ," 275; *Office*

THE IMPERIAL INTELLECT

Newman, John Henry (*continued*)
and *Work of Universities* (see *Rise and
Progress*); *Oxford University Sermons*,
85, 207–8, 233–4; *Parochial and Plain
Sermons*, 152, 208; "Philosophical
Temper, First Enjoined by the Gospel,"
233–4; *Present Position of Catholics*,
132, 135, 150, 154, 211; *Prophetical
Office of the Church*, 155; *Rise and
Progress of Universities*, 115, 153, 169,
173, 186, 274; *St. Bartholomew's Eve*,
13; St. Isidore's oration, 142; "Site of a
University," 169; *Stray Essays on Con-
troversial Points*, 316 (n. 70); "Tam-
worth Reading Room," 259; *Under-
graduate, The*, 13
Newman, Mary, 60–1
Newsham, Dr., 150
Newton, Isaac, 16, 18, 80, 81
Nicholas, Rev. George, 1, 5, 283 (n. 127)
Niebuhr, Barthold, 59, 249
Nil admirari, 83, 209, 211
Noetics, the, 35–7, 38, 39, 58, 63, 64, 77,
228, 257

Oakeley, Frederick, 112
O'Callaghan, Rev. John, 144
O'Connell, Daniel, 124–5, 126
O'Curry, Eugene, 311 (n. 37)
O'Faolain, Sean, 280 (nn. 16, 19)
O'Ferrall, James, 143
Ogle, J. A., 12–13, 47
O'Higgins, Bishop, 128
Oratory of St. Philip Neri, Edgbaston, xi,
xiii, 3, 94–5, 123, 141, 273
O'Reilly, Rev. E. J., 263
O'Reilly, Surgeon John, 147
O'Reilly, Myles, 133, 315 (n. 66)
Oriel College, Oxford: anniversary cele-
bration (500th), 63; collections, 65,
71, 77–8; common room, 35–7, 44–5,
115, 120; communion and chapel, 52,
56–7; deanship, 88; Fellows, 26, 35–
45; Fellowship examination, 26–7, 29,
31–5, 148; Fellowships, open, 26, 65;
intellectual pre-eminence, 8, 18, 21, 26,
35–7, 73–4; in Middle Ages, 89–91;
quarrel of Hawkins and tutors, 64, 66,
68–74, 85–6, 91, 292 (n. 105); rowdi-
ness of undergraduates, 52–7; tutorial
system, 52, 65–8, 75, reformed by JHN,
65, 67–9, 77–8
Oriel Noetics. *See* Noetics
Orleans, schools of, 253
Ornsby, Robert, 138, 140, 142, 143, 144,
305 (n. 23)

Ovid, 2, 5, 278
Oxford University, 1–130 *passim*; attacked by *Edinburgh Review*, 220–1;
clerical chancellor for, 98; compared
with CUI, 134, 158–9, 161, 162–4;
dissipation of undergraduates, 6–7,
52–7, 281 (n. 60); and Ireland, 123;
JHN's use of in *Discourses*, 138, 140–1,
143–4, 145, 146; moral philosophy
professorship, 97; New Examination
Statute (1800), 8, 37; New Examination Statute (1830), 117–18; opposition to London University charter, 99–
101; reform, periods of, 115; Regius
Professorship of Divinity, 97; subscription to the Articles at, 101–15; type of
Religion of Philosophy, 228–9
Oxford University Bill (1854), 120, 134,
158, 296–7 (n. 39)

Paine, Thomas, 4, 228, 279 (n. 14)
Paley, William, 36, 107, 267, 297 (n.
41)
Palmer, William, of Worcester College,
36, 296 (n. 32)
Paris, University of, 174, 179, 253, 254,
255
Pater, Walter, 131, 154
Pattison, Mark, 116; quoted, on Oxford,
26, 36, 73, 75, 77, 91, 115, 117, 119;
relation to JHN, 74, 88, 92, 115, 119,
261
Paul, St., 243
Paxton, Sir Joseph, 211
Peacock's *Visit for a Week*, 276
Pearson's *Exposition of the Creed*, 107
Peel, Sir Robert, 100; stands for re-
election, 69–71, 87; proposes Queen's
College Scheme, 125–6; gives Tam-
worth address, 259–60
Penny Magazine, The, 99
Perceval, A. P., 296 (n. 32)
Perrin's *Elements of French Conversa-
tion*, 275
Persian language, 24
Persius, 2, 278
Peter, St., 145–6, 148
Philip Neri, St., 242–3
Phillpotts, Bishop, 297 (n. 51)
Philo, 184
Philosophia prima, 182, 184–7
Philosophic habit, 82, 190, 191, 193, 195,
209–10, 211, 212, 233–4
Philosophy, 182–5, 190, 219, 221, 227,
265, 269; word explained by Pythag-
oras, 213; medieval definitions of, 184

INDEX

[325]

THE YALE PAPERBOUNDS